7-11-11   Sea of Mud

To Bob

Enjoy your trek through the Sea of Mud

Greg

Pl. 45.

COSTUMES MEXICAINS.
Filisola Calabrais.
Général de Cavalerie, commandant de la place de Mexico.(d'après nature en 1826.)

Costumes Mexicains. Filisola Calabrais. By Claudio Linati, 1828. Lithograph
(hand-colored), 12 ¼ × 9 ³/₁₆ inches. *Courtesy of the Amon Carter Museum, Fort
Worth, Texas.*

SEA
OF
MUD

The Retreat of the Mexican Army after San Jacinto, An Archeological Investigation

GREGG J. DIMMICK

Texas State Historical Association
Austin

Library of Congress Cataloging-in-Publication Data

Dimmick, Gregg J.

Sea of mud: the retreat of the Mexican army after San Jacinto, an archeological investigation/ by Gregg J. Dimmick.

"Published by the Texas State Historical Association in cooperation with the Center for Studies in Texas History at the University of Texas at Austin"—T.p. verso.

    p.   cm.

Includes bibliographical references and index.

    ISBN 0-87611-215-7 (alk. paper)

    1. Mexico. Ejército—History—19th century. 2. San Jacinto, Battle of, Tex., 1836. 3. San Jacinto Battleground State Historical Park (Tex.)—Antiquities. 4. Texas—History—Revolution, 1835–1836—Antiquities. 5. Texas—Antiquities. I. Texas State Historical Association. II. University of Texas at Austin. Center for Studies in Texas History. III. Title.

    F390.D55 2004

    976.4'13303—dc22

                             2004013511

5   4   3   2   1   06   07   08

Published by the Texas State Historical Association in Cooperation with the Center for Studies in Texas History at the University of Texas at Austin.

Funded by a grant from the Summerfield G. Roberts Foundation in Dallas.

Design by David Timmons.

The paper used in this book meets the minimum requirements of the American National Standard for Permanence of Paper for Printed Library Materials, Z39.48-1984.

Contents

Maps

Figures

Preface

IT IS NOT AN EASY TRANSFORMATION to convert oneself from a general pediatrician in the small Texas town of Wharton to a published historical avocational archeologist. How it came about may be no less a product of the fates than the defeat of the Mexican army in Texas in 1836.

In 1996 I was very adept at circumcisions, spinal taps, and treating asthma but I must say that I knew next to nothing about Texas history. Oh, I had been to the Alamo when I did my residency in San Antonio but I must admit that it held no real interest for me. Due to the fact that I was not even from Texas (unless you consider that my home state—Wyoming—used to be part of Texas) and had never had a course in Texas history, I probably had a valid excuse.

Over the years I had dabbled in the archeological excavation of some prehistoric Indian sites with members of the Houston Archeological Society. I found that they gladly accepted help from anyone who showed the slightest interest—especially in the very important job (so they told me) of screening all the dirt that comes out of the pit.

One day in 1996 I was examining a patient—the daughter of one of our local ranchers, Jim Williams. His wife, Luann, mentioned that there was a man who was finding Civil War artifacts on their property. Suffering from the empty-nest syndrome (my youngest was off to Texas A&M), I headed out to their place and spent an entire Saturday following the gentleman around like a shadow. He found a few Minié balls, an old pocketknife and a brass button, and I was hooked.

I decided I had to know more about the Civil War in our area to see if there were other sites to be located and documented. Please let me stress the "documented" part of the equation. Artifacts with no provenance or historical record are interesting but are of no real historical or archeological value. Having found very little information on the Civil War in our area (not too surprising considering how little action actually took place in our neighborhood) I decided to expand my horizons.

At this point I need to interject what to me is an amazing fact. Out of the blue, I decided to try to find evidence of the Mexican army. With absolutely no knowledge of where exactly they had been in our area, or any awareness of any previous artifacts found, I got this crazy idea in my head that we might be able to find some remnant of the Mexican army from 1836.

I had been reading about the history of Wharton County and came across a short blurb about the small community of Spanish Camp.[1] The local lore is that the Mexican army camped at Spanish Camp and left a cannon full of gold in Peach Creek. Being an avocational archeologist (never call yourself an amateur archeologist— to the professionals that means you are not an archeologist at all), I was doubtful of the gold story but very curious as to the possibility of Mexican army artifacts. I dusted off my father's twenty-five-year-old metal detector, which I did not know how to operate, and struck out to find the Mexican army. Needless to say, my digging buddy, Ed Person, and I found just about everything but the Mexican army. We discovered a lifetime's supply of barbed wire, spent shotgun shells, and the dreaded aluminum-can pull tabs, but nothing that seemed the least bit old. There was absolutely nothing that indicated the presence of Santa Anna and his *soldados*.

It took very little time, digging up trash in abundance, to convince us to go back to the drawing board. It occurred to us that we knew next to nothing about the Mexican army and where they had traveled in Texas. We realized that we did not even know if it was indeed the Mexican army—after all, the town is called Spanish Camp, not Mexican Camp. All else having failed, we decided it was necessary to educate ourselves. A quick perusal of the Texas history

1. Annie Lee Williams, *The History of Wharton County* (Austin: Von Boeckmann-Jones Co., 1964), 223.

∞

section at the Wharton County Junior College Library produced two books. The first was José Enrique de la Peña's *With Santa Anna in Texas* and the second was Vicente Filisola's *Memoirs for the History of the War in Texas*. After studying the two sources we had no new information concerning Spanish Camp, nor could we find any mention of Peach Creek. However, further study of the two books did reveal that both sources repeatedly referred to the Bernardo rivers. Somehow the Mexican army had become stuck in the mud between what had to have been the San Bernard River and the West Bernard Creek.

Not knowing where to proceed from this point, I called up our region's archeological steward, Joe Hudgins. Joe is a local rancher and past president of the Houston Archeological Society. He is extremely dedicated to the preservation of the history and archeology of our area. When I informed him that I thought we could find the remnants of the Mexican army somewhere between the Bernards, Joe responded in his typical man-of-few-words manner: "That's a lot of territory." I am convinced to this day that the only reason we were able to locate the path of the Mexican army is that we were actually crazy enough to believe that we could.

One would think that at this point a tremendous task faced us, and in reality it did. However, as it turns out, due to pure dumb luck, we had no real problem finding the Mexican trail. We knew that years ago people used to dig for Spanish gold in the town of East Bernard—also supposedly left by the Mexican army. We put out the word through the local family practitioner, Dr. Mike Farrell, and within a week we had a bite. One of the residents of East Bernard, whose children happened to be my patients, had discovered a cannonball near her home nearly thirty years ago. We went to her home to examine and photograph the cannonball. Had we known what we now know, we likely would have thanked her and left. As it turns out the cannonball was much too large to have been left by the Mexican army. Luckily we were not aware of that fact and we excitedly began a survey of her property. Even though we were unable to unearth any artifacts at that time we were now equipped with a good metal detector with which we were slowly gaining proficiency. Our streak of good luck took another giant step forward when she informed us of a recent find. About two weeks prior, her neighbors, from half a mile down the road, had discovered a cannonball while they were digging a small pond on their property. She wondered if we might be interested in meeting them.

The property owners were more than happy to show off their new treasure, a heavily rusted iron ball that to my untrained eye seemed to be a cannonball. We weighed, measured, and photographed the prize and arranged to return to do a site survey on their property. Ed and I had not been at our work for more than half an hour when we found a twin cannonball. Soon other items began to appear, a rusted iron lock for a trunk, several large musket balls and a brass side plate for an India Pattern Brown Bess Musket. We actually knew what the musket piece was as Joe and the Houston Archeological Society had previously excavated a Republic of Texas army post, Post West Bernard. This site had been a gun repair center and contained many pieces of captured Mexican muskets.

Upon obtaining proof that this was indeed a Mexican army site we shut it down and contacted the Houston Archeological Society to help us properly excavate this site. A mere two weeks after deciding that we might be able to find artifacts that the Mexican army dropped in the mud 160 years earlier, we had done just that. Now if that does not qualify as dumb luck, what does?

The original site that we discovered was excavated with the help of the Houston Archeological Society, several members of the Fort Bend Archeological Society, and two local East Bernard citizens, Terry Kieler and John Robert Wicke. Terry has become one of the main contributors to our project and has spent far more time in the Mar de Lodo than the Mexican army ever did. Bruce and Susan Badger, the landowners, have been very cooperative and have provided some of their artifacts for display at the Alamo and San Jacinto. The original excavation has been documented in *A Campsite of the Retreating Mexican Army, April, 1836 41WH91, Wharton County, Texas.*[2] At the time of publication the authors considered this site as the likely campsite of April 28. After further research it is now felt that the site is more likely the location of the bogged-down artillery and wagons from the night of April 29. It turned out that finding the original site was a piece of cake compared to finding the trail into or

2. Joe D. Hudgins and Gregg Dimmick, *A Campsite of the Retreating Mexican Army, April, 1836, 41WH91, Wharton County, Texas,* Houston Archeological Society Report No. 13 (1998).

SEA OF MUD

out of the site. After months of trudging through rice fields, in the general direction we expected the Mexican army to have moved, I finally found *one* musket ball. We have found hundreds of musket balls in our endeavors but without a doubt this was the most significant. This lead musket ball gave us a second point in the line of march. Now we knew where to look between the two points. The race was on to find and document as much material as possible while trying to keep things quiet so as not to have a hoard of pothunters congregating in our sites.

My interest for the subject has grown into a passion (according to my wife, an obsession) and I am now practicing pediatrics to pay for my archeological and historical research.

One of my best early moves was to contact historians who knew far more about the subject than I. We needed experts to officially identify the artifacts that we were discovering. No one was going to pay attention to an archeological publication with Gregg Dimmick, Terry Kieler, and Joe Hudgins giving their opinions as to what they had discovered. And who could have blamed people if they had been suspicious, as it turns out that we really did not know the full significance of the relics we had unearthed.

Luckily I found a copy of *Texian Iliad; A Military History of the Texas Revolution* by Stephen L. Hardin. I noticed that Dr. Hardin was from Victoria, Texas, and since that is very near Wharton, I thought I would call him up. He still laughs when he reminds me that I called him up and informed him that I thought that we had found remnants of the Mexican army. I'm sure he thought I was a little crazy, but luckily he at least decided to give me a chance. He brought "the" Mexican army expert, Kevin Young, to Wharton to identify our artifacts. I think we impressed him by having table after table of Mexican army relics laid out in the St. Paul Lutheran Church educational building for his perusal. I believe Kevin commented that we already had more Alamo period Mexican army artifacts than anyone he was aware of—including the Alamo and San Jacinto! It was at that point that I knew we were on to something significant.

I need to add that the artifacts that have been recovered from the Mar de Lodo are, for the most part, still together as a collection. Many of the better items have been on display at the Alamo for the past two years. This opportunity to allow our artifacts to be seen by the general public came about due to the efforts of Dr. Bruce

∞

Winders, historical director of the Alamo. We have just begun working with the San Jacinto Museum to create a display of some of the Mar de Lodo artifacts along with the new items that have been excavated from San Jacinto. We have also been talking with the Wharton County Museum about a display of artifacts. There needs to be a display in our community—after all it was our local mud that originally caused this collection to accumulate!

Kevin Young did me another huge favor when he told me that I needed to call a professor at North Carolina State University, Doctor (not an MD but a real Doctor) James E. Crisp. I must admit that I was curious as to why I should call North Carolina to learn about Mexican army history. It became immediately apparent when I first talked to Jim. He sent me places that I never would have ventured. He warned me that I could not always trust the English translation of the original Spanish. I could not have imagined it at the time but I now speak passable Spanish and consider myself a fair translator. He is the person who most impressed upon me that to truly understand and explain the archeology I had to learn the history as well. Jim convinced me that Joe, Terry, Ed, and I had stumbled upon one of those special, yet nearly forgotten, episodes in history.

As a result of Jim telling his many connections of our work, I have had the honor of speaking about our site to several groups—including the Texas State Historical Association, the Texas Archeological Society, the Daughters of the Republic of Texas, and the annual San Jacinto Symposium. Our little group of Mexican army archeologists had the honor of appearing on the History Channel and the Discovery Channel as a result of our work contributing to the debate about the Peña memoirs.

I would be remiss if I did not mention one other person I met when I was speaking at a Mexican army conference organized by Kevin Young. Another speaker at the conference was an architect from Port Isabel, Texas, Manuel Hinojosa. Manuel and I didn't realize it at first but we now know that we are long-lost brothers. We just have to be when you consider our shared passion for the Mexican army! Manuel introduced me to a new level of interest. Our expeditions now take us into Mexico where we try to find the location of the campsites as the Mexican army worked its way north into Texas. We have been to Hermanas, San Juan de Sabinas, Bajan, and Tanque de San Felipe. We have stood at the La Laja crossing of the Salado River and were thrilled as we retraced the steps of the 1835–1836 army. We have driven thirty miles on dust-choked roads and marveled at the fact that the Mexican *soldados* had to endure much worse for hundreds and hundreds of miles.

Manuel was the obvious choice to illustrate my book. He knows and loves the Mexican army (he may well have had a relative or two fighting with General Urrea), and is an extremely talented artist. If you look closely you will see many of the artifacts from the Mar de Lodo in his illustrations.

I need to mention several special groups. We appreciate all the landowners and farmers that have put up with us for the past several years. I hope this helps them to understand those crazy guys who were trudging around in the mud in the 100-degree heat for all those hours. We also could not have done this without all the great people at the Houston and Fort Bend Archeological Societies. Along with Joe Hudgins they made sure this was all being done with proper technique. It was also calming for us to have Anne Fox reassure us that in the middle of a six-hundred-acre rice field there are no good data points and GPS would have to do.

I have also been blessed with very helpful staffs at the Daughters of the Republic of Texas library, the Center for American History, the Benson Latin American Collection, the Texas State Library, the General Land Office, the Wharton County Junior College Library, and our own Wharton County Public Library. The ladies in the pediatric department at South Texas Medical Clinics have tolerated my obsession since the very beginning. Special individuals were Jane Garner at the Benson, Dora Guerra at the DRT, Jerry Smaistrla at the Wharton County Library, Cassie Dimmick who researched the holdings of the Sterling C. Evans Library at Texas A&M University, and Evelyn Nolen, proofreader extraordinaire.

Several researchers have provided me with material from their own research. One of the most diligent in getting me information was Thomas Ricks Lindley. He provided me with an entire copy of Filisola's *Análisis del diario militar del General D. José Urreá durante la primera campaña de Tejas* before I was aware that it existed. Homero S. Vera, one of the archivists at Texas A&M University–Kingsville, brought me a copy of J. Sánchez Garza's *La rebelión de Texas* all the way from Mexico City.

When I was lucky enough to be asked to speak in Goliad concerning our site I had the pleasure of meeting an energetic and enthusiastic lady, Lupita Berrera. She was the director of the Fannin Battlefield State Park at the time. Through her efforts and those of Art Black, archeologist with the Texas Parks and Wildlife Department, we were allowed to help conduct a site survey of the Fannin battlefield. We were able to verify that the Fannin-Urrea battle took place exactly where the old veterans of the battle indicated it did.

My team of metal-detecting avocational archeologists was also recently allowed to work with Roger Moore, Joe Sanchez, and the other professional archeologists at Moore Archeological Consulting in the early site surveys at San Jacinto. Their archeological photographer, Kelly Houk, was kind enough to photograph the artifacts for my book. Once again we have been able to help locate artifacts that will eventually clear up many of the unanswered questions as to the actual site of the battle and subsequent flight of the Mexican army. It is doubtful that we would have been allowed this privilege if not for the friendship and influence of Jeff Dunn, Jan DeVault, Ted Hollingsworth, and Bill Dolman.

When this book was near completion I e-mailed the whole manuscript to Jim Crisp. He read the book for me and suggested various changes. His major recommendation was that I get all the documents, including those previously translated by others, retranslated. He recommended the very talented and knowledgeable Dora Elizondo Guerra. She has been wonderful and has worked far more hours than I had the right to ask of her. Having served as the head of the DRT library gave her the background that is so important in translating period pieces. During her tenure at the University of Texas at San Antonio she was the "keeper" of the Peña papers so it is fitting that she did the translation of the portion of the Peña memoirs that Urrea included in his diary (Appendix No. 1), as well as the Peña deposition from the Filisola court-martial (Appendix No. 2).

Lastly, I would like to thank my wife Debbi for tolerating this obsession. She had to put up with dirty artifacts in the sink, filthy family vehicles, using her jeep to pull my truck out of the Mar de Lodo, and all the Spanish that I spoke to her while learning the language. Someday, maybe I can get her to go digging with me.

After my book was finished—I thought—I received an e-mail from Jeff Dunn, chairman of the San Jacinto advisory committee

∞

and president of the Dallas Historical Society. Jeff, who has an amazing talent for finding obscure sources and documents, told me that he was searching WorldCat on the internet for anything he could find on the battle of San Jacinto when he came across something he thought might interest me. It was a master's thesis written in 1970 by Dorothy Virginia Barler Montgomery, while she was a graduate student at Sul Ross University in Alpine, Texas. The title of her thesis is "Movements of the Mexican Army in Texas after the Battle of San Jacinto." I had not found any reference to Montgomery's thesis in the published literature on the Texas Revolution, nor had I encountered any scholar who was familiar with her work.

Needless to say, I was simultaneously thrilled and nervous at the prospect of seeing this thesis. I had thought that my research was both complete and original—now I wondered if it would be either. When I read Montgomery's work, I was impressed. The 535-page thesis contains 225 pages of documents—some of which I had not seen before—translated by the author. I found that Montgomery's thesis complemented rather than compromised my own, and that her conclusions about the Mexican retreat were very similar to mine.

Montgomery did not give near as much detail about the Sea of Mud as I have included, as the focus of her thesis was much broader and included the retreat of the Mexican army all the way to Matamoros. In another of her chapters, dedicated to other actions related to the retreat, Montgomery gives an excellent account of the actions of Agustín Alcerreca and Gen. Adrian Woll. Her detail regarding the latter phase of the animosity between Urrea and Filisola (and the eventual replacement of Filisola by Urrea) is very well done. It should be remembered that she was working at a disadvantage because, at the time she was writing, neither the Peña memoirs nor the Filisola *Memorias* had yet been translated. Montgomery did manage to include part of the Peña memoirs without knowing it when she included part of the diary of the anonymous officer (who we now know was Peña) that is included in the Urrea diary. She apparently was unaware of Sánchez Garza's 1955 edition of the Peña memoir.

I have taken the opportunity to include some details from Montgomery's thesis in this book, and have profited from reading several documents from her bibliography that I was not previously aware of. She found several documents in the Matamoros newspaper, *El mer-*

curio del Puerto de Matamoros and the national Mexican newspaper, *Diario del gobierno de la República Mexicana*. Montgomery noted that these newspapers were in the Matamoros archives. She added that these archives have since been destroyed, though parts of them have been copied and are at the University of Texas. None of her translations that were new to me are directly relevant to the story of *Sea of Mud*, and thus none have been included in this book.

The existence of this fine work for the past thirty-four years, unacknowledged by scholars of the Texas Revolution, supports my contention that the history of the retreating Mexican army has truly been forgotten.

There have been a few minor changes made for the paperback edition. Adrian Woll was French, not Belgian. The commander of the Mexican force at Victoria was not Ugartechea but Captain Telesforo Alavez, husband or boyfriend of the famous angel of Goliad, Francita Alavez.[3] Clarence Wharton discounted Lubbock's report in regard to Elizabeth Powell's staying at home during the Mexican occupation of her homesite. "Other inquires [unfortunately Wharton does not document these] lead to the conclusion that Mrs. Powell was off with the runaways when the Mexican armies came by and that her house was destroyed; that she never saw any of the things which Governor Lubbock says she related to him. He was often free with facts and after sixty years, when he wrote his memoirs, he may have imagined that the widow Powell told him these things."[4]

At the time of this printing I am considering donating the majority of the Sea of Mud artifacts to the Cushing Library at Texas A&M University. A sampling of the artifacts will be given to the Texas Archeological Research Laboratory for future studies by researchers. The collection at the Cushing is to be incorporated into a traveling exhibit that will be available to local museums for public viewing. It is my desire to make sure that the fascinating story of the unfortunate participants of the trek through the Sea of Mud remains in the public eye.

3. Vicente Filisola, *Memoirs for the History of the War in Texas*, trans. Wallace Woolsey (2 vols.; Austin: Eakin Press, 1986, 1987), II, 214.

4. Clarence R. Wharton, *Wharton's History of Fort Bend County* (San Antonio: Naylor Co., 1939), 68.

Introduction

IT IS ALL TOO OFTEN TRUE that history is written by the victors. And, for the most part, this produces a distorted account. Human nature being what it is, victors do not give an accurate, unbiased presentation, do not tell the tale from the viewpoint of the vanquished, do not recognize the humanity of their opponents, and often do not admit their own shortcomings. The resulting one-sided story does not present the whole picture, but it is preferable to the alternative—which is conflict with no history, struggle with no explanation, and battle with no account.

It is better that history be distorted than obliterated. Misrepresented events can be reassessed, but those that are completely unrecorded and historically forgotten can only be resurrected archeologically. Archeological studies are a critical part of the happenings of the past but without the adjunct of the historical record, conjecture raises its ugly head.

The fate of thousands of Mexican soldiers in Texas after the battle of San Jacinto on April 21, 1836, came perilously close to being one of those unrecorded, forgotten, and unassessed episodes. The history and archeology of the Mexicans' reactions to defeat and their struggle against natural elements as they fled the battlefield have recently been revisited. The newly excavated and researched details can now take their place as an important aspect of the Texas Revolution and a substantial footnote to the history of Mexico.

Previously, historians of the Texas Revolution have given the impression that the conflict abruptly ended with the crushing defeat of Gen. Antonio López de Santa Anna, supreme commander of the

Mexican army at San Jacinto. The accepted course of events has been that Santa Anna was captured the day following the battle and that he immediately sent orders to Gen. Vicente Filisola, his second-in-command, to retreat from Texas with the remainder of the Mexican army. Purportedly, Filisola dutifully obeyed the orders of his supreme commander and fled Texas at the head of a panicked, disorganized army that has been compared to Napoleon's army leaving Russia. In fact, Filisola had approximately four thousand Mexican soldiers at his disposal on April 22, the day after the battle. He and his generals formulated a plan that would allow them to buy the needed time to restart the offensive. It was only a cruel blow from nature that placed the regrouping Mexican army in the midst of a sea of mud, or, as Filisola so aptly described it, *un Mar de Lodo*.

Research of the available sources for this period demonstrates that the activities of the Mexican army were well documented at the time. For the most part this material has been either poorly represented or totally forgotten. Interestingly this seems to be the case in the Mexican literature as well as that of the United States. This holds true not only for the accounts prior to the battle of San Jacinto, but also for those pertaining to the aftermath of the defeat of the Mexican commander and the majority of his best troops.

Of the various archival sources relating to the Mexican side of the story, many have never been translated, and those that have are not completely accurate. One problem is that most of the translators have lacked a basic knowledge of the Mexican army and its involvement in the rebellion of 1835–1836. Carlos Castañeda clearly stated in his introduction to *The Mexican Side of the Texas Revolution*[1] that "great care has been exercised to render with all accuracy the thought of the Spanish originals, but no attempt has been made to give a literal word for word rendition."

In order to make this publication as reliable as possible, great attention has been paid to the translations. All the materials that have not been previously translated into English have now been translated, in consultation with a knowledgeable and experienced Span-

1. Carlos E. Castañeda (trans. and ed.), *The Mexican Side of the Texas Revolution, 1836, by the Chief Mexican Participants, General Antonio López de Santa Anna, Ramón Martínez Caro, General Vicente Filisola, General José Urrea, General José María Tornel* (Dallas: Graphic Ideas, 1970), vii.

ish-language translator. Due to inaccuracies that have been discovered in previously translated documents, the original Spanish sources of said documents were used for resource material. The same translator was consulted for these materials. Particular attention has been given to the literal word-for-word writings of the authors in order to document the small details that can be so important.

In addition to translation challenges, research is further confused by the multiple items written by General Filisola both during and after the campaign. In several articles about the campaign in Texas that were published in Mexican newspapers, he tried to justify his decisions. These articles were later compiled in book form and in 1848–1849 were published by R. Rafael in a two-volume work entitled *Memorias para la historia de la guerra de Tejas* (Memoirs for the History of the War in Texas). In 1849 an entirely different two-volume history of the Texas campaign, also written by Filisola, was published by Ignacio Cumplido. Unfortunately it was given the same title. These are two separate writings, with the Cumplido edition having much more information on the Mexican army during the campaign in Texas, particularly concerning the retreat. The Rafael edition has been translated into English by Wallace Woolsey. Woolsey added a limited portion of the Cumplido version to his translation, but for the most part the Cumplido edition has never been translated into English. To further complicate matters, Woolsey omitted from his translation of the Rafael version some of the original material and gave only summaries of other material. The original Rafael edition was reprinted in Spanish in 1968 and the reprint appears to contain all the original material. The Cumplido edition has not been reprinted, but a copy is available at the Benson Latin American Collection at the University of Texas in Austin. It should also be noted that the portion of the Cumplido version that deals with the retreat is almost word for word from an earlier work by Filisola, *Análisis del diario militar del General D. José Urreá durante la primera campaña de Tejas* (Analysis of the Military Diary of General José Urrea during the First Campaign of Texas). This book was published in 1838. It appears that Filisola used much of that work for his later memoirs. Since there are minor, but significant, differences in the texts, both should be compared for serious study. One should also be aware that Filisola often wrote in the third person and sometimes referred to himself as "Gen. Filisola."

The Mexican writings are often tainted by a bitter rivalry. Filisola, second in command to Santa Anna, and Gen. José Urrea, a division commander, strongly disagreed in regard to the decisions made in the aftermath of San Jacinto. During the retreat the hard feelings started to arise and eventually the two became enemies. The situation evolved to the point that Urrea replaced Filisola as commander on June 13, 1836. Because of accusations made by Urrea against Filisola, the latter was court-martialed and tried on his return to Mexico. He was acquitted, and, in 1838, Urrea wrote his *Diario de las operaciones militares de la division que al mando del General José Urrea hizo la campaña de Tejas* (Diary of the Military Operations of the Division Which under the Command of General José Urrea Campaigned in Texas) in angry response to Filisola's exoneration. Thus, neither Filisola's nor Urrea's writings should be considered precise, complete, unbiased records. They are really memoirs and position papers on the operations in Texas.

An additional problem surfaces in researching the Mexican documentation of the period. It soon becomes obvious that there is a glaring lack of consistency in dates. This is especially true of the various documents written by Filisola over the years. It seems likely that several of the original letters and orders written by Filisola were misdated. When he used these letters to write his defense, or *Representación dirigida al supremo gobierno por el General Vicente Filisola en defensa de su honor y aclaración de sus operaciones como general en gefe del ejército sobre Tejas* (Representation Addressed to the Supreme Government by General Vicente Filisola, in Defense of his Honor, and Explanation of his Operations as Commander-in-Chief of the Army against Texas),[2] to the Mexican government, he used the wrong dates. General Urrea noted in his diary that Filisola's dates were off by one day. Years later, when Filisola wrote several other documents about this period, he corrected his dates. And, as will be demonstrated later, one of General Urrea's letters was misdated as well.

The scope of this project is to provide an accurate account of the interval from April 21 to May 9—from the battle of San Jacinto until the final units of the Mexican army recrossed the Colorado River

2. Vicente Filisola, *Evacuation of Texas: Translation of the Representation Addressed to the Supreme Government by Gen. Vicente Filisola, in Defense of his Honor, and Explanation of his Operations as Commander-in-Chief of the Army against Texas* (Columbia, Tex.: G. & T. H. Borden, Public Printers, 1837).

and set out for Goliad. Archeological findings from Mexican army sites will be discussed[3] but the focus will be on the history that seems to have faded from modern awareness. The archeological details of the book do not constitute a classic archeological report. The information is geared to the general public and is not meant to meet archeological standards. The archeological sections are at the end of the chapter which pertains to the history of that particular site.

Several topics related to but not dealing directly with the Mexican retreat are not addressed. They include an attempt by Col. Augustín Amat, the commander of the Zapadores Battalion, to capture Columbia; the return of Adrian Woll, quartermaster general of the army, to the Texan camp at San Jacinto and his detention there; the panic and flight of Agustín Alcerreca, commander of the Tres Villas Battalion, from Matagorda, and the incursion of United States troops under Gen. Edmund Gaines into Texas. The stories of Alcerreca and Woll are thoroughly documented in the "forgotten" thesis by Dorothy Montgomery mentioned in the Preface.

A full account of what happened to the soldiers and officers of the Mexican army as they stumbled into the Sea of Mud has not been written since the original participants wrote their versions. The majority of their writings have not been translated or addressed in the modern Texas history literature. The most recent source that presents a fair and unbiased account of the story is Hubert Howe Bancroft's *History of North American States and Texas*, published in 1889, and though Bancroft related the story accurately he addressed the matter in a very cursory manner—a total of only two and one-half pages on the subject.

This work will tell the largely forgotten and certainly misunderstood story of 2,500 men, their wives, girlfriends, and children, who, for two weeks in April and May of 1836, stumbled into and somehow traversed the *Mar de Lodo*. The price they paid for this struggle with nature left them deeply wounded. They suffered greatly and survived—and now their story will be told.

3. Several of the excavation sites are documented in Hudgins and Dimmick, *A Campsite of the Retreating Mexican Army, April, 1836, 41WH91, Wharton County, Texas*; Joe D. Hudgins, Terry Kieler, and Gregg Dimmick, *Tracking the Mexican Army through the Mar De Lodo (Sea of Mud), April 29–May 9, 1836, 41WH92, 41WH93, 41WH94, 41WH95, Wharton County, Texas*, Houston Archeological Society Report No. 16 (Fall, 2000).

∞

Introduction

5

This and all other chapter-opening drawings are by Manuel Hinojosa, unless otherwise noted.

CHAPTER I

The Pursuit

BETWEEN FOUR AND FIVE O'CLOCK on the afternoon of April 21, 1836, the Texan army under Gen. Sam Houston dealt a stunning defeat to the Mexican army commanded by Gen. Antonio López de Santa Anna. The resistance of the Mexican army is said to have lasted in the neighborhood of eighteen minutes. From that point on, it turned into a melee of vengeful bloodletting by the Texans, serving as retaliation for the executions at the Alamo and Goliad. According to the San Jacinto account of Col. Pedro Delgado, a member of the general staff of Santa Anna, the Mexicans were literally and figuratively caught sleeping.[1] Santa Anna, Gen. Martín Perfecto de Cos, Ramón Martínez Caro (personal secretary to Santa Anna), and several members of the Tampico Regiment Cavalry, who served as Santa Anna's personal guard, immediately mounted their horses and galloped toward Vince's Bridge. This bridge would have served as a means to cross Vince's Bayou. That accomplished they would have had a clear path to the camp of the Mexican army at Old Fort. This campsite was on the west bank of

---

1. Pedro Delgado, "Mexican Account of the Battle of San Jacinto," *The Texas Almanac, 1857–1873: A Compendium of Texas History*, comp. James M. Day (Waco: Texian Press, 1967), 617–618. "No important incidence took place until about 4:40 P.M. At this fatal moment, the bugler on our right signaled the advance of the enemy upon that wing. His Excellency and Staff were asleep; the greater number of the men were also sleeping; of the rest some were eating, others were scattered in the woods in search of boughs to prepare shelter. Our line was composed of musket stacks. Our cavalry were riding, bare-back, to and from water."

the Brazos River, where the town of Richmond is now located. However, this escape attempt was doomed to failure—for unbeknownst to the fleeing Mexicans, Erastus "Deaf" Smith, by order of General Houston, had burned the bridge earlier that day. This attempted flight from the battle site would eventually, after an unlikely cascade of events, spark the retreat of the Mexican army from Texas.

At nearly every turn, the Mexican forces in Texas seemed to be slapped in the face by fate. This was true prior to, during, and after the battle of San Jacinto. Before reaching the Alamo, they had been hampered by two separate blizzards. For the most part, their oxen had frozen or starved. Their horses and mules had suffered for lack of grass. They had marched nearly four hundred leagues, or one thousand miles, through some of the most desolate deserts of Mexico because they lacked a navy capable of transporting them to Texas. Upon reaching the Alamo, they encountered a stubborn force of Texans who, by all rights, should have obeyed the orders of Sam Houston and retreated like reasonable men. As Mexican soldiers stormed the Alamo they were forced to overcome artillery emplacements that they themselves had constructed within the fortress in 1835. Their supply lines were stretched to the point of nonexistence. They were unaccustomed to the wooded, wet lands east of the Colorado River. And, finally, they were defeated at San Jacinto in a battle that Houston and his out-manned force may well have lost under normal circumstances.

At the close of the battle of San Jacinto the outcome of the Texas Revolution hung in a precarious balance. Prior to the battle there was little doubt that the Mexicans would prevail. With the shocking turn of events at San Jacinto, there was actually hope for the Texan cause. But Houston's troops were disorganized after their victory and were hindered with approximately six hundred Mexican prisoners. Filisola had nearly twenty-five hundred troops within a two- or three-day march of San Jacinto, and both of the main Mexican divisions had partially crossed the Brazos. The events of the next few days would surely tip the balance drastically in one direction or the other. Before San Jacinto, it appeared that the Mexican army had been cursed with bad luck and poor decision making, but then the seemingly impossible happened—their luck turned from bad to worse.

∞

SEA OF MUD

There are various accounts, from participants on each side of the opposing forces, detailing the flight of Santa Anna, Cos,[2] Caro, and a cavalry force of approximately sixty men. The *1868 Texas Almanac* contained a detailed article entitled "Pursuit of Santa Anna and His Cavalry after They Had Commenced Their Flight from the Battlefield of San Jacinto." The recollection was written by William S. Taylor:

When the Mexicans commenced retreating from their breastworks at San Jacinto, on the evening of the 21st of April 1836, Santa Anna, General Cos, and other officers of note among them hastened to join the forces at the old Fort Bend [Old Fort], on the Brazos, under Filisola. Santa Anna and all his cavalry but four attempted their retreat by way of Vince's Bridge, not knowing that this bridge had been destroyed by Deaf Smith, on the morning of that day. About the time this retreat of the Mexicans was commenced, Captain Karnes called for all those having loaded guns to follow him in the pursuit. The following are the names of all I can recollect of those who responded to Karnes's call, namely, James Cook, Washington Secrest, Field Secrest, Deaf Smith, Shell Tunage, Thomas Robbins, Elisha Clapp, Thomas House, and W. T. C. Pierce. These eleven [*sic*] are now all dead, to my certain knowledge. I also recollect a Dr. Alsbury, and a man who had escaped from Fannin's massacre, but do not know whether they are alive or not, as I have not seen them since the summer of 1836. I was also of the number,

2. Martín Perfecto de Cos has been widely reported to have been the brother-in-law of Santa Anna. None of the Mexican sources researched for this book confirmed this fact. Peña documented that Ricardo Drumundo, the purveyor general of the army, was the brother-in-law of Santa Anna. See José Enrique de la Peña, *With Santa Anna in Texas: A Personal Narrative of the Revolution,* trans. and ed. Carmen Perry (1975; expanded ed., intro. James E. Crisp, College Station: Texas A&M University Press, 1997), 59. Filisola also noted that Santa Anna had "family ties" with Drumundo. Vicente Filisola, *Memorias para la historia de la guerra de Tejas* (2 vols.; Mexico: R. Rafael, 1848, 1849); the reprint: Vicente Filisola, *Memorias para la historia de la guerra de Tejas* (2 vols.; Mexico, D.F.: Editora Nacional, 1968); and the translation: Vicente Filisola, *Memoirs for the History of the War in Texas,* trans. Wallace Woolsey (Austin: Eakin Press, 1986, 1987, II, 145.

making fourteen, with Captain Karnes. I think there were four more, making eighteen in all, but I do not recollect the names of these four. The distance of Vince's Bridge from the battle-ground was about four miles, over a very wet muddy plain, and, for perhaps a quarter of a mile, knee deep to our horses in mud and water. Two or three miles from the battle-ground, some three or four Mexicans struck off, (leaving the balance,) in the open prairie, in the direction of the head of Vince's Bayou. Elisha Clapp, having a very fleet horse, started in pursuit of them, and soon coming up with them, fired his rifle, killing one of them. The others, seeing that his rifle was discharged, turned to give him battle, when Clapp was compelled to retreat, not being able to cope with three Mexicans, with an empty gun. The one nearest him discharged his escopet at him, but the ball missed him, though, judging from the whistling, Clapp afterward told me he thought it passed within six inches of his head. But he returned to us unhurt. We continued our pursuit to Vince's Bridge, the three Mexicans, as I afterward learned, making good their escape to Filisola's army on the Brazos, where they reported to him that Houston's army was four thousand strong, and that Santa Anna and all the army were either killed or taken prisoners. While pursuing the Mexicans on the road to Vince's Bridge, we overtook numbers, their horses being too tired to enable them to escape; and as we overtook them, we felt compelled to kill them, and did so, though on their knees crying for quarter, and saying, "Me no Alamo—me no la Bahia," meaning that they were not in either of those horrible massacres. As there were but some fifteen or eighteen of us, and some sixty of the Mexicans we were pursuing, besides Santa Anna, Cos, and several other officers, we saw it was impossible for us to take prisoners, and we had but little disposition to do so, knowing they had slaughtered so many of Fannin's men in cold blood; after they had surrendered as prisoners of war, under solemn treaty stipulations that they should be sent safely to New-Orleans. For about half the distance from the battle-ground to Vince's Bridge, the road was strewed, every few hundred yards, with dead Mexicans, as we took no prisoners in this pursuit. When we arrived within half or three quarters of a mile of the Vince's Bridge, Captain Karnes ordered those in advance to halt till the rear could come up, stating that Santa Anna, was, no doubt, with the other Mexicans, and when they should reach the bridge and find it destroyed, they would certainly make fight, as it would then be their only alternative. We then followed in a body, prepared for and expecting a fight; but, when they reached the bridge and found it gone, they immediately scattered in all directions, some going up and others down the bayou. When we discovered this, every man of us put spurs to his horse, and started after them as fast as possible. When within 300 or 400 yards of the bridge, we discovered Vince's black stallion, with a fine-looking officer on him, dressed in uniform. Captain Karnes, supposing it was Santa Anna himself, (as it was rumored that he was riding Vince's horse,) made for him. When he came up to him, on the bank of the bayou, the officer dismounted, and Karnes asked him if he was Santa Anna. He replied that he was, supposing that quarter would be given to Santa Anna. Whereupon Captain Karnes struck at him with his sword, hitting him a glancing blow on the head, as he stood on the bank of the bayou. When he discovered that no quarter would be showed to him, he jumped into the bayou, saying at the same time that he was not Santa Anna. Whereupon some pistols were discharged at him, killing him in the bayou. We then continued our pursuit up and down the bayou, killing all we overtook, till we had killed all we could find. When we came to the wreck of the bridge, the sun was near setting. Continuing our search, we finally found four horses in a thicket, some few hundred yards above the bridge. We saw that their riders had dismounted and crossed the bayou on foot, wading through the mud and water, and had got into a much larger thicket, on the opposite side. These four afterward proved to be Santa Anna, Santa Anna's secretary, and another officer whose name I do not recollect. By this time it had become too dark to search the thicket for them that night. Captain Karnes then called to Dr. Alsbury, who spoke the Spanish language, to call to Santa Anna in the thicket, (for he had no doubt Santa Anna was one of them,) and say to him, if he would come out, and give himself up, we would take him prisoner and spare his life.[3]

After the retreat, an anonymous Mexican officer wrote a confidential letter to his family in Mexico that described this same occurrence as experienced by one of the pursued.

Seeing that the President [Santa Anna] had no alternative, we began to beat our retreat with a few cavalry, having been chased by the enemy more than four leagues [10.7 miles], until we reached a creek, twelve varas [1 vara = 2.8 feet] wide and very deep. There had been a wooden bridge at that passage but the enemy had ordered that it be set afire that morning after General Cos' division had crossed it. We had not received news of the destruction of the mentioned bridge. When we reached it, we had no recourse but to jump into the water with our horses, as we had no time with the enemy upon us. Santa Anna was undecided about what he would do; but I and Sr. Cos jumped into the water. It was impossible, however, for the horses to climb the opposite side because of a large thick wall that was there. We abandoned them to go out on foot; but since there were enemies on the opposite bank, most that crossed were killed or captured, I had the good luck to escape through the brush. I walked four days on foot through very thick brushwood, by nights, as I could not take the road. Needing to cross the Brazos River, myself and another soldier that accompanied me, accomplished this by constructing a poor wooden raft that we strapped together with our sashes. We managed to arrive on the 25th at the camp of Filisola, who prohibited me from writing to W. the details of this disgrace. Other things happened that I must not trust to the pen. I arrived at this port of Matamoros where I am writing now. I have recuperated and feel better.[4]

3. William S. Taylor, "Pursuit of Santa Anna and His Cavalry after They Had Commenced Their Flight from the Battlefield of San Jacinto," *Texas Almanac, 1857–1873*, pp. 537–540.

4. Mexicano, "Se nos ha entegado en Tejas como borregos de ofrenda" ("We

∞

SEA OF MUD

The author of the pamphlet, from which the above quote is taken, revealed that the writer of the above eyewitness account was "An Officer, perhaps the only one that saved himself on this scorching day of the 21st of April, who in a confidential letter says to his family the following." From statements of his actions prior to the battle and the timing of his arrival at the camp of Filisola there can be little doubt the officer was Capt. Marcos Barragán.

Col. Pedro Delgado documented in his account of the battle of San Jacinto that Santa Anna sent Captain Barragán with a force of dragoons to reconnoiter Houston's movements. He goes on to state that on the morning of April 20 Barragán rushed into New Washington, reporting that Houston was close on their rear.[5] This is consistent with further details given in the letter quoted above, which said that the anonymous writer had been sent from New Washington toward Lynchburg, had discovered Houston's army and rushed back to Santa Anna to report.

Ramón Martínez Caro, personal secretary to Santa Anna, told of his participation in the flight from San Jacinto. He reported that he followed Santa Anna at full speed until they reached Vince's Bridge, only to find it burned. They then retraced their steps a short distance and entered a small thicket. Santa Anna dismounted there and left him. Caro followed a path with Lt. Col. María Castillo Iberri,[6]

---

have been delivered up in Texas like sacrificial lambs"), *Imprint of the Testimony of Valdez* (Mexico: n.p., 1836), 3–4 (a copy of this pamphlet can be found in the Center for American History, University of Texas at Austin; cited hereafter as CAH).

5. Delgado, "Mexican Account of the Battle of San Jacinto," 615.

6. Castillo Iberri was called José María Castillo y Iberri by Filisola. See Filisola, *Memoirs for the History of the War in Texas,* II, 222. He was listed as a brevet lieutenant colonel and aide-de-camp to Santa Anna. Filisola reported that Castillo y Iberri brought the document from Santa Anna that ordered Cos to reinforce him at San Jacinto. Peña mentioned this same officer but spelled his name Castillo Iberry. Peña wrote that Castillo Iberry burned Harrisburg (and that Santa Anna personally participated in the destruction). He also noted that Castillo Iberry died at San Jacinto. See Perry (trans. and ed.), *With Santa Anna in Texas,* 114, 124. He is listed by George Fisher as José María Castillo, 37-year-old brevet lieutenant colonel and a prisoner of war. Archival Correspondence of George Fisher, Galveston 5-26-1836, http://tamu.edu/ccbn/dewitt/fishergeorge4.htm. The Fisher list can also be found in John Jenkins (ed.), *Papers of the Texas Revolution* (10 vols.; Austin: Presidial Press, 1973), VI, 84–85.

Barragán, and some others whose names he did not recall. They all succeeded in crossing the creek, but Caro was cut off from the creek by the approaching enemy.[7]

Lt. Col. José Enrique de la Peña was a cavalry officer assigned to the Zapadores Battalion (sappers or engineers). He kept a diary during the Texas campaign and later reworked his diary into his memoirs.[8] Peña documented the arrival of Barragán in his description of the events of April 25.

> About seven o'clock this morning Captain Don Marcos Barragán, aide to General Santa Anna, Somosa, an officer from the Matamoros [battalion], and a presidial soldier from those dispersed at San Jacinto joined us. Since they found nothing at Thompson's Pass [Old Fort] with which to cross the Brazos, they had to build a barge, tying the logs with their sashes.[9]

The details given by Peña regarding Barragán are consistent with the anonymous officer's report in three respects: the arrival at the Mexican army campsite on April 25, the fact that Barragán was not alone (although the anonymous officer's report failed to mention a third person), and the construction of a wooden raft that was lashed together with their sashes.

7. Ramón Martínez Caro, "A True and Accurate Account of the First Texas Campaign and the Events Subsequent to the Battle of San Jacinto," in Castañeda (trans. and ed.), *The Mexican Side of the Texas Revolution*, 120–121.

8. Peña made several versions of his diary, the last of which was not a diary but a memoir. Only the last version has been translated into English (Perry [trans. and ed.], *With Santa Anna in Texas*). In our Appendix No. 1, part of a version that was included in the Urrea diary is translated. Our Appendix No. 2 is a translation of Peña's deposition from the Filisola court-martial. Both of these translations are by Dora Elizondo Guerra (see "A Note on Translations" in the bibliography). Peña was a brevet lieutenant colonel during the Texas campaign; in some sources he was still referred to as a captain.

9. José Enrique de la Peña, *La rebelión de Texas: Manuscrito inedito de 1836 por un official de Santa Anna*, ed. J. Sánchez Garza (Mexico, 1955), 149; Perry (trans. and ed.), *With Santa Anna in Texas*, 127.

The San Luis Battalion daily report also supported the fact that Barragán was the writer of the anonymous letter as it stated:

> This morning, around 7:00 A.M., there arrived Marcos Barragán and Somosa, officers from the Matamoros [Battalion] and a courier. They had managed to escape from the action of the 21st and they assured us that Santa Anna had gone with them as far as to the edge of the bayou, but that once there, he dismounted, and they were ignorant of his fate.[10]

Even though, in the previous quote, Barragán was said to be of the Matamoros Battalion, he was listed as being a captain of cavalry on Santa Anna's general staff.[11] Peña's account verified that Barragán was on the headquarters staff when he called him an aide to Santa Anna.

According to a list of officers present at San Antonio in March of 1836, Barragán's immediate superior on the staff was Col. Pedro Delgado. Second Lt. Luis Somosa was listed as a member the Matamoros Battalion.[12]

The accounts of Taylor and Barragán, representing opposing sides of the conflict, are so similar that they support each other's accuracy. One item of interest in the Taylor account is his mention of three or four Mexican soldiers who escaped from Elisha Clapp. He related that he later learned these riders were able to escape and reach Fil-

10. San Luis Battalion Daily Log, Apr. 25, 1836, included in the José Enrique de la Peña Papers (CAH).

11. "Relacion de los senores, gefes y oficiales que perteneciente al ejército de operaciones sobre Tejas, pasaron revista en el mes de Marzo en la ciudad de San Antonio Béjar" ("List of the senior commanders and officers who belonged to the army of operations over Texas, and passed in review in the month of March in the city of San Antonio"), Operaciones XI/481.3/1713, Tomo 2, f. (folio) 375–384v (Archivo Historico de Secretaria de la Defensa Nacional [AHSDN], Mexico City, Mexico); provided by Jack Jackson and Thomas Ricks Lindley (cited hereafter as "Relacion de los senores, gefes y oficiales").

It should also be noted that many, if not most, of the Mexican officers participating in the Texas campaign were given brevet promotions prior to departing Mexico. The above document does not give their brevet ranks but their pre-campaign ranks.

12. Ibid.

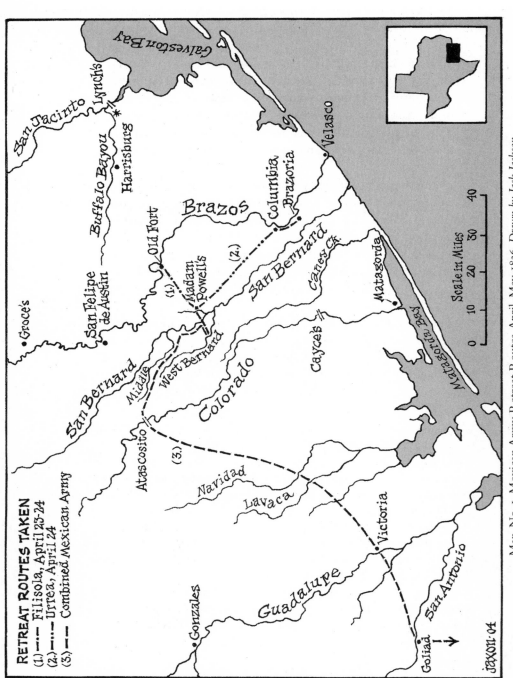

RETREAT ROUTES TAKEN
(1.) —·—·— Filisola, April 25-24
(2.) ······· Urrea, April 24
(3.) ——— Combined Mexican Army

Scale in Miles
0   10   20   30   40

jaxon·04

Map. No. 1. Mexican Army Retreat Routes, April–May 1836. Drawn by Jack Jackson.

isola's camp. He stated that they reported to Filisola that Houston's army was four thousand strong and that Santa Anna and his division were all either killed or captured. This coincides with Filisola's own report of how he first heard about the defeat at San Jacinto:

> came Capt. Miguel Aguirre of the Tampico, wounded in the thigh, two sergeants and four or five men, several wounded, a few healthy, who had aided at the battle; those reported separately to me one by one; it was not difficult to come by the knowledge that the defeat had been complete, and according to their statements, the feeling that the President General was dead or at least had been left a prisoner, was almost indubitable. With respect to the number of the enemy there was no conformity, as some said there had been 1500, others 2000, and finally some exaggerated the number up to 2500, so that the truth could not be estimated as it was an impossibility.[13]

Filisola did not claim that he had been told there were four thousand Texans, as Taylor purported, but it is apparent that the number of Texans was unknown to him and was exaggerated by some of the Mexican survivors.

The role of Capt. Miguel Aguirre was well documented in the Mexican sources. Even though he was not the first soldier to present himself to Filisola at Old Fort, he was the first eyewitness of the battle to do so. A senior Mexican officer, Gen. Eugenio Tolsa, mentioned Aguirre in his deposition for the court-martial of Filisola.[14] He claimed that Capt. Miguel Aguirre, a cavalry officer who arrived wounded in the thigh, confirmed the defeat of the president. He dated the arrival of Aguirre as April 23, 1836.[15] The San Luis Battalion daily log detailed that on April 24 their battalion

13. Vicente Filisola, *Análisis del diario militar del General D. José Urrea durante la primera campaña de Tejas* (Matamoros: Mercurio a Cargo de Antonio Castañeda, 1838), 43.

14. Vicente Filisola was court-martialed after his return to Mexico. This was due to the retreat of the army from Texas. This subject will be addressed in greater detail in subsequent chapters.

15. "La guerra de Texas: Causa formada al Gral. Filisola por su retirada en 1836," *Boletín del archivo general de la nación*, Tomo X, No. 3 (Mexico: DAPP, 1939), 505–509.

[marched] five leagues until 11:00 A.M. and from 6:00 P.M. until midnight [marched] five leagues to reach Madame Powell's, where we joined General Filisola's forces. It was confirmed that the President General's column, that had advanced toward Harrisburg, at San Jacinto on the 21st of the current month, had suffered a complete defeat. Possibly, 1,100 men from all units, plus one piece of artillery [were lost]. Of those, until today, only the wounded Captain Aguirre, of the Tampico Regiment and four or six dragoons, showed up.[16] They assured us that the rest had all perished.[17]

Peña documented that "The captain of the Tampico Regiment, Don Miguel Aguirre, who commanded the general in chief's guard and who returned on the 22nd, is, among others, one of those who affirmed the total destruction of the force."[18]

Aguirre's arrival was also verified by another of the Mexican officers. Col. José Nicolas de la Portilla was initially assigned to the division of General Urrea. According to his diary he was left in charge of the Fannin and Ward prisoners at Goliad and had to make the terrible decision as to whether to obey Santa Anna's orders and execute the Texan prisoners.

Soon after he had decided to comply with the order to execute Fannin's troops he was transferred by Urrea to Filisola's division. Therefore Portilla was in the Mexican camp at Old Fort on April 22 when Aguirre arrived. Portilla documented that Miguel Aguirre, captain of the Tampico Regiment, arrived that day. He said that Aguirre had been involved in the defeat of the troops under the general-in-chief and also that of the troops under General Cos. Portilla went on to say that there was a great deal of movement in camp

16. The dating of this document is confusing. The San Luis Battalion was with Urrea at the time of the battle of San Jacinto. They reunited with Filisola's troops on April 24. Thus, they did not talk with the survivors of the battle, including Aguirre, until April 24. This should not be construed as saying that Aguirre and the other survivors arrived in the Filisola camp on April 24.

17. San Luis Battalion Daily Log, Apr. 24, 1836, Peña Papers (CAH).

18. Peña, *La rebelión de Texas*, 146; Perry (trans. and ed.), *With Santa Anna in Texas*, 123.

that night in spite of the attempts to keep the news of the defeat secret.[19]

There is no proof that Aguirre was one of the Mexican soldiers who escaped from Elisha Clapp as described in the Taylor account. On the other hand, the fact that those mounted soldiers escaped, without pursuit, makes it highly likely they would have been among the first to arrive at Filisola's Old Fort camp. Peña identified Aguirre as the commander of Santa Anna's personal guard, which is very good evidence that he participated in the flight from the battlefield. Note that Filisola reported that Capt. Aguirre was wounded in the action at San Jacinto, not during his escape. This is consistent with Taylor's failure to mention that any of the three officers were wounded in the actual pursuit.[20]

There is another Texan account of the chase of Santa Anna and the Mexican cavalrymen. Y. P. Alsbury participated in the destruction of Vince's Bridge as well as in the pursuit of the fleeing Mexicans from the battlefield. The account is given as it was written by Alsbury in 1859.

> At the same moment the crowd of officers I have spoken of dashed off of the field, bearing in the direction of the Bridge, the Mexican Cavilry droping in their rear, not stopping even a moment to meet the brunt of our charge.
>
> ... at which time thirteen of us remained together and directed our whole attention to the pursuit of their cavilry, believing as we did, that St Anna was among them, each one of us eagerly bent forward in his pursuit, determined on his death of [or] capture .
>
> ... eagerly pressing on his rear, as they strung out according to the respective speed of their horses, and nothing but the bloody scene that followed could equal the excitement of what has so justly been called the bloody chase of St. Anna, for, from that time, ever on, until we reached the smoking ruins of Vinces Bridge, we cut them down in detail, reducing their no. to about twenty, a distance of about nine miles.
>
> I have no doubt, the naughty tyrant must have pased

19. Diary of Lt. Col. Nicolas de la Portilla, Apr. 22, 1836, Peña Papers (CAH).
20. Filisola, *Evacuation of Texas,* 39.

∞

The Pursuit

19

moments of deep anxiety, as ever an on during the exciting chase, the keen yell of the Texian, as he shouted, Remember the Alimo, and Laberdee, Remember our butchird country-men, as such expressions of a just revenge fell upon his ear, accompanied at the same time by the deadly crack of the rifle, as well as the driping point of the crimson blade, all, all plainly told him. Freedom shrieked for revenge, and Texas must, and should be free. But still onward he rode, with apparent ease, on the swift, and splendid black stallion belonging to Mr. Vince little dreaming at the time of the net before him, that had been prepaired to receive him. . . .

St. Anna on seeing the Bridge was destroyed, made a half wheel to the left, and came dashing through both gaps [in the low fence], up the byou at full speed, and in a quartering direction towards us on our left. Now is our time Boys, coolly observed Capt. Carnes, let us meet them.

They must either fight or take quarter, don't let them pass, and by a timely dash to the left, we succeeded in cuting off their retreat up the byou, and forced them either to fight or spring their horses, into the narrow but deep and boggy stream. Several of their number fell trying to cut their way by us. I will relate one incident that will give you an idea of the scene that took place at the point the contending parties met.

One of our party, by the name of Roberts,[21] was unhorsed, at the same time he unhorsed his advisary, both of their fire arms having failed they clinched hand to hand and decided the combat with butcher knives, Roberts killing him, receiving some slight wounds only.

Most of their number sprang their horses in to the byou and after reaching the oposite bank, they made evry exertion to extricate themselves and horses, for a few minutes; during the time most of their number were shot by us from the near

---

21. There is no "Roberts" in the William Taylor account. The closest name to Roberts is Thomas Robbins. Taylor admits that he cannot remember all the men's names and Y. P. Alsbury is one of the men he does not remember. Alsbury actually says there were two brothers named Roberts, and he seems to have forgotten Taylor—just as Taylor forgot him. Taylor, "Pursuit of Santa Anna and His Cavalry," 537–540.

bank literally redning the sluggish stream with human gore.

But one of their number succeeded in getting his horse up the low, boggy bank, and as he mounted the beautiful grey animal, Lieut. James Cook[22] gave him a mortal wound. He, however, rode off at full speed and reached the Mexican Division that night at Fort Bend, now called Richmond, on the Brazos, bearing the first news of their dismal defeat.

The Mexican Genl. Filisola in a conversation with my Brother some time after, stated also, that the wounded express was a Cavilry Capt., and died a few hours after reaching their camp. . . .[23]

Alsbury went on to relate the story of the capture of Santa Anna, General Cos, and Ramón Caro, personal secretary to Santa Anna. Alsbury wrote that on the morning of April 22 he picked up the trail of Mexican officers on a cow path. He returned to camp and informed Deaf Smith and Capt. Karnes, both of whom set out in pursuit. Alsbury reported that after a distance of sixteen miles Karnes and Smith were able to capture Cos and an officer named Nunis.[24]

22. James Cook is listed in the Taylor account. Ibid.

23. Y. P. Alsbury Reminiscences, in Eugene C. Barker Papers (CAH). Alsbury noted later in his account that his brother was H. A. Alsbury. He also gave the story of his brother, a Spanish speaker, calling out to Santa Anna in the brush to give himself up.

Alsbury went on to say that he was unsure of the number of Mexican cavalry they pursued. He said that he agreed with Deaf Smith who said that at that period the Texans had no time to stop to count enemies, dead or living. He did estimate that they were 60–80 strong. He gave the number of Texans involved in the chase as eighteen and listed the following names as those he was able to remember: Capt. H. Carnes, Lieut. Jams. Cook, Lieut. Jams. Elutt, two brothers by name J. Roberts, Jams. Kuzzini, H. A. Alsbury, and Y. P. Alsbury.

24. Santa Anna would later ask Filisola to send him his luggage at San Jacinto. He also requested the luggage of several other officers, including Col. Nuñez. The Col. Nuñez mentioned by Santa Anna was likely Lt. Col. Gabriel Nuñez Ortega. He had served with Urrea at Goliad and Coleto Creek. He then joined Santa Anna as an aide and was captured at San Jacinto. Nuñez Ortega kept a diary of his participation in the Texas Campaign. He wrote that the efforts of one of the Texans, Capt. Coleman, saved him from being killed. Gabriel Nuñez Ortega, "Diario de un prisonero de la Guerra de Texas," *Boletín de archivo general de la nación, Tomo,* IV, No. 6 (Nov.–Dec., 1933), 836.

When they returned, Smith informed Alsbury that had he known for sure that this was Cos he would have shot him on the spot. Apparently Cos had placed a reward of two thousand dollars on Smith's head the year before in San Antonio.

There are several items in the Alsbury account that are of great interest. His report about the Mexican officer that remounted his horse, received a fatal wound, and yet was able to reach Old Fort is not easily explained. The story sounds most like it would be Miguel Aguirre who was wounded in the thigh. Like this officer, Aguirre was mounted. However, the San Luis log entry of April 24 states that Aguirre reported to their battalion on April 24 that all the rest of the division of Santa Anna was dead or captured. Therefore it is known that Aguirre lived until at least April 24 and there is no record of him dying after that point. It is certainly possible that the officer that Alsbury saw wounded never did arrive at Old Fort and that Filisola thought that they were talking about Aguirre. Even that theory has a weakness in that there is no evidence available that Aguirre died from his wound.

It is also very enlightening that Y. P. Alsbury tells of his brother, H. A. Alsbury, a Spanish speaker, having spoken with Filisola, some time later. As will be seen in a later chapter there is ample evidence placing H. A. Alsbury in the Mexican camp on May 7.

Y. P. Alsbury also wrote the following statement that seems unusual for the reports of the period. It may be due to the fact that the account was written over twenty years later when some of the bitterness may have waned.

> Thus ends the chapter of all the particulars that I have any consense off, as connected with the capture of the four survivors of the bloody chase of St. Anna, and strange to tell, a fact that reflects credit upon our enemies, that during the whole chase and struggle the evening before, I do not recollect a single instance of one calling for quarters. They fell, either defending themselves or trying to escape.

Santa Anna and the fleeing cavalrymen were not the only Mexican troops who were trying to remove themselves to the friendly confines of Filisola's camp on the Brazos. Gen. Martín Perfecto de Cos, commanding five hundred reinforcements, joined Santa Anna at San Jacinto on the morning of April 21. This corps, which had left Old Fort on the afternoon of April 18, was composed of the Guerrero Battalion, the remainder of the Aldama and Toluca Battalions, and two companies of the Guadalajara Battalion. What has generally been forgotten is that only about four hundred of the five hundred men in Cos's column ever reached the battle site. The remaining one hundred men were left to the rear as Cos made his forced march to join Santa Anna. This was verified by Santa Anna himself in his manifesto.

At nine o'clock on the morning of the 21st, in full view of the enemy, General Cos arrived with four hundred men from the battalions of Aldama, Guerrero, Toluca and Guadalajara. He left one hundred men under the command of Colonel Mariano García to bring up the baggage that was detained at a bad crossing near Harrisburg. These men never joined us.[25]

General Filisola wrote:

The news of the catastrophe that the commander in chief had in San Jacinto arrived at the general headquarters at Oldford on the twenty-second by means of a presido soldier who secretly delivered to General Filisola a short note from Acting Colonel Don Mariano García in which he informed him, although briefly, of the misfortune.
. . . [A few minutes later] Acting Colonel Don Mariano García arrived with the pack animals and the troops accompanying General Cos; the latter had left them on the way in order not to delay his march.[26]

Filisola gave a few more details in his letter to the Mexican gov-

25. Antonio López de Santa Anna, "Manifiesto que de sus operaciones en la campaña de Tejas y en su cautiverio," translated in Castañeda (trans. and ed.), *The Mexican Side of the Texas Revolution,* 76.

26. Filisola, *Memorias para la historia de la guerra de Tejas* (Rafael, 1848, 1849), reprint, *Historia de la guerra de Tejas* (1968), II, 472–473; Woolsey translation, *Memoirs for the History of the War in Texas,* II, 231.

ernment dated May 14, 1836, from Victoria, in which he reported that on the afternoon of April 23 "a soldier of the frontier dragoons presented to me a small piece of paper, written with pencil, by Colonel Mariano García, first adjutant of Guerrero [Battalion], in which he informed me of the unfortunate occurrence of the afternoon of the 21st."[27] García was listed on the Mexican army roster as being the first adjutant of the Permanent Battalion of Guerrero.[28]

García and his pack wagons sped toward Old Fort after they learned of the defeat at San Jacinto. The fleeing column was being trailed by the Texans. The account given by one of the pursuers, Col. Sterling C. Robertson, in a letter that later appeared in the *Morning Courier and New York Enquirer*, follows.

> I went in pursuit of those that escaped from the field of battle, and those that were in the rear of the reinforcement, commanded by Cos; and left as a guard for his baggage. They appeared to have been frightened, almost to death. Every hundred yards on the road, for 20 miles they had thrown away some of their plunder, and a whole mule load could have been collected, frequently in the distance of a mile; and often the mule with his pack on his back, being run down, was left on the road side. They left the main road, and went through the prairie; and traveled all night, to enable them to reach the Brazos; where the division of Sezma [Gen. Joaquín Ramírez y Sesma] lay, or was crossing the river, at a place called Fort Bend; about 40 miles below San Felipe.[29]

The dates of the various documents are inconsistent, as is discussed in the Introduction, but it seems likely that, being mounted, Aguirre arrived with García's supply wagon on April 22 at Old Fort.[30] Barragán and Somosa rejoined the army on April 25. Peña

27. Vicente Filisola, May 14, 1836, letter to the Mexican Government, in Peña, *La rebelión de Texas*, Anexo No. 22, pp. 281–282, translated in Filisola, *Evacuation of Texas*, 39.

28. "Relacion de los Senores, Gefes y oficiales."

29. Sterling C. Robertson, letter, *Morning Courier and New York Enquirer*, July 8, 1836.

30. The possibility that Filisola intentionally altered the dates in his early documents to give credence to his actions will be discussed in a later chapter.

did mention a presidial soldier along with these two. He also spoke of an artilleryman and a twelve-year-old fifer of the Guerrero Battalion, Luis Espinosa, arriving "later." Filisola reported that along with Aguirre were two sergeants, and four or five others. At most, this puts the total of documented escapees from the battle of San Jacinto at twelve or thirteen, including one boy. The number of Mexicans that escaped from the battle was placed at thirteen by the *Morning Courier and New York Enquirer.*[31]

Another document from the Texan side gives an interesting perspective. In 1883 John J. Linn wrote *Reminiscences of Fifty Years in Texas.* It is one of the better source materials from the colonists' side of the story, but unfortunately it is loosely organized and not indexed. As it was written nearly fifty years after the fact, some details appear to be less accurate than those of the Mexican documents.

> Manuel Escalera (still living [in 1883]), a brother in law of Fernando de Léon, was impressed into the service by order of General Urrea, and, being acquainted with the principal roads through the country, he was sent as a courier with special despatches from Urrea to Santa Anna. Upon arriving at the camp of General Fillasola [*sic*] on the Brazos he found that Santa Anna had gone on to Harrisburg.
>
> Escalera was present on the day after the battle when Capt. Barragán [all the Mexican sources have Barragán arriving the 25th but we know several soldiers and at least one officer, Aguirre, did arrive the 22nd] arrived at the quarters of General Sesma. All were satisfied from his manner that something extraordinary had occurred. To Sesma's inquiry, "What of his excellency and the army?" Barragán replied: "All gone to the devil!" (Lleve el diablo todos) [*sic*]. He [Barragán] gave a vivid narrative of the exciting scenes that he had witnessed. He stated that the Texans were incarnate devils, and that nothing could stop them.

31. *Morning Courier and New York Enquirer,* July 9, 1836. The source of the number is given as "Gen. Wall" (General Adrian Woll). This is the same article, by a correspondent of the *Courier,* which tells of the execution of Davy Crockett. The account is very similar to that given by Peña in his memoirs.

∞

The Pursuit

It seemed that the Mexicans fell dead before them, without even the formality of being fired at.

In about an hour some more stragglers came up, and among them a woman who was wounded in the thigh. As soon as the news reached General Fillasola he ordered that no more troops be posted on the Brazos. The stragglers, some forty in all, related most marvelous stories of escapes by field and flood, and all agreed concerning the diabolism of the Texan soldiers. Each one regarded his escape as a miracle.[32]

The Mexican sources did not reflect the forty refugees and make no mention of a woman. It is interesting that Escalera reported the woman was wounded in the thigh and all the Mexican sources reported that Aguirre was wounded in the thigh. It is possible that some of these "refugees" were from the supply wagon of Cos that came into camp that day, and not all were survivors of the battle.

Once Cos's supply train arrived at the Brazos, along with the few survivors, Filisola needed to formulate a quick plan of action. Should he immediately attack the Texans while he still had the advantage of numbers? Should he hold his ground, communicate with the other Mexican forces in the area, and take time to consider his situation? Should he withdraw to a safer location and come up with a plan of action at a later date? It was to be his most important decision of the campaign.

32. John J. Linn, *Reminiscences of Fifty Years in Texas* (1886; reprint, Austin: Steck Co., 1935), 284–285. A Manuel Escalera is also mentioned in the court-martial of Filisola. It is possible that this is the same Escalera who is mentioned as a presidial soldier sent by Urrea to get a secret message to the captive Santa Anna. See "La guerra de Texas: Causa formada al Gral. Filisola por su retirada en 1836," Tomo X, No. 2, pp. 375–378.

CHAPTER 2

Old Fort

THE REARGUARD OF SANTA ANNA'S ARMY was camped at Old Fort on April 21, 1836. Old Fort was located on the Brazos River at the current site of Richmond, Fort Bend County, Texas. This settlement was variously referred to as Holfort, Hold Fort, Oldfort, and Thompson's Crossing. This force was under the command of Gen. Vicente Filisola, the second in command of the army, and numbered just over fourteen hundred men. The size of his force there was never an issue, but its ability to function as a fighting unit became a major item of contention after their return to Mexico. To truly understand Filisola's situation at Old Fort on April 21, several factors need to be considered: the quality of his troops, the large number of noncombatants, the quantity and condition of the supplies, and the morale of the division.

Santa Anna had handpicked the select troops to advance beyond the Brazos and accompany him on his quest to capture the Texan cabinet. The most accepted theory for Santa Anna's bold advance from Old Fort was his obsession with the capture of his nemesis, noted federalist and vice president of the Texas rebels, Lorenzo de Zavala.

Santa Anna, in his *Manifiesto* to the Mexican government, actually gave two reasons for his advance. He wrote that he had gotten word that the president, the cabinet members of the so-called government of Texas, and the chief leaders of the rebellion were at Harrisburg. He felt that if he could deliver one swift blow at this point it would prove mortal to their cause. After he was unsuccessful in capturing the Texan leaders at Harrisburg he claimed that he had to cut off the retreat of the Texans in order to force a fight.[1]

Another theory as to why he charged across the Brazos, leaving the main body of his army far in the rear, was that he was determined to garner the glory of a victory for himself. It may well have been that it was simply due to the lack of respect that the Mexican dictator had for the Texans as a military threat. Santa Anna, in his report to the Mexican government, stated that when he crossed the Brazos on April 14 he had fifty grenadiers, fifty *cazadores* (light infantrymen), the dragoons of his escort, the permanent battalion of Matamoros, a six-pounder cannon, and fifty cases of musket cartridges. In order to understand how Santa Anna cherry-picked the best troops, it is important to understand the makeup of the Mexican army and their individual units.

The Mexican army of 1836 had two types of infantry battalions. The regular troops were organized into battalions that were called permanent and were named after heroes of the Mexican revolution (Matamoros, Morelos, Jiménez, etc.). The army also had several battalions referred to as active units, which would compare to National Guard units of today. The active units were named after their place of origin (San Luis, Querétaro, Tres Villas, etc.). Each battalion, both permanent and active, had eight companies, six of which were regular infantry. Soldiers of the regular companies were called *fusileros* (a *fusil* was a musket). Each battalion also had one company of veteran troops, called grenadiers, and one company of light infantrymen, called *cazadores*. These last two companies were referred to as the preferential, chosen, or select units and were considered the elite troops of the army. The cavalry of the Mexican army was composed of regiments that were named for famous battles in Mexican history (Dolores, Tampico, Cuautla, etc.). They, too, were designated as permanent or active.[2]

Filisola was not exaggerating when he pointed out that Santa

1. Santa Anna, "Manifiesto que de sus operaciones en la campaña de Tejas y en su cautiverio," translated in Castañeda (trans. and ed.), *The Mexican Side of the Texas Revolution,* 22–23.

2. Angelina Nieto, Joseph Heftner, and Mrs. John Nicholas Brown, *El soldado mexicano, 1837–1847: Organización, vestuario, equipo* (Mexico, D.F.: privately printed, 1958), 55.

Anna had assigned about thirteen hundred of the best troops to his own force. He noted that the commander-in-chief's force had three permanent battalions (Guerrero, Matamoros, and Aldama), the Active Battalion of Toluca (which Filisola considered the best of the active battalions), the two preferential companies of the Active Primero Mexico Battalion, two select (preferential) companies of the Guadalajara Battalion, fifty or sixty cavalrymen of the Tampico and Dolores Regiments, the complement of artillerymen for a six-pounder cannon,[3] and the entire headquarters staff. Filisola was left with the remnants of the division that had bivouacked at Old Fort. They were primarily active battalions and two of them were now missing their preferential companies. There is no certainty that Filisola's force at Old Fort would have been able to defeat the Texans in battle. He did have a slight edge in numbers, but if the quality of his units is taken into account, he was at a great disadvantage.

It is true that many of the Mexican troops were battle-tested veterans, having put down several uprisings in Mexico during the preceding years. Just prior to his campaign in Texas, Santa Anna and several of the units had fought and soundly defeated a much larger army from the state of Zacatecas. However, it is also true that a portion of the Mexican army was composed of conscripts, criminals, and untrained Indians from the Yucatán. Gen. Eugenio Tolsa, in his deposition for the Filisola trial, claimed that during a military review in Monclova, Mexico, prior to entering Texas, a full two-thirds of his brigade of two thousand men had muskets that would not fire. He

3. The cannon that was captured at San Jacinto has been described in various sources as a 6-pounder, an 8-pounder, a 9-pounder, and a 12-pounder. Houston called it a double-fortified medium 12-pounder brass cannon in his report to the Texan government detailing the battle of San Jacinto (Jenkins [ed.], *Papers of the Texas Revolution*, Apr. 25, 1836). Dr. Labadie called it a 12-pound piece (N. D. Labadie, "San Jacinto Campaign," *Texas Almanac, 1857–1873,* p. 158). Santa Anna called it a 6-pounder in his report to the Mexican government (Castañeda [trans. and ed.], *The Mexican Side of the Texas Revolution,* 74). Filisola called it a 6-pounder in three places: in *Representación*, in his letter to the Mexican Government of May 14, and in his *Análisis* of General Urrea's diary, p. 42. Pedro Delgado called it a 6-pounder and named the commander of the piece as Lt. Ignacio Arenal (Delgado, "Mexican Account of the Battle of San Jacinto," 613). This piece has often been referred to as the Golden Standard.

∽

Old Fort

went on to say that this was not remedied, despite his complaints, for lack of a gunsmith.[4]

The status of the Permanent Morelos Battalion on April 21 is a good example of the condition of some of the units in Filisola's command. This unit had been sent to San Antonio de Béjar in 1835 under the command of General Cos. Its mission was to quell the increasingly violent behavior of the more aggressive recent immigrants from the United States. There were, however, only about 150 men in the unit when they proceeded to San Antonio. To strengthen the unit nearly four hundred "volunteers" were conscripted and forced to march to San Antonio under the command of Col. José Juan Sánchez-Navarro. Their trip to Texas was filled with adversity as they traversed hundreds of miles of desert occupied by hostile Indians. These men, upon arrival at San Antonio December 9, 1835, were considered a hindrance rather than relief. They were untrained, undisciplined, and did little more than help eat the scarce food that remained in the San Antonio garrison after six weeks of siege.

Several days after they arrived Cos surrendered and signed an oath that neither he nor his troops would ever return to Texas to fight. Under this condition the troops were allowed to return to Mexico. Thus the Morelos Battalion replacements, after just four days in San Antonio, did an about-face and marched back through the desert to Laredo. Upon arriving there, Filisola was stunned when Santa Anna ordered them to continue their march all the way to Monclova. During this trip of over two hundred miles, thirty-two men, as well as many women and children, perished. Filisola described the condition of Cos's detachment as follows:

> More than half the men in this detachment were the rein-forcements who on the very day of the retreat of General Cos had arrived at that city [San Antonio] almost naked, barefooted, with sore feet and almost emaciated and without any strength whatsoever for the sufferings that they underwent in about four hundred leagues [just over one thousand miles] which they did strung out and poorly cared for in every respect. Thus in addition to the discouragement that

4. "La guerra de Texas: Causa formada al Gral. Filisola por su retirada en 1836," Tomo X, No. 3, p. 506.

they must have been caused by the retreat and the surrender of Béxar, they were the least useful because they had only the slightest training in the use of arms, etc.[5]

He further described the Morelos replacements on the march south of Laredo, during which they were without water for nearly two days.

> It did not happen that way with the unfortunate replacements from [the] Morelos because they were so weak and so little accustomed to the fatigue of the marches that they had fallen far behind. Although water was sent to them, with all haste, several of them never managed to drink because they were already dying: others died as they drank: and others finally got through with a thousand difficulties after having drunk.[6]

Cos and his troops finally arrived at Monclova on January 20, 1836. A mere twenty-two days later, on February 11, the Permanent Morelos Battalion left Monclova for Texas. The force of the unit, as they left Monclova, was 393 soldiers, with more than half being replacements.[7] This obviously violated the oath of General Cos that they would fight no more. Between November of 1835 and April 22, 1836, the total distance they marched, on foot, under the worst of conditions, was approximately fifteen hundred miles. Can there be any question why the Morelos Battalion was not one of the units that Santa Anna chose to join him in his dash eastward across the Brazos? For the same reason, this was not the type of unit that Filisola could expect to utilize in a rapid advance against the victorious Texans and exact revenge for the action of April 21st.

5. Filisola, *Memorias para la historia de la guerra de Tejas* (Rafael, 1848, 1849), reprint, *Historia de la guerra de Tejas* (1968), II, 271; Woolsey translation, *Memoirs for the History of the War in Texas*, II, 121.

6. Filisola, *Memorias para la historia de la guerra de Tejas* (Rafael, 1848, 1849), reprint, *Historia de la guerra de Tejas* (1968), II, 275; Woolsey translation, *Memoirs for the History of the War in Texas*, II, 123.

7. Filisola, *Memorias para la historia de la guerra de Tejas* (Rafael, 1848, 1849); Woolsey translation, *Memoirs for the History of the War in Texas*, II, 150.

Another salient point was later raised by Filisola in a letter written to the newspaper *El Mosquito*. He stressed that Santa Anna not only handpicked his force but that his division was unencumbered by sick and wounded.

> It was not a simple vanguard division that suffered that debacle at San Jacinto, in fact it was one whole third of the forces that crossed the Colorado. It was a select portion of the army, unshackled by the sick, the wounded, etc., including all the rest that was his. In short, it was the commander-in-chief and all of his senior officers.[8]

The exact number of the sick and wounded at Old Fort is not known, but a general idea of the numbers can be reached. Filisola reported that on April 28, 1836, he had over one hundred men who were sick and wounded. It should be noted that this was after Urrea had joined him. Urrea may have had more wounded as his division had participated in the battle at Coleto Creek. Filisola may have had some of the less severely wounded from the Alamo.[9]

Filisola listed the following units, along with their numbers, as being under his command at Old Fort on April 24 (this should be April 22 or 23 as he was not at Old Fort on April 24): Artillery—50 men, Permanent Zapadores (sappers) Battalion—144 men, Permanent Morelos Battalion—382 men, First Active of Mexico Battalion—206 men, Active Battalion of Guadalajara—254 men, Active Battalion of Guanajuato—285 men, 46 men of the Dolores Cavalry Regiment, 21 men of the Tampico Cavalry Regiment, and 20 presidial (frontier) cavalrymen. His total force was listed as 1,408 men.[10] In his entire force he had only the sappers, the substandard Morelos Battalion and a few cavalrymen that were regular or permanent troops. Of the three active units under his command, two (First

8. Peña, *La rebelión de Texas,* Anexo No. 2, p. 214; translated for G. Dimmick by Dora Elizondo Guerra.

9. Filisola, *Análisis del diario militar del General D. José Urrea durante la primera campaña de Tejas,* 95.

10. Filisola, *Memorias para la historia de la guerra de Tejas* (Rafael, 1848, 1849), reprint, *Historia de la guerra de Tejas* (1968), II, 474–475; Woolsey translation, *Memoirs for the History of the War in Texas,* II, 232.

Active of Mexico and the Guadalajara) were significantly weakened, as Santa Anna had taken all of their preferential companies. This fact is supported by the smaller numbers of men that Filisola listed in both of these units.

As seen from the above numbers Filisola had only eighty-seven soldiers in his cavalry force at Old Fort. The cavalry of the Mexican army was considered to be its backbone. The condition of the cavalry horses at Old Fort was likely to have been very poor. This is substantiated by the fact that on April 4, 1836, Gen. Juan José Andrade, commander at San Antonio, wrote the minister of war that more than two hundred of their horses had died and that the rest were useless. He mentioned that there had been no grain or good pastures and that the horses had been exposed to cruel temperatures. If anything, the horses at Old Fort should have been in worse condition than those in San Antonio, considering the extra miles they had traveled.[11]

The only branch of his force that could possibly be considered as superior to that of Santa Anna or Houston is the artillery. Filisola did not document the number or sizes of his cannons at Old Fort. Considering that the Mexican army had eight pieces of artillery in the retreat and subtracting the three cannons Urrea brought, he apparently had five cannons.

This number does not add up with the count of cannons that should have been there. In his *Representación* Filisola stated that on March 29 the Zapadores and Guadalajara Battalions left San Antonio for Gonzales with two eight-pounders, two four-pounders, and one howitzer.[12] In the Rafael version of his *Memorias* Filisola documented that Ramírez y Sesma left San Antonio with two six-pounders and that Gaona left with one eight-pounder, and two four-pounders. (Gen. Antonio Gaona and his division had been covering Santa Anna's left flank; he was to proceed to Bastrop and then on to Nacogdoches.) Subtracting the six-pounder cannon that was lost at San Jacinto, this should have left Filisola with one six-pounder, three eight-pounders, four four-pounders, and one how-

---

11. "La guerra de Texas: Causa formada al Gral. Filisola por su retirada en 1836," Tomo X, No. 3, p. 583.

12. Filisola, *Evacuation of Texas,* 11.

itzer, for a total of nine pieces of artillery.[13] If Filisola's count of cannons taken by various forces as they left San Antonio is correct, there are four unaccounted for. Considering all the acrimony among the Mexican officers, it seems almost impossible that any of their cannons could have been abandoned without criticism (as Filisola criticized Urrea for the lost twelve-pounder at Matagorda). Even if he had only five pieces, this would be considered a slight advantage over the three pieces that Houston possessed (which included the Mexican cannon captured at San Jacinto).

It could just as easily be argued that the artillery would have been a disadvantage, considering that speed would have been of the essence in attacking Houston and the Texans before they could regroup and prepare for another battle. This is presumably why Santa Anna sent for five hundred additional troops to join him but specifically stated that he wanted no artillery.

Another factor to be taken into account in evaluating Filisola's position at Old Fort was the presence of a large number of noncombatants. Peña showed nothing but disgust for them.

> At least three fifths or one-half the number of our soldiers
> were squadrons composed of women, muledrivers, wagon-
> train drivers, boys, and sutlers [assuming 6,000 troops this
> would put the number of noncombatants at anywhere from
> 3,000 to 3,600]; a family much like the locusts that destroy
> everything in their paths, these people perpetrated excesses

13. The numbers of the artillery pieces do not add up correctly. Filisola reported in his memoirs that Sesma took two 6-pounders with him as he left San Antonio on March 11 (Woolsey translation, *Memoirs for the History of the War in Texas*, II, 208). In the same source Filisola wrote that Gaona left San Antonio on March 24 with two 4-pounders and one 8-pounder (ibid., 206). Col. Morales left San Antonio, to join Urrea, on March 11 with three artillery pieces, probably a 4-pounder, a 12-pounder, and a howitzer (Perry [trans. and ed.], *With Santa Anna in Texas*, 65). In his *Representación* Filisola said that on March 29 Col. Amat left with the Zapadores Battalion, the Guadalajara Battalion, two 4-pounders, two 8-pounders, and a howitzer (Filisola, *Evacuation of Texas*, 11). Urrea had a 4-pounder with him as he left Mexico. One 12-pounder was lost by the Mexicans at Matamoros and a 6-pounder at San Jacinto. This should have left Filisola with one 6-pounder, four 4-pounders, three 8-pounders, and one howitzer at Old Fort.

difficult to remedy, and naturally all hatred fell on the army and those who commanded it.[14]

Peña gave more details concerning these noncombatants, which indicate that Filisola's position was even worse than might be expected:

This morning [April 18] Lieutenant Colonel José M. Castillo Iberry, aide-de-camp of the commanding general, has returned from the vanguard with an order that General Cos initiate a march with five hundred infantrymen and no artillery to rejoin his Excellency.... Also we saw the women, who up to now had shared hardships with the soldiers, suffering today the pain of having to separate from them, a measure already taken by the general in command, which, though apparently harsh, was nevertheless expedient for the success and speed of the operations.[15]

Thus, not only was Filisola encumbered by the camp followers of his troops but those of Santa Anna and Cos as well. If Peña's more conservative estimate of one noncombatant for every two soldiers is accepted, Filisola may have had nearly fifteen hundred camp followers, or *soldaderas*, as part of his force.

It might be argued that Filisola could have abruptly abandoned these *soldaderas* at Old Fort to chase down Houston's Texans in short order. There is little doubt this would not have been an acceptable alternative to the soldiers in his command. A lengthy footnote from Filisola's 1848 Rafael version of *Memorias* not only gives an insight into the feelings of the Mexican troops for these women but a glimpse into his own opinion as well.

Here then is one of the serious inconveniences of the ill-advised custom practiced by our army that tolerates the company of families, women and the boys who also tag

14. Peña, *La rebelión de Texas*, 35; translated in Perry (trans. and ed.), *With Santa Anna in Texas*, 22.

15. Peña, *La rebelión de Texas*, 137; translated in Perry (trans. and ed.), *With Santa Anna in Texas*, 113.

∞

Old Fort

along with them. Beyond that, there are more devastating consequences. We see that the worst of it is not the discomfort and scarcity they cause within the Divisions, but there are other more injurious consequences that trespass morality and good behavior. If these men happen to have young women in tow, or have daughters of a certain age, squalor and circumstance drives them to prostitute themselves. From this comes not only desertion, but also corruption, disease, so common among our troops, altercations and even murder.

However, let us assume, without really conceding it, that none of these things would happen, and that these unfortunate wrecks remained loyal to their [Division's] flags, how would that benefit the army? To begin with, these men are already old, weary, and sickly, and as a result they spend more time in the hospital than out of it. When on the march, they are slow and undisciplined. They begin to fall back, either because they simply cannot keep up, or because when they fail to see their wives and children in their immediate surroundings, they become contentious and choose to look for and to accompany their women, or to carry their children in their arms. Once they fall out of formation, they revert to stealing and extortion, assaulting residents and transients along the way, and perpetrating all sorts of despicable mischief.

Furthermore, without diminishing its relevance, there is the fact that with each regiment is a convoy of children and women who without fail, pillage, destroy and annihilate everything in sight, so that by the time the poor soldier, who happens to remain true to his duty, arrives at camp, can't even find water to drink because this rabble, like locusts, have left nothing.

When the moment to engage in battle arrives, all of these married soldiers, and those soldiers who are friends of their wives or daughters and who are concerned about their safety are totally distracted. Instead of paying attention to their commander's orders about where to direct their fire, and instead of advancing and maneuvering swiftly according to their orders, they are only waiting for the right moment to abandon their formation, in order to find and to take care of their women. In doing so, they weaken the lines, and the gaps created in their lines makes the enemy's fire appear to be more effective. Their fellow soldiers then become disheartened and begin to abandon their own positions.

Meanwhile, the women, on the one hand and the children on the other are running around among the rearguard crying and screaming, and running around among the troops and their flanks, and all attempts at stopping this chaotic behavior goes unheeded. All efforts to stop this confusion simply add to it, and it engenders fear. Such disorder, seen from the enemy's vantage point, encourages him to interpret our situation as a dismal retreat or as his victory.

Even when it is explained to this rabble that their behavior interferes and gives our enemy the upper hand, they refuse to refrain from their behavior, even when it means that they are helping the enemy to win a battle. Instead, they become recalcitrant, and they slip into the battle lines to steal from the wounded and the dead, and they encourage their kinsmen to follow their example. The men, instead of fulfilling their duty and holding rank, fall back and participate in the looting. This not only weakens any chance at a victory, but also puts the army at risk in case of a sudden forward move by the enemy, who seeing our confusion and the breakup in our pursuit of them, quickly renews his advance, and finding our men otherwise occupied literally rolls over them.

These misfortunes become even greater and have a more terrible impact when faced with the unfortunate possibility of having to abandon our position to the enemy in what one would hope would be an honorable and orderly fashion. In such an event, the situation really worsens: these wretched families of women and children line the road, impeding passage and raising to high heaven their screams and groans asking everyone not to let them fall into the hands of the oncoming enemy. They not only slow down an orderly march, but they also make it heart wrenching and end up impeding it. Husbands and fathers are torn between their duty as soldiers and their duty to their screaming and moaning loved ones. In the end, the men abandon the march, either to give support to their beloved life companions who have shared in all their labor and misery, or to lift their tender children into their arms, amid the tears and sobs of these already exhausted and starving children who look to their fathers for protection.

They begin with this simple and natural act of compassion, but before long fatigue sets in and in effort to lighten their load, which is now a heavier burden between the weight of their gun, their ammunition, their wives and their children, they, without any doubts in their minds, choose to remain loyal to the objects of their affections and loves of their lives. They drop their guns and ammunition, becoming defenseless, because by that point, under the pursuit of the enemy, their equipment has become more of a problem than an asset, especially in the face of too soon becoming prisoners. If they manage to escape the enemy, it is under the most extreme, almost super human effort on their part. They slip away down a different road. They hide in ravines or take refuge in the dense woods.

That is how they abandon their flags. The cries of their women and compassion for their children incline them against ever returning. They turn away from taking new risks and from enduring further suffering, and in doing so they increase the terrible consequences and the disgrace that comes with having to give up a position to the enemy. Yet, is there anything more natural [than to want to protect one's own]?

If there is, you tell me dear reader, assuming you have a wife and children. What would you do in like circumstances?

THE AUTHOR. [Filisola][16]

There is no denying that the presence of these women and children presented a huge dilemma for Filisola and would have severely hampered his ability to hastily undertake a forced march to San Jacinto.

16. Filisola, *Memorias para la historia de la guerra de Tejas* (Rafael, 1848, 1849), reprint, *Historia de la guerra de Tejas* (1968), II, 277–279; translated for G. Dimmick by Dora Elizondo Guerra.

∞

The amount, condition, and availability of supplies at Old Fort became a major issue in Filisola's trial. This matter was used by Filisola in his own defense as one of the primary reasons he had to retreat from Old Fort. In his May 14 letter to Mexico he described the condition of the army as follows:

> The march of the army had been as far as the right bank of the Brazos River, and it marched like the wind; its primary focus was to push forward toward victory; the soldiers had borne every kind of privation and fatigue with inimitable heroism, their clothing destroyed in the passing of rivers, [in the miserable] condition of the roads, and during the long and painful marches which had been performed without any rest, and without even being able to take a day to wash themselves. The greater part of the troops were barefoot, wanting clothing, shelter and everything necessary to endure a campaign at such an immense distance. . . . I had behind me two large rivers, unguarded by any detachment, a number of sick without physicians, without medicines, and without the hope of any provisions in the wide desert in which I found myself. What few houses and supplies had existed had been reduced to ashes by the owners themselves.[17]

Other officers in Filisola's command gave their depositions at the court-martial. They were each specifically asked about the condition of the army and its supplies at Old Fort. Col. Agustín Amat, commander of the Zapadores Battalion, gave the following report about the armaments and supplies:

> [T]hat he did not think much of the condition of the armaments mainly because of the dew of the nights and the strong sun of the day, since they had no canopies for their protection; that as to the amount of munitions he believed that they had suffered considerably due to the constant jolting of the march, since the cartridges that were in cartridge belts had to

17. Filisola, May 14, 1836, letter to the Mexican government, *La rebelión de Texas,* Anexo No. 22, p. 282; translated in Filisola, *Evacuation of Texas,* 40; retranslated for G. Dimmick by Dora Elizondo Guerra.

be remade frequently; that as to the amount of supplies, most were very scarce, therefore the mess was regularly reduced to only meat and once in a while beans; that the animal fat that they had was thrown away, for the most part, before they arrived at Hold-Fort, as it had become rotten.[18]

Gen. Eugenio Tolsa not only echoed the feelings of Filisola and Amat, but painted a bleaker picture of the condition of the weapons, supplies, etc.

We had several rivers at our back and no possibility of receiving the supplies which the army so badly lacked, since in the stores there existed only 50 loads of corn and three or four casks of wine; that the number of sick was growing at an astounding number due to the lack of shelter and of healthy food which was seldom evenly distributed; in addition one could not count on having medicines or any other means for healing [the sick]. The arms were useless for the most part, which problem I noted at the review of arms that took place in Monclova by my brigade of 2,000 men, of which two thirds would not fire, without having been remedied this evil could bring so many consequences, to regret those frequent representations which in effect I did; the dew of the night is very heavy in this country, equal to a rain storm, so that the arms rusted and required continuous cleaning, and from this resulted another misfortune, that was the loss of some pieces, and the disablement of others, without being able to repair them for lack of gunsmiths; the munitions also suffered this misfortune that was produced by the continuous jolting of loading and unloading on such a prolonged march, in addition to that it resulted from traveling on the backs of mules.[19]

Not all were in agreement, however. Lt. Col. Peña wrote that it was

18. "La guerra de Texas: Causa formada al Gral. Filisola por su retirada en 1836," Tomo X, No. 2, pp. 400–403.

19. Ibid., No. 3, pp. 505–509.

a deception to say that we were lacking supplies; this was nothing but a pretext to justify the necessity and expedience of retreat. At Matagorda, Columbia, and Brazoria, flour, rice, sugar, and potatoes were plentiful. Cattle and pork were to be found in all directions, the former seeming to flow forth from the woods, the latter to be found in the corrals of many homes along the Colorado and Brazos. Between the Brazos and the San Jacinto there were also great quantities of supplies. Although the army needed no more than a month's supply to end the campaign and hoist its eagles on the banks of the Sabine, it would have had supplies for more than six months had it been ordered to remain in Texas; during that time it could have received, in spite of any possible delays, those supplies so frequently offered, part of which later fell in the hands of the enemy because of the retreat.[20]

It needs to be pointed out that Peña, in spite of his claim that supplies are ample, repeatedly cried out about the terrible sufferings of the soldiers and officers of the army. He added that the suffering is not due solely to the lack of supplies but also to the greed of the general-in-chief.

My daily occupations have prevented me from noting the pitiful state of the army. We have given an idea during the course of this diary of the happenings up to the departure from Béjar, and in part up to Gonzales, but we should record for the history of this campaign that at the Colorado the soldier's half-rations of corn tortilla terminated, and his total diet was reduced to one pound of meat and a half-ration of beans. Think of the soldier so poorly fed, clothed and shod even worse, sleeping always in the open, crossing rivers and swamps, exposed to heavy downpours, and even during hours of rest having to protect his firearms from the rain, as he had no protective covers for them, though the campaign required crossing wilderness. No one would object if these sufferings were all the results of circumstances and not of the

20. Peña, *La rebelión de Texas*, 163–164; translated in Perry (trans. and ed.), *With Santa Anna in Texas*, 141–142.

∞

Old Fort

disregard and neglect with which the poor soldier has been treated up to now; yet despite these conditions, this half-starved soldier guarded loads of corn and strictly followed the orders of the general in chief that no one should make use of it. When by accident a sack would tear, we have had the unpleasant experience of seeing the soldiers and the women who accompanied them gather around like chickens in order to pick up the last grain, and further, with their bare hands making certain that no single grain was left. In these cultivated lands around the houses, we have seen them dig up and expose seeds of sweet potatoes and Irish potatoes that had not yet had a chance to germinate.

If the fate of the soldier is pitiful, that of the officer is no less so. Few of them are fed any less poorly than the soldier, and frequently they are seen begging for a tortilla from the muledrivers. There are many here on the Brazos River who have often begged to buy one for eight or ten reales. Shocked, we have seen a muledriver make as much as fifty pesos and four reales for a single liter of corn. In this sad situation the soldier has suffered without complaint, and no one has seen him mutiny for the sake of food, as any but a Mexican soldier would have done. This suffering among our soldiers is not necessarily because they are stupid, but only because the Mexican soldier is the most long-suffering in the universe. If they do not complain, this does not mean that they are not ready to criticize among themselves. Their criticism is as just as it is cutting and sometimes so sharp and amusing that one is compelled to laughter, even in the midst of the compassion that it inspires. Occasionally during the march these complaints are made loudly, intended to be heard by their immediate superiors, but even the most severe among these are compelled to overlook it, for no one dares to reprimand a soldier who is disgruntled because he is not given the rations that have been charged against his pay in advance. The insulting reprimands that some thoughtless officers have made at times have been the more unjust, for the officers themselves have also complained.[21]

21. Peña, *La rebelión de Texas*, 138–139; translated in Perry (trans. and ed.), *With Santa Anna in Texas*, 114–115.

∞

The truth probably lies somewhere between these two diverse accounts. There can be no doubt that these troops had suffered greatly since leaving Monclova in January and February of 1836. Certainly their supplies had been stretched thin by the great distance from Mexico, the poverty of the Mexican government, the scorched-earth policy of the Texans and particularly by the poor condition of the army and its equipment when first leaving Mexico. It is likely that the scorched-earth policy was more widespread than is generally recognized. Peña told of a conversation he had with Doña María Francisca de los Reyes, a young lady of Béjar, who had lived among the colonists for six years. She told him some of the families of Texas did not support the war, and decided to wait for the Mexican army to save them from the rebels. These loyalists were unable to do so as armed men set fire to their dwellings.

When comparing these accounts, a trend starts to unfold. It is obvious the retreat of the Mexican army was a highly emotional issue among the Mexican participants. Both the Filisola, pro-retreat, supporters and the Urrea, anti-retreat, pundits were so involved with the issue that they were very prone to exaggeration. More often than not they twisted the facts to support their particular beliefs and actions during the campaign. As the retreat progressed, the animosity between the two generals and their supporters became more apparent. By the time the army had returned from Texas, and for years afterward, the two camps continued to attack one another. In 1837 Filisola and Peña had a back-and-forth war of words in the Mexico City newspaper. In 1838 Urrea published *Diario de las operaciones militares de la división que al mando del General José Urrea hizo la campaña de Tejas* in response to Filisola's *Representación* to the Mexican government. Later the same year, Filisola published a response to Urrea's manuscript. In many ways the bickering was almost comical. Every little detail of the retreat was dissected with a fine-tooth comb trying to find any means for one of them to criticize the other. One needs to keep this in mind when evaluating the various writings. For the most part, the earlier the writing, the less the bias involved. Documents dated after May 14, 1836, when Filisola began to feel the need to justify his actions, reflect an ever increasing degree of bias.

In addition to lack of supplies, General Filisola used the morale of the soldiers as an excuse for undertaking the withdrawal: "Alarm and discouragement was general amongst all classes, for it was

∞

Old Fort

believed that all the prisoners, the president included, would have been shot as a reprisal for the conduct observed in Béxar and Goliad with theirs."[22]

In regard to this statement, the deposition of Colonel Amat did not support the opinion of Filisola. Amat testified

> that the morale of the army was good, since the arrival of this notice [the defeat at San Jacinto], it [the army] controlled its emotions, and it was consequently upset by this unexpected misfortune, and although the opinions about it were diverse as they should be, and the faces generally sad, they acted to control it, and order and subordination were kept.[23]

Peña quoted Filisola's evaluation of the army as being discouraged, and addressed it specifically.

> Such an assertion was an injurious falsehood about the army, which as a whole had opposed the retreat, since they would have been shamed at being stopped within sight of the enemy's weakness when heretofore not even the enemy's entrenchments nor the thought of his substantial numbers or the superior quality of his force had detained them. They became indignant against those who held them back and outraged to see honor debased and a country sacrificed, which they had been charged to defend; they showed resentment and pain upon seeing that through folly and weakness without parallel, their cruel sufferings their sacrifices, so numerous and great, had been rendered fruitless. Only weak souls are crushed in the presence of adversity, the strong on the contrary, are stirred by fortune's blows; they grow in stature and rise above the whims of this fickle deity. General Filisola measured the sentiments of the army by his own, so it is pleasing to me and very satisfying to affirm for the sake

22. Filisola, May 14, 1836, letter to the Mexican government, *La rebelión de Texas,* Anexo No. 22, p. 282; translated in Filisola, *Evacuation of Texas,* 40.

23. "La guerra de Texas: Causa formada al Gral. Filisola por su retirada en 1836," Tomo X, No. 2, pp. 400–403.

of truth, and the honor of my comrades-in-arms, and for my own sake as a Mexican and a soldier, that his judgment was in error. This dismay to which General Filisola refers was not evident at Thompson's, except among certain persons he had taken as counselors, who did not counsel him well and who compromised his reputation and that of the army. Generals Gaona and Woll were there, but neither they nor the commander of artillery showed any noticeable dismay, nor did any of the lower ranks of the army. In the Sapper [Zapadores] Battalion, with which I made the campaign, there was, except for its commander [Colonel Amat], not a single individual who did not raise his voice against the retreat from the very moment he was ordered to retrieve everything that had been transported to the left bank of the Brazos. . . . It is true that some, who thought we were taking too much time to get away from the enemy, loudly protested against the retreat when they saw that we were already incapable of taking the offensive.[24]

Lt. Col. Portilla gave a hint that things were less than calm in the Mexican camp on April 22. He wrote that generals and some officers were anxious about the division of General Urrea as strong protection. Portilla had spent most of the campaign in Urrea's division so it was natural that they questioned him. They asked him about the division's state and strength. He replied that nowhere was there a column of fighting Mexicans so filled with pride from many and repeated triumphs. According to Portilla, the army spent the night of April 22 under arms and all the generals and officers remained in their respective positions. There were only a few officers that Portilla knew well enough to discuss the main decision of that unfortunate day. Among these friends he listed "Col. of artillery—Ampudia, Captains of the Zapadores Peña and Ricoy, and the major of this corps, Romulo Dias de la Vega."[25]

24. Peña, *La rebelión de Texas,* 162–163; translated in Perry (trans. and ed.), *With Santa Anna in Texas,* 140–141.

25. Diary of Lt. Col. José de la Portilla, Apr. 22, 1836, Peña Papers (CAH). Peña and José Maria Ricoy were brevet lieutenant colonels but were sometimes referred to as captains. This was their pre-campaign rank. Romulo Dias de la Vega is listed as

∽

Old Fort

John Linn also gave us Manuel Escalara's impression of the effect of the news of San Jacinto upon the Mexican army.

> The army was thoroughly panic-stricken and demoralized by the excited tales of these refugees.
>
> During that day the army was withdrawn from the river, and guards posted so as to prevent a surprise. Before authentic reports of the disaster reached them General Sesma, thoroughly frightened, could stand the strain no longer and set out for Mexico to bear the tidings as he had received them from the fugitives.
>
> Munson, formerly a resident of San Felipe, and a watchmaker by trade, was a prisoner in the hands of the Mexicans, and was forced to take charge of the ferry at Richmond [Old Fort], which post he filled several days under guard; and his statements coincide with those of Escalera, just related. Upon the withdrawal of the Mexican forces he was set at liberty.
>
> If General Sesma was a fair sample of the Mexican officers—and it is probable that he was—the result of the battle of San Jacinto is less surprising and more readily accounted for.[26]

In a separate statement, Peña verified that prisoners were used as rowers and boatmen in crossing the Brazos. He also reported the Brazos was wider and swifter than the Colorado. He commented that with no barge available, the crossing of the Brazos was made even more difficult.

Looking at the account of Escalara, as told by Linn, it is apparent that many of the details given are not true. Ramírez y Sesma obviously did not hightail it for Mexico at the news of San Jacinto. He stayed with Filisola until after the crossing of the Colorado, at which point Filisola ordered him to Mexico. It is interesting that Escalara

---

the 1st adjutant of the Zapadores Battalion on the "Relacion de los senores, gefes y oficiales." Ricoy is mentioned on the same document as a captain and company commander in the Zapadores Battalion.

26. Linn, *Reminiscences of Fifty Years in Texas*, 285–286.

SEA OF MUD

does back up Filisola's contention that the army was in a panic and demoralized.

Taking into account the above factors regarding the condition of Filisola's forces on April 22, his actions can be more fairly evaluated. He contended his initial movements were based upon these factors, as well as the poor military position of the point he occupied at Old Fort.

When Filisola learned of the defeat of Santa Anna, his force was in a vulnerable position. The seven hundred troops under the command of Gen. Antonio Gaona had occupied Bastrop on their way to occupy Nacogdoches. After leaving Bastrop they proceeded to lose their way between there and San Felipe de Austin. In his April 8 orders to Filisola, Santa Anna had decided that Gaona would be sent instead to Harrisburg. By April 13 Santa Anna had still not heard from Gaona so he instructed Filisola to send a detachment to San Felipe to find Gaona and direct him to Old Fort to await further orders.[27] Gaona's force did not arrive at Old Fort until April 21 and began to cross the Brazos on April 22. Gaona's command had been ordered to continue its march to Nacogdoches but the crossing was halted when word of the defeat arrived.

Even before the wounded Captain Aguirre arrived, Filisola began to take action. He immediately crossed the Brazos accompanied by Col. Pedro de Ampudia, commander of the artillery of the Mexican army. Filisola directed the construction of a bridgehead with cotton bales around one of the houses on the left bank of the river.[28] This fortress was large enough, in Filisola's estimation, to enclose a battalion of infantry and the three artillery pieces that had already crossed the Brazos. He then placed the *cazadore* companies of the Morelos Battalion and the Guadalajara Battalion at a distance, along the only road that led to Harrisburg. Needing more information about the enemy, and hoping to find stragglers from the battle, he dispatched Lt. Macedonio Castillo of the Tampico Regiment. Castillo, along

27. Richard G. Santos, *Santa Anna's Campaign against Texas, 1835–1836, Featuring the Field Commands Issued to Major General Vicente Filisola* (Waco: Texian Press, 1968), 94, 96.

28. The Mexican participants in the Texas Revolution often wrote of the "left bank" or the "right bank" of a river. To determine which is which, act as if you are facing downstream and then the left bank is the one on your left.

with twenty cavalrymen described as the best riders, proceeded to "the end" of the Harrisburg road. Peña also reported that troops were sent toward San Jacinto but gave some different details.

> Lt. Col. Nicolás de la Portilla[29] has told me that he requested some cavalry in order to search for the stragglers and also to see if he could locate his brother, Don Manuel, aide to the commander in chief, and that this had been denied him; but on the 22nd a cavalry patrol and some infantry were sent as far as the exit from the woods. No doubt our general has remained very proud in the thought that he has exhausted every means of reuniting the scattered troops, but he has misled himself miserably, and I am forced to conclude that because he is a foreigner [Filisola was Italian by birth], he is not interested in the fate of Mexicans.[30]

In his diary entry of April 23, 1836, Lt. Col. Portilla confirmed what Peña stated about wanting to find his brother Manuel. He wrote that he pleaded with Filisola to cross the Brazos with four dragoons to see if he could determine his brother's fate. "He denied me."

Filisola utilized the small cotton-bale fortress on the opposite (east) side of the river as his headquarters. He immediately began to recross Gaona's brigade. Most likely this was so that he could personally supervise removal of the exposed troops from the east bank. This fort and the smaller outpost on the Harrisburg road were deemed necessary because Filisola felt his divided force to be at considerable risk if attacked.

The place where I said the type of bridgehead was built by

---

29. Diary of Lt. Col. Nicolás de la Portilla, Apr. 23, 1836, Peña Papers (CAH). Manuel Portilla, the brother of Nicolás Portilla, was on the general staff of Santa Anna and was captured at San Jacinto. There is a letter in the James Morgan Papers at the Rosenberg Library in Galveston from Manuel de la Portilla, who was a prisoner, to James Morgan, commander at Galveston. These two brothers are often confused and Nicolás is often listed as killed or captured at San Jacinto.

30. Peña, *La rebelión de Texas,* 148; translated in Perry (trans. and ed.), *With Santa Anna in Texas,* 125–126.

Sr. Ampudia was surrounded by a dense forest, having been cleared by ax, an area of about 150–200 varas in radius; the clearing forming a semicircle with the river: it seemed to me then that it should be my command to immediately continue passing the troops on the other side, back to this side. Those that had carried out the relief on this operation, that lasted until the morning of the 24th, were Generals Gaona, Ramírez y Sesma, Tolsa, Woll and myself in person; because in those circumstances if the enemy had approached, in the numbers that had been suspected by the witnesses; it is indubitable that the forces that I had there, separated almost in half by a large river that required 38 minutes for each passage; and having no more that one solitary barge, or so called canoe for carrying it out; they could not have been more exposed and compromised than they were.[31]

Filisola continued with a thorough description of the house, near their campsite, on the right (west) bank of the Brazos. He also mentioned a nearby cotton gin. This is likely to have been the gin of Thomas H. Borden and his small settlement called Louisville (also Bordentown).[32] He described the large loop in the river that surrounded his campsite, and gave this as one of many reasons the position was not defensible militarily. He mentioned that the left bank was covered by a thick wood which would hide snipers. He also noted that the left bank was higher and thus dominated the right bank. Additionally, there were several fords of the river nearby making it easy for the enemy to cut off any retreat. Filisola gave all these details as proof of the camp's strategically poor location. In arguing for his need to withdraw from Old Fort, he remarked that the area in the loop of the Brazos was full of swamps with frequent creeks and thick woods that formed a labyrinth. He decried that his maps of the area were full of inaccuracies and he had no guides or scouts with knowledge of his position.

31. Filisola, *Análisis del diario militar del General D. José Urrea durante la primera campaña de Tejas,* 43.

32. Moses Lapham, "Moses Lapham: His Life and Some Selected Correspondence, II," ed. Joe B. Frantz, *Southwestern Historical Quarterly,* 54 (Apr., 1951), 466–468. In Thomas Borden's letter of March 8, 1835, he told of building a large

As the units under Gaona's command began to return to the west side of the Brazos, there occurred another incident that was to later become a point of contention between Urrea and Filisola. Peña reported that many barrels of brandy were destroyed and other provisions thrown into the river for lack of transportation. He noted that these provisions, for the basic needs of the soldiers, had previously been rationed to the point of deprivation. Additionally, equipment was set on fire, most of it belonging to officers who had fallen at San Jacinto. Knapsacks were burned, which Peña felt should have been distributed among the Guadalajara Battalion and the auxiliaries of the Guanajuato, which had none.

General Urrea, in his declaration for the Filisola trial, mentioned the following about the destruction of supplies at Old Fort:

> From the information of various officers it was felt that they
> [Filisola's troops] had the needed supplies for one month,
> and that some of the supplies were destroyed the same day
> that the army began the retreat. It was reported that they
> burned some baggage of the prisoners, backpacks and other
> various things, among which was the only barge that was in
> Old Fort. This destroyed the only chance of salvation for our
> stragglers from San Jacinto.[33]

Peña noted in a letter written to the newspaper *El Mosquito* on February 3, 1837, that Filisola retreated after burning the only flatboat that was at that point of the river. In his reply to Peña on February 5, 1837, Filisola vehemently denied ordering the burning of the flatboat: "false, infinitely false that the ferry was burned, as it is

---

cotton gin on his new place. In his letter of November 7, 1833, he said he had decided to call his new homesite "Louisville." In a letter of August 9, 1836, Borden reported that they had experienced the devastating aspects of a horrid and brutal war. He said that he had lost all of his personal property, including buildings and fences, which were burned. He was unable to save his own clothes. Borden's cotton gin could be the one Filisola described at the Mexican campsite at Old Fort; the fact that Peña and Filisola documented that the houses at the Old Fort campsite were burned as the Mexican army left that position strengthens this possibility.

33. "La guerra de Texas: Causa formada al Gral. Filisola por su retirada en 1836," Tomo X, No. 3, p. 528.

equally false that the ferry was not used for crossing the river, or that it was not available for the stragglers."[34]

The burning of the ferry or raft was verified by Portilla in his diary entry of April 23. He called the ferry the only means that they had to cross the river which could have saved some of the stragglers. He even added that other acts were committed that he was not going to include in his diary because they could be considered criminal. It should be noticed that there is an amazing consistency in the statements of Urrea, Peña, and Portilla. It is suspicious that the diary of Portilla, like that of Peña may have been written or at least revised after the return to Mexico.[35]

By the afternoon of April 23 a large portion of Gaona's section had completed the recrossing of the Brazos. In most of his writings Filisola simply stated that Old Fort was such a poor position militarily he decided to withdraw to the homesite of Madam Powell. Elizabeth Powell was a widow who came to Texas from New Orleans in Austin's second 300. She ran a tavern at a major intersection of the Columbia-to-San Felipe road. Filisola said he instructed Urrea to join him there and began the movement toward Powell's on April 23 (some of his earlier writings dated it April 24). Yet, in his *Análisis del diario militar del General D. José Urrea durante la primera campaña de Tejas*, Filisola gave a totally different account of how his division ended up at Powell's. He wrote of a homesite eight miles upstream from Old Fort along the San Felipe road. It was on the west bank of the Brazos and a good meeting place for his scattered forces. In this version he claimed that he left Old Fort that afternoon, intending to march to said homesite, leaving General Gaona and the Guadalajara Battalion to finish recrossing the Brazos that night.

The march had progressed only a few miles when Filisola called a halt. He wanted to wait for some supplies and make sure he did not get too far ahead of Gaona. When the mules arrived carrying these supplies, he claimed that not only were the items poorly packed but the mules were overloaded as well. He claimed the confusion of the situation was aggravated not only by all the baggage (that of Santa Anna and his staff, the generals and the officers) and all

34. Peña, *La rebelión de Texas,* Anexo No. 2, p. 214; translated for G. Dimmick by Dora Elizondo Guerra.

35. Diary of Lt. Col. Nicoláas de la Portilla, Apr. 22, 1836, Peña Papers (CAH).

the maintenance gear of the companies and corps that had been at San Jacinto, but by the multitude of accompanying orderlies and women. As this operation was proceeding, darkness fell and the poor roads created a great hindrance to the march; their path was poorly traveled and obscured by the undergrowth, and the area was criss-crossed with cattle trails and small streams, making it easy to stray from the road.

Apparently, one N. Cárdenas, who had come from Urrea's division to see his brother-in-law Col. José Antonio Treviño,[36] assured Filisola that he knew the location of the dwelling Filisola was trying to reach. He said Urrea had camped there the night of April 20, and offered to lead Filisola and his troops to that spot.[37] General Filisola claimed he had no knowledge of the whereabouts of Urrea and was assured by Cárdenas that the road was adequate. After three to four hours, the general realized they should have by now arrived at the homesite. He chastised Cárdenas and they made camp near a stream to await the dawn and get their bearings. He sent messages to Gaona and to Urrea notifying them where to meet him on April 24. At dawn Filisola could see that instead of paralleling the river as he had intended, they had marched perpendicular to it, headed southwest, toward Madam Pow-ell's dwelling. As he had already come this far, he decided to wait for General Gaona before proceeding on to Powell's to await Urrea.

This account provides insight into the consequences of the haste with which Filisola left Old Fort. He certainly could have waited for Gaona to finish crossing his force instead of dividing his troops. The threat from the Texans was not imminent, nor of such magnitude that a forced night march, during which he became lost, was justi-fied. Filisola's later writings failed to give this version and claimed he specifically chose Powell's as a meeting place. When examining Fil-isola's orders to Urrea, instructing him to abandon Brazoria and

36. Filisola, *Análisis del diario militar del General D. José Urrea durante la primera campaña de Tejas,* 45. This is likely the same officer who is listed as Col. Antonio Tre-viño, killed in action at San Jacinto. See Archival Correspondence of George Fisher Galveston, 5-26, 1836, http://tamu.edu/ccbn/dewitt/fishergeorge4.htm.

37. José Urrea, "Diario de las operaciones militares de la división que al mando del General José Urrea hizo la campaña de Tejas," in Castañeda (trans. and ed.), *The Mexican Side of the Texas Revolution,* 249. The diary verifies that Urrea's division spent the night of April 20 at Powell's.

Columbia and join him immediately, his account of being lost in the dark seems credible.

The first message sent by Filisola to Urrea was dated April 23, 1836, from Hold-Fort. In his diary, Urrea pointed out that the date given on this document was a mistake. As he received it at nine or ten in the morning on April 23, it could not have arrived by that time if written on the same day. It was likely written on April 22, as Filisola got the news of San Jacinto that afternoon and claimed he sent orders to Urrea even before Garcia and Aguirre arrived that evening.[38] In this first communiqué Filisola told Urrea of the defeat of Santa Anna and ordered him to immediately join him. He instructed him to bring all his troops to "this point"—referring to Old Fort.

Filisola's next letter to Urrea was dated April 24 (should be April 23). Subsequently he had changed his instructions and told Urrea to follow the guide he had sent to the place where he (Filisola) awaited. It is apparent that when Filisola sent the second letter he did not know he was headed to Powell's. If he had, he would have told Urrea to meet him at Madam Powell's. Filisola sent this second letter the night of April 23, when he was unsure where he was or what his exact destination would be.[39]

Peña's description of his exit from Old Fort was consistent as to dates and times, although he made no mention of the army being lost. This is not surprising as it is unlikely he would have been privy to such embarrassing information.

> The night of the 22nd the Sapper [Zapadores] Battalion received orders to approach the banks of the river, and we commanders and officers were under the impression that we were going on the offensive to hold the crossing while the rest of the army went over it, a natural assumption; but we occupied the whole bank, not without some surprise and indignation at the recrossing of the loads of ammunition and supplies that had already crossed to the other side for General Gaona's march. Yesterday morning [April 23] as we

38. The early documents written by Filisola said that he got the news April 23, not April 22. This will be discussed later.

39. "La guerra de Texas: Causa formada al Gral. Filisola por su retirada en 1836," Tomo X, No. 3, pp. 535–536.

∝

Old Fort

retreated toward the camp we found our tents down, but we did not begin the countermarch until sundown, leaving the aforementioned general to look out for the recrossing of the loads that still remained on the opposite side. On the same night of the 22nd we noticed a sort of aurora borealis on the side where the encounter had been[40] under the circumstances, some of us attributed this brilliant reflection to the cremation of our dead. We had already marched a few hours and darkness obscured some objects when we noticed that the houses we had left were on fire.[41]

The issue of dates became a point of contention after the retreat. Filisola tried to claim he received the news from San Jacinto on April 23 and began the retreat on April 24. One possible explanation is that he was trying to support his claim that it was too far from Old Fort to San Jacinto to attack the Texans quickly enough to catch them unprepared. In his *Representación* to the Mexican government he claimed that it was forty-five leagues (120 miles) from Old Fort to San Jacinto. If, as he claimed, it was 120 miles, it was unlikely the Cos supply train and those that escaped San Jacinto could have reached Old Fort in twenty-four hours. Peña countered that it was only fifty-four miles from Old Fort to San Jacinto. He later quoted

40. This quote by Peña is taken from his diary entry for April 24. Therefore when Peña writes "yesterday" he may have been speaking of April 23. This glow on the horizon was possibly the explosion and fire of the Texan ordnance that is described by Pedro Delgado in his account of the battle of San Jacinto. Delgado dated it as April 23 (Delgado, "Mexican Account of the Battle of San Jacinto," 622). If one reads the Peña account it seems as though he may have meant to date it April 23, as he said, "on the same day," and he had just been talking about April 23. This date still does not agree with the fact that Marcos Barragán and Somosa reported to Filisola that they heard many musket volleys on April 22 and thought the Mexican prisoners were being executed (Filisola, *Análisis del diario militar del General D. José Urrea durante la primera campaña de Tejas*, 63). It is possible that this was the exploding munitions that Delgado reported and from which Peña may have noticed the glow.

41. Peña, *La rebelión de Texas,* 147; translated in Perry (trans. and ed.), *With Santa Anna in Texas,* 124; retranslated for G. Dimmick by Dora Elizondo Guerra. This is the passage where Peña verified the burning of the homes at Old Fort as reported by Thomas Borden.

Lt. Col. José María Castillo, a prisoner from San Jacinto, as stating the distance was more like seventy-five miles. According to the *Texas Atlas and Gazetteer*, it is closer to forty-five miles. It should be noted that a Mexican mile equals .893 English miles,[42] making Peña's fifty-four Mexican miles equal forty-eight English miles. His distance, therefore, was nearly right on. In later writings, after his trial, Filisola corrected the dates and reported that the news of the defeat arrived at Old Fort on April 22. Thus the Peña account seems to be the more accurate in regard to the dates and distances involved. Filisola appeared to have exaggerated both the timing and the distance, possibly in order to justify his failure to attack Sam Houston.

In order to better understand Filisola's options, the average distance the Mexican units could march in a day needs to be considered. The San Luis daily log is an excellent source for this information because it documented the distance the battalion traveled each day. In order to be fair to Filisola, only the days just prior to San Jacinto will be considered. This is when the traveling conditions would have been similar to those that the Mexican army would have encountered in an advance on San Jacinto. Taking the nine days prior to their arrival at Powell's (using only the days that it appeared they marched a full day) the average distance was 7.1 leagues or just under twenty miles. Looking over the entire document, there are no days that the battalion marched further than twelve leagues (thirty-two miles). Overall the most common distance seems to have been about six leagues (sixteen miles). Considering these distances it is reasonable to state that Filisola could have reached San Jacinto within two to three days, once he had finished crossing the Brazos River.

When Filisola learned of the defeat of Santa Anna he had to make a crucial decision, and he needed to do so in a timely manner. One of his options was to finish crossing the Brazos immediately, send orders to Urrea to do the same, and meet Urrea on the road to San Jacinto. At that point he would have been in position to attack the Texans before they could reorganize, get reinforced, and dispose of the Mexican prisoners. Filisola later argued it would have required ten days to cross the Brazos and advance to San Jacinto.

42. Manuel de Mier y Terán, *Texas by Terán; The Diary Kept by General Manuel de Mier y Terán on His 1828 Inspection of Texas,* ed. Jack Jackson, trans. John Wheat (Austin: University of Texas Press, 2000), 210.

However, even using a conservative estimate, he should have been able to finish crossing the Brazos by April 24 and attack the Texans by April 26 or 27. Filisola seems to have conveniently forgotten that Cos had made the march from the east side of the Brazos, leaving Old Fort on the afternoon of April 18, and arriving at San Jacinto at nine in the morning on April 21. Admittedly, when Cos arrived at San Jacinto, his troops were exhausted. Their panic upon being awakened by the attacking Texans may have been a major factor in the overwhelming Texan victory. It is true that not only did Cos leave his supply wagons and camp followers behind, but he also had no artillery to slow him down. Even considering these factors, one would think Filisola should have been able to finish crossing the Brazos and arrive at San Jacinto within four to five days. It is impossible to say for certain, but it is highly likely that this scenario would have caused the Texans serious problems.

Another choice would have been to await Urrea at Old Fort. Even though Filisola asserted that he was in a poor military position and that the left bank of the river dominated the right, the fact was, he controlled *both* banks. He would have been able to find an adequate defensive position on the left bank to protect the army as it finished crossing the Brazos. Urrea could have joined him by April 25 at the latest, and he would have been able to march to San Jacinto by April 28 or 29. This scenario would have left the Texans more time to prepare, but they might still have been disorganized.

His third option was the one he chose. He decided to fall back, regroup, join up with Urrea, and see what the consensus of the generals was concerning a plan of action. This was the conservative choice and, by all accounts, Filisola was a conservative leader. If he had been able to foresee the future this plan would have been unacceptable, but at the time it probably was the best decision.

In retrospect, since they ended up mired in the Mar de Lodo, the first option—to cross the Brazos and meet Urrea on the road to San Jacinto—would have been the best, but even that was a long shot. Filisola was hindered by the sick, wounded, and noncombatants. He could have pressed forward and gambled that the Texans would not attack those left behind at Old Fort. Granted, his force was composed of many of the least formidable troops in the Mexican army, but Urrea's forces were of higher quality, and battle-tested. Sam Houston was wounded and may not have been able to function in his role as commander of the Texans. Another consideration is the probable effect of the horrendous rains that were to commence April 26. Arguably, these rains would have been even more devastating to an advancing Mexican army than a retreating one. At best, it would seem Filisola had only a fair chance of short-term success with this venture. At worst, it could have meant the destruction of the entire Mexican army in Texas.

Filisola was asked the following questions at his court-martial: What steps had he taken after the outcome of the San Jacinto expedition was known? Had any means of attacking the enemy been found? What enemy forces were there, and at what places? What were his motives for abandoning the position that he held? His answer to the interrogation was as follows:

> [T]hat the afternoon of the 23rd [should be April 22], after he received the disastrous notice of what happened to his excellency, the General in Chief, as I was ignorant of the strength of the enemy that attacked him, the distances, and whether his excellency was dead or captured, and thinking that if a prisoner he may have been shot in reprisal, that the enemy might advance, either toward Old Fort, exploiting the closeness of the forces, or by the road from San Felipe, or to the Atascosito Pass on the Colorado, to cut off the retreat of the army, those supplies that might arrive, and communication, it was arranged immediately to reunite all the forces between the Brazos River and the Colorado at the homesite of Madam Powell.[43]

At this critical moment in the Texas Revolution the outcome was hanging in the balance. If a bold, aggressive leader, i.e., Urrea, had been second in command it is quite possible the Mexican army would have attacked. However, a successful outcome from such a maneuver would have been very much in doubt. As it was, with the more conservative Filisola in charge, the Texans never had to prove that the victory at San Jacinto was not a fluke. Indeed, Filisola argued later that he had saved the Mexican army to fight another day. His critics may well ask—to what avail?

---

43. "La guerra de Texas: Causa formada al Gral. Filisola por su retirada en 1836," Tomo X, No. 2, pp. 386–387.

CHAPTER 3

Urrea

GEN. JOSÉ URREA COMMANDED the division of the Mexican army that had advanced along the Texas Gulf Coast. When he left Mexico, his division was composed of 293 cavalrymen and three hundred infantrymen of the Active Yucatán Battalion. The latter unit was composed primarily of Indians and considered one of the least effective of the entire Mexican army. His artillery consisted of only one four-pounder cannon. Just before the division arrived at Goliad, they were reinforced by the Active San Luis and Permanent Jiménez Battalions and three pieces of artillery,[1] under the command of Col. Juan Morales. Soon after, they were joined by the Active Tres Villas Battalion.

Filisola argued that his division was very poorly supplied. Urrea's troops, on the other hand, were in very good condition in terms of

1. Sources disagree on the size of the three pieces of artillery. The San Luis Battalion daily report entry of March 11, 1836, said that the unit left San Antonio with the Jiménez Battalion and a 12-pounder, a 6-pounder, and a howitzer. They were ordered to join Urrea. On their entry for March 20 they reported that two 8-pounders arrived at Coleto. The problem is that Urrea had no 8-pounders. Col. Nicolás de la Portilla reported in his diary entry of March 19 that he took two 4-pounders to the battle site. (A portion of the Portilla diary is included with the Peña Papers at CAH.) Urrea reported in his diary that on March 20 two 4-pounders and a howitzer arrived at the battle site. Considering these various sources it seems likely that the three pieces that were sent from San Antonio to Urrea were a 12-pounder, a howitzer, and a 4-pounder. The 12-pounder was lost to the Texans at Matagorda, so Urrea probably brought a howitzer and two 4-pounders with him when he joined Filisola at Powell's.

supplies. Urrea had captured Matagorda, Columbia, and Brazoria—
towns the fleeing Texans had not burned as they had Gonzales and
San Felipe—and at both Matagorda and Columbia a large stash of
goods was captured.

Urrea's division was not only well supplied but, by all accounts,
extremely confident and ready to fight. On February 25, 1836,
Urrea's troops met and defeated a small detachment of Texans at San
Patricio. All the Texans, save three and their commander, Frank
Johnson, were killed in the action. On March 2 the division vanquished Dr. James Grant, the commander of the Texan campaign
against Matamoros, at Agua Dulce, killing Grant and forty of his
men and taking six prisoners. On March 14, 1836, they made a
frontal attack against Col. William Ward and his Georgia Battalion, at
the Mission Refugio. In this action the Mexican forces reported
thirteen dead and forty-three wounded.[2] Ward and his troops
slipped out of the mission that night but were later captured and
executed with Fannin's men at Goliad. The Texan force under Capt.
Amon B. King was surrounded in the woods south of Refugio,
attacked by the Mexicans and forced to surrender. On March 19
Urrea's troops surrounded and battled the Texans under the command of Col. James Fannin at Coleto Creek. Fannin surrendered his
command the following morning after the Mexican artillery
arrived. According to the more reliable sources, both opponents
took moderate losses in the action, most likely twenty-five to thirty
men were killed on each side.[3] Additionally, the Mexicans captured
a large store of arms, munitions, artillery, etc., during this action.

2. Filisola, *Memorias para la historia de la guerra de Tejas* (Rafael, 1848, 1849), vol. II;
Woolsey translation, *Memoirs for the History of the War in Texas,* II, 194, 232. The
Morning Courier and New York Enquirer of May 30, 1836, printed a letter from a
"Mexican general to his wife. It was intercepted by the Texians." The letter was
written from Goliad on March 25, 1836. It is unlikely that the officer was a general
as he was with Urrea, who had no other generals in his command. This letter put
the total dead and wounded Mexicans from assault on the Refugio mission at 40.
He went on to tell of the horror of the execution of the captured Texans from this
action.

3. In his *Diario,* Urrea placed the number of Texan casualties at 27 dead and 97
wounded (Urrea, "Diario de las operaciones militares . . .," in Castañeda (trans. and
ed.), *The Mexican Side of the Texas Revolution,* 236). He claimed that there were 11
Mexican dead and 54 wounded (45 soldiers and 5 officers). Col. Garay's account

The route that Urrea took during his advance to the north, eventually ending up in Brazoria, is very poorly documented in most Texas history sources. It is important to be aware of his route because he ultimately convinced Filisola to take the same path south during the retreat. From Goliad, Urrea advanced to Victoria and on to a small village called Santa Anna. He then proceeded to cross the Colorado River at Cayce's Crossing which was near present-day Bay City. From here he headed south, paralleling the Colorado, to capture Matagorda. After leaving the Tres Villas Battalion at Matagorda, he countermarched and camped the night of April 17 at the same site where he had spent the night following the division's crossing of the Colorado on April 12.[4]

Both Urrea and the San Luis log stated that they advanced along the San Bernard for the next few days. This was most likely Caney Creek and not the San Bernard. The road that the San Luis report indicated they took out of Matagorda was called the Bay Prairie Road. It paralleled the Colorado and skirted the Caney as well. If the distances given by the San Luis report are evaluated, they are

---

(included in Filisola's *Análisis del diario del General D. José Urrea*, 22) stated that the Mexicans were unaware of the number of Texan dead as they had buried all but 5 in the night. He listed the Texan wounded at 64. He listed the Mexican dead as 33 dead and 98 wounded, including 4 officers. Dr. Joseph H. Barnard (see Linn's *Reminiscences of Fifty Years in Texas*, 158, 163) put the number of Texans dead at 7 with 60 wounded. He stated that they were unsure of the number of Mexicans killed, but stated that there were 15 bodies near the Texan line. He placed the number of Mexican wounded at 100. The San Luis Battalion Log claimed that there were 50 dead and wounded Texans. It placed the casualties from their own battalion at 2 dead and 30 wounded. It should be noted that some of the Texan sources, i.e. Herman Ehrenberg and Mrs. George W. Cash, placed the number of Mexican casualties at 740 and 600 respectively. Those estimates are far higher than the number of Mexican troops participating in the battle. Natalie Ornish, *Ehrenberg; Goliad Survivor—Old West Explorer* (Dallas: Texas Heritage Press, 1993, 1997), 225; Sons of DeWitt Colony Texas Website, http://www.tamu.edu/ccbn/dewitt/goliadframe.htm.

4. San Luis Battalion Daily Log, Apr. 17, 18, 20, 1836. Urrea reported that the campsite of April 17 was on the San Bernard River but the San Luis Battalion Log stated that it was the same place they camped on April 12 when they crossed the Colorado. The log also noted that on April 16 they left Matagorda on the same road on which they had entered.

∝∞

Urrea

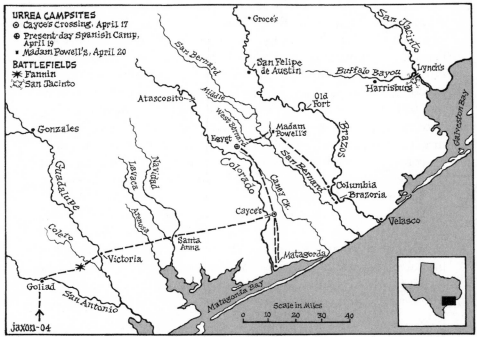

Map No. 2. Probable Route of Gen. José Urrea's division, from Fannin battle site to Brazoria. *Drawn by Jack Jackson.*

more consistent with their being on the Bay Prairie Road (see Map No. 2). Recent Mexican army archeological finds along the west side of the West Bernard Creek can be explained only by Urrea taking this route north. On April 20 Urrea crossed the San Bernard and camped at Madam Powell's. In addition to the Urrea *Diario de las operaciones militares de la division que al mando del General José Urrea hizo la campaña de Tejas* and the San Luis log documenting this fact, there is a 1936 historical marker at the Powell homesite stating that Urrea camped there. This path places Urrea much further north than most Texas history maps indicate when showing his advance. From Powell's he proceeded south, occupied Columbia and marched on to Brazoria. Indeed, if he had come up the coast, as most Texas history books claim, he would have reached Brazoria first and then Columbia.

Filisola reported that on April 24 Urrea's force included the fol-

SEA OF MUD

lowing units: artillery—20 men, Permanent Battalion Jiménez—273 men, Active Battalion of San Luis—394 men, Active Battalion of Querétaro—258 men, Permanent Regiment of Cuautla—102 cavalrymen, Permanent Regiment of Tampico—97 cavalrymen, and the Guanajuato Auxiliaries—21 cavalrymen. This totals 1,165 men under his command. It is not specifically stated in the records but it is likely that Urrea's men had their camp followers as well. Using Peña's estimate of one *soldadera* for each two soldiers, an estimate of five hundred noncombatants is not unreasonable. Urrea had three pieces of artillery at his disposal, a seven-*pulgado* (or 6.5 inch) howitzer and two four-pounders.[5]

It is important to note that even though most of the sources describe Urrea's division as confident and full of fight, it had undergone significant losses. The Jiménez and the San Luis Battalions had sustained heavy fire at the Alamo as well as at Coleto Creek. Comparing the strength of the battalions under Urrea's command on April 24 to the rosters when they first left Mexico, it is evident they had suffered significant losses due to battle, illness, and desertion. The Jiménez Battalion had twenty-seven fewer men, the San Luis was down sixty-six, the Querétaro had ninety men fewer, the Cuautla Regiment was missing forty-six men (almost 33 percent), the Tampico Regiment was actually up thirty-four (possibly they had been reinforced from another part of the Tampico that left Mexico with the cavalry brigade, but I find no record of this), and the Guanajuato Auxiliaries was down fourteen men. In total, at least 209 men were dead, wounded, or missing from the six units. Certainly, this must be taken into account when considering their readiness to engage the Texans so soon after San Jacinto. It should be noted that each battalion was intended to have eight companies of 50 to 100 men. Thus a battalion at full strength would have been 400 to 800 men. Of all the battalions entering Texas, only three had the requisite four hundred men and then just barely. This indicates that the units were undermanned even before they left Mexico.

5. Filisola, *Memorias para la historia de la guerra de Tejas* (Rafael, 1848, 1849), vol. II; Woolsey translation, *Memoirs for the History of the War in Texas,* II, 232. Urrea also had a 12-pounder cannon and the Tres Villas Battalion under his command, but they were left in Matagorda. The 12-pounder was lost and the Tres Villas did not participate in the retreat of the main Mexican army until they rejoined the army at Victoria.

At Columbia, Urrea left the Jiménez Battalion, all the cavalry and some pickets of the San Luis and the Querétaro,[6] under the command of Col. Mariano Salas. On April 22 he proceeded with the rest of the corps, a howitzer, and a four-pounder to Brazoria, which he occupied at ten that morning. In Urrea's diary he wrote that many of Brazoria's citizens awaited him, having been assured by Dr. Harrison that they would meet no harm. Harrison, an American, had been captured in Victoria and sent ahead with a letter from Urrea to calm the fears of the colonists. This mysterious Dr. Harrison was widely believed to be the son of President William Henry Harrison, and is mentioned in many of the period sources. There were reports in the U.S. newspapers that Dr. Harrison, son of William H. Harrison, had been captured, castrated, and disemboweled by the Mexicans.[7] This was not the case as Harrison later showed up at Lynch's Ferry.

William Fairfax Gray, a land purchaser from Virginia, noted in his diary entry for April 15: "Dr. Harrison also came in the steamboat [from Harrisburg with many of the Texas cabinet]; the son of General William H. Harrison, who was reported to have been massacred at Victoria." Gray went on to say that Urrea had treated Harrison well, had given him a fine horse, a saddle, and a hundred dollars. This was because Urrea had served as the Mexican minister to the country of Columbia at the same time William H. Harrison represented the United States.[8] It is interesting to see the contrast between the

6. José Urrea, "Diario de las operaciones militares de la división que al mando del General José Urrea hizo la campaña de Tejas . . .," *Documentos para la historia de la Guerra de Tejas* (Mexico: Editora Nacional, 1952), 26. Castañeda (trans. and ed.), *The Mexican Side of the Texas Revolution*, page 249, wrote "Guerrero" but the original Spanish of Urrea's diary said "Querétaro," not "Guerrero." This should be the case as the Guerrero Battalion did not serve under Urrea. Castañeda also translated *obus* as a "mortar" and a "howitzer" would be more accurate.

7. *Morning Courier and New York Enquirer,* May 9, 1836. The whole report is as follows: "We also learn that Dr. Harrison, son of Gen. Harrison of North Bend, Ohio was while traveling with three American gentlemen, taken by the Mexicans, castrated, his body cut down, and his bowels torn out and left in that situation before life was extinct! The wife of Dr. Harrison came as a passenger on the *Invincible*."

8. William Fairfax Gray, *The Diary of William Fairfax Gray: From Virginia to Texas, 1835–1837,* ed. Paul Lack (Dallas: William P. Clements Center for Southwest Studies, 1997), 154–156. The entire quote is as follows: "Dr. Harrison also came down in the steamboat: the son of general William H. Harrison, who was reported to have been

"evil and vile" Mexicans described in the New York newspaper and the very humane treatment that Harrison apparently received from them.

---

massacred at Victoria. He was taken prisoner, but General Urrea having been Minister from Mexico to Colombia at the time that General Harrison was also the Minister from the United States, out of respect and regard for the father, he protected the son. He was entertained in the General's tent, and was permitted to return to the United States on his parole. The General, on his departure, gave him a fine riding horse, $100, a cloak, and also permission to bring off an American prisoner as a servant. He brought off Ben Mordicai, of Richmond Virginia, who was thereby saved from the general massacre that took place of Fannin's men. Colonel Garay conducted him away from the Mexican camp, and at parting presented him with his sword. He speaks highly of Urrea and Garay—latter is Governor of Durango, and commands the southern division of the invading army [this should read the former, not the latter], Siezma commands the center, which is that now at San Felipe; the northern division is destined for Nacogdoches, under _____, Harrison says the report in camp was that the division had proceeded up the Colorado 300 miles, without meeting a white man. It will strike across the upper country to Nacogdoches. He says Urrea was very indignant at the massacre of Fannin's troops; said it was done without his orders or knowledge. And that he intended to resign his command and return to his government as soon as the army reached Brazoria. Speaks highly also of Garay. He also confirms the report of a revolution or trouble in Mexico, which had caused the return of Santa Anna." [Santa Anna did briefly consider a return to Mexico right after the Alamo. It was reported by many Texans and picked up in U.S. newspapers that he had done so.]

In his entry for April 16, 1836, Gray noted that Harrison went on the steamboat with the members of the cabinet, on his way to the United States. Gray wrote that Harrison sold Urrea's gift [horse], including the bridle and saddle to Colonel Houston for $50, and presented the sword to President Burnet.

There is a footnote from the editor of the Gray diary that gives the following information about Dr. Harrison: "There has been considerable skepticism expressed about this story, but the circumstances described by Gray are corroborated by other evidence. Dr. Benjamin Harrison (1806–1840) was the sixth of ten children fathered by William Henry Harrison. He suffered from alcoholism and family turmoil and failed a cure designed by his father in the form of an extended western trapping expedition in 1833–34. In all likelihood he arrived on the Texas coast in March of 1836 and quickly fell into the hands of the Mexican army. Harrison returned to Ohio, where he died on June 17, 1840. Harbert Davenport, *Dr. Benjamin Harrison*."

An excellent discussion on Harrison is included in Pat Ireland Nixon, *The Medical Story of Early Texas, 1528–1853* (Lancaster, Penn.: Lancaster Press, 1946), 227–233.

The Harrison story took another interesting twist when the good doctor, who supposedly had been impaled, showed up in Galveston. According to the *Morning Courier and New York Enquirer,* Harrison was "boasting of being an officer in the Mexican service (Surgeon General), and actually came in before the battle with some of Sezma's proclamations to distribute."[9]

General Urrea made a comment in his *Diario* entry on April 22 that revealed how tenuous Houston's situation was at the time. Urrea reported that, through several informants, he had discovered Houston's intention had been to occupy Galveston and defend it until the families and possessions there could be evacuated. Apparently there were Texans willing to aide Urrea in his efforts against Houston,

> and he [Houston] who in the course of unfavorable circum-
> stances could have obtained no glory as a soldier and might
> have perhaps disappeared from the scene, presented himself
> now as the conqueror and the hero. Men were not lacking,
> of those who had served under him, who now offered to
> lead me to that formidable Houston. There were even those
> who voluntarily offered to contribute to his defeat, for they
> desired it because the greater part of the men under his
> command were adventurers who were worse enemies of the
> colonists than we ourselves.[10]

Urrea claimed that he crossed the Brazos on the afternoon of

9. *Morning Courier and New York Enquirer,* July 9, 1836. It is unlikely that Harrison had proclamations from Ramírez y Sesma. These were likely the proclamations that were given to Harrison by Urrea.

10. Urrea, "Diario de las operaciones militares," *Documentos para la historia de la guerra de Tejas,* 27–28; translated in Castañeda (trans. and ed.), *The Mexican Side of the Texas Revolution,* 251. This statement seems to hold some truth and may be more factual than is known. Urrea had prepared the way for his advance by sending Dr. Harrison ahead to reassure the Texans that they and their property would be safe. Neither Columbia nor Brazoria were burned upon his arrival. There had been, and continued to be, a large chasm between the newly arrived Texans and the earlier, landholding colonists. Also, at the time Urrea entered Brazoria things looked very bad for the Texans. The colonists were likely trying to cover their bases in light of what looked at the time to be a sure Mexican victory.

∞

SEA OF MUD

April 22 with the preferential companies of the San Luis and Querétaro Battalions. He had received word that there were 300 to 400
colonists garrisoning Velasco. They were said to be on the east bank
of the Brazos, congregating at its mouth. On the morning of April
23, he indicated he was about to start for Velasco and, later, Galveston, when he received a "mysterious executive order of General
Vicente Filisola." He was directed to march immediately to Old Fort
with his entire force, making no stops en route. At least, this is how
Urrea reported the situation at the time he received the news concerning San Jacinto.

The official order from Filisola was:

> Army of Operations—Main—It is absolutely essential that
> your excellency, at the moment which you receive this,
> without making any stops, come to this position with all the
> forces that you have at your command, as this best serves the
> interest of the nation.
>   God and Liberty—Hold Fort, April 23rd, 1836—3:00
> PM—Vicente Filisola—General José Urrea[11]

Filisola sent a personal note to Urrea, along with the official
order to retreat, that simply stated: "The President has suffered a misfortune according to a dispatch sent to me by a colonel who says
that he will be here tonight. It is necessary therefore, for you to do
everything you can to reach this place [Old Fort] with all your force
as soon as possible."[12] This note supports the fact that Filisola said he
sent the order to Urrea and Salas, even before the arrival of Colonel
García and Captain Aguirre.

In his *Análisis del diario militar del General D. José Urrea durante la
primera campaña de Tejas* Filisola included a related quote from the
diary of Col. Francisco Garay. Garay was a brevet colonel who
served on the staff of General Urrea. It addressed several of the issues
previously discussed, i.e., Dr. Harrison, the supplies, etc.

11. "La guerra de Texas: Causa formada al Gral. Filisola por su retirada en 1836,"
Tomo X, No. 3, p. 535.

12. Urrea, "Diario de las operaciones militares," *Documentos para la historia de la
guerra de Tejas,* 28; translated in Castañeda (trans. and ed.), *The Mexican Side of the
Texas Revolution,* 252.

When the division left Matagorda it left there the garrison of the Tres Villas Battalion under the leadership of its commander, who was also the commander of the port, Colonel Agustín Alcerreca. The Lt. Col. of engineers, Juan José Holsinger, was left in charge of building a small fort in which they could place a 12 pounder and two three pounders that they had captured: to this leader 15 prisoners were assigned for helping with the work.

Much has been talked about the supplies the division is said to have taken from Matagorda. This is slander, because what was found at that place was not easy to transport, and the division had no means to convey it; they were scarcely able to carry foodstuff and some liquor, which is what was most needed.

The division occupied Columbia on the 20th: on their journeys of the 16th, 17th, 18th and 19th nothing occurred that is worthy of mention, only the arrival of some slaves that in succession were headed for Guadalupe [Victoria] since none wanted to remain beyond the Colorado: such was the fear that inspired them, the fear that they would return to be captured by their masters, that this class of person did not render us any service.

Columbia was abandoned: and most of the houses were vacant, only in two were found some cases of wine and other fine liquors; they were being sheltered. Two miles from Columbia is the small town of Marion, situated on the Brazos River, which really came to be the port of the first. . . . Marion has few houses, but all are grand and all serve as warehouses: in one of these were found two hundred plus muskets.

On the 21st General Urrea ordered that Col. Mariano Salas, with the Jiménez Battalion under his command, two cannons and a picket of dragoons, remain in Columbia, and occupy Marion as well; and that Señor [Urrea] with the rest of the division head toward Brazoria which is also along the Brazos, four leagues from the first [Columbia].

Since we had been told that the [Texan] garrison at Velasco had occupied that city [Brazoria], necessary arrangements were made to do battle; however there were no more than seven or eight families there whom Dr. Harrison had persuaded to wait for us; among them was the mayor and justice of the peace and other similar officials; the first put in the hands of Col. Garay a letter from said doctor vouching for the integrity and favorable feelings toward the Mexicans from all those that remained.

The mayor was questioned as to the town's warehouses, and he disclosed that there were fourteen. Guards were posted to guard them, but an inventory of their contents was left for later. Col. Morales and Garay took this task, but the sad event that occurred on that same day at San Jacinto did not permit them to discharge it.

The troop was quartered with comfort and committed no disorder.

The mayor and other neighbors informed us that the garrison from Velasco had retreated the night before but that they suspected that part of them were still on the other side of the river watching our movements. General Urrea heard this and commanded that a hundred men be placed at that place; but as this order was not communicated a soldier from the San Luis Battalion who had gone down to drink water was killed by a rifle shot, none the less nobody attempted to oppose the crossing of the troops that were protected by our cannons with some canister. [The San Luis Battalion log verifies the death of the soldier: "April 22 At Brazoria—They killed Eulogio Correa of the 4th" (company).][13]

Brazoria was the place designated by the general-in-chief to be the headquarters of the army after the campaign. No place, however could be less appropriate; acknowledged as very unhealthy, it is surrounded by the thickest forests that extend for five or six leagues in each direction, and half the year they are covered in waters. The city has not progressed since 1830, in spite of its closeness to the sea, which is only eleven leagues away, and with the foundation of Columbia, although four leagues more up river, it is probable that it [Brazoria] will decline completely because [Columbia] is situated on a beautiful plain and has clear roads from all parts

13. San Luis Battalion Daily Log, Apr. 22, 1836.

throughout the year. Dr. Harrison had come straight to this city after he had left us at the Colorado. Trusting his popularity more than his better judgment, he read Santa Anna's proclamation at a [town] meeting, and spoke of the good treatment that he had received from the Mexicans. He told them that the Mexican army was at war only with the volunteers and not with the colonists. The unabashed frankness of his words, plus his enthusiasm to convince those people to renounce their loyalty to Texas and to side with the Mexican cause, plus his liberal and very public spending of Mexican money, that had been given to him, made him appear as a spy in the employ of the Mexican government. As a result, the Commander of Velasco ordered his apprehension and was prepared to execute him. However, after some reflection over the matter, he chose instead to send him to Houston, and Dr. Harrison was hauled away in shackles, which probably saved his life as has been written about previously.

On the 23rd in the morning, as he was going to inspect the warehouses, General Urrea received the ill-fated news of San Jacinto. He suspended said operation, and covertly arranged for the exit of our forces. The General began his march at noon, entrusting Col. Garay to remain with the rearguard until after sunset, endeavoring to withdraw the boats, without giving any suspicion to the neighbors of plausible excuse for boarding them.

As he passed through Columbia, Col. Garay rendered useless the muskets that were there and he burned the boats as they arrived from above on the river, permitting those that had rowed to return to their homes. In the evening he caught up with Gen. Urrea, who had stopped in order to unite all of his forces. He learned of a new march for the homesite called Madam Powell's, where they arrived at 12 midnight. Now the division was incorporated into the army of operations under the command of the Commander-in-chief Vicente Filisola.[14]

---

14. Filisola, *Análisis del diario militar del General D. José Urrea durante la primera campaña de Tejas,* 49–51.

∞

This account of the actions of Urrea's division by one of his own staff members revealed some pertinent facts. It is significant to note that, in spite of the fact that plentiful supplies existed in Columbia and Brazoria, there seemed to be no way to transport them. It is hard to imagine how these supplies could have been made available in a timely enough manner to be used by Filisola's forces in an attack on Houston's army.

It is also apparent there was more cooperation from the towns-people in Brazoria than from those in Gonzales or San Felipe. Some of the Brazorians were seemingly convinced by Dr. Harrison to change their allegiance to the Mexican cause. The mayor, the justice of the peace, and other officials were there to meet Garay and apparently cooperated. Also it should be noted that Brazoria had not been burned by its citizens, as, on Houston's orders, the towns of Gonzales and San Felipe de Austin had been. Once again, it must be remembered that, at the time, it looked as though nothing was going to stop the Mexicans from totally defeating the Texans. In contrast to Brazoria, the Texans at Velasco must have felt less cooperative, as they arrested and almost executed Harrison. Without a doubt, Urrea's division was better fed and supplied than that of Filisola, partly due to the cooperation of the locals.

Garay's diary told of another detail that is pertinent in the evaluation of Urrea's statements. Although he reported that the troops were crossing the Brazos under the guard of their cannons, Garay mentioned that Urrea was in the process of inspecting a warehouse on the morning of April 23, not preparing to leave for Velasco and Galveston as Urrea's diary claimed. It is also tempting to question the validity of Urrea's statement that he was headed to Velasco with four preferential companies to attack the three or four hundred Texans at that point. The four preferential units likely were comprised of no more than 160 to 170 men.[15] However, remembering that Urrea rushed forward at Goliad to cut off Fannin's retreat, and attacked a larger force possessing eight or nine artillery pieces, it is possible that he would have carried out this maneuver.

15. The San Luis Battalion had 394 men with eight companies or approximately 49 men per company × 2 preferential companies per battalion = 98 men. The Querétaro Battalion had 258 men for an average of 32 men per company × 2 = 64 men; for a grand total of 162 men.

Filisola's response to Urrea's statements about these days reflected the bitter animosity that had developed between these two men by the time Filisola wrote his *Análisis* of Urrea's diary in 1838.

Here is a truthful, straight forward account [the account of Garay given above] of the actions that General Urrea disguises with so much verbosity. It alone is sufficient to refute all that this Señor has said in his diary, especially when it focuses on the days of the 23rd and 24th up to midnight when he joined me at the homesite of Madam Powell. Since he has audaciously introduced a number of falsehoods and suppositions that offend my honor so much and that of my companions that had been there with me, I can't help but refute them one by one.

Well then he [Urrea] said, "The 23rd I was about to march toward Velasco and was to continue to Galveston, when I received the mysterious executive order from General Vicente Filisola that ordered me to march to Old Fort with all the forces under my command without any stops. This order was dated the 23rd at three P.M. and I received it the same day between 9 and 10 in the morning. It proved to be an unforgivable mistake." If Sr. Urrea will allow me to point out his error that makes it clearly obvious that he has a bad memory. He had no orders to march toward Velasco, much less to continue to Galveston. Furthermore, he has forgotten, probably because of the many and grave issues he had in mind, that in his communications with His Excellency the President, with me, and with General Ramírez y Sesma, dated the day before, that he had begged the President to allow him to establish his main headquarters in Columbia, giving as his reasons Brazoria's terrible climate, its dense forests and general poor location, the lack of pasture for the horses, and the marshy lands that surround it, etc., etc. In addition, is it not obvious to the reader that those who had been assigned to march toward Velasco were the Señores Cos and Ampudia. In reference to his continuation to Galveston, that is empty talk designed to give himself importance. Instead it has shown lack of respect for the general public, because Galveston is an island. Where did Señor

Urrea have the necessary ships to embark his troops and transport them there?[16]

As discussed in Chapter 2, it is likely that Filisola did get the dates wrong. As to whether that was unforgivable, as Urrea asserted, it would seem not. It is interesting that in Urrea's *Diario* entry for April 23 he claimed that he was about to begin the march to Velasco when he got the order from Filisola. Garay's diary reported that Urrea was inspecting a warehouse at the time. Note that in a continuation of the Urrea diary entry for April 23 (see below at text footnoted no. 18), Urrea claimed that he was four leagues into a thick forest when he got Filisola's message. He acted as though he was within hours of attacking the Texan force at Velasco. Here Urrea seems to contradict himself within the same paragraph of his *Diario*.

Even though there is no evidence that Urrea had any plans or orders to advance against Galveston, there is documentation that he felt that this strike should be undertaken. He had previously offered the opinion that this needed to be done just as soon as possible. Urrea wrote a letter to General Ramírez y Sesma on April 22, the day prior to his receiving the news of San Jacinto and the order to join Filisola.

Señor general D. Joaquín Ramírez y Sesma.—Brazoria, April 22, 1836.—My very dear friend: I am responding to your most welcomed letter from the day before yesterday, and am thanking you for the news that it contained. Like you, I think that by striking a blow against Galveston the matter would be completely concluded. It would put an end to [their] assembly, independence, etc. etc.: but it is imperative that we strike soon, because rain is about to be upon us, and if, at this stage, we are caught in it, we will be trapped for the rest of the year.

By my dispatch to general Filisola, you will learn of my occupation of Columbia, and of this position [Brazoria], by the division under my command, and of the situation of the rebels in these parts, and the reasons that influenced me to

16. Filisola, *Análisis del diario militar del General D. José Urrea durante la primera campaña de Tejas,* 51.

∞

Urrea

choose the first [Columbia], in which to establish my head-quarters.

I am happy at the arrival of friend Gaona; but I would have been more pleased if he had marched directly to Nacogdoches.

I regret that you did not receive the biscuits, I will repeat the effort at the first opportunity.

If you want flour, order it from me; right now we don't have a shortage.

Our colleagues send their regards to you and to the clerk whose old horse you left behind.

It will make me happy if you remain without [bad] news, and that as always you will consider me a true friend, who greatly admires you and kisses your hand. I kissed that hand again . . . You already know why.

My best wishes to all of you, and know that you can issue whatever orders you deem necessary to your friend who values your friendship from the bottom of my heart.—José Urrea.

PS—Let us leave this land soon, where I have not had one single good day. Do everything in your power so that we can push forward on this ragtag rabble, and get it over with, and then we can go to our homes.[17]

Urrea was also upset with Filisola for removing his rearguard. When Filisola sent the order to Urrea to join him at Old Fort, he sent the same order to Colonel Salas in Columbia. Salas immediately obeyed and marched toward Old Fort (and eventually Powell's) without awaiting the approval of Urrea, his immediate commander. General Urrea, still claiming he was in the process of a march to Velasco, had this reaction:

The same order had been transmitted directly to Col. Salas, who, without waiting for orders from me, immediately complied with it. As a result of this operation my rearguard was

17. Urrea to Sesma, Apr. 22, 1836, in Jenkins (ed.), *Papers of the Texas Revolution*, VI, 20.

left unprotected, since I was four leagues ahead in a very thick and marshy woods where not even the rays of the sun penetrated. Velasco is almost as far from Brazoria as this point is from Columbia and, had I undertaken the operation I had planned a few hours before the receipt of the said order, attacking the enemy in their stronghold, I would have found myself in dire distress without the support of a force upon which I depended for my operations. It never occurred to me that this force would be removed without my knowledge. There are many instances where superior orders must be obeyed regardless of the manner in which they are transmitted, but there are others in which exception must be taken and this, in my judgment, was one of them.[18]

Urrea agreed that Garay was left in Brazoria as a rearguard, as stated in Garay's own account. The main force of the troops in Brazoria apparently started the withdrawal toward Columbia at 11 A.M. on April 23. Urrea related that he had assumed he was being ordered to reunite with the main force of the army in order to advance on the enemy. Once again in his diary, Urrea seemed to have forgotten the fact that he was supposedly already across the Brazos and advancing on Velasco at the time he received the order. It seems unlikely, if indeed he was across the Brazos with the four preferential units, that Filisola's order could have arrived sometime between 9 A.M. and 10 A.M. and Urrea's troops had been able to leave Brazoria by eleven.

Urrea reported that after the march from Brazoria to Columbia was underway he

sent his aide, Capt. Pretalia with a cavalry escort to see Señor Filisola and to inform him of the high spirit of my division, showing him how advantageous it would be to advance upon the enemy before it could receive reinforcements. It was impossible for me while on the march to set down the great many ideas that rushed to my mind at the time. I

18. Urrea, "Diario de las operaciones militares," *Documentos para la historia de la guerra de Tejas*, 28; translated in Castañeda (trans. and ed.), *The Mexican Side of the Texas Revolution*, 251–252.

∞

Urrea

instructed Pretalia not to lose a single moment in fulfilling the important commission entrusted to him, and to use all possible means to influence Señor Filisola to advance upon the enemy without the loss of a single moment. Among the instructions given to this officer, I charged him to explain the means that I had for crossing the Brazos quickly at Columbia, if the enemy was between this point and general headquarters, and that if I was being called to him, in order to advance from there upon the former, I could [more effectively] undertake this operation from where I was, before wearing out my soldiers and without losing precious time, since I had the means with which to do it.[19]

This statement, on the surface, sounds well and good. However, with Urrea already on the march, it is doubtful Pretalia was going to be able to find Filisola (who Urrea thought was at Old Fort), get his reply, and return before Urrea's column advanced beyond Columbia. Filisola specifically debunked this purported mission to encourage an attack upon the enemy. In fact he clearly stated that Pretalia gave him no such message.

At about 8 in the morning [on April 24] Capt. Pretalia, of the command of General Urrea, arrived [at the campsite of the night of April 23, between Old Fort and Powell's]. [Pretalia], instead of telling me the many ideas of Señor Urrea, which he had been supposedly charged to tell me, proceeded to complain about his commanding General's inefficiency, and about the confusion among all the ranks, that he himself had been witnessing from Matamoros to the present, where he left him. Not once did [Pretalia] mention the slightest hint of the myriad of ideas of Señor Urrea, as he describes the events of that day, in his report.[20]

Urrea started the march at 11 A.M. on April 23 and Pretalia probably left within a few hours. Thus it took him approximately eight-

19. Ibid., 253; retranslated for G. Dimmick by Dora Elizondo Guerra.

20. Filisola, *Análisis del diario militar del General D. José Urrea durante la primera campaña de Tejas,* 46.

∞

een to twenty hours to reach Filisola. Even if Filisola had immediately replied, it likely would have taken the greater part of half a day for Pretalia to rejoin Urrea's section. It is doubtful he would have been able to return in time to save the troops the unnecessary march, as Urrea claimed to have desired. Considering Filisola's statement and the timing issue, it seems dubious that Urrea ever gave Captain Pretalia this critical mission—to convince Filisola to advance upon the enemy with all haste.

Urrea reported that he arrived in Columbia at 5 P.M. on April 23. Awaiting him there was his personal escort under the command of Lt. Col. Angel Miramón. The remainder of Salas's troops had already marched to join Filisola. Miramón gave Urrea some of the details given to him by Capt. Ruiz, Filisola's aide, who had delivered the orders for Salas and Urrea. According to Urrea, the details involved the army's plans to withdraw from Old Fort, and he described his reaction as follows:

> When I learned that the place which our dispersed soldiers [from San Jacinto] would naturally make their way [Old Fort] was to be abandoned and that a retreat was to be undertaken, a thousand contending sentiments rushed over me and my displeasure was shared by the part of the army under my command. A few hours before, we thought only of flying to avenge our companions and our general-in-chief, but the first rumors of turning our back upon them in their misfortune began to be heard. Such a change, could not but arouse extreme feelings of despair and dismay, of shame and indignation.[21]

He went on to say he loaded as many mules as possible with the supplies in Columbia but did not destroy the rest as he still did not know what Filisola had planned. He ordered the two hundred muskets and powder thrown in the river and ordered his escort to burn the two barges there. He marched immediately but due to the muddy road, made it only one league.

21. Urrea, "Diario de las operaciones militares," *Documentos para la historia de la guerra de Tejas,* 29–30; translated in Castañeda (trans. and ed.), *The Mexican Side of the Texas Revolution,* 254.

∞

Urrea

Filisola related some key points about the above statements in his *Análisis del diario militar del General D. José Urrea durante la primera campaña de Tejas.* To begin with, he noted Lieutenant Colonel Ruiz (Urrea called him a captain), who was not his aide, left from Old Fort before any of the survivors from San Jacinto had arrived. Therefore Urrea could not have been concerned about the stragglers due to information he received from Ruiz.[22] However, the deposition of Lt. Ignacio Salinas, at the trial of Filisola, supported the Urrea version; at least the information about San Jacinto. Salinas was commander of Urrea's escort, and claimed that he learned of the battle of San Jacinto from two lieutenant colonels in Columbia.[23] Secondly, Filisola argued Ruiz would have had no knowledge of what the army was to do when he left camp April 22, as Filisola himself did not yet know whether they would advance or retreat. Moreover, he asked why in the world would Urrea have burned the barges before knowing the results of Pretalia's alleged mission to talk Filisola into attacking?

The second order that Filisola sent to Urrea was dated April 24. It is likely that this was the order that Filisola stated he wrote Urrea when they stopped their march late on the night of April 23. If he wrote it after midnight that night the date would be correct.

> Gen. José Urrea—Camp, April 24th, 1836, My dear friend: I suppose you are on the march and that without a doubt we will be reunited today, so that we can talk about everything. Meanwhile, I am returning the scout that will guide you to the place where I await you. It is more urgent each moment that we meet. What I told you about our P. [President?] is even much more than it appeared; therefore, it is my judgment that you accelerate your march, and that you proceed with caution. From your dear friend that holds you in great esteem. Truly.—Vicente Filisola—P.S.—Do not leave any troops either in Columbia or any where around there.[24]

22. Filisola, *Análisis del diario militar del General D. José Urrea durante la primera campaña de Tejas,* 58.

23. "La guerra de Texas: Causa formada al Gral. Filisola por su retirada en 1836," Tomo X, No. 3, pp. 552–554.

24. Ibid., 535.

Examination of one of the letters Urrea sent to Filisola, prior to his arrival, gives more details of Urrea's frame of mind at the time.

His Excellency General Vicente Filisola—Camp four leagues from Columbia—April 25th, [should be the 24th] 1836—My General and very dear friend: By your memorandum of yesterday, which I received at 11:30 A.M., I understand with great regret, that you had to abandon the camp you occupied along the Brazos River, but what is worse is learning that our commander-in-chief still has not yet been heard from.—I am suspending judgment, because I am not aware of things, but already I can notice the damage to the honor of the Mexican Army and the Nation.—I am eager to join you and as your valor and your skill are well known to me, I do not doubt that this time you will know how to save the reputation of the Mexican soldiers, who know instinctively that they would rather die than appear weak, especially in the face of their current enemies who are cowards, insignificant, and incapable of confronting our forces on the battle-field. I want to tell you many things, but I fear that the information will not come across with the importance it should have, because I am ignorant of all the details. I am uninformed of everything. I am almost beside myself and I cannot calm down until I see the national honor vindicated and see at the same time our worthy commander among us. I conclude my general and friend as I can do no more.— Before I close, I will tell you that I have obeyed your orders to abandon Brazoria and Columbia yesterday; arriving, with the guide that you sent me, at this point, which is seven leagues distant from the place you quoted.—I await here until two companies of infantry and a picket of cavalry, that I left as my rearguard, with the purpose of observing, can join me. This evening I will have all of my forces united and later will continue the march.—Yesterday I dispatched Capt. Rafael Pretalia to meet with you so that he might inform you verbally about my departure from Brazoria, which I have already notified you. Very few hours remain until one part of this division is reunited; it has forces in Matagorda, Guadalupe Victoria, Goliad and Cópano. You will know how

∞
Urrea

81

to resolve what will be best in their regard.—Goodbye, my general, you will soon see and be able to embrace your heartbroken friend and servant Q.S.M.B. [Que su mano besa]—José Urrea[25]

This letter is not only informative, but it shows how the relationship between Urrea and Filisola later changed dramatically. Certainly it could be argued that Urrea was just paying due respect to Filisola, as he was now in charge of the army. On the other hand, it seems as though, early in the retreat, Urrea truly cared for and respected Filisola. Urrea never specifically argued for immediate action against the enemy. He did, however, make it clear that he was anxious to redeem the honor of the Mexican army. He argued that, on the battlefield, the Texans could not stand up to the Mexican soldiers, but it must be remembered that he had no details of the battle of San Jacinto and especially how one-sided the defeat was.

In this letter Urrea seemed to prove that he did indeed know that the position at Old Fort was to be abandoned. However, this was on April 24, late in the afternoon, not at 5 P.M. on April 23, as Urrea had earlier claimed. Of course the exact definition of the word "retreat" may well have been in dispute at this point. Did the retreat start the moment that Filisola abandoned Old Fort, or when the Mexican army left Madam Powell's, or possibly even when they eventually abandoned Victoria?

Urrea's letter also mentioned the mission of Captain Pretalia but did not clarify that Pretalia was to convey Urrea's desire for immediate movement against the enemy. Also, it is important to remember that Urrea did not know for sure there were no enemy troops between him and Filisola, so he seemed to have taken caution not to give too many details in the letter, in case it fell into enemy hands. It should also be noted that the date of this letter was wrong—it should have been April 24. According to his own diary, Urrea was at Madam Powell's by midnight of April 24 and spent the entire day of April 25 at that location. In the papers from the court-martial, Urrea stressed that the above letter (as well as the letter quoted below, dated April 25), should have been dated April 24.

Urrea wrote a second letter on that day to General Ramírez y

25. Ibid., 536–537.

∞

Sesma, who was with Filisola and his division. Later in his diary, Urrea quoted the following letter and the above letter written to Filisola as proof that he objected to the retreat from the outset.

Señor General Joaquín Ramírez y Sesma.—April 25th [April 24] of 1836.—My dear friend, as none of you have told me anything about what you know, I am on the verge of insanity with all kinds of demons in my head. I am desperately yearning to join all of you. It seems like the devil has taken us. Is it not true? What happened with the President? Has he died, and has this been verified to be true? Can we not at least rescue his remains? What a terrible predicament we find ourselves in! Well then, I repeat that I am ignorant of everything, and I will reserve judgment about all that has happened; although, I believe that there wasn't such urgency to abandon the Brazos River to where stragglers from the recent action could go. Do you have any [stragglers]?— Good bye dear friend. Pardon me if I explain it thus. It is not my intention to question the valor of our second in command, even less so that of my comrades, nor the army's commitment or its honor, nor our nation's vulnerable destiny. It is the ever-constant change that drives my heart. Mainly I keep silent, but will talk when we see each other, hopefully soon. Meanwhile I send you an embrace and my affection. From your friend and servant. José Urrea[26]

Urrea did briefly mention that, in view of the stragglers, it might not be the best idea to give up Old Fort. But his letter said nothing about being against a retreat after that purpose was fulfilled. He definitely said nothing about advancing on the enemy, other than the vague reference to recovering the remains of Santa Anna. On the other hand, it should be noted that Urrea had not seen Filisola or Ramírez y Sesma since their last meeting in Mexico, probably in February. He knew very little of the condition of the army at Old Fort, the units and their strengths, or the mindset of the other generals. Basically, he was operating independently of the rest of the army, and had been for months. It seems, in both letters, Urrea was

26. Ibid., 537.

very hesitant to put everything in writing. It is clear he had much more to say to Filisola and Ramírez y Sesma, but he knew he would be seeing them later that day so he did not go into greater detail.

The last letter that Urrea wrote on April 24 at 11:30 P.M. was perhaps the most honest. It is the only time that he seems to openly oppose the sudden movements of the army and his orders to immediately join Filisola. This shows that he likely was against any quick movements to the rear, but since he wrote it to one of his subordinates and not Filisola or the other generals he had to know that it would have no effect on future actions.

> Camp—April 25 (should be 24 [this is Filisola's note]) of 1836—Colonel D. Francisco Garay.—It's 11:30 and I have arrived at the first house that we encountered on the march the day that we arrived at Columbia, and I have just received another needy note from General Filisola summoning me to the house at which we slept the night prior to our arrival at Columbia. This is already a disgraceful flight of the army of which I can not approve, but it is necessary to obey, and so it is that you need to begin your march without leaving the boat that I suppose will come on the wagon. How good it would be if 10–12 men on good horses could return to Columbia and burn the warehouses. . . There is not risk in my judgment but Señor Filisola fears it, and precaution is always needed. Advance without stopping to this position, since it is indispensable to move with promptness in order to calm our companions. Once again my affection.—José Urrea[27]

In his analysis of Urrea's diary, Filisola was outraged by the above letter. He claimed that this letter was a combination of sedition, rumor, atrocity, and much that is ugly in a military man. He went on to ask where in any of his letters to Urrea did he give the impression of being needy.[28]

Once again, we seem to have two disparate sets of documents

27. Filisola, *Análisis del diario militar del General D. José Urrea durante la primera campaña de Tejas,* 60.

28. Ibid.

about the events that occurred immediately after the battle of San Jacinto. All the orders and documents that were written at the time gave the appearance of respect and cooperation between Filisola and Urrea, maybe even friendship. In the documents that were written after the retreat, following the removal of Filisola as commander and his replacement by Urrea, the relationship got downright nasty.

On the surface, Urrea's diary seems to have slightly more inconsistencies than the writings of Filisola. Urrea continued to try to paint a picture of himself as having championed the cause of attacking the Texans immediately. He claimed to be the sole voice, among the leaders, in strong opposition to the retreat. There are several points in Urrea's diary that make his arguments less believable.

First, there seems to be no evidence that he crossed the Brazos and was advancing on Velasco, as he claimed. His own staff officer, Garay, placed him in Brazoria when the notice of San Jacinto arrived.

Second, he claimed to have sent Captain Pretalia on a special mission to convince Filisola to attack, yet Filisola flatly stated that Pretalia said nothing of this to him. Urrea's letter to Filisola mentioned Pretalia but gave no hint that he was to speak directly to Filisola, and express, in the strongest terms, Urrea's desire to attack. Moreover, it seems unlikely that Pretalia could have accomplished the mission in time to stop Urrea's movement to join Filisola.

Third, Urrea claimed to have been informed at 5 P.M. on April 23 that the army was going to abandon Old Fort. It seems very unlikely Urrea could have learned that the army was pulling back from Old Fort until sometime on April 24. In his letter to Filisola on April 24 he even went so far as to say that he understood the necessity for the abandonment of Old Fort, even though he did indicate that it pained him that they had to do so.

Under the surface, however, there is still a gnawing feeling that there is much truth to what Urrea said. Considering the fact that Urrea had not been a part of the main army, and did not know the politics of the headquarters staff, he appeared to be very hesitant to state his case strongly early in the retreat. After all, he barely knew any details of the defeat, and was not likely to want to step on any toes until he had been able to glean more information about the specifics of the situation. Unfortunately for Urrea's claims as to his actions in regard to the retreat, there is little hard evidence that he openly opposed Filisola's movements during the early stages of the withdrawal.

There is no doubt Urrea's division, though slightly smaller than that of Filisola, was in better shape to take the offensive on April 23, when he received the news of San Jacinto. He had (not including his detachments in Matagorda, Goliad, etc.) 1,165 men, with about 273 of those in Columbia and the rest in Brazoria. His division was far better supplied than that of Filisola and had captured numerous arms at Goliad. Their morale was still high as they had been victorious in several battles. And though they had probably only just begun their crossing of the Brazos, they did have two barges or flatboats at their disposal and may well have been able to cross in a fairly timely manner. However, it must be kept in mind that had Urrea done so, he would still have had the Texan garrison in Velasco to contend with. Also, since he did not receive word of San Jacinto until April 23, at the earliest, and allowing at least one day to get approval from Filisola, one day to cross the river, and two days' march, the soonest he could have reached San Jacinto would have been April 27. Considering there was a severe thunderstorm that started at noon on April 26 and lasted for nearly two days, it is very likely that the delay would have been much longer. This would have allowed the Texans ample time to regroup and react to his advance.

Texas historian John Henry Brown claimed that General Gaona, had he been able to advance on Nacogdoches as ordered, would have encountered sufficient volunteers from the U.S. to have defeated him. Brown wrote that there were four to five hundred men on the Nacogdoches road moving to join Houston. He also noted that Capt. John A. Quitman and twenty-five men reached San Jacinto on April 22, and that another 174 men from New York, under the command of Maj. Edwin Morehouse, arrived at the battle site the same day. He also noted that Capt. Jacob Eberly was camped on Galveston Bay with fifty men. Thus, the concern of the Mexican commanders, that Texan forces would be swelling, seems well founded.[29]

Urrea, unlike Filisola, had no decision to make. He was under direct orders to join Filisola. He knew so little of the circumstances

29. John Henry Brown, *History of Texas, 1685–1892* (2 vols.; Saint Louis, Mo.: L. E. Daniel, 1893), II, 46–47.

of the battle that it would have been very difficult for him to have had a strong opinion at that point. It is probable that Urrea was considering the battle merely a defeat—not the total disaster it was. It is obvious from his initial letters that he was stunned by the defeat and anxious to exact revenge. Overall, his claim, from the outset, of strong opposition to the retreat doesn't hold up to close scrutiny. It was especially telling for him to insist that he opposed the retreat before he could have known there was to be one!

With both major divisions of the Mexican army closing in on the Powell homesite, timing would become even more critical. Did the combined Mexican force now have the necessary strength and willpower to attack? Filisola claimed that he had not decided what course to take at this moment. Not knowing what action was best, he decided to call a council of war with his generals—not an indication that he was an aggressive, bold, or independent leader.

CHAPTER 4

Madam Powell's

MADAM POWELL'S TAVERN was located on the south-east side of Turkey Creek in what is now Fort Bend County, Texas. It was situated at a major intersection of several roads, about halfway between San Felipe de Austin and Columbia. This location made it a natural stopping point for travelers in early Texas. Roads led from Powell's to San Felipe de Austin, Columbia, Matagorda, Old Fort, Santa Anna, and the Atascosito Crossing of the Colorado. Elizabeth Powell, commonly referred to as Widow Powell, and her children ran the tavern. Madam Powell's homesite was prominently mentioned in many of the documents of the Mexican army.

The Mexican army visited Powell's on three separate occasions. While making his way from San Felipe to Old Fort, Santa Anna and his vanguard spent the afternoon of April 10 near the tavern. After taking a short rest for water there, he proceeded on to Thompson's Crossing at Old Fort. Urrea's division was the next Mexican force to camp at Powell's. His troops spent the night of April 20 and left the next morning for Columbia. On April 24 the combined forces of Filisola and Urrea met at Powell's and camped there for two nights before leaving on the morning of April 26.

There is no mention in any of the available Mexican documents of Elizabeth Powell or her children being at the site when the Mexican army was there. However, there is an interesting account by Francis R. Lubbock, who reported in his memoirs that he visited the home of Mrs. Powell, her two sons, a daughter, and a widowed daughter. He dated the trip as being in the spring of 1838. He wrote that her home was beautiful, everything there bright and cheery. This would have been her rebuilt home as the Mexican army burned her tavern when they withdrew the morning of April 26. Lubbock related the following information about Madam Powell:

> The intelligent student of Texas history will not fail to note that this was the Mrs. Powell in whose house Filisola held a council of war after concentrating his army a few days subsequent to the battle of San Jacinto. It was the unanimous verdict of the council of war to fall back and get out of Texas as fast as possible. So the famous retreat of the Mexican army began, never to halt on the east side of the Rio Grande. Mrs. Powell was a true Texan and retained a vivid recollection of Generals Filisola, Urrea and Gaona, who staid [*sic*] over night at her house. She also saw Santa Anna and Almonte[1] on their march to Harrisburg.[2]

That Madam Powell did not flee as a part of the runaway scrape in the face of the Mexican army is evidenced in her statement to Lubbock. Filisola, Urrea, and Gaona did spend the night at or near her home, while Santa Anna and Almonte stopped there only for a while. It is unlikely that she would have known this had she not been present at the time.

The fact that Santa Anna and his troops passed by, but did not camp at, Madam Powell's was verified by two separate Mexican officers. Col. Juan Almonte wrote in his private journal that on Sunday, April 10, "At half past 5 o'clock we made a short halt at the farm of the Widow Powell, or rather at a stream called Guajolote [Turkey]; leaving the road from Brazoria on our right, we took the left."[3]

Col. Gabriel Nuñez Ortega, another aide to Santa Anna, docu-

---

1. Col. Juan Nepomuceno Almonte was a special advisor to Santa Anna. Almonte's 1834 inspection of Texas and his role in the 1836 campaign are thoroughly detailed in Jack Jackson (ed.) and John Wheat (trans.), *Almonte's Texas: Juan N. Almonte's 1834 Inspection, Secret Report, and Role in the 1836 Campaign* (Austin: Texas State Historical Association, 2003).

2. Francis R. Lubbock, *Six Decades in Texas; or, Memoirs of Francis Richard Lubbock, Governor of Texas in War Time, 1861–63 . . .* , ed. C. W. Raines (Austin: Ben C. Jones & Co., 1900), 78–79. For more on Madame Powell, see my Preface, p. xviii.

3. Jackson (ed.) and Wheat (trans.), *Almonte's Texas*, 400.

mented in his diary entry of April 10: "At noon we began our march on the Columbia road [this would have been the same road as the Brazoria road that Almonte mentioned] until the house of Mad. Paula [sic] and from there we headed in the direction of Thompson's Pass."[4]

General Filisola awaited Gaona the morning of April 24, on the road from Old Fort to Powell's. After Gaona's arrival, they began the march between nine and ten in the morning. Upon their arrival at Powell's in the mid-afternoon they encountered Colonel Salas and the Jiménez Battalion, a part of Urrea's division, just arrived from Columbia. Peña reported that it was between two and three in the afternoon when they arrived at some houses and found the Jiménez Battalion. He added that the soldiers of the Jiménez were in possession of rich booty from Columbia.

Filisola gave a detailed description of the Powell homesite.

> The position of the dwelling which takes the name of Mrs. Powell's is on the left bank of one of the various arroyos that form the San Bernard, which traverses at that point almost north to south. The location was picturesque: the house was wood and had two parts each six varas square [1 vara = 2.8 feet], between which was a type of corridor and a garden in back of about 20 varas square. There were also two or three other shacks, one of which served as the kitchen and the others served as servant's quarters. In front there are various oak trees to the east; and on the road that goes to Brazoria, there is another group of trees and from these to the arroyo in front of the house the land forms a type of elevation that is nearly imperceptible, because of this the house is in a hollow, so that one can not see a great distance from it. On the middle of this [elevation], supported on the right by the mentioned group of oak trees and on the left to the arroyo, the corps was ordered to form with its line being cut into two almost right angles by the road to Old Fort. At the right edge of the arroyo another very battered dwelling was found at a distance from the main house of 800 to 1000 paces.[5]

4. Ortega, "Diario de un prisonero de la Guerra de Texas," 835.

5. Filisola, *Análisis del diario militar del General D. José Urrea durante la primera campaña de Tejas,* 47.

Sometime during the day of April 24 Filisola issued the following proclamation to his division:

To The Military

A cowardly and disloyal enemy has, quite by chance, been able to overcome that section of the army under the personal command of the President General, no doubt due to the disdain in which the latter has held the former; otherwise the valor of his troops could not have been deterred.

This small, but notable event, stirs one to vengeance and increases the indignation of the Mexican Army toward the villainous enemy against which it does battle.

To The Soldiers

We are strong, and our nation's honor compels us to avenge its illustrious son, General Santa Anna. Are we not to avenge him? We would die first rather than to commit such infamy. Let us prepare ourselves. Let us go to battle certain of victory, and certain that that perverse bunch that has dared to think it could steal a part of our nation will feel our wrath over its accidental victory.

Your general has no doubt about the valor of the troops under his command, and he, (like his troops) always shares in the same deprivations and labor as well as in the danger.

In The Field [Campo], 24 april, 1836[6]—Vicente Filisola

The fact that this proclamation was written at Campo, the same as the second order to Urrea, indicates it was written very early on the morning of April 24, prior to Filisola moving on to Powell's.

Not too surprisingly, Filisola almost ignored this strongly worded statement in his writings. Peña, however, was more forthcoming.

It has been said, and believed by some, that our first reverse maneuver was intended to disengage us from what was useless and to reunite with General Urrea in order to pursue the enemy, and General Filisola has so stated in some of his

6. Peña, *La rebelión de Texas*, Anexo No. 18, p. 273.

∞

dispatches, but the destruction of the meager means at our disposal for crossing the Brazos [burning the rafts] served only to consolidate the enemies victory. A courageous proclamation addressed to the army on the 24th was a further move to nourish the hopes of the many who wished far more to advance, since retreat was so distasteful. What honor, what glory, would have been General Filisola's had he carried out in deed what he offered in his speech, as the country and duty categorically demanded!

In undertaking the narrative of the events in Texas, I am also compelled to assume the role of accuser, as I have already done in my diary, though I greatly regret having to do so against a general who merits personal consideration and whose private virtues command my esteem. Were General Filisola as well trained and courageous as he is honest, he would be among the first commanders of the Republic.

Frankness and sincerity are qualities that speak highly for men, but they should particularly characterize a soldier. To say what one does not feel for personal considerations or because of fear, is, to say the least, a base act.

Having declared this, I shall make some minor observations about a proclamation that misled the hopes of the army, the contents of which was contradicted by the facts and by subsequent dispatches. If General Filisola was convinced on the 24th of April that the victory obtained by the enemy was purely accidental and caused by the disdain with which General Santa Anna regarded the enemy; if he judged the enemy perfidious and cowardly and incapable of vanquishing us, and considered us strong; if it is true that the honor of the nation and the avenging of its first magistrate and also our comrades had been entrusted to us; then why abandon the field to the enemy? Why consolidate his own temporary victory, why sacrifice so shamelessly the honor of the nation and abandon so pitilessly our unfortunate compatriots? Should they be left unavenged? General Filisola asked himself, restricting this question to General Santa Anna. No! Rather die than commit such infamy. If, therefore, he could describe as infamous the failure to avenge this commander, how much greater infamy to have sacrificed the national

Madam Powell's

93

honor, to have departed without avenging the insult our arms had received? If General Filisola has judged himself as he deserves, why should he take offense when I reiterate what I have said? Not having fulfilled what he offered the army, that to which he invited it, that to which he had excited its indignation and provoked its fury, he appeared as a despicable buffoon and gave the enemy cause for laughter.[7]

Urrea also reacted to Filisola's bold proclamation in his diary entry of April 24.

A spirited proclamation issued on the 24th promised the army an advance to avenge national honor and the blood of our companions. Enthusiasm filled all hearts and no one could doubt that such solemn promises would be kept. Imagine my surprise at hearing from the very lips of General Filisola his determination to abandon the scene of war! I expressed my opinion that now was the opportune time to advance upon the enemy; I offered to do so with my division, emphasizing the probabilities of our triumph; but although I did everything I could do to have my opinion accepted, my advice was not heeded.[8]

Filisola briefly mentioned this proclamation in his analysis of the Urrea diary. His response to Urrea's accusations was worthy of a slick lawyer.

It is a falsehood that I expressed such a resolution on that night, because [at that point] I still believed that the General-in-chief would be able to rejoin us and would then act accordingly. Until then I had no thought other than to reunite the army, as I have already stated, but Señor Urrea

7. Peña, *La rebelión de Texas,* 160–162; translated in Perry (trans. and ed.), *With Santa Anna in Texas,* 138–140; retranslated for G. Dimmick by Dora Elizondo Guerra.

8. Urrea, "Diario de las operaciones militares," *Documentos para la historia de la guerra de Tejas,* 30; translated in Castañeda (trans. and ed.), *The Mexican Side of the Texas Revolution,* 255.

continuously contradicts himself, at every turn and from line to line. Why? Why does he claim such surprise? Could it be that it was a lie that he knew beforehand of the retreat of the army.[9]

He cleverly denied that he issued the proclamation on that *particular* night but did not deny that he issued the proclamation. In all likelihood he actually issued the proclamation the night before. It may have been after midnight, technically April 24, or he may have misdated it as he did several other documents. Ignoring the fact that he had still not explained why he had made such a bold statement and done nothing to back it up, he turned the table on Urrea. He questioned why Urrea had claimed that he was shocked when he learned of the retreat at Columbia on April 23—when subsequently Urrea proceeded to talk of the irony of having first heard of the retreat directly from the mouth of Filisola himself. Filisola not only caught Urrea in a contradiction, but moreover, he swept aside the whole issue of the proclamation.

It can only be conjectured as to why he actually sent out this fiery notice to his troops. Possibly he was worried about the total collapse of the army in panic. Perhaps he wanted to make a statement that would show his strength as a leader. And the possibility that he actually meant what he said in the proclamation should also be entertained. Had things worked out differently, he may well have led the Mexican army in an offensive strike at a later date.

In his diary entry for April 24, General Urrea noted that he marched eight leagues and then halted for his rearguard to join him. While halted he received the order from Filisola that was written the night before, in which Filisola told Urrea to follow the guide he had sent to the place where he (Filisola) would await him. He pointed out that Filisola did not know at the time where he would go. This was consistent with the fact that Filisola was lost and had no intention of meeting at Powell's until after he took the wrong road. The choice of the road they took while exiting Old Fort would soon become a point of contention. Urrea and Peña would later strongly criticize Filisola for not taking the well-traveled road to San

9. Filisola, *Análisis del diario militar del General D. José Urrea durante la primera campaña de Tejas*, 61.

∞

Madam Powell's

Felipe instead of the one leading toward Powell's. Possibly Filisola was too embarrassed to admit that they took the wrong road and that he had originally intended to go to San Felipe.

Urrea arrived at the camp at Madam Powell's at about midnight on April 24. He indicated that he came through Columbia on his countermarch to Madam Powell's, so there is little doubt he would have come by the same route as Salas. Filisola acted as though Urrea came to Powell's via a direct route from Brazoria, but there was apparently no such separate road (i.e., another road from Brazoria that did not come through Columbia).[10] As mentioned above, Urrea stated that when he spoke with Filisola on April 24 he argued for advancing against the enemy, and offered to use his division to do so. In response, Filisola gave a totally different account of their interaction at Powell's on April 24.

> At about twelve midnight, having retired and resting from the fatigue of that day, Col. Francisco Garay, along with General Adrian Woll came in to advise me that the missing sections of Gen. Urrea's division had joined us, and to get an assignment for the position that they should occupy in the line. Scarcely had he finished indicating it when Señor Urrea appeared in person with the same purpose. I repeated what I had told the aforementioned officers, then I ordered Gen. Woll to verbally report to each of the brigades that were already in position, of the incorporation of Gen. Urrea, so that there would be no mistakes that would have unfortunate consequences due to these changes. The only thing Gen. Urrea requested of me was that I permit him to camp the cavalry that was with him, on the other side of the stream, near the small wooden house that I mentioned in my description of this location. [His request] would have made his forces useless in the event of any sudden movement that could present itself. As I have already mentioned, the said stream had steep banks and a muddy bottom, and presented great difficulty in crossing the horses, even one by one. I

10. There is a possibility that Colonel Salas left Columbia immediately and headed for Old Fort, as ordered. If he was part way there when he received a second order to go to Powell's, he might have arrived on a different road than Urrea.

made several pertinent observations, but he insisted in his request, and I acquiesced. At the time I could not understand the grounds for such outlandishness, but later I came to know that his purpose was so that I would not see the scant force that his Cuautla Regiment had, because he had left them scattered from Matagorda to Victoria. It is uncertain whether he might have made other propositions that night, as His Excellency claims. I wanted to retire and rest, so I dismissed him after a few moments during which I made known the placement of his division. He said that he also was going to rest from his arduous march, and that in the morning we would settle as to what ought to be our conduct in the future. I don't remember well, but I think that witnessing this were Señores Tolsa, Sesma and Gaona, who arrived at that moment to greet Señor Urrea. With regard to the irony in the proclamation to which he refers, the proclamation speaks for itself, and is clear as to whether up to that point mention had even been made or thought had even been given to a retreat, a retreat that was later initiated. This is one more piece of evidence of the injustice and frivolity of his letter directed to Señor Garay and of the groundlessness of his rantings about the occurrences of the 23rd and 24th.[11]

Once again we are faced with markedly divergent views of the very same events. As more and more Mexican-army accounts surfaced after the battle of San Jacinto, it seems as though most were biased by the Filisola–Urrea paper war, and therefore not totally reliable. Common sense would argue that the earlier the document was written the less it was slanted by the animosity. Thus the early letters probably give us the most reliable look at what actually occurred. However, even these letters are tainted by the apparent hesitancy of these writers, especially Urrea, to put their true feelings on paper. It is obvious that most of the Mexican eyewitness accounts were written with an agenda and are full of inconsistencies, exaggerations, and even lies. The documents cited up to this point make it clear that

11. Filisola, *Análisis del diario militar del General D. José Urrea durante la primera campaña de Tejas*, 61–62.

none of the accounts of Filisola, Urrea, or for that matter most of the others, can be accepted at face value. Unfortunately, in most cases, when there was obvious disagreement between the two opposing camps, the truth of the matter remains nebulous.

Early on the morning of April 25 General Filisola sent Lt. Pedro Rodríguez of the frontier dragoons back to Old Fort. He took along a picket of cavalry from the Dolores and Tampico Regiments and some presidial dragoons to scout for the enemy and look for stragglers. The lieutenant did not return until the next day and found no soldiers from San Jacinto. He did bring back a young boy, a muleteer, and a woman who had remained on the other side of the Brazos. Apparently the mule driver was afraid to cross the river because he had accidentally lost the papers of the Aldama Battalion in the river and invoked the wrath of Gen. Gaona. It thus appears unlikely that the papers of the Aldama Battalion's participation in the Texas campaign will ever be located.[12]

As related in chapter one, Marcos Barragán and Somosa arrived from San Jacinto on April 25. In his analysis of Urrea's diary Filisola gave an interesting detail that was not included in his other writings. He stated that the information that these two officers gave him about the battle and the commander-in-chief was about the same as that given by the other survivors that reached the Mexican camp on April 22. Filisola did note, however, that these two officers reported that earlier they had been very alarmed—due to the fact that on April 22 they had heard many musket volleys. Barragán and Somosa told Filisola that they had little doubt that all the valiant soldiers had now perished and that Santa Anna and his general staff had been shot after having been captured. They felt like this was in response to the same treatment of Texan prisoners by the Mexican army.[13]

It should be recalled that Peña documented that the arrival of Barragán and Somosa at the Mexican camp took place at 7 A.M. on April 25. This means that for the next fifty-six hours, when Filisola

12. Vicente Filisola, *Memorias para la historia de la guerra de Tejas* (2 vols.; Mexico: Ignacio Cumplido, 1849), I, 210–211. This is a totally different book than the Rafael book with the same title. The Cumplido book has never been translated into English.

13. Filisola, *Análisis del diario militar del General D. José Urrea durante la primera campaña de Tejas,* 63.

SEA OF MUD

and his staff were making major decisions as to what steps to take in response to the news of the defeat, they were all under the impression that Santa Anna and the rest of his forces had likely perished at the hands of the Texans. Apparently the opinions of Barragán and Somosa were not taken as gospel as the generals continued to voice a concern for the well-being of possible prisoners and the desire to find out the fate of Santa Anna.

Filisola then decided to call a meeting to discuss several matters regarding the army—its command and what actions should be carried out in response to Santa Anna's defeat and his death or capture. Initially it was decided to have all the generals, colonels, and unit commanders in attendance, but that was later changed to only the generals and Col. Pedro Ampudia, commander of the artillery. Needless to say, this did not sit well with the younger officers who were more opposed to the withdrawal than their superiors. As a result, a rift seemed to develop between several of the younger officers and the older generals. Peña lamented: "this sacred love of country finds an easier dwelling place within the breasts of the young than in those of the old, whose hearts seem dead to all noble passions, susceptible only to those which degrade."[14] The rift came to a head when on May 10, the first night after leaving the Colorado, Filisola had to call a meeting of officers and demand an end to the malicious talk against the retreat. He specifically mentioned Peña and three other young officers as the offenders. Peña was the only officer he mentioned by name.[15]

Peña gave this candid opinion on the change of plans for who was to attend the meeting:

On the memorable day of the 25th, when the generals were summoned for a council of war, the unit commanders were also summoned, but, since their opinion had been previously sounded and their opposition to the retreat was known, they were ordered to withdraw under the flimsy pretext that they had been called so that they might be charged with guarding

14. Peña, *La rebelión de Texas,* 167; translated in Perry (trans. and ed.), *With Santa Anna in Texas,* 145.

15. Filisola, *Memorias para la historia de la guerra de Tejas* (Cumplido, 1849), I, 251–252

the camp while this meeting was taking place in its very center. No one should have been listened to more than the unit commanders on this occasion, for, being so close to the troops, they could accurately assess the real attitude among the soldiers, and no one would have responded more favorably than they to an advance toward the enemy.[16]

Peña's argument had several gaping holes. To begin with he forgot that an army is seldom run as a democracy. A good commander should take into account the feelings of the officers and troops, but there is no vote when the final decision is made. His argument was also lacking in that he himself said the unit commanders had already been sounded, and it was known prior to the meeting that they opposed the retreat. If indeed this was the case, why would the unit commanders need to be at the meeting and report to Filisola what was already known?

Once again Peña's argument mirrored Urrea's diary entry of April 25.

A council of war, composed of all the generals and ranking officers of the various units, was attempted, but when it was learned that the greater part of the latter were opposed to a retreat—in my own division there was not a single man who favored it—it was decided that the council be composed only of generals, ordering all other officers to their respective camps and telling them that they had been assembled only to recommend to the care of their respective commands while the council was being held.

No one could know the attitude that prevailed among the troops better than their immediate officers. Because of this fact, their opinion should have been more important than that of the generals who could judge of the spirit of the army only by their own feelings. It is true that there were cowardly men, as is always the case, but they were by no means in the majority.[17]

16. Peña, *La rebelión de Texas,* 169; translated in Perry (trans. and ed.), *With Santa Anna in Texas,* 147–148.

17. Urrea, "Diario de las operaciones militares," *Documentos para la historia de la*

Like Peña, Urrea seemed to want to make the army a democracy and act according to the will of the troops. Had Filisola listed only the morale of the army as his excuse for retreating, their point may have been well taken. However, since that was not the case, this point seems desperate and trivial.

Comparing these two quotes reinforces a common link that has been seen in earlier chapters. Peña's memoirs and Urrea's diary are so similar that it appears that one is practically quoting the other. Urrea's diary was published in Durango in 1838 and Peña's final draft was still not completed as late as November 1839.[18] Peña, however, had prepared an edited version of his diary in the summer of 1836. Additionally, he started publishing letters in the Mexican newspapers as early as February 3, 1837, in which he stated that he intended to make a review of the campaign in Texas. Peña was aware that Urrea had used a quote from Peña's own diary when Urrea published *Diario de las operaciones militares de la division que al mando del General José Urrea*. Peña footnoted the exact portion of his diary that Urrea quoted as being from the diary of an anonymous officer.[19] The fact that we know Urrea borrowed from Peña leads us to suspect that many of the other similarities were Urrea reflecting Peña's more eloquent arguments.

Filisola was not about to let any point of contention made by Urrea, even a trivial one, go unanswered.

In fact, I had ordered all the Generals, Colonels and unit commanders to gather, with the purpose that I will discuss later. Some of the Generals, who I can't remember individually, having shown up, thought it best if the meeting was attended by only the generals. I then ordered that this information be made known to the unit commanders, exactly as

---

guerra de Tejas, 30–31; translated in Castañeda (trans. and ed.), *The Mexican Side of the Texas Revolution*, 255–256.

18. James E. Crisp, "The Little Book That Wasn't There: The Myth and Mystery of the de la Peña Diary," *Southwestern Historical Quarterly*, 98 (Oct., 1994), 261–296. Peña stated in his pamphlet, *Una víctima del despotismo* (Mexico: Imprenta del IRIS, dirigida por Antonio Diaz, 1839) that he was still working on the final draft.

19. Peña, *La rebelión de Texas*; translated in Perry (trans. and ed.), *With Santa Anna in Texas*, 166.

Gen. Urrea tells it. However, it is absolutely ludicrous and illogical to suppose that the revision might have been adopted because it was believed that the majority of the unit commanders were against the retreat, given that up to that point, even I had not considered it, nor had I discussed it with any of the generals or unit commanders for fear that they might become suspicious.[20]

Filisola blamed the generals for this sudden switch in plans, yet seemed to have conveniently forgotten which generals suggested it. He claimed that the revision of the meeting plans was not made on account of a pervasive opinion against the retreat, as he had not discussed the issue with anyone and knew nothing of the feelings of the officers.

The meeting at Madam Powell's did take place. The future of the Mexican presence in Texas and the fate of the rebellion were riding in the balance. San Jacinto was the first major blow to the Mexican campaign in their northern-most state. Little did they know they were soon to suffer a second, and in some ways more devastating, setback.

ARCHEOLOGY OF MRS. POWELL'S

The Houston Archeological Society has excavated a small portion of the Powell homesite. The fieldwork was carried out in 1999–2000 and the findings are presently in the process of publication. When the fieldwork began it was unknown as to whether the site was, in fact, the actual Powell homesite. Also in question was whether the Mexican army actually camped there and if so, where.

Local historians and avocational archeologists were aware of the site due to a 1936 Texas centennial historical marker on the property. Unfortunately, records from the placement of the marker were destroyed in a fire in Austin. Therefore the documentation of this being the actual site has been lost. Since the site was on private property, permission to investigate was obtained from the current landowner, Elizabeth Darst. Including the Powells, the Darsts are

20. Filisola, *Análisis del diario militar del General D. José Urrea durante la primera campaña de Tejas,* 62.

one of only three families that have owned the property since the original land grant.

Excavations near the marker indicated that there was indeed a long-term occupation on the small hill near Turkey Creek. The location was found to be almost exactly as Filisola described it in his 1836 book analyzing Urrea's diary. Especially noteworthy is the fact that from the homesite there is a low ridge to the south and east that gives the impression that the site is in a hollow.

When the area was originally surveyed, ground-penetrating radar was performed but gave no productive information. Metal detecting was also undertaken over a wide area in an effort to locate the position of the campsite of the Mexican army. When the initial survey was started, the Filisola description of the site had not yet been found. In spite of extensive surveying with the metal detectors, the position of the Mexican campsite remained a mystery. There was no knowledge as to how far the army would have camped from the home itself and there was significant doubt as to whether the army, having camped there only two nights, would have left enough artifacts to have survived the 160-plus years since the event.

In the initial survey, near the homesite, a brass buttplate [Fig. 4-1] and a brass trigger guard [Fig. 4-2] were found. Both of these were from an India Pattern Brown Bess Musket. Even though there was no doubt the brass pieces were from India Pattern muskets there was no proof they were from the Mexican army.

The India Pattern musket was the main weapon carried by the Mexican soldier in the Texas campaign. It was a smoothbore flintlock musket and had a .75 caliber bore weighing approximately ten pounds. This musket was first manufactured for the East India Company as an inexpensive alternative for the short land pattern musket. In order to increase production, the English adopted the India Pattern musket as its primary firearm. It was manufactured from 1793 until 1815, with only one modification during that time. In 1809 the cock, or hammer, was reinforced from its original gooseneck configuration. The India Pattern musket had a shorter barrel of thirty-nine inches and had only three ramrod pipes, instead of the four in the short pattern. It fired a round lead ball that was packed into a paper cartridge with gunpowder. In the Mexican army the balls were not measured in diameter but by weight. The musket balls were listed as weighing both seventeen and nineteen *adarmes* [one *adarme* = $\frac{1}{16}$ of an ounce].[21] There were twelve orders and eighteen separate steps in loading and firing the musket. Each soldier was supposed to be able to fire three rounds per minute.

Because the musket had a smooth bore it had a range of only about eighty yards with any reasonable accuracy. Since the accuracy was rather poor, the seventeen-inch bayonet was considered the most effective part of the weapon. A musket sideplate was discovered, at a site that will be described later, which turned out to be from a New Land Series musket. This particular firearm was manufactured after 1802.

There are documents that show the Mexican army carried Baker rifles, as well as the smoothbore muskets. The Baker was also manufactured in England and had a .625-inch bore with a rifled barrel. Andrade mentioned, in his list of items he destroyed as he abandoned San Antonio, fifteen hundred rifle balls, nine *adarmes* each. To give an idea of how common the rifles may have been, it was reported that they destroyed 49,990 musket balls. In our sites we have found no confirmed items from Baker rifles. This is not unexpected as the Bakers were used by the *cazadores* and most of them were at San Jacinto.

Later, by using General Filisola's description of the Mexican line

21. José Enrique de la Peña, unpublished clean copy of his diary, pp. 100–101, Peña Papers (CAH); Nieto et al., *El soldado mexicano,* 53. In his first draft Peña documented a list of the items abandoned or destroyed by Gen. Juan Andrade at Béjar when he evacuated that town in May 1836. Among the items listed are 49,990 musket cartridges with balls weighing 17 adarmes or 1 $\frac{1}{16}$ ounce. He also listed 1500 rifle cartridges with balls weighing 9 adarmes or $\frac{9}{16}$ ounce. Thanks to Thomas Ricks Lindley for finding this list.

In *El soldado mexicano,* Joseph Heftner quotes Gen. Nicolas Bravo as saying, in 1836, that his forces in Texas (Bravo was still in Mexico) had English muskets with cartridges with powder and balls of 19 adarmes or 1 $\frac{3}{16}$ ounce. It should be noted that during this period the Spanish word *fusil* was translated as musket, and rifle was spelled the same in both languages. As there are, for the most part, no longer any muskets, *fusil,* in modern times, is translated as rifle or musket.

Musket balls of different sizes have been discovered at Mexican army sites and it is possible that both sizes mentioned by Bravo and Andrade were manufactured. Re-enactors have communicated to the author that smaller balls could be loaded more quickly in the heat of battle but larger balls would have been more accurate. The difference between the size of the bore of the musket and the diameter of the ball is referred to as windage.

∞

being on top of the elevation and divided at a 90 degree angle by the road to Old Fort, the search area was vastly narrowed. A significant number of artifacts were discovered right where Filisola said they would be. Many musket balls were found at the location along with several items that proved it to be a Mexican army campsite. Two eagle buttons marked *Republica Mexicana* were excavated [Fig. 4-3a, 4-3b]. It is suspected, due to their rarity, that the eagle buttons were likely from officers' uniforms. A Mexican silver coin, dated 1782, was recovered from the army campsite [Fig. 4-4]. There were a variety of plain brass military buttons, many with backmarks indicating English manufacture. A brass coin from the state of Zacatecas was excavated. This coin supports the known history, as many of the Mexican forces in the Texas campaign had recently returned from suppressing a revolt in Zacatecas prior to entering Texas.

Some of these coins from our site had a small hole punched into their tops. One theory for this is that the Mexican soldiers were so poor they sewed their coins into their pockets. Near one of our coins a small brass lock and key were unearthed [Fig. 4-5]. These may have been part of a small moneybox.

A rectangular button was found at the far end of the Mexican army line. It has a shank and appears to be silverplated. It is decorated with a fancy floral design and the back mark reads "plated." This item does not appear to be a military artifact [Fig. 4-6]. Several shards of ceramic were found in the same general area. It is possible that this area is where the camp followers were located.

Several items were found at or near the actual homesite. Another eagle button was found [Fig. 4-7]. This one-piece button was fashioned after a Mexican coin and had a date of 1828. On the reverse it was inscribed with the phrase "Libertad in la Ley," or "Freedom in the Law." A one-piece numbered button was discovered at the homesite as well. It had the number six on the front of the button, with a pinched shank, and no backmark [Fig. 4-8]. The number six most likely refers to the Sixth Battalion. The Mexican army numbered their battalions from 1823 to 1832, and again after 1839. Therefore, this button was very likely manufactured between 1823 and 1832. The Sixth Battalion from that era became the Aldama Battalion in 1832.[22] Since the Aldama Battalion was at San Jacinto, and not in the retreat, it seems likely that the uniforms of the Sixth Battalion,

22. Nieto et al., *El soldado mexicano*, 55.

∞

Madam Powell's

which would have become surplus items after the Aldama got their new uniforms, were passed on to another unit—very possibly one of the active units. Another possibility is that the button is a surplus button from the Sixth Regiment Cavalry. Once again, in this event, it would represent a pre-1832 artifact.

An unusual decorative item was found in the Mexican line. It is made of silver and may have decorated a saddle, cartridge box, etc. [Fig. 4-9]. This is a good example of one of the many items found that seem to be previously unknown to Alamo-period Mexican army historians. Each of these "new items" adds one more piece of the puzzle in rediscovering the accoutrements of this force.

On the other side of Turkey Creek, near the crossing, a large number of Mexican army artifacts were found. A brass "exploding bomb" insignia was discovered that was worn on the helmet (shako), or the cartridge box flap, of a grenadier [Fig 4-10]. In the same area a horn insignia was unearthed that was worn by a *cazadore*, or light infantryman, once again on the helmet or cartridge box flap [Fig. 4-11]. Several "6" buttons were also found, along with several two-piece "ball" or "bullet" buttons [Fig. 4-12]. Other items found here were musket balls, brass tacks, a small brass chain, and multiple plain brass buttons. It should be noted that this site could also include artifacts from Santa Anna's division as it is likely they used this crossing on April 10, 1836. The advancing division of Urrea may also account for some of these artifacts, since they camped at Powell's the night of April 20 and would have used this crossing.

One other site has been located that verifies what the Mexican documents describe concerning their position at Madam Powell's. Nearly half a mile upstream from the crossing, on the west side of Turkey Creek (opposite side from the homesite), a site was located that had many iron square nails and a few old pieces of ceramic. Also found were several decorative brass buttons and a number of large musket balls for the India Pattern musket. This is likely the site of the "battered dwelling," across the creek, that Filisola mentioned as the campsite of Urrea's cavalry.

Fig. 4-1. India Pattern musket brass buttplate (partial). *All photographs, unless otherwise noted, were taken by Kelly Houk, Moore Archeological Consulting, Inc.*

| 1 cm |

| 1 cm |

Fig. 4-2. India Pattern musket brass trigger guard (partial).

| 1 cm |

Fig. 4-3a. Brass eagle button.

Fig. 4-3b. Silver-plated brass eagle button.

Fig. 4-4. Silver 1782 Mexican coin.

Fig. 4-5. Brass lock and key.

Fig. 4-6. Rectangular, silver-plated button.

Fig. 4-7. 1828 brass eagle button.

Fig. 4-8. Sixth Battalion coat and cuff buttons.

Fig. 4-9. Silver decoration.

Fig. 4-10.
Grenadier
exploding
bomb
insignia.

Fig. 4-11. *Cazadore* horn insignia.

Fig. 4-12. Brass "bullet" button.

CHAPTER 5

La Junta

O N APRIL 25, 1836, GENERAL FILISOLA held a meeting of the senior Mexican generals at the homesite of Madam Powell. At the meeting a decision was reached that was to have a major impact on the course of the Texas Rebellion. Down through the years the decisions made at that meeting, and even the fact that the meeting ever took place, have been virtually forgotten. This is true of the Mexican historians as well as the Texas history experts.

At the time of the meeting Filisola had 2,573 men under his direct command at Powell's. Additionally there were 1001 men (many of whom were wounded) under the command of General Andrade in San Antonio, 60 men at Cópano, 5 at Refugio, 174 in Goliad, 189 in Matagorda, 40 in Victoria, 21 men of the Active Durango, and 15 presidial troops. All total there were 4,078 Mexican soldiers in Texas. When deciding upon a plan of action, Filisola and his generals had to take into consideration all the scattered Mexican forces in Texas, not just those at Powell's.

Many Texas history sources refer to the movements of the Mexican army, after San Jacinto, as a *retreat*. Collins Spanish dictionary translates *retirada* (the word primarily used in the Mexican documents to describe the action) as a retreat *or* a withdrawal. It is a fine point, but an important one, to realize these were not defeated troops retreating in the face of an enemy who posed an immediate threat. If indeed the Mexicans were retreating in mass confusion, as usually described in the Texan accounts, would this general staff meeting have taken place? It is reasonable to describe their movements as more of a withdrawal than a retreat. As the events of the meeting are recounted and better understood, the word "regrouping" may fit the situation even better. If they were fleeing in a state of panic, would the Mexican army have taken a whole day at Powell's to rest, reorganize, and come up with a plan of action? Would General Urrea have held a review of arms on the morning of April 28? The truth is that there is ample evidence that, until their unfortunate entrance into the Mar de Lodo, the Mexican army was withdrawing in a disciplined and orderly fashion.

When the principals at this meeting returned to Mexico and the accusations began flying, Filisola claimed that his primary purpose in holding the meeting was to resign as commander.

> My intention for arranging the meeting was to renounce the indisputable right that would be handed to me, the command as General of the Army, because of the fact that I was not born in this country, I also did not believe that I had the prestige or sufficient knowledge in those ill-fated circumstances. I had not been informed of the plan that had been proposed by His Excellency, General Santa Anna, or of the instruction from the government relative to this. . . . In view of this, I was hoping that one of the senior generals—Sesma, Tolsa or Urrea—would have taken command, since they possessed all the qualifications that I and generals Gaona and Woll [foreigners] lacked. However, I was determined to obey blindly, and to resign myself to whatever fate might befall the army.[1]

Despite the fact that Filisola had moved to Spain at age six, and had worked his way through the ranks, first in Spain, and later in New Spain and Mexico, he was still dogged by the fact that he was Italian. Peña was especially vociferous in his denunciation of the foreign influence in the Mexican army.

> Although I may appear discourteous and may be judged falsely to be a man preoccupied with selfish ideas, I must call to the attention of whoever may read this, that in an assem-

---

1. Filisola, *Análisis del diario militar del General D. José Urrea durante la primera campaña de Tejas,* 62–63.

∞

SEA OF MUD

blage of three thousand Mexicans, of those seven leaders, who without judgment and consideration, resolved to seal the disgrace of all, only three were Mexicans by birth, who naturally should have greater interest in the good name and prosperity of the homeland than those who had abandoned their country to adopt ours, although there are honorable exceptions. The four remaining were: the commander in chief, Italian; the major general [Woll], French; and the commander of the First Brigade [Tolsa] (according to the new organization of the army, in effect from the very beginning of the campaign), from Havana; the commander of the artillery [Ampudia], who passes for a Cuban, is thought by some to be Andalucian, which his character verifies. It is most painful and degrading for Mexicans, but this is the sad condition to which we have been condemned, for our release from the Spanish yoke had been followed by a series of foreign commanders, many of them unworthy of this honor.[2]

In his diary entry of April 25 Urrea stated that his troops were strongly opposed to the retreat. He mentioned also that several officers made known to him they were against the retreat (Peña said he spoke to Urrea against the retreat). He claimed that he himself was against the retreat and voiced this publicly. He offered the following excuse for not strongly opposing the retreat from the start: "though always ready to abide by the decisions of the general-in-chief, as I was duty bound to do."[3] He then proceeded to argue that his letters

2. Peña, *La rebelión de Texas,* 170–171; translated in Perry (trans. and ed.), *With Santa Anna in Texas,* 149. In footnote no. 89 on page 171, J. Sánchez Garza, the editor of *La rebelión,* points out that Peña did not know that Gaona was Cuban. Sánchez Garza added that of the seven generals at the meeting that decided the fate of Texas, only two were native-born Mexicans and one of those was the "intimidated" Ramírez y Sesma. Gen. Adrian Woll has been called Belgian by several authors (including the first edition of this book), but he was actually French. In the quote above, Filisola mentioned Gaona as foreign but listed Tolsa as Mexican.

3. Urrea, "Diario de las operaciones militares," *Documentos para la historia de la guerra de Tejas,* 31; translated in Castañeda (trans. and ed.), *The Mexican Side of the Texas Revolution,* 256.

∞

La Junta

to Filisola and Sesma on April 24 proved his opposition to a retreat, even before he rejoined the main army. As has been discussed, those letters, at most, showed a vague hint of his disdain for any retrograde movement.

It is obvious that Peña was a staunch supporter of Urrea. This is particularly interesting considering that Peña never served with Urrea or his units during the entire Texas campaign. At the time he finished the final draft of his memoirs, Peña was in prison. He had been incarcerated for supporting Urrea's federalist uprising against the centralist national government. In spite of his loyalty to Urrea, he was greatly disappointed in the general for not stepping up and doing his part to avoid the retreat.

> Doubtless we would have achieved it [victory], had there only been a commander who would have led us into it and who could have appraised the advantage to be gained by not showing the enemy our backs; we would have conquered had there been among those in charge a single one desiring glory, who could have foreseen the renown that would have been his if he had taken that resolution, for which no great heroism was necessary. General Urrea seemed destined to play this brilliant role and everyone pointed to him as the best suited to carry it out, but he let himself be influenced by the ideas of his comrades. He was disgusted by the retreat from the moment he knew that it had been initiated, even more by the haste with which it was executed: the language he used with General Filisola and Ramírez y Sesma during some moments of conflict will always do him honor, but he did not oppose it openly, as he did later,[4] and on the 25th of April his energetic opposition would have been enough to have exchanged our shame for laurels.
>
> Most of the army would have followed him gladly to rectify the disaster of San Jacinto, had he wanted to place him-

---

4. Carmen Perry pointed out in *With Santa Anna in Texas,* page 147, that Urrea was later to write to the Mexican government and to Filisola, expressing his deep resentment against the retreat, which he considered shameful and against all military principles. Filisola was subsequently removed from command and Urrea replaced him as commander.

self at their head. Several of us officers, indignant to learn that our disgrace was to be consummated, invited him to do so; but a misguided principle of delicacy made him gently reject our invitation, expressing his appreciation for our good intentions.[5]

Peña was not the only witness who reported that Urrea was indeed against the retreat. In his deposition for Filisola's trial, Lt. Ignacio Salinas had this to say about the meeting of April 25:

Question: If he knew the cause of the initiation of the retreat after the reunion of the Army at the habitation of Madama Powell? He said that when they gathered at that habitation, after the division of Sr. Urrea had made camp on the other side of the creek, separated from the rest of the camp, the witness accompanied the mentioned General to the billet of Sr. Filisola, where the rest of the generals were, among whom they had a conference about what ought to be done, and that only Gen. Urrea was of the opinion that they should go battle the enemy, the rest being of a separate opinion, not having been informed of the reasons of anyone as I was left outside tending the horses.[6]

Luckily there is a record of what was discussed and each general's opinion at the April 24 meeting. In the papers from the Filisola court-martial there was a document submitted by Filisola that tells of the meeting. He described the document as being

from the summary of the opinions declared by each of those present at the meeting of the generals on the 26th [should be April 25] at the homesite of Madam Powell, Señor Ramírez y Sesma's declaration shows that at the meeting there was no mention of the army's definite retreat, as

5. Peña, *La rebelión de Texas,* 168–169; translated in Perry (trans. and ed.), *With Santa Anna in Texas,* 146–147.
6. "La guerra de Texas: Causa formada al Gral. Filisola por su retirada en 1836," Tomo X, No. 3, pp. 552–554.

La Junta

implied by General Urrea in his private memorandum to the Minister of War, dated May 11th.[7]

While reading this summary it should be remembered that Ramírez y Sesma was, both during and after the campaign, a staunch backer of Filisola.

Summary of the opinions expressed by the senior general staff that attended the meeting of war held on the 26th of April, [April 25] 1836, at the house of Madam Powell.

At the house of Madam Powell, on the 26th day of April of 1836, the Commanding General, Don Vicente Filisola, brought together the senior generals of the army, Don Antonio Gaona, Don Joaquín Ramírez y Sesma, Don Eugenio Tolsa, Don Adrian Woll, Don José Urrea and Commanding General of the Artillery Don Pedro Ampudia [Ampudia was a colonel but was serving as general of the artillery].

His Excellency [Filisola] said that knowing of the total loss of the President's division, plus suspecting the possible loss of the President himself; and knowing that the responsibility [for the army] fell upon him; and being confident that the generals, as well as all those individual members of the army would obey him; he nevertheless wanted to hear the opinion of the generals present, in order to better weigh their opinions, and to be better prepared to develop whatever movements or operations might subsequently follow. Forthwith Commanding General of the Artillery [Ampudia] took the floor and he recommended that presidial soldiers be assigned to go in search of the President, and if after three days he could not be found, the division should then proceed toward Matamoros, where they could not only restock the resources that the army lacked, but they could also be in contact with the interior of the Republic; which, in the absence of General Santa Anna's leadership was vulnerable.

General Urrea declared that he was satisfied with the experience of His Excellency, the second in command of the army, as well as with his valor and loyalty to the national

7. Ibid., 557.

SEA OF MUD

cause. He stated that he was ready to comply with whatever was asked of him, notwithstanding the army's regrettable position as it contemplated abandoning the campaign.

Gen. Woll stated that having lost the line of operations along the Brazos River, a new one should be taken along the Colorado, especially since the enemy has the resources for crossing rivers that the army does not.

General Urrea added his regret at having to abandon the line, but repeated that his division would follow orders without question.

General Tolsa declared that, except for the division of General Urrea, all the rest lacked resources, and having lost the majority of the chosen troops [the grenadiers and the *cazadores*] of the corps, leaving for the most part, recruits, surprised by the incident of the loss of the President's division, His Excellency agreed with Señor Woll that the base of operations should be on the other side of the Colorado, taking the territory occupied by General Urrea, and that even though he considered the enemy was without military knowledge, he thought that now, with the victory that it had obtained, it would gather many more forces; consequently he thought that certainly the suggested base of operations should be taken, but always in a manner that would preserve the honor of the army.

General Gaona said: that yes, there was a precedent for having a base of operations, and that knowledge of the terrain was needed; and indeed, knowing [the enemy's] military position was essential; but given that none of that was known, and knowing that our rearguard detachments are a sham, as our present situation proves it, even though it had been the rearguard's obligation to obey; therefore his opinion was to move to the Colorado, or elsewhere, to establish a base of operations in a way that our detachments were protected.

General Ramírez stated that given that the present campaign was in a foreign country unfamiliar to the convened forces, and committed to never leaving its rearguard behind; it was essential that before moving one step forward, the rearguard's status must first be confirmed. Also it was important to acknowledge that not everything had been abandoned. Impassable rivers had divided the army, because the army lacked the necessary resources [to cross them]. In addition, the army continued marching, without any other thought but to advance. In view of all this, his opinion was that a new base of operations be formed and that it be situated with a view to covering the line to Matamoros. By doing so, the army could not only reorganize, but it could also attune itself to the interior affairs of the Republic.

General Gaona spoke again, and reiterated that the line of operations, as mentioned by His Excellency [Ramírez y Sesma] be set in a way that will make it possible for it to be in contact with the Republic so that all the concerns expressed by the generals could be addressed. He repeated that he was in agreement with the opinions expressed.

His Excellency, the second in command, based on the opinions of the rest of the generals, in addition to the opinion of others in the same vein, and with the same objective, gave a speech in which he stated that in the final analysis, he believed that it was indeed necessary to move the line of operations to the Colorado River and make it the army's base, and that once the reorganization was complete, and further instructions were received, and resources were replenished, then he would be better able to resolve the next move in accordance with the circumstances.[8]

In spite of the fact that this document may be biased against Urrea, it seems consistent with what Peña contended: Urrea did not stand up and oppose the retreat at this time, as he later claimed. It is possible that his claim that he and his division would "blindly obey" the orders of Filisola was a backhanded way of objecting to the retreat. However, this possibility is certainly not obvious and did not seem to have been taken that way by Filisola or the others.

Several recurring themes arose at this meeting. It was brought up that Santa Anna's fate was unknown and that his leadership would be missed. The lack of supplies and experienced troops, for all but Urrea's division, was pointed out by Tolsa. The need to protect the detachments to the army's rear was mentioned by Gaona.

8. Ibid., 561–563.

SEA OF MUD

There was a new concept that surfaced at the meeting as well. Three of the seven officers specifically addressed this issue. Ampudia, Ramírez y Sesma, and Gaona commented that the security of the Mexican interior was a concern. The loss of Santa Anna's leadership in Texas was probably not as significant in the long run as the instability it was likely to bring about in Mexico City. The Texas Campaign was only a part of an ongoing civil war in Mexico between the Federalists and the Centralists. It is obvious that there was a concern at the meeting for the survival of the sitting government of the day. It is certainly a stretch of the imagination but not totally inconceivable that Urrea, being a Federalist, may not have been in a hurry to support the Centralist government.

In his *Representación* to the Mexican government, Filisola further addressed Urrea's opinion at the meeting of April 25.

> It is true that Mr. Urrea, who was the second to speak, declared that he was sorry that the army should have to retrace their steps; but that his want of knowledge made him place a blind confidence in the experience and capacity of the second in command; and to what individual of the army did not the retreat, as well as the event that originated it, cause sorrow?[9]

It is likely that Urrea agreed with or at least was willing to tolerate this initial plan, which in no way included leaving Texas or halting hostilities. Remember that Ampudia was the only officer present at the meeting who wanted to delay the withdrawal. It is apparent that what was planned was an orderly withdrawal to the opposite bank of the Colorado. There they could get resupplied, organize the other detachments scattered throughout Texas, and communicate with the government in the interior of the Republic. It should be noted that Tolsa emphasized that the maneuver should be undertaken in a manner so as to preserve the honor of the army. Woll was

9. Vicente Filisola, "Representación dirigida al supremo gobierno por el General Vicente Filisola en defensa de su honor y aclaración de sus operaciones como general en gefe del ejército sobre Tejas," included in "La guerra de Texas: Causa formada al Gral. Filisola por su retirada en 1836," Tomo X, No. 1, p. 164; translated in Filisola, *Evacuation of Texas*, 21.

also correct in assuming that the victory was having a positive effect on the size of the Texas army with new recruits streaming in as they received the news of San Jacinto.

When Filisola was court-martialed after his return to Mexico, he was specifically asked what his motives were for abandoning the position at Powell's. His response was as follows:

The part of the army that was there was, in no way, able to undertake going to look for the enemy. 1) Because, as he had said before, of lack of supplies. 2) Because the majority were recruits with the least training. 3) Because, having lost the army's Commander-in-Chief, with all the prestige it implied; having lost its general staff, that, with respect to the rest of the forces, meant losing more than one third of its preferential troops, it caused morale to be at its lowest ebb. 4) Because the army had all the sick, all the equipment, all the support staff, and the rest of the non-combatants, so many from the units that had been lost the 21st, as well as those from the units that had now gathered, including the artillery, munitions, wagons etc., it would have been necessary to fortify a definite position in order to protect all the immense accumulation of hindrances that we would have to leave behind. Or we would have had to have them march to Béjar or Goliad with a sufficient escort that would have divided the force in half. In either case, it would have been necessary to garrison the roads to the Colorado and to the Brazos Rivers, in order to find support when needed, and to be able to cross the rivers, if needed; in which case the army's numbers would be greatly reduced. 5) because in the case of going to look for the enemy it would have been necessary to return to the Brazos on the 26th, looking for means to cross it and effecting that operation would have taken until the 29th or 30th, afterwards it would have required a march of 40 leagues [107 miles] to where the enemy was, which would have taken eight or more days of marching, considering the numerous streams that had to be passed and the enemy having destroyed the means to do so, and these and others could have been utilized by the enemy in moving all their forces, looking for advantageous positions at which to await us, or they may have shot our prisoners, embarking on steamboats and other small crafts that they had there to retreat by the Galveston lagoon, placing themselves on that island, or to take the Brazos up the coast to destroy those detachments that had been left there and at the Colorado, or those at Matagorda, Cópano and Goliad, as none of these had support from the sea, or possibly to await us along the right bank of the Brazos to impede our countermarch when we had wanted to do so, all of this supposes that we would have had supplies for those days that this operation demanded, and that afterwards there never would have been the torrents of rain that fell on the 27th and 28th [26th and 27th], that would have disabled the major part of the munitions and the roads making the whole military operation impossible because the terrain is muddy and frequently cut with streams and bad passes.[10]

Certainly Filisola's reply to the trial judge was wordy and full of exaggeration. His claim that the Texans were able to use steamboats to ferry their entire force here and there was a gross exaggeration. His claim that it was forty leagues to San Jacinto, even though trimmed down from other estimates, was still about double the actual mileage. And the time estimated to travel this distance was probably about double as well. On the other hand, his overall assessment of their position was essentially accurate and the plan of action settled upon at Powell's was likely the best one at the time.

Peña gave this highly emotional account of his opinions concerning the meeting of April 25:

Assembled at General Filisola's tent were Generals Urrea, Ramírez y Sesma, Tolsa, Gaona, and Woll, and Lieutenant Colonel Ampudia of the artillery, all firmly agreed to continue the retreat. The mystery with which the meeting was held, with no one allowed to come close enough to hear the discussion, augured ill and prevented my knowing the reasons that inspired this resolution, but doubtless they would

10. "La guerra de Texas: Causa formada al Gral. Filisola por su retirada en 1836," Tomo X, No. 2, pp. 388–389.

have differed from those made public. The seven persons who of their own accord decreed in a few moments the loss of the most valuable and interesting part of our territory, they who with little thought resolved to sacrifice the national honor, the army's and their own, they who in a weak moment contributed with General Filisola in thrusting the nation into a bottomless sea of misfortunes, these men, to say the least, share in the opprobrium of that general, even if the responsibility is his alone. In taking a resolution so difficult, so delicate, and of such vast import, and such far-reaching consequences, they forgot the extreme sacrifices the nation had made and the great difficulties it had to overcome to organize the expedition even halfway; they never thought of the greater difficulties a second expedition would encounter after they had allowed the enemy to take heart and to gain strength; they never gave a thought to the effect a retreat has on the morale of a soldier; the abundance of blood already shed carried no weight in their thoughts, nor did the fact that many more victims and sacrifices of all kinds would be required to reconquer the abandoned territory and to repair the losses that a retreat always incurs; when all that was needed to dam up the torrent of calamities that the retreat was bringing upon us and restore the good name of our arms and change into glory the face of the Republic was to take the one step that patriotism, honor, and duty urgently demanded; but in all this they acted childishly and shamefully failed.[11]

Peña may have been young and inexperienced in military matters. It is likely that he was not considering all the factors that Filisola had to take into account, i.e., the lesser overall quality of his units, the camp followers, the sick and wounded, and the lives of the captured Mexican troops. However, one cannot help but be moved by the heartfelt emotion that flowed from the young officer in this time of anguish.

Notice that Peña stated that the meeting was in Filisola's tent.

11. Peña, *La rebelión de Texas,* 167; translated in Perry (trans. and ed.), *With Santa Anna in Texas,* 145–146; retranslated for G. Dimmick by Dora Elizondo Guerra.

∞

This would be consistent with Filisola later documenting that he was in his tent when he got the news of Santa Anna's defeat.[12] It also should be noted that on the evening of April 27 the Mexicans had a second meeting and it was held in Filisola's tent.[13] It can be confusing that the meeting place is often translated as being "at" Madam Powell's home or "in" Madam Powell's home. This is due to the fact that the original Spanish usually said "en la habitación de Madama Pawel." The Spanish word "en" can be translated as "in," "on," or "at." As there are at least two sources documenting that the meeting was in Filisola's tent, it seems likely that the meeting took place in the tent, at the homesite of Madam Powell.

On the same day as the meeting at Powell's, Filisola wrote a letter to José María Tornel, secretary of war, in Mexico City. Since this letter was written from Powell's on April 25, it is less likely to have been tainted by Filisola's subsequent problems than his deposition given above. At this point there was no obvious animosity between Filisola and Urrea and the information Filisola sent Tornel likely would have been accurate. It is very telling that Filisola flatly stated that they planned to resume military actions after this new base of operations was established.

> Army of operations over Texas. —Excellent Sir—
> The esteemed president general in charge of this army left, on the 14th of this month from Old Fort, to the left bank of the Brazos River with 750 choice men of the divisions with one six pounder. He left at Old Fort, on the right bank, the rest of the corps that he had personally commanded. I arrived there on the 16th and General Ramírez y Sesma, of course, surrendered to me the command. I set up permanent camp in accordance with the orders and instructions which His Excellency had left me as he marched.
> On the 18th he ordered me to place 500 men under the command of General Cos, which I did immediately. However, the entire force was defeated on the 21st near New

12. Filisola, *Memorias para la historia de la guerra de Tejas* (Cumplido, 1849), I, 216–217.

13. Urrea, "Diario de las operaciones militares," *Documentos para la historia de la guerra de Tejas,* 33.

Washington, a short distance beyond Harrisburg. Only three officers and six men have escaped. Therefore I united the forces of the army which came from different directions. Those gathering include the Generals Gaona and Urrea. Lacking a well supplied base of operations, because His Excellency had never established one, and lacking every indispensable means of self preservation; I am going to establish a base of operations on the right bank of the Colorado River from where I will, not only be able to receive the necessary assistance, but also make this saddest of circumstances less difficult for your excellency; while simultaneously reorganizing the army to begin a new offensive. Please pass on to His Excellency, the Interim President, this information I'm giving you, and let him know the concerns that occupy my fellow officers and me.

God and liberty: From Madam Powell's, five leagues from the Brazos River. April 25 1836. Vicente Filisola.—Esteemed Sr. Secretary of war and navy.[14]

At the end of his diary Urrea gave a summary of his defense and his case against Filisola. He stated that the above letter proved that Filisola thought there were only nine survivors from the battle of San Jacinto. He also claimed that this proved the retreat was not carried out to save the lives of Santa Anna and the six hundred Mexican prisoners. He correctly noted that Filisola did not even know if there were any prisoners and, if so, whether they had been executed. However, this seems to be yet another example of the way Urrea and Filisola went about twisting each others' words in order to discredit one another. Filisola did not seem to suggest that there were only nine men that survived the battle at San Jacinto, but that there were nine that escaped the battle and made their way back to the Mexican army.

Filisola wrote another letter on April 25, from Powell's, which supported the fact that his plan was indeed to recross the Colorado and set up a new line of operations. The letter was sent to Col. Domingo Ugartechea,[15] commander of Goliad.

14. Filisola, *Memorias para la historia de la guerra de Tejas* (Cumplido, 1849), I, 212–213.

15. Col. Domingo de Ugartechea was the military commander of the state of

Army of operations.—The supplies and money that you ought to have received from Matamoros, send to Guadalupe Victoria, consistent with orders from the General-in-Chief and from General Urrea, not to dispose of any amount that exceeds the allocated one thousand pesos, and taking care [not to waste] the scarce supplies. Frugality is essential.

The horses sent from Matamoros are for your use. Also in compliance with the orders issued by General Urrea, you are to inform me the minute you carry out this order.

God and liberty. At the home of Madam Powell, April 25, 1836.—Vicente Filisola.—Señor colonel D. Domingo Ugartechea, Military Commander at Goliad.[16]

It appears from this letter that Filisola indeed wanted all the supplies, money, and horses sent to Victoria, the nearest population center across the Colorado to the southwest. If Filisola was planning on continuing the retreat all the way to Mexico, why would he have bothered sending these supplies north? Had he been able to carry out the plan that was agreed upon during the meeting at Powell's, without the calamities that were to befall him and the army, it is likely he would have been able to hold this line and eventually renew the offensive.

It is really impossible to judge the "retreat of the Mexican army from Texas" as a whole, since it is not one maneuver but several small actions almost independent of one another. When the Mexican officers returned to Mexico following the disastrous retreat, they seemed to lump the whole withdrawal together and spoke strongly either for or against its necessity. Urrea's slowly growing opposition to the retreat is a notable example of the ever changing sentiments of many of the officers as the countermarch progressed. It is apparent that initially Urrea had only a mild distaste for giving up the position at Old Fort, primarily due to the fact that he was concerned for the well-being of the escapees from San Jacinto. When he first heard of the defeat it is likely that he thought there would be

---

Coahuila y Texas in 1835. He served at Béjar under Cos in the 1835 siege by the Texans. As commander of Béjar he ordered the cannon at Gonzales to be confiscated.

16. Filisola, *Memorias para la historia de la guerra de Tejas* (Cumplido, 1849), I, 213.

many more soldiers to flee the battle than there apparently were. After all what were the odds that the disastrous battle could have been that one-sided? It was only later that he began to strongly object to the retreat, as events went from bad to worse and it became apparent that the army would have to return to Mexico. He first officially opposed the retreat in his letter to the Mexican government from Victoria on May 11. He did not do so publicly until after June 10, when he was placed in command of the army.

The retreat is best understood if it is broken down into stages (see Map No. 1). The first phase was the countermarch from Old Fort, Columbia, and Brazoria to meet at Powell's. If any stage of the retreat was a mistake, this is the most likely candidate. Although Filisola was in a poor position militarily—in the middle of a large bend of the Brazos River—he controlled both banks of the river. Most of Gaona's division had already crossed to the east side. Urrea was also nearly ready, or had actually begun, to cross the Brazos River. However, his division had been greatly weakened by leaving so many troops in Victoria, Matagorda, and Columbia. Had Filisola acted at once and advanced on San Jacinto with his division and that of Urrea, the Texans may have been caught unprepared. However, considering the quality of troops that Filisola had at his disposal, the very poor condition of the cavalry horses and transport mules, the lack of adequate guides for the area, the terrible weather that we now know was to hit April 26, the poor state of the arms of Filisola's division and the time it would take Urrea to gather his troops, the success of such an offensive seems unlikely. Perhaps the most glaring problem that hindered the Mexican army from immediately taking the offensive was the lack of a daring leader to take charge. It is likely Urrea was such a man but he was not in position to act at the time. He was unable to influence Filisola's initial reaction to San Jacinto due to the distance that separated them.

There seem to have been several factors leading to the first stage of the retreat. Filisola obviously wanted to join Urrea as quickly as possible. However, he could have waited for Urrea to join him at Fort Bend. Filisola was probably spurred to action both by his cautious nature and his extreme lack of knowledge of the strength and position of the Texans. By the time Urrea had joined Filisola at Powell's, all hope of quickly attacking the Texans had been lost.

Stage two of the retreat can be thought of as the planned relocation to the opposite side of the Colorado. As planned, it was a reasonable decision. Since the opportunity for quick action against the Texans was now past, it made sense to put the Colorado between them and their enemies. There was also the matter of the other fifteen hundred Mexican soldiers in Texas with which they could be reinforced. Santa Anna had just lost the battle of San Jacinto due to impatience and his disdain for the Texans as a fighting force. Apparently, Filisola and the other generals were not anxious to do the same. At this point the Mexican generals still knew nothing of the fate of Santa Anna. All seemed to agree that the best thing to do was to fall back, regroup, and let the Mexican government act now that Santa Anna, the autocrat, was not there to make all their decisions for them. This probably was the best plan at the time but, as we now know, things were not to go as planned.

Stage three of the retreat occurred after the crossing of the Colorado. And as will be shown, by this time the Mexican army had few choices. Circumstances had developed, through no fault of their own, that drastically limited their options. Their effectiveness as a fighting unit had been severely diminished due to fatigue, loss of equipment, and low morale. And if that were not enough, a rift had developed between their general-in-chief and Urrea, the commander of their best surviving division. The condition of the army deteriorated so significantly that they never again united as a single force after crossing the Colorado.

Other matters were addressed at the meeting at Madam Powell's. The army was given a new organization. The first brigade would now be composed of the Permanent Morelos Battalion, the Active Guadalajara Battalion, the auxiliary from Guanajuato, two six-pounder cannons, and a howitzer. The first brigade was to be commanded by General Gaona. The second brigade would be led by General Tolsa and was to include the Zapadores Battalion, First Active Battalion of Mexico, the Active Querétaro Battalion, two eight-pounder cannons, and a howitzer. The reserve division, under the command of Urrea would be made up of the Permanent Jiménez Battalion, the Active San Luis Battalion, all the cavalry, and two four-pounder cannons. General Sesma was to be Filisola's second-in-command and General Woll would serve as major general of the army.[17]

17. San Luis Battalion Daily Log, Apr. 25, 1836; Peña, *La rebelión de Texas,* Anexo

The only other matter that still needed the attention of Filisola was which road to take when recrossing the Colorado. Filisola clearly stated that they were going to retrace the path Urrea had taken as he advanced from Victoria to Powell's.

It had already been decided to retreat. Now nothing was left but to find the shortest road with easy access for the units, and with resources which could serve all the operations planned. General Filisola did not know of any other roads than that they had taken from Bexar to San Felipe and on to Old Fort, but General Urrea informed all the participants [of the meeting] that the shortest and most convenient road, on which they could still get some aid and with the easiest crossing of the Colorado, was the same road that he had taken.[18]

Both Urrea and Peña later criticized Filisola for taking the road toward Cayce's Crossing, instead of taking the road to San Felipe. It seems unlikely that Urrea would have objected strongly to taking the road that he was familiar with and which he knew would lead them toward his other units at Matagorda, Victoria, etc. It should be noted that Urrea never did claim in his diary that he recommended taking the San Felipe road or that he objected to taking the route that was chosen.

The same day, Filisola sent troops ahead to secure the crossing on the Colorado called Cayce's Crossing.[19] This is the same crossing

No. 6W, p. 252–253. This is an excerpt from the order of the day for April 25, 1836. It stated that the first brigade would have two 8-pounder cannons and a howitzer. The second brigade was also to have two 8-pounder cannons and a howitzer. The rearguard was to have two 4-pounder cannons (*La rebelión de Texas*, 183). There is a disagreement in these two sources as to the size of the two cannons of the first brigade. In the last reference, Peña stated that the first brigade had two 6-pounder cannons and a howitzer. It is tempting to favor the accuracy of the daily order found in the battalion log, but the archeological evidence favors the latter, i.e., that the first brigade had two 6-pound cannons. The iron cannon balls seem to be for a 6-pound cannon and the solid copper cannon ball seems to be for a 4-pound cannon.

18. Filisola, *Memorias para la historia de la guerra de Tejas* (Cumplido, 1849), I, 211.

19. Thomas Cayce owned a league of land near what is now Bay City,

that Urrea had used from April 6–11, passing to the left bank of the river.

> For that purpose he [Filisola] sent Col. D. Francisco Garay ahead with a detachment of troops and various craftsmen from the prisoners to prepare all possible means for repassing that river [Colorado] at a place called Casey. Indeed the Col. left that same day with a force of 125 men from the infantry and cavalry, artisans and their tools, as listed: 50 infantrymen of the activo Btn. San Luis, 25 soldiers from the permanente cavalry regiment Tampico, 25 of the same from the squadron auxiliary de bajio, 25 of the same from the presidial cavalry and 20 artisans, carpenters and canoeists etc.[20]

Since these troops left Powell's on April 25, they were able to arrive at Cayce's and waited there for the main army—which never came. They were eventually joined by most of the Tres Villas Battalion, which had been occupying Matagorda, and finally met up with the main Mexican army at Victoria.

For better or worse, by the evening of April 25 the die was cast for the Mexican army to start its movement to recross the Colorado. There was no way for them to suspect that the worst of their struggles still lay ahead. How could they have known they were about to confront a quagmire that Filisola would later refer to as "un Mar de Lodo" or "a sea of mud."

Matagorda County, Texas. It was on the right (southwest) bank of the Colorado. Cayce did operate a ferry on the Colorado but it may have been on the league north of his land (he had purchased part of the league just north of his grant). Despite extensive research by Mary Belle Ingram of Bay City, and many hours of fieldwork by the author and by Gary Ralston of Port Lavaca, Texas, the exact location of this crossing has not yet been established.

20. Filisola, *Memorias para la historia de la guerra de Tejas* (Cumplido, 1849), I, 211–212.

PL. 8.

XIXe Siècle.

COSTUMES MEXICAINS.

Dragon. Troupe de Ligne.

Chapeau rond garni d'une bande de Mousseline

Imp. de Decouvre Platsacks, lith. de la Cour

Costumes Mexicaines. Dragon. By Claudio Linati, 1828. Lithograph (hand–colored), 12 ¼ × 9 ¼ inches. *Courtesy of the Amon Carter Museum, Fort Worth, Texas.*

CHAPTER 6

The Storm

THE ORDER OF THE DAY for the Mexican army at Powell's, on April 25, called for the march to begin the next morning in the following order:

> At the vanguard, two companies from the first brigade; followed by the wagons, all the loads of ammunition, luggage, and supplies; next, will be the second brigade, which will follow the first. The rearguard will be covered by the reserve. THE FIRST BRIGADE: Morelos, Guadalajara and Guanajuato, with two eight pounders and one howitzer. THE SECOND BRIGADE: Zapadores Battalion [Sappers], First Active, and the Querétaro. Reserve: Jiménez and San Luis, all the cavalry and two four pounders.[1]

Peña and Filisola documented that after the march commenced the various dwellings at Powell's were burned. Neither seemed to know who was responsible but Peña noted the feeling of great loss such a fire produced.[2]

The road that the army used as they exited Powell's that morning is still not known. Filisola gave several different descriptions of the route they took on April 26. In his earlier documents he did not

---

1. Peña, *La rebelión de Texas,* Anexo no. 6y, p. 253.

2. *La rebelión de Texas,* 181; translated in Perry (trans. and ed.), *With Santa Anna in Texas,* 160; Filisola, *Memorias para la historia de la guerra de Tejas* (Cumplido, 1849), I, 219.

mention which road was taken or the distance traveled that day. As noted before he often mistakenly dated April 26 as April 27.

In 1838, when Filisola wrote *Análisis del diario militar del General D. José Urrea durante la primera campaña de Tejas,* he had corrected the date to April 26 and added the following information: "El dia 26 emprehendieron la marcha las tres brigades. . . . A las dos leguas dejamo á la derecha, el camino que va para S. Felipe de Austin, y á cosa una legua mas, nos encontramos con un arroyo de los various forman el S. Bernardo." This passage is a good example of the possible pitfalls of translation. The correct translation of the above is: "The day of the 26th the three brigades began the march. . . . After two leagues [5.36 miles] the road to San Felipe was left to our right, and after one more league we encountered one stream of the various that form the San Bernard." If not carefully translated this phrase could make it seem as though after two leagues on the San Felipe road the army took a right turn. On the contrary, it actually says that after two leagues they left the San Felipe road to their right, i.e., they took a left turn.[3] After approximately one more league they encountered one of the streams that make up the San Bernard. Filisola may have found this terminology confusing as well because in his 1849 Cumplido edition of *Memorias* he omitted the term "á la derecha." Thus according to Filisola's later accounts the army took the San Felipe road north from Powell's for two leagues (5.4 miles) and then took a left turn and marched for one league (2.7 miles) where they encountered the San Bernard River (the San Bernard is the first of the three branches of the San Bernard that the Mexican army would have come upon if traveling west from Powell's). After crossing the San Bernard they continued the march. Filisola's account did not say how far past the river they marched before they made camp.

Peña reported that they went eight to ten miles on April 26, but it must be remembered that he was referring to Mexican miles, not English miles. One Mexican mile is equal to .893 English miles

---

3. Another example of this type of usage in the writings of the times is found in Juan Almonte's journal when he wrote: "from thence, leaving the road from Brazoria on our right, we took the left." Jackson (ed.) and Wheat (trans.), *Almonte's Texas,* 400.

(2.68 English miles equal one league which equals three Mexican miles).[4] Thus he said they went a total of 7.1 to 8.9 English miles.

The San Luis Battalion log recorded the distance traveled that day as two leagues (5.4 English miles). Unfortunately the log did not give any indication as to the route taken. The San Luis log is included in the Peña Papers. It was probably used by Peña to fill in the gaps when he had no personal knowledge of events.[5] The fact that Peña does not give the same distances as the San Luis log supports the contention that he did indeed keep a diary which he consulted when he compiled his memoirs. It should also be noted that his distances are not only different from the other sources, i.e., Filisola and Urrea, but taken as a whole his distances seem to be as accurate as the others, or even slightly more so.

When comparing these sources certain facts need to be considered. To begin with, it should be noted that Filisola's early writings did not include the detail of his later writings. Apparently it was only in 1838, after he was criticized by Urrea and Peña for not taking the San Felipe road, that he conveniently remembered that he did set out on said road but left it after about five miles. Another general truism is the fact that the distances given by the San Luis log and by Peña appear to be more accurate than those offered up by Filisola. This judgment is to be expected considering the fact that the writers of the San Luis log recorded the distances they traveled every day of their trip whereas Filisola rarely gave distances in his accounts.

Even more convincing evidence regarding the route taken by the army can be found in the San Luis log and the Urrea diary. The combination of these two documents gives a good sense of their route from Goliad—across the Colorado at Cayce's, south to Matagorda, and then back north to eventually reach Madam Powell's place on April 20. If the distances they give are used on the Stephen F. Austin Connected Map of Texas, their path, as they advanced from Matagorda, can be postulated with a reasonable degree of certainty.[6]

4. Mier y Terán, *Texas by Terán*, 210.

5. This can be clearly seen in Peña's description of the Mexican army arriving in San Antonio on February 23. Since Peña did not arrive in San Antonio until March 3 he obviously used the San Luis Battalion Log to describe the events of February 23 through March 2.

6. The San Luis Battalion Log stated that on April 16–17 the battalion went

The Storm

Using the distances that were given in the San Luis log, two things become apparent. First, the mileages recorded seem to be quite accurate. Second, there does not seem to be any way to match the direction and distances that were given by Filisola for April 26 with those of the San Luis as they approached Powell's on April 20. The two should match as Filisola repeatedly stated that his plan was to take the same path to Cayce's Crossing as Urrea (and the San Luis Battalion) had taken on their advance (see Map No. 2).

This speculation is interesting but there is actual archeological evidence that the Mexican army headed almost due west—not up the San Felipe road. On the west bank of the West Bernard Creek various Mexican army artifacts have been found. As the retreating Mexican army was never able to cross the West Bernard, due to the flooding, these artifacts could not have been left by them. It is likely that these artifacts are from the crossing site of Urrea's division as it headed east, from the campsite of April 19, to Powell's on April 20 (see Map No. 2).

If indeed all this conjecture is true, and it does seem to add up well, it is very likely that this is the same path, in reverse, that Filisola planned to take to Cayce's Crossing. If the army was retracing Urrea's path, they would have headed to the west, not five miles up the San Felipe road as Filisola reported. It is just over four miles from Powell's to the San Bernard River as measured on the road shown

---

eight leagues from Matagorda and camped at the same place they had camped the night of April 12. This was Cayce's Crossing on the Colorado. On April 19 they said that they were on the bank of the San Bernard and had traveled eight leagues. It seems likely that they were actually on the bank of Caney Creek, not the San Bernard. If they were on the San Bernard the seven leagues they traveled the next day would have put them well past Powell's, which is where they camped the night of April 20. Urrea also reported that they were on the San Bernard, but if indeed they spent the night of the 18th at Cayce's Crossing, they were on the Bay Prairie Road. This road led straight north and not to the east and the San Bernard. The path via the Bay Prairie Road would have intertwined with the Caney, which is not often shown on the old maps.

Also there is a small community in Wharton County called Spanish Camp. Reportedly at least two Mexican army artifacts were found there in the 1950s but this is not documented. If the San Luis distances are used from Cayce's on April 18 to Spanish Camp on April 19, then on to Powell's on April 20, they are nearly correct.

∞

SEA OF MUD

on Stephen F. Austin's Connected Map of Texas. Taking the San Luis log's estimate of two leagues traveled on April 26, which is about one and one-half miles less than Peña's lower estimate (7.1 English miles), the campsite of the night of April 26 should have been one and one-half to three miles west of the San Bernard River. The crossing shown on the Austin map is less than one mile above the current crossing of Highway 59 over the San Bernard.

Even though the exact road and crossing site on the San Bernard River are as yet undiscovered, much is known of the happenings of that gloomy day. The various reports stated that sometime between 10 A.M. and noon a heavy rain commenced. One of the better descriptions of that day is found in the Cumplido version of Filisola's *Memorias*. He described the crossing of the San Bernard as follows:

> This stream runs very narrow, its bed is very muddy, and the passage extremely narrow. Consequently it was a difficult crossing. The baggage, munitions, etc. were taken to the front, and while they were filing by, the brigades were ordered to halt and form into battle formation with the front toward the rearguard. This left the entire division formed in three lines.
>
> The operation of crossing the river was troublesome because it was necessary to make a new crossing with branches, fragments of wood, etc. so the artillery would not be buried. Double pulls of mules were placed on each one [cannon] and the carts, in order to make the climb up the other side. The Zapadores [sappers], with the help of the grenadier companies and the officers, officials and generals, were persistently busy working on that laborious operation. It must be said to honor justice that Sr. Urrea himself did not work the least.
>
> The operation was not half done when the sky was suddenly obscured. Thereupon it started raining, worsening gradually, until it ended in a deluge. The last troops had hardly finished crossing when the crossing was left useless by a huge abundance of water coming down the river. The march was continued, water falling in torrents upon the troops, as far as a little wooden dwelling, about five varas

square [1 vara = 2.8 ft.], that was almost swimming in water. Because beside this [dwelling] runs a creek: all the ground was converted into a lake. The night was near and the rain continued with force. The brigades were scattered some distance from one another. It was necessary to unite them in the light of day to see that the position was good militarily, for passing the night and for preparing mess for the troops etc. I commanded the brigades to form a square, although irregular. The right side of the square, the road we had taken, was occupied by general Tolsa, the front by general Gaona and the left of the square by general Urrea. When he [Urrea] arrived it was nearly nightfall. Forming the fourth side, or the back if you will, was the mentioned creek. As a result the safest point, in any event, was that occupied by Urrea. I believe that the safest point should go to the cavalry so that in any event they might have time to saddle up etc. It was not because I felt those troops to be inferior to the rest of the army.

The night was spent with much trouble, the corps passed it squatting with their muskets right in their hands, the water reaching to their backsides.[7]

Peña reported that the crossing took nearly three hours. Urrea added that the crossing of his units was delayed even more as the other divisions had made the crossing impassable with their wagons and herds.

In his *Representación* to the Mexican government Filisola stated that on that night Urrea occupied the position to the left on the "square" formed by their units and the creek. He intimated that Urrea chose this position and did so from fear. Urrea responded to this in his diary entry for April 26.

When Señor Filisola narrates the events of this day (which he designates as the 27th) [this correction of the date is from Urrea] he does me a great injustice and makes such a ridiculous statement, permit me this remark, that, like all his other

7. Filisola, *Memorias para la historia de la guerra de Tejas* (Cumplido, 1849), I, 214–215.

∞

statements which depend for their faith upon his word, it has no value. He says on page 23: "We camped that night in a small house and Messrs. Gaona and Tolsa covered the most exposed posts with their brigades, while Señor Urrea took care of the best protected location." . . . This base insult not only to my person but to the brave men under my orders, who covered themselves with laurels and on whom victory turned her back, proclaims a heart possessed of all the ignoble passions, incapable of justice, and unwilling to admit its own errors. When did Señor Filisola see me show signs of cowardice? When was I ever known to turn my back upon, or to fear danger? If my presence was so unimportant, why was I called with such haste only to be given a worthless position in the army? Was it because of the fear that possessed General Filisola? Let those who saw me campaign in Texas, and those who read the diary of my operations decide the question. As for the rest, I do not believe that I owe his Excellency any thanks, for on that night there was no danger, the general having exercised his usual prudence to avoid it.[8]

After Urrea and Peña took him to task for such a claim, Filisola later, as we have seen above, admitted that he chose the positions for the purpose of allowing the cavalry to saddle up in the event of an engagement.

Also note that even though there was a terrible storm, the army was still marching and performing as a unit. Peña complained that the retreat of the army in a single column went against good military judgment, but the fact remains that they were functioning as a single unit and care was being taken to address their military situation. The forming of the square is evidence that care was being taken to protect them from an enemy attack.

In June 2001 the Houston area was hit by tropical storm Allison. Some areas in and around Houston received up to thirty-eight inches of rain over a period of two or three days. There is no way to know how much rain fell on the Mexican army on April 26 and 27,

8. Urrea, "Diario de las operaciones militares," *Documentos para la historia de la guerra de Tejas,* 31–32.

1836, but there is little doubt that it was significant. Peña gave an idea of the severity of the first day of the storm.

> Between eleven and twelve in the morning, rain began to pour, continuing heavily until nightfall, when we made a halt. The rear guard, protected by General Urrea with a reserve brigade, had not yet arrived when it began again, to continue through the night without interruption and consequently without any rest for us.[9]

We know that it was a very wet spring to begin with. Several times the Mexican army was hindered by high waters. A good example of this was Urrea trying to pass the Colorado, at Cayce's, as he was advancing from Victoria to Matagorda. Urrea arrived at the Colorado on April 6, and due to rising waters had to construct barges for crossing the army. He was not able to get under way again until April 12. There is also corroboration of the wet spring in the Texans' statements. In both the Taylor and Alsbury accounts of the flight of Santa Anna from San Jacinto it was mentioned that the prairie was so wet that the horses were knee deep in mud.

There is other documentation of this storm. William Fairfax Gray, a land purchaser from Virginia, was traveling in Texas and kept a diary of the events of that day. Even though he had actually left Texas on April 25, 1836, he was just across the border in western Louisiana. He wrote in his diary that on April 27 he was overtaken by a heavy shower of rain early in the day. Later the same day he documented traveling through a boggy prairie in a hard rain. The weather cleared for a while but he added that "it rained excessively hard in the night. The thunder resembled the discharge of cannon." Gray added that the rain ceased on April 28 but in crossing a swollen bayou his horse fell in the water and he was soaked. On April 29 it rained hard all morning. He was unable to continue his travels due to the rain. Later that day, having resumed his trip, he was hit by another very heavy shower of rain.[10]

Extensive fieldwork has been undertaken in the area of the sus-

---

9. Peña, *La rebelión de Texas,* 181; translated in Perry (trans. and ed.), *With Santa Anna in Texas,* 160.

10. Gray, *The Diary of William Fairfax Gray,"* 163–164.

pected crossing and in the neighborhood of the suspected campsite of April 26. At the time of this writing no evidence has been discovered that proves this was the route, other than the probable Urrea site on the west side of the West Bernard. When the *Análisis* of Urrea's diary was obtained, the focus of the search was shifted north five miles, as Filisola said they went five miles up the San Felipe road before turning west to cross the San Bernard. Once again the river and the surrounding areas were searched but to no avail. The Urrea site was actually discovered after months of looking for the northern crossing. After this site became known the focus shifted back to the southern crossing near Highway 59. The distances covered each day, as reported by the various sources, are more compatible with the southern crossing, but even they vary greatly. Currently the "southern route" is the "best guess" as to the route of the army on April 26, but until the crossing and the campsite of that night are found, nothing will be set in stone.

ARCHEOLOGY OF THE URREA SITE

At the present time the archeological report for the site located on the west side of the West Bernard Creek has not been published. The site was initially discovered by a farmer who found a six-pound iron cannonball in a field that he had recently plowed. It was originally thought that this site may have been associated with Post West Bernard, a Republic of Texas facility just south of the site on the West Bernard. This is still possible as the function of Post West Bernard was gun repair and many of the guns they repaired were captured Mexican muskets. But this possibility seems unlikely, as all the military artifacts at the site appear to be Mexican.

The site is also very unlikely to be from the retreating Mexican army, as it was unable to cross to the west side of the West Bernard due to the flooding mentioned above. Based on the distances recorded by the San Luis Battalion on April 19, it is believed that this site was not a campsite. The campsite of April 19 was probably near present-day Spanish Camp, Texas. If this is correct it is theorized that the site discovered on the West Bernard is where Urrea and his division crossed the river during their advance. It is possible that these artifacts were discarded at the site as the units awaited their turn to cross. The artifacts from this site are consistent with the above theory.

There are very few of the items most commonly found at the other sites deemed to be campsites. There are basically no musket balls or canister shot, yet there are an inordinate number of gun parts and other brass items. These are in very poor condition leading one to think they may have been discarded because they were irreparable.

There were many broken pieces of India Pattern Brown Bess butt plates at the site, many more than would have been expected when compared to the number of ramrod pipes, sideplates, nosecaps, etc. This site also seems to contain greater numbers of trigger-guard tangs. Overall, these musket parts seem to be in much worse condition and much more fragmented than at the other sites. One thought on these artifacts is that they were trash that was dumped by a blacksmith or gunsmith prior to the crossing.

There were also pieces of a brass stirrup found at the site. Approximately one-third of the stirrup was found but it is broken into two pieces [Fig. 6-1]. A brass ring that would have attached to a candleholder was excavated. And there was an iron blade from a Bowie knife at the site [Fig. 6-2], with the handle showing a coffin-handle configuration. A brass pommel-cap, which may have fit the Bowie knife, was also excavated [Fig. 6-3].

One of the most interesting items unearthed was a piece of a brass wax-stamp. The item had a backwards, block "G" on the face. It seems probable that only one of the higher officers would have had a wax stamp. Searching the available lists of officers in Urrea's command on April 20 reveals one officer whose last name began with a "G"—Col. Francisco Garay. It is interesting to conjecture that this could be his wax stamp. It is possible that someday this may be proven as Garay was a tariff collector at Matamoros prior to the Texas campaign and may have used this stamp for official business. If so, there might still exist evidence of this very same stamp being used on his documents [Fig. 6-4].

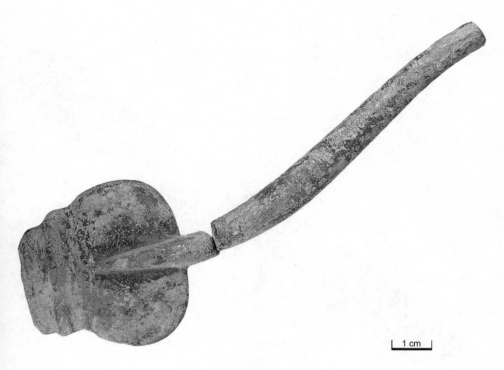

1 cm

Fig. 6-1. Brass stirrup fragment.

1 cm

Fig. 6-2. Iron "Bowie" knife.

Fig. 6-3. Brass knife pommel.

|_ 1 cm _|

|_ 1 cm _|

Fig. 6-4. Brass wax stamp engraved "G".

Soldado Mexicano Presidial.

Soldat des presidios des Etats Internes du Mexique

Soldado Mexicano Presidial. By Lino Sanchez y Tapia. Watercolor on paper.
Courtesy of the Gilcrease Museum, Tulsa, Oklahoma.

CHAPTER 7

Santa Anna's Orders

AFTER SPENDING THE NIGHT squatting in the mud, the Mexican army faced a persistent hard rain as the next day broke. After mess[1] the march in the mud proceeded. One source claimed that the whole day they marched through mud up to their knees, while another claimed the mud was up to their thighs. Both Filisola and the San Luis log reported that they went three leagues prior to encountering another of the branches of the San Bernard. However, as will be discussed in chapter eight, there is a conflict in the distance Filisola said they traveled that day. Peña stated they had marched no more than five miles (4.5 English miles) before they had to stop as it was impossible to cross the second Bernardo. The distance from the proposed campsite of April 26, just west of the San Bernard, to the West Bernard, opposite the Urrea site, is just under about 4.75 miles. This is almost exactly what Peña reported but almost three miles less than that reported by Filisola and the San Luis log. Examining map No. 3, it can be seen that the road that leaves from Powell's to the west is far enough south that it would totally miss the Middle Bernard Creek. This fact argues for the more southern road from Powell's, since, if they had taken the San Felipe road and cut east, as Filisola claimed, they would have encountered the Middle Bernard Creek first. The distance between the San Bernard River and the Middle Bernard Creek is so small that this would not have allowed for Peña's 4.5 miles, much less Filisola's three leagues.

---

1. Filisola used the word *rancho* for mess.

Once again the locations of these campsites are educated guesses and have not been proven. However, along the West Bernard, opposite the Urrea site, a brass spur and two musket balls have been discovered. It cannot be determined whether these artifacts were from Urrea's advancing division, after he crossed the West Bernard and headed east to Powell's on April 20, or from the retreating Mexican army's campsite of April 27. Considering the small number of artifacts it seems highly unlikely that this is the campsite, but the search goes on.

Filisola claimed to be at a disadvantage due to a lack of good maps. It is very likely that the series of streams that form the San Bernard system was very confusing to the leaders of the Mexican army. Even today residents of the area who have lived their whole lives in the vicinity of the three rivers often mix up the various branches when quizzed about the specifics. In reviewing the various sources, and listing them by date, there is noted to be a great diversity as to what the Mexican authors called the various Bernard branches.

April 26—when the Mexican army was crossing the San Bernard, the river was called: (1) one creek of the various that form the San Bernard, (2) the first of the rivulets of the San Bernard, (3) San Bernard Creek, (4) first fork of the San Bernard, (5) one of the three Bernardos.

April 27—when the Mexican army was camped along the flooded West Bernard, the creek was called: (1) the principal rivulet of the three that form the San Bernard, (2) the second rivulet, (3) another of the creeks that form the San Bernard, (4) the second branch of the San Bernard, (5) the second Bernardo.

April 28—when the Mexican army was camped on a river that was most likely the San Bernard, the same as April 26, the river was called: (1) the middle rivulet of the San Bernard, (2) second branch of the San Bernard, (3) the same rivulet crossed the 26th.

April 29–May 2—when the army was stuck in the mud along the Middle Bernard, the creek was called: (1) the principal rivulet of the several that form the San Bernard, (2) middle creek of the San Bernard.

Comparing the various titles given to the rivers, it is understandable that the Mexican officers were not always sure which branch of the San Bernard was which. In examining map No. 3, it can be seen that the path of the Middle Bernard is confusing, as it loops to the

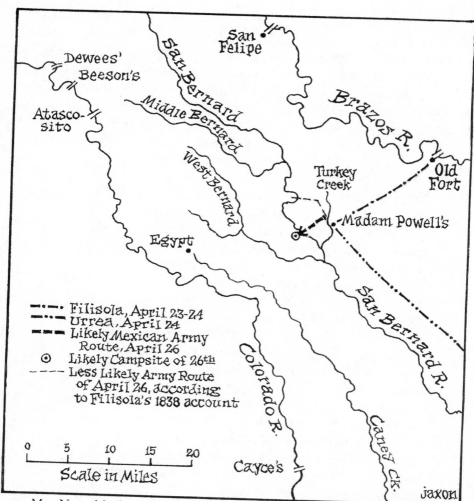

Map No. 3. Mexican Army Routes, April 24–26, 1836. *Drawn by Jack Jackson.*

northeast just before it enters the San Bernard. If the Mexican army eventually (on April 28) traveled north along the west side of the San Bernard, as it seems they did, and then turned northwest along the Middle Bernard, it would have been easy for them to have mistaken the Middle Bernard for a continuation of the San Bernard.

Filisola claimed that, on the morning of April 27, he instructed General Urrea to send an officer and a few of his best riders, toward the river they had crossed the day before. Their objective was to search for stragglers and gather information concerning the enemy. Urrea mentioned the same action but claimed that he, not Filisola, instituted the mission. Urrea's version was that he sent two good scouts to check out the roads on which the enemy might advance. He reported that the scouts were given orders to advance as far as the Brazos, cross it if possible and bring back any stragglers from San Jacinto.

When Filisola arrived at the flooded West Bernard it was obvious that there would be no crossing of the creek that day. In his Cumplido edition of *Memorias* he described the situation at that point.

After a march of three leagues, part of which we had water up to mid-leg, another fork of the several that form the San Bernard was encountered. It runs meandering from the northwest to the southeast, in immense turns. After diligently trying it was not possible to find any means of passing it. In addition to all the water carried in its width, and the mud of its banks, it had a multitude of oaks that impeded the passage. It was necessary to wait until the next day to see if during the remainder of that day and that night it would run lower. Meanwhile General Woll was sent to reconnoiter the river toward its origin, to see if there was a better place to cross the river.

We camped on the left (east) bank of the river at a point that seemed less muddy. However, when the men stayed a little while in one place their feet submerged. The army formed a single line facing the rear. The stream supported both flanks because it made a type of angle projecting toward the south. Thus the line of battle came to be the base of an irregular triangle, with the stream embracing our flanks and backs. The position could not have been more desperate, and this was reported to the other generals by Filisola. However there was no ground that was better. In case of attack, the only means of retreat would be to cross the stream as they were encircled everywhere by other swamps and marches. Consequently it was absolutely imperative to rid the troops of any idea that salvation would not be based on victory.[2]

2. Filisola, *Memorias para la historia de la guerra de Tejas* (Cumplido, 1849), I, 215–216.

SEA OF MUD

Filisola gave a slightly different version of the site on the West Bernard in his letter to the Mexican government of May 14, 1836.

On the following day I continued the march to the second rivulet, the troops being up to their knees in water the whole distance; when I came upon it I found that it was not fordable, as the rain had swollen it so much, and the guides assured me that it would take at least eight days to go down, and that afterwards it was necessary to pass through a forest for five leagues, full of bamboo[3] and swampland, which on account of the storm would be very difficult to get out of.[4]

Once again the matter of translation comes up. Filisola commented that on April 26 he sent General Woll to the "nacimiento" of the river. This should be translated as the origin, not the mouth as it was written in the Woolsey translation of the Rafael edition of Filisola's *Memorias*.

Urrea wrote in his diary on April 27 that between three and four in the afternoon the scouts he had sent out that morning returned with a presidial soldier who had papers for Filisola from Santa Anna. The presidial soldier informed Urrea he had been sent from Béjar with dispatches for Santa Anna. When the courier arrived at the Brazos he had been met by Smith[5] and two other Anglo-Americans,

3. There was no bamboo in the area but there was an abundance of sugarcane. There are descriptions by the early settlers of forests of cane, which were referred to as cane breaks.

4. Filisola, May 14, 1836, letter to the Mexican government, *La rebelión de Texas*, Anexo No. 22, p. 283; translated in Filisola, *Evacuation of Texas*, 41–42; retranslated for G. Dimmick by Dora Elizondo Guerra.

5. On page 182 of *La rebelión de Texas*, editor Sánchez Garza added that this was Benjamin F. Smith. In Pena's original handwritten document it says only "Col. Smith." It is likely that Sánchez Garza is mistaken and that this colonel was Erastus "Deaf" Smith. Another document has been located that proves that the "Smith" that Urrea mentioned was indeed Deaf Smith. A Republic of Texas claim in the Texas State Library and Archives, filed by L. Dickinson, requests reimbursement for a horse. The claim is accompanied by a statement from John Chenoweth. In his statement Chenoweth included the following: "Said horse was taken on the morning of the 21st by Col Forbs at the request of Deaf Smith to go at the request of the Com-Gen—or by his order to burn the bridge on Vince's Bayou. Smith afterward

who were searching for Filisola to deliver him dispatches from Santa Anna. The soldier stated that these men had taken the correspondence that he was carrying for Santa Anna and had given him that intended for Filisola. Urrea learned from Santa Anna's dispatches, as well as from the pass that Smith had given the presidial soldier signed personally by Santa Anna, that the Mexican commander-in-chief was indeed a prisoner of the Texans. He noted that all the members of his brigade were overjoyed as they had all thought Santa Anna had been killed in the battle. As Urrea read the news to his troops he urged them to turn upon the enemy. The general reported that this is exactly what the soldiers desired. Bugles were sounded immediately and all the troops broke out into loud acclamations and hurrahs. Urrea felt that this clearly showed the enthusiasm for battle that existed among all the classes of soldiers.

Urrea sent the presidial soldier with one of his aides to find Filisola, who had already encamped on the West Bernard. Filisola reported that he got the news at two in the afternoon, even though Urrea put the time at between three and four o'clock. Interestingly enough, in his Rafael version of *Memorias,* Filisola stated that he received this news the following day. In all other sources he stated that it was the same day. This is not a translation error as the original Spanish confirms that he wrote "del dia siguiente." It should also be noted that Filisola often wrote in the third person and referred to himself as "General Filisola" or "Filisola."

In the Cumplido edition of his *Memorias* Filisola described the circumstances of his first learning of the survival and captivity of Santa Anna.

> About 2:00 in the afternoon, Filisola found himself in his tent, and heard sounds of jubilation in camp. He arose to discover its cause. Scarcely had he reached the door when a mounted presidial soldier appeared with two other men.

---

informed me that he rode the horse when he was the bearer of a dispatch to the Mexican army from Santa Ana [*sic*] when he was fired upon and compelled to retreat and after retreating about 20 miles his horse failed and bogged and he left him bogged down ner [*sic*] Mrs. Powells [*sic*] ..." L. Dickinson Audited Claim, R25, F740 (Texas State Library and Archives, Austin, Texas). Provided by Thomas Ricks Lindley.

∞

They were the same men whom I ordered General Urrea to send back along the road that we had taken the day before. While surrounded by the crowd of officers and men celebrating General Santa Anna, the first [the presidial soldier] placed in General Filisola's hands several documents. [Filisola], without paying attention to the documents, asked, 'Where is the General-in-chief?' He believed him to be in camp already. 'No sir, he is in the camp at San Jacinto,' was the reply. Little satisfied with this response, he entered the tent to read the papers that contained the official document that follows:[6]

ARMY OF OPERATIONS

Most Excellent Sir.—yesterday, [as a result of] a small division acting in my control and having had a disastrous encounter, I find myself a prisoner of war among the insurrectionists. I have retained [in my possession], as much as has been possible, all dispatches. In view of this, I command Your Excellency to order General Gaona to countermarch to Béxar to await my orders, which Your Excellency will also do with the troops under your command. Likewise direct General Urrea to withdraw with his division to Guadalupe Victoria. An armistice has been drawn up with General Houston while negotiations are under way to bring the war to an end for ever.

Your Excellency can make arrangements for the maintenance of the army—which from now on is under your orders—from the sums of money that have arrived at Matamoros and the supplies that should be in said point and Victoria, as well as the $20,000 that should be in that treasury and were taken from Béxar. I hope that without fail Your Excellency will carry out these instructions, advising me in reply of your beginning to put them into execution.

God and Liberty. Field at San Jacinto, April 22, 1836. —

6. Filisola, *Memorias para la historia de la guerra de Tejas* (Cumplido, 1849), I, 216–217.

Antonio López de Santa Anna.—His Excellency Division
General Vicente Filisola[7]

The second letter addressed the issue of protecting the property
of the Texans during the retreat.

No. 2 Army of Operations:
Excellent Sir,
     In as much as I have ordered your excellency by official
note of today that you cause the troops to retire to Béxar
and Guadalupe Victoria, I charge you to instruct the Com-
mandants of the several divisions, not to permit any damage
done to the property of the Inhabitants of the country, hoping that these dispositions will be punctually complied with.
God and Liberty, Camp of San Jacinto, April 22, 1836.
                          Antonio López de Santa Anna.

There was a third letter included in the Santa Anna documents.
This addressed the issue of prisoners which was to become another
point of criticism directed at Filisola after his return to Mexico. It
was claimed by several of the participants that Filisola released most
of the Texans without arranging for the freedom of any of their own
soldiers.

No. 3, Army of Operations:
     Excellent Sir,—You will immediately order the Military
commandant at Goliad, to put all the prisoners made at
Goliad, at liberty, and send them forthwith to San Felipe de
Austin, and for which purpose your Excellency will dictate
such Orders as may be conducive to the object.
God and Liberty, Camp of San Jacinto, April 22, 1836.
                          Antonio López de Santa Anna[8]

These three directives contain several items of great interest. It is

7. Filisola, *Memorias para la historia de la guerra de Tejas* (Rafael, 1848, 1849), II,
481.
8. Santa Anna to Filisola, Apr. 22, 1836, in Jenkins (ed.), *Papers of the Texas Revolution,* VI, 16.

∞

obvious, when looking at the details of Santa Anna's orders for the withdrawal, that these orders were never carried out, nor was there any attempt to do so. Santa Anna ordered Filisola and Gaona to withdraw to San Antonio and await further orders. Urrea was to proceed to Victoria with his division. Obviously the entire force continued the march on the same path. None of the troops ever withdrew to San Antonio. It is interesting to postulate that had Santa Anna's orders been carried out, the Mexican army may have been in a much better position, militarily, than by taking the course of action that they chose. The army would have been divided, thus easier to supply and feed. More importantly, Filisola and Urrea would have been divided by a greater distance, possibly lessening their animosity and freeing Urrea to act more boldly, had he so chosen.

It is also interesting to note that Santa Anna did not order Filisola to arrange an exchange of prisoners. He directed him to release the Texans who had been captured at Goliad and gave him no directions as to arranging or requiring a release of Mexican soldiers. Certainly, it could still be argued that Filisola should not have obeyed any of the orders of the captured commander-in-chief.

As was often the case, Santa Anna enclosed a personal letter to Filisola as well. Filisola must have noticed a glaring fact in this letter.

> Private secretariat of the president of the Mexican Repub-
> lic.—Commander in chief of the army of operations.—His
> Excellency Division General Don Vicente Filisola.—San Jac-
> into Pass, April 25,[9] 1836—My esteemed friend and com-
> panion. Since I do not know how long I shall remain here,
> and you and your men must return to the interior, I want
> you to send me my baggage, that of Colonel Almonte, of
> Castrillón, of Colonel Núñez and a trunk belonging to my
> secretary Señor Caro, which will be found in the living area
> next to my own things. Take care that there be a person
> whom you trust with the mule drivers and a guide that will
> accompany them to this camp. You will give him the

9. In both the Cumplido and Rafael editions of his *Memorias* Filisola dated this letter April 25. The same letter in *Papers of the Texas Revolution* is dated April 22. As the first and third letters in the same series are dated April 22 as well, this seems more likely to be the correct date.

∞

Santa Anna's Orders 155

enclosed safe conduct so that there will be no difficulty along the way. You will have the baggage of the leaders and officers returned so that in due time they will be received by their respective owners. I recommend to you that as soon as possible you carry out my order concerning the withdrawal of the troops since this is conducive to the safety of the prisoners, and in particular that of your most affectionate friend and companion who sends you his deepest regards. Antonio López de Santa Anna[10]

In spite of the fact that General Castrillón was killed in action at San Jacinto, Santa Anna was requesting that his baggage be sent along with that of the other officers. Surely Santa Anna was well aware of the pressing need for every pack mule that the army possessed. Yet he was asking that the baggage of all fifty-two captured officers be hauled from there to San Jacinto.

Gen. Filisola was later to claim that he was none too happy to receive these orders. He reported that his initial reaction to the documents was one of anger. He noted that General Ramírez y Sesma had entered his tent and he had commented to the general that he could not believe that Santa Anna did not trust him to have things in order and was upset that, in spite of the fact that Santa Anna was a prisoner, he was still giving orders. Sesma then motioned to Filisola that he should calm down as several other officers and men were gathering around and Filisola would not want to be heard criticizing Santa Anna.

By this time most of the division had gathered around Filisola's tent, so he came out and made the announcement of the status of Santa Anna and the other officers and soldiers captured at San Jacinto. Filisola called them "companions in his disgrace." The troops gathered around the tent requested that they sound *dianas* (a bugle call) and fire a volley in celebration of the news that Santa Anna was alive. Filisola refused this request, saying that even though the desire was admirable, the disgraceful defeat at San Jacinto was a national

10. Filisola, *Memorias para la historia de la guerra de Tejas* (Rafael, 1848, 1849), II, reprint, *Historia de la guerra de Tejas* (1968), II, 482; Woolsey translation, *Memoirs for the History of the War in Texas,* II, 236; retranslated for G. Dimmick by Dora Elizondo Guerra.

misfortune. He felt that instead of celebrating with demonstrations of rejoicing, all good Mexicans should be filled with grief and bitterness. After his decision the troops calmly and quietly left to return to their camps to prepare to continue the march.

Filisola next decided to question the presidial soldier who had delivered the documents from San Jacinto. In the interview the soldier informed him that he had been proceeding to San Jacinto when he was met by two rebels, one calling himself Colonel Smith.[11] The soldier reported that Smith had found the burned buildings at Old Fort, Madam Powell's, and the shack where Urrea's cavalry had camped at Powell's. Smith decided not to continue further and handed the presidial soldier the papers meant for Filisola. Smith informed the soldier that his troops were very angry and he was concerned that they would continue hostilities and shoot the prisoners.

The accounts of both Urrea and Filisola indicate that Smith never entered the Mexican camp. The presidial soldier that was captured by Smith was brought to Urrea by the scouts that Urrea had sent out earlier that day. Smith had given this soldier the dispatch from Santa Anna and Urrea sent him on to Filisola's camp. One obvious reason that Smith did not enter the Mexican camp or approach Urrea's division was that he was fired upon by Mexican soldiers—probably the scouts that Urrea had dispatched.[12]

Filisola later wrote that the news of the president's survival, as well as that of the other prisoners, in no way improved the situation of the army. Nor could it alter the decision to repass the Colorado. On the contrary, he noted that the munitions, harnesses, and gear for the mules were in very poor condition, as they had been standing in water, and that the army was surrounded by swamps, marshes, and streams. Even worse, the river that they had crossed on April 26 and the river on which they were currently camped were both flooded. He recalled that the presidial soldier who had delivered the papers from Santa Anna had had to swim the flooded river behind them, not without great peril to himself and his horse, floating his saddle over on a small raft he had made from some sticks and branches.

General Filisola then called a second meeting of his generals to discuss this new development. In the Rafael edition of his *Memorias*

11. See note 5 above.
12. Ibid.

Filisola pointed out that he was aware at the time that the president was no longer commander-in-chief, and that as a consequence his orders were not to be obeyed. After all were gathered he showed them the orders from Santa Anna and let each express his opinion of the situation. The opinions given at this meeting are not as well documented as those at the previous meeting at Powell's on April 25, but the decisions reached are telling, in light of the fact that they now had the orders from Santa Anna to retreat. If they were indeed going to follow these orders, as most Texas history accounts and many Mexican ones claim they did, this would have been the time to change their plans and proceed to San Antonio and Victoria as Santa Anna had directed. On the other hand, if indeed this news emboldened them to fight they would have held their ground or retraced their steps from this point.

General Urrea actually gave the most information concerning the meeting of the evening of April 27 at the West Bernard campsite.

Late that evening I was called by order of General Filisola to appear at his tent. All the generals of the army having gathered there, Señor Filisola read to us the letter and dispatch which Santa Anna, now a prisoner, had sent to him with instructions for the army to retreat agreeable to an armistice entered into with Houston.

I perceived some confusion among several of my companions, but I cannot say what it was. The retreat had already been undertaken by orders of General Filisola and the dispatch of General Santa Anna was taken to be only a safe conduct so that the army would not be disturbed by the enemy. It was decided to reply to General Santa Anna, giving the impression that our movement was being executed agreeable to his orders.

I called the attention of General Filisola to the fact that it was indispensable to explain why the Brazos had been abandoned before the receipt of his communication. This was done by telling the general, now a prisoner, that our first movement had had for its purpose the abandonment of useless posts to concentrate our forces and then turn upon the enemy. No other excuse could be thought of, for in fact, we had sufficient forces to have kept our position upon the Bra-

∞

zos, holding all the useless posts, and to have organized an excellent division which, by advancing upon the enemy, could have obtained victory and vindicated the honor of the army and of the nation.

In the above mentioned council, I insisted on turning back upon the enemy, and not succeeding in having my proposal accepted, because the enemy was thought to be very numerous, I proposed to Señor Filisola that I be permitted to go to Houston on pretext of taking to His Excellency his mail and bringing back the armistice. The army could await the result of my mission in the vicinity, from where, once the information as to the weakness and impotency of the enemy was obtained after my return, it could march upon it. Many objections were offered to my plan though its importance was recognized, and it was decided finally that General Adrian Woll should undertake the commission, but that the army should continue its retrograde movement although with assurances, at the time, that a position would be taken on the Colorado.[13]

Filisola's report of the meeting was somewhat different. There was no mention that Urrea ever opposed the retreat during this meeting.

So it was that they met together so that they might give a reply, seeming to conform, so that we could finish the movement with ease that Gen. Santa Anna had asked. Also to provide better treatment for him and the rest of the prisoners and to take time, if possible, to receive new orders and instructions from the supreme government and to find out the reaction to the news of the defeat at San Jacinto in the interior of the republic. Additionally for making all the rest of the preparations that were left from before, in order to take the offensive at an opportune time.

To give the appearance of better formality to this seem-

13. Urrea, "Diario de las operaciones militares," *Documentos para la historia de la guerra de Tejas,* 33; Castañeda (trans. and ed.), *The Mexican Side of the Texas Revolution,* 258–259.

ing submissiveness and for better safety for Gen. Santa Anna, we decided that one of the generals of the army would travel to the camp at San Jacinto. Not to negotiate with the enemy rebel leaders, because we did not want to get involved in any way, until we received the orders of the supreme government, but to see the president, to give him much honor, and to have the enemy believe that indeed he had come for everything that his excellency had agreed to with them. At the same time the commissioner would acquaint himself with the number and the position of the rebels, their armaments, munitions, resources, etc., etc. It is true that Generals Urrea, Woll, and others presented themselves immediately for this, but General Filisola decided on the second [Woll]. Besides his knowledge and excellent ways he assisted, he had the valuable advantage of speaking English, with which not only could he converse with the commander of the enemy and the other leaders, but also it was easy to make use of the conversations of the crowd. Troops without discipline or order forget to express terms discretely and betray the true intentions of all of them. Furthermore, for certain, the presence of Gen. Urrea in that camp would have put the president and the other prisoners at a greater risk, as it was known that the same were very close to being victims, because they already knew of what occurred at the mission and Goliad with his prisoners.

Consequently, the following replies were written to the president, understanding in the end what would be seen, because the enemy would inspect the letters before he would see them.[14]

Army of Operations

Most Excellent Sir.—As soon as I learned through some officers and scattered troops of the unfortunate encounter which Your Excellency has communicated to me in your note of the twenty-second, I executed the maneuvers that seemed proper to me for pulling the army together. When

14. Filisola, *Memorias para la historia de la guerra de Tejas* (Cumplido, 1849), I, 220–221.

this had been done, I marched on this flank in order to be relieved of some useless and bothersome items and to resume the initiative against the enemy. However, in keeping with the aforementioned communication from Your Excellency and the circumstances expressed therein, wishing to give proof of my regard for your person and for the prisoners of which Your Excellency speaks, I am going to recross the Colorado, and I shall cease hostilities provided the enemy gives no cause to continue them.

Generals Gaona, Urrea, and Ramírez y Sesma with their divisions have now joined me, as I mentioned above. Your Excellency is well aware of the forces at my disposal with which I can operate with these divisions; consequently, you will know that I am ceasing hostilities in spite of my responsibility to the supreme government. I repeat that I do this only out of consideration due your person and the peace of the Republic. However, on the other hand, I wish also to know that this consideration and that of the prisoners will be completely respected as is that of several of the enemy whom I have in my power.

When hostilities cease, as I tell Your Excellency, properties will be respected also, and we will take only what is most necessary for the army, and if the owner appears he will be paid religiously, just as he would have been if he had not left his home and possessions abandoned and for the most part burned. Some small wooden homes have been fired, to my indignation and that of the generals under my command. This deed committed by marauders who are always around in armies attracted our attention to such a degree that as a consequence I imposed the pain of death upon the first who repeated this, even before receiving instructions from Your Excellency.

Since Your Excellency tells me that you have reached an accord with General Houston concerning an armistice and do not explain to me the basis for it, General Adrian Woll is on his way to inform himself concerning this so that we may carry out our part and to be able to demand compliance from the enemy. With the above all that Your Excellency tells me in the said note has been attended to, and I have the greatest satisfaction in expressing again my esteem and consideration.

God and liberty. San Bernard Creek, April 28th, 1836.— Vicente Filisola. His Excellency the President and Commander in Chief of the army of operations, Don Antonio López de Santa Anna.[15]

Filisola's reply to Santa Anna raises several interesting questions. To begin with, Filisola had the date wrong again. Santa Anna noted this fact in his *Manifiesto* to the government. He mentioned that the letter from Filisola was dated April 28 and "simulated dignity," while General Urrea's letter was dated April 27 and "gave expression to the high spirits of the army."[16] Santa Anna also noted that General Houston was unable to discern the true intentions of General Filisola and feared the respectable force that could easily destroy him. If indeed Houston could not decide what Filisola was up to by his response to Santa Anna, then the stated purpose of the letter, i.e., to give the appearance of submissiveness to Santa Anna without compromising the Mexican position in Texas, may well have been accomplished.

If Filisola was just trying to convince the Texans that he still considered Santa Anna to be in charge and that he would obey the captive general's orders, it might be said that he was overplaying his hand. His response regarding the simple direction of Santa Anna to

15. Filisola, *Memorias para la historia de la guerra de Tejas* (Rafael, 1848, 1849), reprint, *Historia de la guerra de Tejas* (1968), II, 483–484; Woolsey translation, *Memoirs for the History of the War in Texas,* II, 237–238; retranslated for G. Dimmick by Dora Elizondo Guerra.

16. Santa Anna, "Manifiesto que de sus operaciones en la campaña de Tejas y en su cautiverio," translated in Castañeda (trans. and ed.), *The Mexican Side of the Texas Revolution,* 86. Urrea did write to Santa Anna on April 27 from the Arroyo de San Bernardo as Santa Anna mentioned. However, when reading the letter it has no mention whatsoever about the spirits of the army. The letter has no real information (as would be expected in sending a letter to a prisoner). It simply says that Urrea is thrilled to find out that Santa Anna is alive and that Generals Ramírez, Tolsa, and Gaona send their affections. Santa Anna, *Manifiesto que de sus operaciones en la campaña de Tejas y en su cautiverio dirige á sus conciudadanos el General Antonio López de Santa Anna* (Vera Cruz, Mexico: Imprenta Liberal, á Cargo de Antonio María Valdez, 1837), 89–90.

respect the property of the Texans was so dramatic that it leads one to believe that Filisola was putting on a show for the Texans. Filisola responded to Santa Anna by saying that he planned to repay the Texans for any supplies used by the army (and of course he had no money to do this). He claimed that he had gone so far as to order a sentence of death for the next soldier who burned one of the Texan homes. There is a Texas source that confirmed Santa Anna's order to Filisola to respect the property of the Texans. John Henry Brown's *History of Texas, 1685–1892* documented that Santa Anna proposed to Houston that he would write a letter to Filisola, ordering him to leave Texas. Gen. Thomas Rusk, Texan secretary of war, replied to Santa Anna that Filisola would not obey the orders of a prisoner. Santa Anna assured them that the officers and soldiers of his army were so attached to him that they would obey. Brown stated that Rusk demanded that Santa Anna order his troops to surrender to the Texans, but that Santa Anna had refused. Brown further noted that, along with the primary order, two other notes were sent by Santa Anna to Filisola. In these Filisola was instructed to tell all officers not to permit any injury to the inhabitants of the country; and to order the commander at Goliad to release Miller's eighty men and all other Texans held prisoner at that locale.[17]

The site that Filisola used as his address—San Bernard Creek—is a clear indicator that he did not know exactly where he was during these days. He and the Mexican army were camped on the West Bernard Creek when the letter was written.

The unknown author of the San Luis daily log actually gave credence to the fact that they were not going to obey Santa Anna's orders, and that they were going to carry out the initial plan as agreed upon at Powell's. San Luis log, April 27:

> Continued raining until 11 today. Retreated three leagues, and we received papers from General Santa Anna announcing that they were prisoners of the enemy as a result of the misfortune they had suffered, along with 21 or 23 officers and generals. He ordered that the Division of General Urrea situate itself at Guadalupe [Victoria] and the rest of the troops under General Filisola return to Bexar. General Woll

17. Brown, *History of Texas,* 45–46.

∞

Santa Anna's Orders   163

took the reply to the prisoner president in which it was stated that the army was retreating to the Colorado to await orders from the Supreme Government, since only they had the authority to remove the existing forces, while he remained imprisoned. [In the camp] bugles played, when it was learned that the General-in-Chief was alive.

This is clear evidence that the understanding of the rank and file was that they would only obey the orders of the Supreme Government. It also verified that there were celebrations in the camp of the rearguard, as Urrea had reported. The San Luis Battalion was in the rearguard at the time the news arrived. Unlike Urrea, Filisola refused to allow the divisions in his camp to cheer the news of Santa Anna's survival.

Filisola replied to the personal letter of Santa Anna with one of his own. Once again the date should read April 27, not April 28.

God and Liberty. San Bernard Creek. April 28th, 1836.— Vicente Filisola. His Excellency the President and Commander in Chief of the army of operations. Don Antonio López de Santa Anna.

Personal letter.—His Excellency Division General, President of the Republic, Don Antonio López de Santa Anna.— San Bernard Creek, April 28th, 1836.—My esteemed companion and friend and leader, through your good letter of the twenty-fifth I have been greatly pleased to know that you are alive and that they have given due consideration to your character. My companions are as delighted as I, and in their name I congratulate you. Your baggage and that of Señores Almonte, Castrillón and Núñez is not here, for as I have told you officially I wished to get rid of encumbrances in order to begin again the operations against the enemy, but I shall see that they are sent to you from Guadalupe Victoria, and they will be accompanied by trusted people so that you may receive them as quickly as possible and without damage. Concerning your official communication my answer is that it will be attended to as your person is high in our esteem.

The safe conduct that you sent will be used by the bearers so that you may receive this communication. You will try to see that they bring it back so that it may serve those who take the baggage.

Generals Urrea, Ramírez, Gaona, Tolsa and Woll send you their cordial greetings, and they have been most pleased at the news that you are alive. I was equally so. I send greetings to your unfortunate companions and I express to you again my friendship and that I am at your service. Your faithful and obedient servant.—Vicente Filisola.[18]

The fact that Filisola said that he received the letter from April 25 supports the fact that Santa Anna either misdated this letter or wrote it at a later date. There is no evidence that the letter from Santa Anna was delivered separately from the first three.

As all of Filisola's letters were undoubtedly read by the Texans prior to letting Santa Anna see them, it can easily be seen how the Texans may have suspected that Filisola was still totally devoted to and willing to obey Santa Anna, in spite of the fact that he was a prisoner. It is obvious from the above references that, in no way was that the case, but that the Mexicans wanted to make it seem as though it were.

Peña, however, never bought into this idea that Filisola was trying to convince the Texans and thought that he was only giving the pretense of obeying Santa Anna's orders in order to make the retreat easier. He claimed that all the arguments that Filisola had stated for his ordering the retreat were shifts and pretexts with which he tried to excuse his grave error.

Filisola did let Santa Anna know that the baggage that he requested had already been sent to Victoria and that he would arrange for its return. This fact is verified in a May 6 letter from Urrea to Garay (who was still at Cayce's Crossing). In this letter Urrea told Garay that Santa Anna wants the baggage returned to him as quickly as possible. Urrea instructed Garay to bring said baggage immediately to Atascosito Crossing so that it might be sent on to Santa Anna. Of all the things that he requested of Garay, Urrea

---

18. Filisola, *Memorias para la historia de la guerra de Tejas* (Rafael, 1848, 1849), reprint, *Historia de la guerra de Tejas* (1968), II, 484–485; Woolsey translation, *Memoirs for the History of the War in Texas,* II, 238.

said that the most important was the return of the equipment that the president asked for.

Urrea wrote Garay again the very next day. He ordered Garay to begin his march from Cayce's for Victoria immediately with the baggage that Santa Anna had requested. Urrea told Garay that he would like to personally arrange for the return of this gear to the president but that his brigade had been ordered to leave the Atascosito Crossing for Victoria. Urrea added that he felt that Garay should keep Santa Anna's sword and give it to his señorita as he had no use for it in captivity. He also informed Garay that he had Cos's equipment with him. In a postscript for this letter Urrea informed Garay that there was news that Santa Anna had been moved so it was decided that the baggage of the president would not be returned to him as previously planned.[19]

These two letters indicate that even after the Sea of Mud, Urrea was still very anxious to please, if not obey, the captive Santa Anna. Certainly sending the president's baggage to him in the enemy camp was not going to alter the outcome of the struggle. It still seems that at this time Urrea was in accordance with the plan to give the appearance that they were following the wishes of Santa Anna.

General Filisola wrote a third letter on that day that seemed to support his argument that he did not change his plans based on the arrival of Santa Anna's orders. It was written to General Tornel, the secretary of war, in Mexico City. Like the other two letters of the same day, and same address, it is misdated April 28.

> Army of Operations.—Your Excellency.—Today I have
> received the official and personal communications from His
> Excellency, president D. Antonio López de Santa-Anna, that
> I forward to Your Excellency. As I should have and did begin
> my march, for the advantage of better operations, as I
> informed Your Excellency in my note of the 25th of this
> month; for this reason, for others that I can amplify more at
> an opportune time to Your Excellency, and for that indicated
> by His Excellency general Santa-Anna, I have answered him
> as follows: (which I have left attached)

19. Filisola, *Análisis del diario militar del General D. José Urrea durante la primera campaña de Tejas*, 100–101.

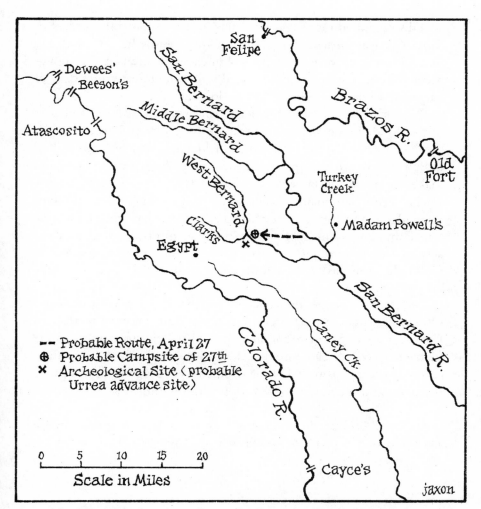

Map No. 4. Mexican Army Route, April 27, 1836. *Drawn by Jack Jackson.*

I want to advise Your Excellency that you give an
account of everything to His Excellency the interim president, for his best resolution.

God and Liberty. San Bernard Creek, April 28th, 1836.—
Vicente Filisola.—His Excellency secretary of war and
navy.[20]

20. Filisola, *Memorias para la historia de la guerra de Tejas* (Cumplido, 1849), I, 224.

Filisola did admit that he had taken into account the orders of Santa Anna and listed this as one of the reasons he retreated. He made it clear however that he had already undertaken the movement prior to the orders and wanted to get the interim president of Mexico[21] to decide what he was to do next.

As April 27 ended the Mexican army was delayed on the banks of the flooded West Bernard Creek (see Map No. 4). This creek, like the San Bernard River, is located in low, flat prairie lands. When these rivers flood they spill from their banks for great distances and make any passage impossible, usually for days.

The army had finally learned of the fate of Santa Anna and their comrades at San Jacinto. They now had their orders from their captive commander-in-chief. From their accounts, as well as their actions, they did not seem to have changed their plans to recross the Colorado, consolidate their forces, and await orders from the government in Mexico City.

What did change their plans was the flooded West Bernard Creek. The high waters prevented them from taking the road to Cayce's Crossing and eventually on to Victoria. To make matters worse they were well aware that the San Bernard, which lay to their rear, was flooded as well. Filisola decided to bed down his troops for the night and see how the river looked in the morning.

21. Miguel Barragán, the president of Mexico had died during the campaign and was replaced by interim president José Justo Corro who had been minister of justice.

CHAPTER 8

The Countermarch

ENERAL FILISOLA FACED a tough decision as he awoke
the morning of April 28. The original plan was to cross
the West Bernard Creek and then proceed toward Cayce's Crossing
on the Colorado. It is interesting to note that in his letter to the government of Mexico, written on May 14 from Victoria, Filisola
reported that he made the decision the afternoon of April 27. He
said that the guides told him it would be eight days before the river
subsided and even then it would be necessary to pass through a forest of reeds and high grass that extended for thirteen miles past the
crossing.

In his later writings he implied that the decision was made the
next morning (the 28th) and gave more details about his decision-
making process. He reported that, as of nine in the morning, the
river's crest had lowered. He consulted one of Urrea's scouts as to
how much delay they might expect in waiting for the river to sub-
side. The scout advised that, as the land was so flat and the current of
the river so slow, it could be twelve to fifteen days before the crossing was safe to use. He commented that even then the opposite bank
would be so muddy that it would be impossible for the horses,
mules, artillery, and carts to be extracted from the riverbed. Once
again he mentioned the thirteen miles of reeds and added that the
reeds were so thick the mules would have to proceed in single file.

The guide informed Filisola that there was a way to head (go
around the source of) the West Bernard. If they would backtrack to
the wooden dwelling where they had camped the night of April 26

they could take the Contrabando road[1] to the Atascosito Crossing of the Colorado River. Filisola knew of this crossing, as most of the Mexican army had used it during the advance. Filisola reasoned that he would not be able to return by way of San Felipe, since the San Bernard was flooded. Even if he had been able to do so, this would have maneuvered them in the opposite direction of their detachments in Matagorda, Victoria, etc. General Filisola argued that if he had encountered the enemy in the San Felipe area it would have taken five or six more days for reinforcements to reach him.

Filisola also consulted General Woll, who had reconnoitered the West Bernard the day prior. Woll informed him that he had gone two leagues upriver, trying to find a better crossing, and discovered only a swamp and an immense lagoon. Filisola sent other scouts to look for a crossing downstream. Like Woll, they were unable to locate a site to ford the river. After taking all this into consideration Filisola decided to abandon the road to Cayce's, countermarch to the dwelling where they camped April 26 and proceed from there to the Atascosito Crossing (see Map No. 5).

Before they began their march, General Woll, along with two sappers, an officer from Urrea's command, and a Spaniard, left on the road to San Jacinto. Finding the San Bernard still flooded, they had to swim it, floating their saddles on makeshift rafts.[2]

There also were several other loose ends to tie up. Word was sent to General Andrade in San Antonio of the fate of Santa Anna. Andrade was warned that he should be prepared to depart San Antonio if need arose. Filisola warned Urrea to be prepared to send word to Matagorda for that detachment to fall back to Victoria. Capt.

1. Further mention of this road was made by Maj. John Forbes of the Texas army: "I accordingly proceeded with the troops and munitions up the Brazos River to Columbia as a starting point, selecting the old contraband trace leading from there to the Colorado, as the line of march to Headquarters." Stephen L. Moore, *Eighteen Minutes: The Battle of San Jacinto and the Texas Independence Campaign* (Dallas: Republic of Texas Press, 2004), 124.

2. Filisola, *Memorias para la historia de la guerra de Tejas* (Cumplido, 1849), I, 224. In a letter to the secretary of war (Tornel), Urrea identified the officer that he selected to accompany Woll on this mission. He wrote that he sent his aide, Sub Lt. Ambrosio Martínez because of his spirit and his perfect English. "La guerra de Texas: Causa formada al Gral. Filisola por su retirada en 1836," Tomo X, No. 3, pp. 565–566.

SEA OF MUD

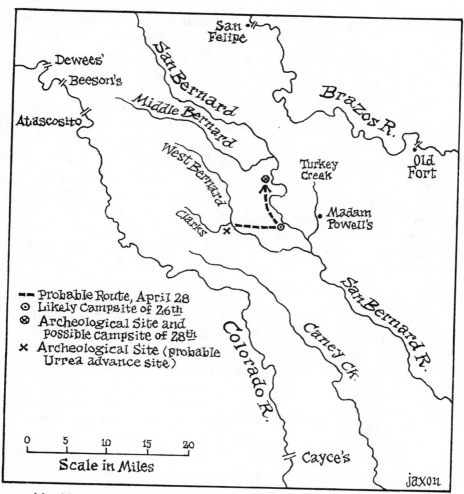

Map No. 5. Mexican Army Route, April 28, 1836. *Drawn by Jack Jackson.*

Alavez, commander at Victoria, was ordered to send any supplies that he had in Victoria to the Atascosito Crossing on the Colorado. Filisola pointed out that in his camp he had not one horse that was capable of making the trip to Victoria to forward the dispatches to the Mexican government and to Andrade. He was forced to buy a horse from Urrea for one hundred pesos and another from Lt. Col. Gregorio Gonzáles, for forty, for his couriers to make these trips.

Filisola wrote that on the morning of April 28 General Urrea was chastising two of his scouts, Salvador Cuellar and N. Rodríquez because they had given advice to Filisola about the roads. Filisola overheard Urrea tell the scouts that if the commander wanted information, he should come to him, not his scouts. Filisola noticed that when Urrea saw him he hushed and motioned to the scouts not to say anything.

General Urrea requested that morning that his division be allowed to remain two or three days to the rear of the army. He told Filisola that the enemy could not advance upon the main army, as he would have the rear blocked. In his diary he stated that his purpose in this request was two-fold. First, he said that he wanted to make the retreat less embarrassing. Secondly that, as they had served for two days as the rearguard and had been delayed on the road, his brigade needed a rest. He hoped that they could have time to eat, clean their guns, etc. Urrea stated that Filisola would give him only one-half day of delay and "instructed him, nay, begged him" to follow that afternoon.

The movement of the Mexican army on April 28 is very well documented. So much so that the various documents conflict on several key points and actually confuse the issue. There is no doubt that they retraced their steps to the vicinity of their April 26 campsite. The best guess for that position, as was described in chapter six, is one and one-half to three miles west of the San Bernard, slightly north of due west from Powell's. Recall that in his *Memorias* Filisola stated that on April 27 they traveled three leagues from the campsite of April 26 to the next branch of the Bernard. However, in that very same document, Filisola stated that they went five leagues on April 28 and added that they went three leagues past the campsite of April 26. As it had to be the same distance coming and going, this would leave two leagues from the beginning of the march of April 28, at the West Bernard, to the campsite of April 26, not three leagues as he claimed they had traveled on April 27. If indeed the distance from the campsite was two leagues, 5.4 miles, this would nearly match the 4.5 English miles quoted by Peña.

The next item of confusion in the various documents is where they went after reaching their campsite on April 26. In the English translation of Peña's account, he stated that the army countermarched in search of another road and another crossing for the Colorado. He said they passed by the place where they camped the night of April 26 and made a forty-five degree turn to the left, then continued their march. In the original Spanish document Peña wrote: "Pasamos por el lugar en que acampamos el 26, dimos un cuarto de conversión por la izquierda y continuamos la marcha." The proper translation for this turn is not a forty-five degree turn but a ninety degree turn to the left.[3] This left turn would have been onto the road Filisola referred to as the "Contrabando road." If indeed the road on which they backtracked from the campsite of April 27 to the campsite of April 26 was headed almost due east, the ninety degree turn to the left would place them paralleling the San Bernard in a northerly direction. If they had taken a forty-five degree turn to the left they would have run into the San Bernard River.

The distance from the campsite of April 26 (where they made the ninety degree turn to the left) to that of April 28 varies with the different sources. Peña said that they made ten Mexican miles that day, but on looking at the first draft of the document included in the Peña Papers, he said ten to twelve miles. Subtracting the five Mexican miles that he said was the distance between the campsite of April 26 and that of April 27 leaves the army five to seven Mexican miles, or 4.5 to 6.25 English miles, north of the intersection with the Contrabando road on the night of April 28.

Filisola mentioned that they went three leagues, or eight miles, past the intersection. The San Luis report estimated their march for April 28 to have been four leagues. As they stated they went three leagues on April 27, this would have left them only one league or 2.7 miles past the intersection. However, if indeed the distance traveled on April 27 was only two leagues, as can be argued from the Filisola distance for April 28 and the Peña distance of April 27, they would have proceeded two leagues or 5.7 miles past the intersection.

Another item that is very confusing is the fact that Filisola gave different descriptions of the location of the April 28 campsite. In his *Representación* to the Mexican government, which he penned soon after his return to Mexico, he wrote:

El 29, no hallando vado en el arroyo en cuya orrilla
estábamos campados, contramarchamos con la cabeza de la
derecha por el mismo camino que habíamos traído el día
anterior, y campamos sobre la orilla derecha del arroyo de en

3. Thanks to Dr. James E. Crisp for this important translation correction.

medio de los de San Bernardo ya mencionados, que habíamos pasado, como dije, el 27, y estaba todavía invadeable. [Once again the dates are one day off].[4]

Castañeda, stating that he was not giving a word-for-word translation but accurately reflecting the thoughts of the writers, gave the following translation of the above passage:

Not finding a crossing on the creek where we were encamped, we countermarched on the 29th [28th] to the right, following the same route over which we traveled the day before. We pitched camp upon the right bank of the second branch of the St. Bernard, which we had crossed as before stated on the 27th [26th], and which was still impassable.[5]

Comparing this translation to one from December 1836 by George Hammeken, a friend of Stephen F. Austin, it is seen that there is a variation that could be critical in searching for these positions.

On the 29th [28th] not having been able to ford the stream, on the banks of which we were encamped, we countermarched, the right wing in advance, by the same road that we had come the day previous, and encamped on the right bank of the centre rivulet of San Bernard already mentioned, which we had passed as I observed, on the 27th [26th], as it was not yet fordable.[6]

Hammeken gave the more detailed translation when he translated the campsite of April 28 as having been on the center stream of

4. "La guerra de Texas: Causa formada al Gral. Filisola por su retirada en 1836," Tomo X, No. 1, p. 163.
5. Filisola, "Representación dirigida al supremo gobierno por el General Vicente Filisola en defensa de su honor y aclaración de sus operaciones como general en gefe del ejército sobre Tejas," in Castañeda (trans. and ed.), *The Mexican Side of the Texas Revolution*, 188.
6. Filisola, *Evacuation of Texas*, 19–20.

the branches of the San Bernard. His translation implied that the center stream was the same stream that Filisola had crossed April 26, and that was not the case. Looking at the original Spanish again, it could be argued that Filisola is stating that they camped on the right bank of the middle stream of those branches that make up the San Bernard, which he crossed April 26. This translation would not mean that the Middle Bernard and the river that he crossed April 26 were one and the same, which indeed they were not. Another possibility is that Filisola thought that he was now on the Middle Bernard, despite the fact that he was on the San Bernard, which he had crossed April 26. It may well be that both of the above translations are not quite right and he knew only that this was one of the several branches of the San Bernard, and he knew he crossed one of them on April 26.

The issue, surprisingly, gets more confusing when looking at other Filisola documents. In his letter to the Mexican government, dated May 14, and thus the first document written after the fact, when the events were the freshest in his mind, Filisola described his actions of April 28: "lo continué el día 29 [28], que campé junto al mismo arroyo que había pasado el 27 [26], aunque cosa de tres leguas más arriba camino para el Atascosito."[7]

Hammeken translated the above as follows: "I continued it (the march) on the 29th [28th], when I encamped near the same rivulet that I had passed on the 27th [26th]; although about three leagues above is the road for the passage called Atascosito."[8] This certainly indicates that Filisola camped the night of April 28 on the same river that he passed on April 26, which supports the idea that Filisola was mistaken in the *Representación* statement, when he said they camped on the Middle Bernard that night. It is possible Filisola was confused because the next several nights the army was camped along the Middle Bernard.

However, the above quote leads to a new question about the translation of the last phrase in the sentence. It is almost like Filisola left out a word before or after "arriba" in the sentence. Hammeken translated it as "is above" but there is no "es" in the original Spanish

7. "La guerra de Texas: Causa formada al Gral. Filisola por su retirada en 1836," Tomo X, No. 1, p. 78.

8. Filisola, *Evacuation of Texas,* 42.

version. If Filisola left out a word it would seem as though "en" would make more sense. Then the phrase would be translated as "although three leagues above on the road for Atascosito (note that Hammeken added "passage"). This would make more sense since the intersection of the Contrabando road, which Filisola said led to the Atascosito Crossing, was near the campsite of April 26. Filisola said they camped three leagues past that point. Thus the campsite should have been three leagues up the road toward Atascosito. In the Rafael version of his *Memorias* Filisola added that the road was terrible, and the horses, carts, and cannon bogged down continually.

In the Cumplido edition of his *Memorias* Filisola gave a version of that day's travel that seemed to verify the points argued above.

> At about three in the afternoon they arrived at the place
> where they were to take the road that had been pointed out
> to them. The road they had just traveled, and the one they
> had now taken were extremely muddy; consequently, the
> artillery and the carts moved with great difficulty, especially
> the latter. In view of this, Filisola decided to camp on the
> right bank of the stream they had passed on the 26th,
> although it was about three leagues farther upstream, at
> about a two league march on the new road, and about five
> from the camp they had abandoned that morning.[9]

The above paragraph is difficult to translate well. It is also contradictory. Filisola said that on the night of April 28 they camped three leagues upstream from the campsite of April 26. Then he went on to say that they marched two leagues on the new road. One possible explanation is that the intersection of the new road and the old was one league past the campsite of April 26. Certainly another explanation is that he simply made a mistake. The preponderance of the evidence is that it was two leagues from the West Bernard campsite to the April 26 campsite.

General Urrea indirectly supported the contention that it was two leagues to the intersection mentioned above. He stated that on April 28 his rearguard began the march from the camp of April 27.

---

9. Filisola, *Memorias para la historia de la guerra de Tejas* (Cumplido, 1849), I, 228.

After about two leagues they came upon all the wagons and black-smith equipment of the army, stuck in the mud. Since Filisola had claimed that the terrain was much worse after the turn at the inter-section, it would be a reasonable conclusion that this is where Urrea found them stuck. The San Luis Battalion log documented a coun-termarch from the bank of the San Bernard Creek (probably the West Bernard) in order to take a different road that led to the Atas-cosito Crossing. The log reported that the road was covered with water and mud, and that the battalion marched four leagues that day. This would have put them two leagues past the intersection if Urrea's two leagues are subtracted from their four league total.

Taking into account all this variable and confusing information, there are two details that seem likely. The Mexican army camped the night of April 28 on the San Bernard River, not the Middle Bernard as Filisola stated in his *Representación*. Second, the army took a left turn, near the campsite of April 26, onto the Contrabando road and proceeded north for about four and one-half to six miles (Peña); 5.4 miles (Urrea/San Luis log); or eight miles (Filisola) toward the Atas-cosito Crossing of the Colorado River (see Map No. 5).

Members of the Houston Archeological Society have found Mexican army artifacts on the west bank of the San Bernard River about six miles north of the postulated campsite of April 26. The artifacts will be discussed below in the archeology section but at this point it is unknown whether the artifacts are from a campsite or from the trail. Either way they show that the Mexican army was in the area. This could be the site, or near the site, of the campsite of April 28.

General Urrea, in his diary entry for April 28, made a claim that was to become a major point of contention between him and Fil-isola after they returned to Mexico. Urrea claimed that early that morning Filisola declared to him

> how cumbersome he considered the wagons and even the
> artillery, and told me that he had decided to abandon every-
> thing that might tend to hinder the speed of the march
> which he believed essential until the Colorado was reached,
> adding that in view of the armistice arranged with Houston,
> whatever was left by the army was safe, since the Texans
> would take care of it. I was surprised to hear such an opin-

∞

ion from the general in command of the army, and I exerted myself to disabuse his mind with reasoning, repeating what I had already expressed. I said that, "the armistice and the retreat of the army, as stipulated in the dispatches of General Santa Anna, are nothing but the orders of the Texans to save themselves from the blow which they expect, since they have no other way out of the danger; and General Santa Anna has merely availed himself of the opportunity offered to resume communication with us." This was my opinion, and General Gaona supported me in combating the idea of abandoning the artillery.[10]

Peña agreed with the contention that Filisola proposed abandoning the artillery, but he did not give a specific date this occurred. Thus it is unknown if he was talking of the morning of April 28, or later, when the artillery was stuck in the mud. He went on to talk about the extraction of the artillery from the mud, which will be discussed later.[11]

Filisola responded as follows to the claim that Urrea saved the artillery:

> Sr. Urrea also says, at the beginning of page 34 of his diary, that on that morning I talked about my intention of abandoning the carts as well as the artillery, in order to reach the Colorado as quickly as possible, trusting the armistice with the colonists etc., and at the start of pg. 35 he added: that I had demonstrated great fear that it would be difficult to quickly occupy the Atascosito Crossing on the Colorado River; because I believed that the enemy was making preparations to begin to move against us, and that, possibly, we could be captured by them at the aforementioned crossing; with a multitude of other suppositions all meant to reproach and denigrate me.

10. Urrea, "Diario de las operaciones militares," *Documentos para la historia de la guerra de Tejas*, 34; translated in Castañeda (trans. and ed.), *The Mexican Side of the Texas Revolution*, 260.

11. Peña, *La rebelión de Texas*; translated in Perry (trans. and ed.), *With Santa Anna in Texas*, 159.

Anybody, other than Sr. Urrea would notice at first glance the gross contradiction that the poor Sr. incurs; because, in short, was I trusting or afraid of the enemy? That it was not the first, could not have been more obvious, when I gave him the order to march with his lightened brigade to take said crossing; neither could that prudent move be classified as being from fear, as the Sr. expresses; but one of opportune precaution in a circumstance where any other enemy other than the Texans, would have made us pay very dearly for the slightest mistake. I would ask Sr. Urrea. What would we have done at the exit of that immense swamp in which we had to march one by one with the water up to our knees; the artillery, munitions, baggage, wagons etc. etc. bogged down and horribly spread out, incapable of using either the first or the second, without any means of subsistence, and without firewood with which to at least cook the very few beans that we still had; and needing to exit toward a forest situated along the elevation; with the potential for finding it occupied by 600 men [of the enemy]? The result of this is easy to infer for all who understand military matters, or have read some history, ancient as well as modern.[12]

At the beginning of the statement it seemed as though Filisola was going to answer Urrea's accusing him of wanting to leave the wagons and artillery, but it should be noted that, once again, Filisola skillfully skirted the issue. He did not deny that he considered leaving the wagons and artillery at that point. He did however shift his discussion to a totally different point—Urrea's saying that he (Filisola) acted out of fear yet claimed to trust the Texans due to the armistice.

There is no known confirmation of the conversation described by Urrea, even by Gaona, who Urrea claimed to have witnessed the conversation. Gaona did comment about the artillery in a letter sent to the president of Mexico during the Filisola trial.

It is false that Sr. Urrea saved the artillery; it remained sub-

12. Filisola, *Análisis del diario militar del General D. José Urrea durante la primera campaña de Tejas,* 92.

merged in an immense marsh in which we had spent 11 days to travel five leagues, and it is well published that when Sr. Filisola arrived on the left bank of the Colorado Urrea had already crossed with his brigade, and that he was beginning his march the following day for the colony of Guadeloupe Victoria, with the assigned artillery. The artillery was saved by the persistent work of the troop, assigned to its care under the direction of Lt. Col. Pedro Ampudia, and by the orders of the Commander-in-chief. If any artillery piece was left, in effect, abandoned; falling into the hands of the enemy, it was one that Sr. Urrea had under his immediate responsibility at Matagorda, and about which he yet has not made necessary explanations.[13]

It is interesting to note that Gaona, like Filisola, seemed to skirt the issue of the conversation of the morning of April 28. Gaona addressed the issue of the artillery only after it was stuck in the mud commencing April 29. There can be little doubt that Urrea's claim to saving the artillery was referring to the morning of April 28 when he stated that he talked Filisola out of abandoning it. It must be recalled, however, that Gaona wrote this statement after his return to Mexico when he and most of the other generals seemed to align themselves with Filisola. Their statements as to what happened were in no way unbiased.

Urrea wrote that Filisola set out with the first and second brigades at seven in the morning on April 28. General Urrea and his troops remained at the West Bernard camp. They busied themselves, cleaning their arms, washing their clothes, etc. Urrea held an inspection of arms and munitions at three that afternoon and then commenced the march, following in the tracks of the other two brigades. This is additional evidence that the Mexican army was not retreating in some sort of mad dash. An inspection of the troop's arms and munitions is hardly the action of an army in a flight of panic.

Another interesting event happened the afternoon of April 28. Urrea stated that he had traveled two leagues when he came upon all of the army's wagons and smithing equipment stuck in the mud.

13. "La guerra de Texas: Causa formada al Gral. Filisola por su retirada en 1836," 134–137.

SEA OF MUD

He said the officer in charge of the wagons was unaware of the path the army had taken and no guides had been provided them. Urrea did not feel that he could free the stranded wagons and carts as they were loaded with arms, munitions, food, dirt sacks, and utensils as well as with a number of sick men, among them Col. N. Infante.[14] Urrea went on to say that he sent his aide to find Filisola and inform him of the condition of the bogged-down carts and ask that any unloaded mules be sent back to lighten the loads of the wagons and carts, in order that they might be freed from the mud. Urrea noted that he also ordered members of his brigade to help free the wagons by taking what items they could from them. He documented that all the officers and troops, including Col. Juan Morales, commander of the San Luis Battalion, and Col. Mariano Salas, commander of the Jiménez Battalion, pitched in and carried most of the sacks to firm ground. After being unloaded the carts and wagons were set in motion again. About that time the unloaded mules arrived to help. The preferential companies of the San Luis and Jiménez Battalions were assigned to escort the wagons and mules on to the camp. Urrea said he arrived at Filisola's camp at nightfall, and about 10 P.M. the carts and mules arrived. He quipped that, for the time being, the sick were saved. Urrea felt that had he not done what he did, the sick would not have survived the harsh night, or would have fallen into enemy hands.

Filisola's account of the above incident was, as expected, quite different. He put the time of his departure later in the morning, around ten or eleven. He agreed that Urrea stayed at the camp so that his troops might dry their clothes. He felt that the delay would not be a problem because he knew the march would be slowed by the carts and artillery on the nearly impassable road. Filisola had no doubt that Urrea's brigade, traveling light, could catch up to his column. He reported that the first and second brigades arrived at their campsite at about five that afternoon. He immediately ordered that the mules be unloaded of the treasury, ammunition, equipment, pro-

14. This was probably Bvt. Col. Miguel Infansón. He is listed as keeper of the orders for the first brigade of the second division by Filisola in the Rafael edition of his memoirs, page 150 (Woolsey translation). In the Cumplido edition of his memoirs, page 230–231, Filisola mentions him as being one of the sick who were stuck in the carts on April 28. He spelled the Colonel's name "Infanzon."

∞

The Countermarch

visions, etc. He ordered them back, under the command of Lt. Col. Juan Cuevas, to help lighten the load of the carts. The operation lasted until ten or eleven that night, as the carts, their wheels in mud up to the hubs, were very hard for the mules to pull, even unloaded. He agreed that Urrea arrived with his brigade at about twilight but made no mention of Urrea helping in the operation or requesting aid for the bogged-down carts.

In the Cumplido edition of his *Memorias* Filisola gave a lengthy response to Urrea's description of the happenings of the afternoon of April 28, and raised some valid questions about Urrea's facts.

General Urrea, speaking of the march of this day, on page 34 and part of page 35 of his diary, said that Filisola left camp with the first two brigades at seven in the morning. [He stated] that he, at three in the afternoon, had a review of the arms and munitions of his brigade, then he began the march. After two leagues march, he encountered the forges and carts bogged down with the sick, supplies, munitions, etc., etc., without an escort or guide, abandoned. [He said] that the troops, leaders, and officers of his brigade carried many things to lighten the load and that he sent information to Filisola with one of his aides. [He said] that he requested [from Filisola] cargo mules to take part of their cargo. [He said] that he left an escort composed of the preferred companies of the Jiménez and the San Luis Battalions. [He said] that at nightfall he arrived with his brigade at Filisola's camp, and that at 10 P.M. he checked on the carts and the escort. [He said] thereby, that he had saved, for then, the sick, who had the case been different, some would have died in the night etc. etc.

Regarding Filisola [Filisola is speaking in the third person here], we have already mentioned that he set out from the camp on the San Bernard at 10 to 11 in the morning. They [Filisola's column] arrived at about 5 in the afternoon at the new camp named for the Contrabando road. So apparently six hours passed in walking the five leagues from one point to the other.

We examine now the grade of truth that encircles the other assertions of General Urrea.

∞

SEA OF MUD

First—He says that at three in the afternoon his brigade passed in a review of arms and munitions. In which operation he might have taken at least an hour. Was there indeed such a review? However, it's clear that he initiated the march at four in the afternoon.

Second—That after two leagues of walking, he came upon the bogged down campaign forges, carts, etc. Are we supposed to believe that in walking the two leagues it took less than two hours on the troublesome roads covered in mud, arriving at the point of the carts at six in the evening.

Third—He encountered these totally abandoned, without escort or any help, by which they could continue. [He encountered also] the sick, including Col. D. Miguel Infanzon, left to die at the hands of the enemy and in abandonment. This certainly is not true as the army retreated by the same road on which they had come the day before. It was the only one on which they might encounter the enemy, in a labyrinth of unfordable streams, swamps and marshes. Also, how does he say they were abandoned and without escort? Could it be that his brigade is insufficient when it has no other mission than to cover the retreat with all the units that were attached to him. What? Did he [Urrea] estimate that there were so few under his command that he [Filisola] had to give another escort and safety and aid that he [Urrea] was able to lend to the carts and the sick, when his [Urrea's] entire brigade composed of artillery, of the best battalions and all of the cavalry, was a small army? Without guides for them to continue! Come now, is it necessary to have guides when marching in the rearguard of 2500 troops, six cannons, their respective gun carriages, other wagons, about 1200 cargo mules, and an enormous number of unattached people? What? Would they not leave enough tracks to proceed safely, that he needed to have guides? That the sick were abandoned! What were the accommodations that awaited those unfortunates in camp? Was it not water and mud? Where were they better off? In this element or on the carts on which they had come? Perhaps they left from these [carts] when they arrived at camp and this was proven to be true.

Fourth—That he sent Filisola one of his [Urrea's] aides to tell him to send him the mules that had already been unloaded, and to also tell him [Filisola] that he [Urrea] would not move from that point until the mules arrived. It was thus carried out. His brigade, with the help sent, and including that of colonels Morales and Salas, unloaded everything, lightening the carts. The preferred companies of the Jiménez and San Luis were left to guard them, after which he began his march and arrived at Filisola's camp at nightfall. As I have said before, according to the writings of Gen. Urrea himself, he arrived at six in the evening where the carts were, and at nightfall at the camp where the troops were. It was in the month of April when night fall is at 6:30. Therefore all of these operations, and marching to the new camp, only took Urrea half an hour. About having an aide go to see Filisola to request mules; within [that half hour] [Urrea's] aide had to have gone to Filisola to request the mules, these then had to be rounded up, because we must assume that they had already been put out to pasture and needed to be rounded up, and only then be taken to where Urrea was waiting. [One might ask] at what distance from where Filisola and the rest of the forces were camped, was Urrea, the wretched carts, and the brigade?

Furthermore, his duty was to, not only have done what he says he did at that place, but it was also his duty to remain there until the last man was out. That is the obligation and duty of a rearguard unit, especially one like his that had been specifically formed to serve as a rearguard![15]

Certainly Filisola presented a valid argument when he commented that it was unlikely Urrea could have marched—depending on which source is consulted—from ten to thirteen miles in a matter of two to three hours, on a very muddy road made worse by the army having traveled half of it two days in a row. However, since they both agreed that Urrea arrived at twilight, there can be little doubt that Urrea misjudged the time when he left the West Bernard.

15. Filisola, *Memorias para la historia de la guerra de Tejas* (Cumplido, 1849), I, 229–232.

The most valid point, and a humorous one at that, was Filisola's reaction to Urrea's criticism of the carts being abandoned with no guides. Filisola made an excellent observation in asking how the force left behind, stuck in the mud, could possibly have needed guides to follow the tracks of a large army in terribly muddy conditions.

Filisola realized that by the end of April 28 his position was far from optimal. He called the situation very critical. He went on to describe the army's status at the time. He said they were obstructed in all directions by the waters of the creek on which they had camped and noted that the creek was to their north. If indeed he mistook the Middle Bernard for the San Bernard, the Middle Bernard would have been to the north. He went on to say that the creek from which they had left that morning (West Bernard), to the south, was flooded as well. Had he been on the San Bernard or the Middle Bernard, the West Bernard would be to his west but would have coursed to the southeast, thus eventually passing to his south. He stated that the land to their backs, the east, was totally covered with small streams, forests, and impenetrable swamps. As if this were not enough, he commented that to add to a bad situation, the trail toward the Atascosito Crossing looked like it was becoming a swamp.

The above details were written in the Cumplido edition of Filisola's *Memorias*, which was not written until 1849. It is interesting to note that most of the material in that source is the same as the description of the retreat in *Análisis del diario militar del General D. José Urrea durante la primera campaña de Tejas*, written in 1838 by the same author. However, this analysis of his position was not included in the earlier work. It could be argued that the fact that this information was written some thirteen years later makes it less reliable than some of his earlier writings.

Regardless, the point is still well made that the army was in a terrible position with no good options. The West Bernard empties into the San Bernard south of the position of the Mexican army. As both were flooded, the army could take only one path—northwest through some of the worst conditions imaginable for moving an army.

The area that Filisola was entering is considered by geologists to have been an ancient seashore. Even today it is primarily used for rice farming. The locals refer to the ground in that area, known as the Lissie Prairie, as quicksand. It is still nearly impossible for even large tractors to get into these fields when they are saturated with rain. Filisola actually described that area quite well. He stated that nearly all of Texas is like this, which is certainly not true. When wet, this locale is much worse than most of the rest of Texas. Filisola reported that in dry times the soil is boggy and sandy, and allows animals to be buried up to their chests in the bog. After a few hours of hard rain, immense swamps form. Later, the soil becomes saturated—deep, sticky, and impassable.

The general also observed that, due to their knowledge of the area the enemy was not affected by these problems. He concluded that the best thing to do, militarily, was to send a force to occupy the Atascosito Crossing before the enemy, counting on the ongoing negotiations with Santa Anna, decided to do so. Additionally, they were not impeded by artillery, carts, cargo, wounded, etc., which his forces had in abundance. He was concerned that the rebels might take the road from San Jacinto to San Felipe and on to Atascosito before he could get there with his army.

Both Urrea and Filisola agreed that Filisola ordered Urrea's brigade to march the next morning to the Atascosito Crossing on the Colorado River. Urrea was to leave his artillery and baggage, on orders from Filisola, so as to move quickly and occupy the crossing. Urrea told the story with a twist, saying that General Filisola could imagine only alarming and terrifying ideas. According to Urrea, these imaginary scenarios could not possibly have materialized under the circumstances. Urrea claimed that he had a long discussion with Filisola to try to make him see reason. However, it was impossible to free him from the concerns that caused such fear and anxiety. Urrea promised to obey the orders which, according to Urrea, Filisola had basically begged him to carry out.

Urrea also mentioned that the army had left the main road and was now stuck in a mud hole where the men were hardly able to stand up. He brought up this issue once again later in his diary when he commented:

Let his own reports of the retreat be read and let the reader judge for himself whether an army marching under such conditions can do it in order and comfort, keeping in mind particularly that the sad plight of the army, in the middle of marches, was due entirely to the fear and inefficiency of its general, who in his anxiety to get as far away from the enemy as possible, decided to make his way through the lowlands, leaving the good road of San Felipe de Austin to his right. He could have followed this road without difficulty by undertaking an extra march of a little more than two leagues, avoiding all the trouble and inconvenience of the long march through the marshes. General Filisola has recounted acts which he never performed, he has omitted those details that reflect upon him, and he has denied those that may reflect credit upon me.[16]

Urrea raised some valid points but his argument as to the choice of the route of the retreat is questionable. The following are Filisola's comments on the choice of roads:

Gen. Urrea protests also, saying on page 42 of his manifesto or diary, that he had been stuck in that horrible swamp because we left the high San Felipe road, by which they had come, to go on those we took. In the first place, all the roads in Texas, with few exceptions, are the same. Particularly during those days, the San Felipe road was no better, and secondly, he himself, was the one that persuaded us at the meeting of the 25th at Madam Powel, that they should take that [road] to Casey's pass, arguing that it was better and shorter. As was mentioned elsewhere, the other generals didn't know another road, other than the San Felipe, which they had taken to go to Holds-Fort, nor did they have any other guides or experts that were not their own. So if there were any complaints to be made, he would have to complain about himself at finding himself reduced to that fatal and horrible situation. All the rest that suffered the consequences, and very particularly Filisola, can attribute it to him. However, neither General Urrea nor anyone, could have foretold

16. Urrea, "Diario de las operaciones militares," *Documentos para la historia de la guerra de Tejas,* 42–43; translated in Castañeda (trans. and ed.), *The Mexican Side of the Texas Revolution,* 273–274.

or surmised the deluge of water that fell. Neither can there exist a rational motive for placing the blame of that misfortune. When that course was proposed, there is no doubt that it had been made in good faith, and with the same it was adopted. Consequently all that he said about this particular could not be more unjust.[17]

It is logical that Urrea would have argued in favor of retracing his steps, when making the withdrawal. Filisola also made an excellent point in asking how they were supposed to predict the storm. When they set out on the road to Cayce's they had every reason to believe that their path was traversable. Urrea had just used the same route the week prior. Filisola made a valid argument in stating that choosing the San Felipe road would have been no better. Certainly all the roads in Texas are not the same but after a deluge like occurred on April 26 and 27 it is likely all the roads in that part of Texas were nearly impassable. Additionally, Filisola likely reasoned that to move north on the San Felipe road would have been to head back into the heart of the Anglo settlement.

ARCHEOLOGY OF APRIL 28

The path of the Mexican army is not known with certainty, as demonstrated above. There is evidence, both in the archives and in the artifacts, which allows us to make an educated guess as to the path that they took that day. The archives show varying accounts that are fairly similar and, as discussed above, with relatively consistent distances. The artifacts that are believed to support the proposed path have a very interesting story of their own.

Soon after the project of tracking the Mexican army was undertaken, and just after the first actual campsite had been discovered, word was received that a local real estate agent, who lived on the San Bernard River just south of the town of East Bernard had some sort of artifacts. He was unaware as to what the odd items were but was willing to let them be examined. The six objects were easily recognized as brass canister shot. The landowner reported that his father

17. Filisola, *Memorias para la historia de la guerra de Tejas* (Cumplido, 1849), I, 233–234.

∞

had found them, over the years, lying on the ground, some in the garden and some on the old dirt road into town.

Upon further exploration of the area with metal detectors, several more brass canister shot were found, as well as a trigger guard for an India Pattern musket. Also excavated were several lead musket balls of approximately .69–.70 caliber. These items were discovered in a fairly limited area only, but the site is surrounded by thick woods and underbrush that make metal detecting nearly impossible. Many of the artifacts were discovered along a line, which suggests that the items may have been dropped on the trail. This seems to indicate that they are from the path of the Mexican army as they moved through the area. Multiple excursions into all the surrounding fields have yet to reveal any artifacts that would indicate a path into or out of the site.

Sufficient artifacts have been found at this site to state that it is from the retreat of the Mexican army. In trying to put together the riddle of the exact route taken, it fits best as a part of the path taken on April 28. It is possible, but less likely, that this is the location of the campsite of the night of April 28.

COSTUMES MEXICAINS.

Soldat en petite tenue.

Veste et Pantalons de Toile. Coëffé de Schako en Mousseline

Imp. de Desarene Plelincke, lith. de la Cour

Costumes Mexicaines. Soldat en petite tenue. By Claudio Linati, 1828. Lithograph (hand–colored), 12 × 9 inches. *Courtesy of the Amon Carter Museum, Fort Worth, Texas.*

CHAPTER 9

"El Mar de Lodo"

THE MORNING OF APRIL 29 found the main force of the Mexican army camped either on the San Bernard River or the Middle Bernard Creek. As discussed in the previous chapter, the San Bernard seems the more likely of the two. Col. Francisco Garay remained at Cayce's Crossing on the Colorado River, preparing for the army's arrival. Other than Garay, and Adrian Woll, who was at San Jacinto, all the Mexican personnel that gathered at Powell's on April 24 remained united as a single force.

However, the laborious task of fighting the mud on April 28 had significantly affected the spirit of the army. This is evidenced by the fact that for the first time there was no mention of their military position for the campsite of the night of April 28. At Powell's, and the next two nights, Filisola was careful to describe where the units camped and what the military position of the entire force was at the time. There is no mention, by any of the participants, of their position on the morning of April 29, either in regard to each other or the river.

A significant event took place early the morning of April 29 when General Urrea, per order of Filisola, left the main body of the army with his brigade. Urrea's division then became the vanguard of the army, in spite of the fact that his force was still occasionally referred to as the reserve. Urrea reported that he and his soldiers departed camp a little before seven in the morning. Filisola ordered him to leave his brigade's two artillery pieces with General Gaona's brigade in order to speed up his march. He also left his baggage to be brought up by the rest of the army.

General Urrea described that day's march to the Atascosito Crossing as "very painful." He documented that the road lay along a muddy lake[1] which threatened to engulf the men and animals. It is interesting to note that he also reported that he had no signs to guide him, other than the general direction they were traveling.[2] He likened the travel through the prairie to a ship on the ocean. A party of his cavalry reached the crossing on the Colorado at five in the afternoon, some of the infantry arrived at six, and by seven the entire brigade was encamped there.

It is important to note that Urrea did spend the first two days of the march as the commander of the rearguard. When they returned to Mexico, Urrea pointed out that he had held the more dangerous position, as the enemy was behind them. In a letter to the president of Mexico, dated September 15, 1836, General Gaona seemed to have forgotten that, at the outset, Urrea's brigade had indeed been at the rear of the march. In two separate places in the letter Gaona claimed that, from Powell's on, Urrea had always occupied the vanguard, a large distance from the army.[3] Once again the deep schism between the Filisola and Urrea camps revealed itself. It became more apparent that none of the major players in the operation seemed interested in telling the whole truth.

The San Luis Battalion log for April 29 stated that only the reserve brigade marched to the Atascosito Pass, without artillery, so as not to slow them down. They advanced through an immense marsh and traveled ten leagues (27 miles). Measuring backwards from where the Atascosito Crossing is believed to have been located, near the old Alley homesite,[4] it is apparent that the 27 miles would

---

1. This may have been present-day Eagle Lake.

2. It is likely that Urrea was talking about physical signs, such as creeks, villages, etc., but it is possible he meant mileage signs. General Mier y Terán mentioned that there were mileage signs on the Old Gonzales road when he traveled it in 1828. See Mier y Terán, *Texas by Terán*, 43. It is highly unlikely that a road as remote as the Contrabando road would have been so marked.

3. "La guerra de Texas: Causa formada al Gral. Filisola por su retirada en 1836," Tomo X, No. 1, pp. 134–137.

4. According to the *New Handbook of Texas* the Atascosito Crossing was near the homesite of Rawson Alley. This was situated on the east bank of the Colorado River about nine miles downstream from Columbus. This is the same crossing that

SEA OF MUD

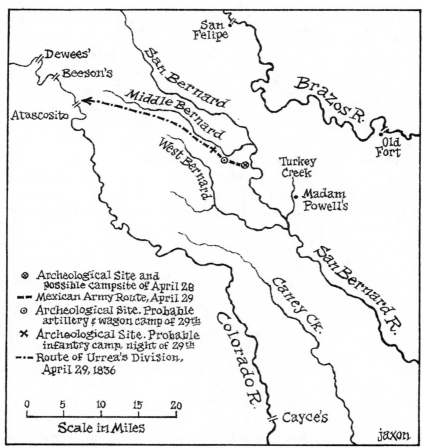

Map No. 6. Mexican Army Movements of April 29, 1836. *Drawn by Jack Jackson.*

be much closer to the suspected San Bernard campsite of the night of April 28 than the possible Middle Bernard site for the same night (see Map No. 6).

The withdrawing Mexican army was now two separate forces and would essentially stay that way (or even more divided) for the entire march back to Mexico. From that time on, as the ill feelings

---

Santa Anna had used to cross the Colorado as he was advancing toward San Jacinto. Rawson Alley was one of five Alley brothers who came to Texas in the early 1820s. "Atascosito Crossing." The Handbook of Texas Online, http://www.tsha. utexas.edu/handbook/online/articles/view/AA/rial.html (accessed July 30, 2003).

"El Mar de Lodo"

between Filisola and Urrea began to openly manifest themselves, the two commanders generally kept their distance from one another.

The morning of the 29th Filisola arranged a meeting of the rest of the generals to plan the advance of the remaining two brigades, the ammunition, armaments, etc. Even though the wagons had proceeded fully loaded up to this point, in order to continue the march they had to be lightened. The muskets that had been taken from the reserve brigade (now the vanguard) were unpacked and stripped down to just barrels and stocks. The ramrods and lockplates were removed and saved. Filisola established a reward for any *zapadore* or grenadier who was willing to carry an extra musket. The few muskets that could not be carried on mules or by the troops were thrown into the creek, along with other "items of style" they carried.

To further lighten the load, Filisola wrote that he had the canvas bags (which were used to make sandbags for fortifications, etc.) distributed to the troops to use as knapsacks and to repair their pants and jackets.

Peña verified Filisola's account of items being thrown into a creek the morning of April 29. He reported that before the march began armaments, munitions, nails,[5] quick matches of rope (used to ignite the cannons), and other appurtenances of the artillery had been thrown into the creek[6] in order to lighten the load of the wagons. He also mentioned the canvas bags and said they were distributed among the corps, three to a man. It should be noted, however, that in a third version (described below) of the Peña account, the one included in the appendices of the Urrea diary and attributed to

5. It is interesting to note, and will be discussed further in the archeology section of April 29, that the word Peña used for nails was *clabasons*. This is most likely the same as *clavazons*, which in the F. C. Bustamante *Nuevo Diccionario Inglés–Español y Español–Inglés* translates as "sets of nails." Nails would have been translated as *clavos*. It should be noted that in many of the period documents a "b" would be used instead of a "v," and an "s" instead of an "x." In the original excavations several "clumps" of nails were found that seemed to be unused.

6. In the unpublished clean copy of his diary Peña said that it was "a creek," not "the creek." This may mean that these items were not thrown into the San Bernard (or Middle Bernard, whichever was the campsite of the night of the 28th) but into a creek that was near the campsite. It is also noted that he wrote "appurtenances of ammunition of artillery."

an anonymous officer, Peña said these items had been abandoned, not thrown in a creek as he said in his first draft and in his final draft.

In the following quote, General Filisola described a situation that was almost beyond belief. After reading this depiction one cannot help but feel the suffering and deprivations endured by the common soldiers of the Mexican army. Santa Anna was reportedly fond of saying that, if nothing else, his army knew how to suffer. One need look no further than this narrative to verify the truth of his claim.

The second brigade undertook the march; but after two hours, when Filisola noticed that the first [brigade] had not yet followed; in spite of the many orders he sent by his aides to speed up, he finally went to see for himself. What he saw was unlike anything he had witnessed in 30 years of service; men, animals, cannons, all that can be named, were floating in a sea of mud [*un mar de lodo*]. We did not doubt for a moment that the mules were sunk in the mud up to their cargo, this alone prevented them from disappearing. This immense swamp, consisting of more mud than water, had small prominences of land scattered throughout.[7] Seven or eight men were able to squeeze together on each one. I ordered then that they unload the mules and that the soldiers, who were buried up to their waists, take the cargo on their shoulders to the little flat-topped hills. They later extracted the mules, also almost on their shoulders. In this way the march was able to progress on that day until a point was reached that was able to accommodate the cargo, men and animals fairly well. Later they had to pass another swamp, although only for a short distance, but it was worse than what they had just gone through. So then, on that day of true grief, men artillery, munitions, equipment, foodstuffs, etc. remained scattered from the point where we had departed. That night it could be said was not without pur-

7. Prior to this area being transformed into rice fields, these prominences were called pimple mounds by the locals. They are naturally occurring. Most of them have been destroyed by the leveling of the rice fields but a rare one still exists. The term that Filisola used for these mounds was *mogotitos*.

pose as everyone was busy seeing that the march would progress the next day.[8]

Peña also confirmed the suffering and misery of April 29. In fact, he reported that on that day their misfortunes reached their limit. The wagons had been delayed from the previous day, and some of the sick died during the night due to lack of medicine and nourishment. He claimed that the sick were ill treated, as if the men were made of bronze and not subject to illness. He wrote that the vanguard (most likely Urrea, even though he did not say so specifically), left at 8 A.M., and that the rearguard had still not been able to move by 10 A.M.

Peña's description of the general state of affairs as the army plodded through this quagmire agrees with the reports of Filisola and adds to our amazement that the troops were finally able to extract themselves.

It was necessary to have seen and experienced it to understand the army's sufferings and the obstacles it had to overcome when it was already exhausted after so many prolonged marches. During the days of the storm, particularly the 29th and 30th of April and the 1st, 2nd, and 3rd of May, we went along roads hardly passable. The corps marching in the vanguard scarcely passed over a road but that it was instantly made impassable; those who followed, divided into platoons, passed wherever they could; no one paid them any mind, since their officers and commanders hardly worried about details. The cannons and the loaded pack mules sank in the mud when least expected, and much time was lost and great effort expended to pull them out of these formidable mudholes. No one alerted the others to the danger; it seemed that each corps marched on its own initiative, and each individual alone, as if their fate did not depend on that of the others. It appeared as if no general orders had been given and no common bond existed among them.

No enemy pursued us, because their forces were just as

8. Filisola, *Memorias para la historia de la guerra de Tejas* (Cumplido, 1849), I, 235–236.

SEA OF MUD

insignificant as they had been before the battle of San Jacinto; nevertheless, our general seemed to wish to move faster. The enemy depended for his safety on our retreat, and he ridiculed and humiliated our prisoners because of it.[9]

Peña gave another description of the situation of that day, but the way it is translated from his final draft is confusing and it is difficult to tell if he was talking of April 29 or April 30. Examining the unpublished clean copy of his diary, it is apparent that the following was written on April 30 but described what happened on the afternoon of April 29.

Today I had to dismount, sinking up to my knees in the mud, falling and getting up, finally loosing my boots, and continuing thus. We walked no more than thirty or forty paces before the soldiers had to help pull out the artillery pieces, an extremely exhausting chore, since they were poorly nourished, and much time was lost in this way. Between five and six in the afternoon, when we had traveled five or six miles at most, each corps camped as best it could, and likewise the commanders and officers, for conditions were beyond discipline. All around one could see groups at a distance one from the other. The artillery remained stuck up to the axles two or three miles away from the point of departure. The loads of ammunition, provisions, and equipment were left scattered along the road and the individual who at great sacrifice was able to bring up his corresponding equipment found it useless. Many loads were lost, many mules were ruined, and the troops could not have mess because it never reached them, nor was there any wood to prepare any if it had. It is difficult to describe our march on this day; it was a complete disaster. Exasperation among the officers and the troops. Grumblings because it was impossible to judge the condition of the roads ahead, before we got mired in them, all the while suffering hunger and other privations. The road to Austin [San Felipe de Austin] was solid

9. Peña, *La rebelión de Texas,* 180; translated in Perry (trans. and ed.), *With Santa Anna in Texas,* 158–159; retranslated for G. Dimmick by Dora Elizondo Guerra.

∞
"El Mar de Lodo"

and on high ground and we had been able to travel on it during heavy rain.[10]

The fact that this quote is indeed from April 29 is proven by the diary of General Urrea. In the Castañeda translation, footnote number 35 quotes a short segment of a diary, written by "an officer who was an eyewitness of the events as they happened." As was established in chapter four, the officer was obviously Peña. In this Peña passage from the Urrea diary the entry for April 29 is almost a word-for-word match for the above quote. Only part of the Peña passage from the original Urrea diary was translated by Castañeda when he compiled *The Mexican Side of the Texas Revolution*. Several more pages are given in Appendix No. 33 of Urrea's original diary. Our Appendix No. 1 is a translation of the entire Appendix No. 33 from the Urrea diary. Part of this appendix has not been previously translated.[11] It is very interesting to compare the original Spanish of the Peña passage in Urrea's diary to that of the Peña first draft, and to the Peña final draft. There are items that are included in the Urrea quote that are not in the first draft yet are in the final draft. Then again there are items that are not in the Urrea quote but are in the first and second drafts. Peña wrote in the Urrea version that he lost his boots this day and had to continue barefoot. This is only one of many examples where the quote from the Urrea diary is different from the first draft and the final draft that are included in the Peña Papers. It is possible that Peña, or possibly Urrea, edited Peña's diary for the Urrea version. Another possibility is that both the Urrea pas-

10. Peña, *La rebelión de Texas,* 185–186; translated in Perry (trans. and ed.), *With Santa Anna in Texas,* 165–166; retranslated for G. Dimmick by Dora Elizondo Guerra.

11. José de Urrea, *Diario de las operaciones militares de la division que al mando del General José Urrea hizo la campaña de Tejas publicado se autor con algunas observaciones para vindicarse ante sus conciudadanos* (Victoria de Durango, Mexico: Imprint of the Government, 1838), 87–92. It should be noted that Urrea quoted most of the anonymous officer's [Peña's] diary from April 29 to May 25. He did not include all of the diary however, as can be seen on page 90 where Urrea states under the date of May 23: "After a description of Texas, of the forests, of its rivers and of its country side, he says: . . ." After this statement he continued to quote the diary. See our Appendix No. 1 for a complete translation of the entire appendix No. 33 from the Urrea diary.

sage from the diary and the diary's first draft were used by Peña to write the final draft. But it is obvious that Peña had not finished his memoirs at the time that Urrea quoted him in 1838.[12]

One mention of the distance traveled by the first and second brigades on April 29 was in Filisola's letter to the government dated May 14, 1836. He stated that in the entire day's march they were able to advance scarcely more than one league. One league would be consistent with the two to three miles (1.8 to 2.7 English miles) that Peña estimated the artillery moved that day.

It is just over three and one-half miles from the area of the proposed campsite of the night of April 28 to the site that is likely to be where the artillery and wagons bogged down on April 29. As will be seen in the archeology section in this chapter there are many artifacts that support this theory. About one and a half to two miles past the site where the artillery and wagons are thought to have bogged down another concentration of artifacts has been excavated. This would be consistent with the Peña description of the other units having marched five to six miles (4.5 to 5.4 English miles) on April 29 (see Map No. 6).

ARCHEOLOGY OF APRIL 29

The archeological site of the trail of the Mexican army from April 29 is widely strewn, covering the area from the point at which the artillery and wagons got stuck to where the infantry camped on the same day. According to Peña these two sites should be separated by about two and one-half miles. Beyond the infantry campsite the army becomes totally dispersed. The likely location of the infantry campsite on the night of April 29 was later traversed by the artillery and wagons as they slowly inched through the mud. Thus the artifacts excavated beyond this point could have been dropped by three separate groups, on separate days, using the same road. Urrea's division completed the entire leg of the journey on April 29. The infantry of the first and second brigades required two to three days

12. For an excellent summary of Peña's unpublished clean copy of his diary and his struggles producing his final publication see Dr. James E. Crisp's introduction to the expanded version of *With Santa Anna in Texas* (College Station: Texas A&M Press, 1997).

to traverse the same trail. The artillery, wagons, etc., brought up the rear and were detained in this area for days, slowly drifting into the Atascosito camp between May 5 and May 8.

Peña gave two lists of items that were thrown into a creek or abandoned on the road on April 29. He reported that arms, munitions, canvas and rope sacks, artillery cords, sets of nails, unlocked trunks, broken packs, and destroyed ammunition boxes were left by the retreating troops. He wrote that among the ammunition boxes were cans of canister[13] which could barely be seen in the midst of the mud.

Several of the above mentioned items were found at this site, including several hundred nails. The nails were not just individual nails, but large clusters of iron, square nails that appeared unused. This is consistent with the fact that Peña called them "sets" of nails, not just nails.

Also found at this site was a collection of three cans of canister. They were found in the same location, as if they may have been dropped together [Fig. 9-1]. The first contained sixty-six lead canister shot which measured 2.17 to 2.24 centimeters (.854 to .882 inches). They weighed 63.4 to 65.1 grams. There were fragments of the metal container as well as wooden fragments from the plug, or sabot, which sealed the open end of the can. The second can had 55 lead shot, the same size as that of the first can. The bottom of the second container was still intact along with twelve balls in place. This has been treated with microcrystalline wax [Fig. 9-2]. The third can held only twenty-nine canister shot but these were larger than those of the first two cans. They were 2.38 to 2.64 centimeters (.937 to 1.04 inches) and weighed 83.7 to 103.7 grams. Many of the shot showed signs of casting with remnants of sprues and seams.

At the battle of Palo Alto the Mexicans and the Americans used different sized canister shot for different sized cannons. Archeology

---

13. Peña used the Spanish phrase *botes de metralla*, which Carmen Perry translated as "shrapnel containers." A better translation might be, "cans of canister," or simply "canister." The translation of the second list of abandoned items in the anonymous officer's diary, given in the Urrea diary, reads somewhat differently than that in the translation of the final draft. It says that "among the abandoned items were unlocked trunks, trampled packs, cans of canister, and much ammunition, that scarcely could be seen in the mud."

at that site revealed both brass and lead Mexican canister shot. The four lead shot found at that site were 1 to 1.03 inches, or similar in size to those of our third can.[14] The brass and lead balls often showed a slight nonalignment of the ball hemispheres owing to a shot mold in need of repair. It is possible that the nonalignment was intentional to get a better spread from the shot. In his unpublished first draft Peña listed the items destroyed or discarded by Gen. Juan Andrade when he abandoned San Antonio. Included on the list were twenty-four cans of canister for a twelve-pound cannon, twenty-seven cans of canister for a seven-inch howitzer, twenty cans of canister for an eight-pound cannon, fifteen cans of canister for a six-pound cannon, and five cans of canister for a four-pound cannon.[15]

A slightly different explanation of the different sizes of canister is given in *Artillery Equipments of the Napoleonic Wars*. It reports that canister was used primarily for short range, generally less than 350 yards. The book goes on to note that both large and small canister were used by the artillery of that age. The large canister shot was made for increased range. There were some instances where large canister shot was used at up to six hundred yards. At times a solid shot and canister shot were used in the same discharge. It was also common to use two canisters simultaneously at very close range.

This source describes a canister as: "a thin tin cylinder, a little less in diameter than the caliber of the piece, with a wooden sabot bottom and an iron lid soldered on. This tin was packed with balls to make up the weight of the projectile, and the cylinder held these balls together during its passage up the bore. Sawdust filled the spaces between the balls. As it left the confines of the barrel the pressure of the charge and the relaxation of the inward pressure of the barrel caused the cylinder to disintegrate so that the balls continued forward, splaying outwards to form a cone of death with a diameter of 32 feet at 100 yards, 64 feet at 200 yards, and 96 feet at 300 yards."[16]

Since there have been just two sizes of canister found at our sites

14. Charles Haecker and Jeffry Mauck, *On the Prairie of Palo Alto* (College Station: Texas A&M University Press, 1997), 147–151.

15. Peña, unpublished clean copy of his diary, pp. 100–101, Peña Papers (CAH).

16. Terence Wise and Richard Hook, *Artillery Equipments of the Napoleonic Wars*, Men at Arms series (London: Osprey Publishing, 1979), 16–17.

∞

"El Mar de Lodo"

it is likely that the two different sizes of shot were for different ranges, not for different cannons. Thus, on the list of materials abandoned at San Antonio, the different sized cans of canister were probably based on the size of the cans, not the size of the canister shot.

In addition two separate iron locks were found that seem to have come from trunks. No remnants of the trunks were found. In the area of the three cans of canister, several musket balls were also found that were .69 to .70 caliber. Also in the vicinity of the canister there were two solid iron cannon balls. The first was the original cannon ball that was found while digging the pond and the second was discovered during the survey of the site. Both were very rusted and had diameters of about 9 centimeters (3.54 inches) and weighed six pounds [Fig. 9-3]. The diameter of the two cannon balls was almost exactly the same as the intact base of the second can of canister, making it likely that the two solid iron shot and the cans of canister shot were for the same size cannon, very possibly a six pounder.

A brass oval plate was unearthed that was inscribed "B.N.1" on the top half and "GRANADEROS" on the bottom half [Fig. 9-4]. As described earlier the grenadiers were the veteran troops. The plate is 7.2 centimeters top to bottom, and 9 centimters side to side. There is a small raised rim all the way around the edge of the piece. There are two small holes on each side to attach the plate. This piece may be from a cartridge box or from a shako. The shakos were the tall leather helmets worn by the infantry. The fact that the inscription indicates that it is from the First Battalion signifies that the piece is pre-1832. Prior to 1832 the Mexican army numbered their battalions and from 1832 to 1839 their regular army battalions were named for heroes of the Mexican independence movement from Spain. It is possible that in the intervening four years not all the permanent units had received uniform pieces with the new battalion names. It is also likely that when they did receive the new items, the old surplus items were handed down to the active units. There have been far more items found that have numbers so it is quite likely that many of the units were still wearing pre-1832 insignia, shakos, buttons, etc.

A rectangular brass cross-belt plate with "clipped" corners was found. This plate served to secure the two belts, one for the bayonet scabbard and one for the cartridge box, which crossed over the soldier's chest. The corners are slightly uneven suggesting that it is handmade. It is 6.5 centimeters top to bottom, and 4.7 centimeters side to side. It is .3 centimeters in thickness and weighs 78.8 grams. On the face of the plate is a scrolled letter "M" [Fig. 9-5]. This most likely stands for the Morelos Battalion rather than the Matamoros Battalion, as nearly all the soldiers from the latter were killed or captured at San Jacinto. (A second identical example of this plate was later excavated; it is unlikely that two soldiers of the Matamoros Battalion escaped from San Jacinto, and that both lost their plates in the mud.) The Morelos Battalion, on the other hand, had 382 soldiers when it left Old Fort. It has also been suggested that the scroll over the letter "M" could make the inscription read "PM." This is possible as the Morelos was a permanent battalion and "PM" could stand for Permanente Morelos. "PM" could also stand for the active unit called Primero Mexico, but this item would more likely have been for a regular unit than for an active battalion.[17]

At the bottom edge of the cross-belt plate is a small hole to which a chain was fastened. Only the first link of the brass chain was still attached to the plate. On the other end of the chain would have been a pick and a brush. The pick was used to clean out the firehole of the musket when it became plugged with powder debris. The brush would have served to brush away the debris after it had been loosened by the pick. It was important in battle to keep the firehole clean. If the powder in the pan exploded but the fire did not get to the barrel nothing would happen but a flash in the pan. There are two raised fasteners on the reverse side of the cross-belt plate, one at the top edge and one at the bottom. Each fastener has a small hole near the top for an attachment; either a wire or a wooden stick may have been used to attach the fasteners behind the belts.

A shako plate was a thin brass plate sewn to a felt or leather helmet (shako). Two brass fragments of a shako plate were found. They were initially connected but broke apart in recovery. One of the fragments has a rounded rim along the outer edge and a smaller raised rim below, which apparently went around the entire plate. On one side there are two small holes that were used to sew the plate to the

17. Since the permanent battalions were named rather than numbered after 1832, this plate would have been nearly new in 1836. Seemingly the regular or permanent units would have been more likely to have the new accoutrements than the active units.

shako. A raised letter "M" is near the top of this plate. Just below that there is what seems to be the wing of an eagle [Fig. 9-6]. This wing appears to be the same as the one shown in a report of artifacts found near the San Jacinto battle site.[18] The San Jacinto plate has a rim as well, and two small holes on each edge for attaching it to the shako.

Several items from India Pattern British Brown Bess muskets were recovered. Three oxidized lockplates were found. These plates contained the main firing mechanism for the musket [Fig. 9-7]. Upon cleaning by electrolysis, the lockplate that was the least oxidized was found to be inscribed "BARNETT," and just beneath that is "London." Barnett was one of several private contractors that manufactured India Pattern muskets in London in the early 1800s.[19] None of the three plates had a hammer attached but an unattached hammer was found at the site. Two of the three lockplates did have their frizzen in place. The lockplates were approximately 17 centimeters long and 3.1 centimeters top to bottom.

Several other items from muskets were discovered. Most of the "furniture" for British muskets are made of brass, making it easy to verify that this was indeed from the Mexican army. The Texans used primarily American made muskets and rifles that had mainly iron furniture. Musket pieces discovered included ramrod pipes, trigger guards, nosecaps and a sideplate [Fig. 9-8]. There was also an iron bayonet socket. The socket has a reinforced collar at the proximal end and the locking slot is visible. The triangular bayonet, which would have been attached to the shank, is missing. This type of bayonet was used on the India Pattern muskets [Fig. 9-9].

Eight Spanish-style horse or mule shoes of various sizes were dug from this site. These have a unique shape [Fig. 9-10]. This type of horse/mule shoe is very rare in Texas and helps differentiate the site as Mexican army. The shoes generally show great wear. There are usually four square nail holes on each side and many of the nails are still in place. Hefter shows similar shoes in his illustrations but his shoes seem to have fewer nail holes on one side.[20] The Mexican

18. Alan R. Duke, "Artifacts from San Jacinto," *Houston Archeological Society Newsletter*, 45 (Apr., 1974), 6.

19. Anthony D. Darling, *Redcoats and Brown Bess,* Historical Arms Series, No. 12 (Canada: Museum Restoration Service, 1971), 52.

20. Nieto et al., *El soldado mexicano,* 34.

army had two campaign forges when they entered Texas. We know that both were with the army as it retreated because Urrea and Filisola used the plural in discussing the forges.[21] Filisola documented that two forges were brought into Texas and Peña reported that one of the forges had to be abandoned.[22]

A conical shaped brass base for a flagstaff or guidon was retrieved. The flag or guidon was carried by mounted troops with the pointed distal end designed to fit into a leather holder attached to the side of a saddle stirrup. The proximal end of the base is rounded and measures 2.5 centimeters in diameter. A small round hole is on one side of the base, .75 centimeters below the proximal end. The head of an iron pin, approximately .5 centimeters in diameter, which held the wooden staff to the base, is visible. When cleaned, remnants of the wooden staff were seen inside. The overall height of the piece is 8.5 centimeters and it weighs 155 grams [Fig. 9-11].

A gilded Mexican eagle was found at the site. The eagle is facing to the left which is very odd for Mexican eagles. Generally Mexican eagle coins or buttons that were made after 1821 had the eagle facing to the right. This eagle may well date back to the insurgency of Mexico against Spain. The eagle is standing in a patch of prickly pear cactus leaves. The wings are spread and curved downward. Its height is 3.5 centimeters, width 3 centimeters, and weight 7.7 grams. On the reverse side are two small raised posts that are approximately .3 centimeters. These posts are blunt-tipped and have no holes in them. The eagle could be from a cockade on the side of an officer's bi-corn hat. Another possibility is from a shoulder epaulet. A third possibility is that it was attached to a belt buckle. The type of metal is unknown but it seems to be different from the other brass items [Fig. 9-12].

21. Urrea, "Diario de las operaciones militares," *Documentos para la historia de la guerra de Tejas,* 34; Filisola, *Memorias para la historia de la guerra de Tejas* (Cumplido, 1849), I, 229. Notice that Castañeda in *The Mexican side of the Texas Revolution,* page 260, translated *fraguas* (forges) as "smithing equipment."

22. Filisola, *Memorias para la historia de la guerra de Tejas* (Rafael, 1848, 1849), reprint, *Historia de la guerra de Tejas* (1968), II, 338. The Spanish for the forges is *fraguas de campaña.* Peña, *La rebelión de Texas;* translated in Perry (trans. and ed.), *With Santa Anna in Texas,* 171 (this is the list of the items the Mexican army abandoned in the Mar de Lodo).

Many personal items were uncovered as well, including a two-pronged fork, a iron blade from a straight razor, two iron-handled pocket knives, one iron ladle handle, two scissors, a plain brass button with a backmark of "E. T. Moore Extra Rich," several iron and brass buckles, a broken iron spur, and two iron woodworking tools.

There was also a broken china plate that was identified as green edgeware dating from 1800 to 1840. Twenty-one fragments of the plate were recovered, comprising over half the plate. Considering the documented looting by the Mexican army, it is possible that this was part of their plunder.

The fact that this site contained three distinct articles that Peña specifically stated as having been abandoned on the road on April 29—the locks from trunks, the sets of nails, and the several cans of canister—makes it likely that this is the area he was describing in his memoir.

This is the first site on the retreat path that contains a large number of items that seem to be abandoned and not just things one would naturally discard. This fact makes it likely that this site is the "gateway" to the actual Mar de Lodo. Past this area, to the northwest, there are a large number of artifacts that have apparently been dropped.

Fig. 9-1. Canister cans in situ. *Photograph courtesy of the author.*

⌞1 cm⌟

Fig. 9-2. Canister end containing twelve lead canister.

Fig. 9-3. Iron solid shot cannon ball.

Fig. 9-4. First Battalion Grenadier plate.

Fig. 9-5. "M" cross-belt plate.

|__ 1 cm __|

|__ 1 cm __|

Fig. 9-6. Fragment of brass shako plate.

Fig. 9-7. India Pattern musket iron lockplate inscribed "Barnett London".

⌐1 cm⌐

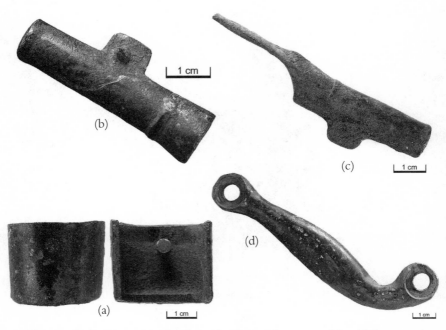

Fig. 9-8. India Pattern musket brass furniture (a) nosecap (b) middle ramrod pipe (c) terminal ramrod pipe (d) sideplate.

Fig. 9-9. Iron India Pattern musket bayonet socket.

1 cm

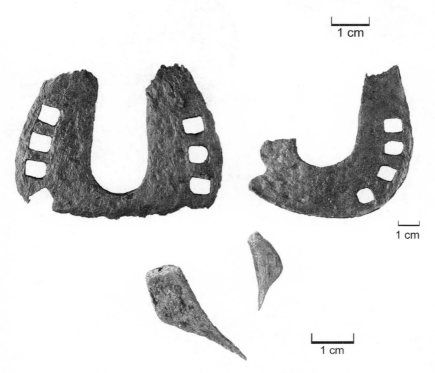

1 cm

1 cm

Fig. 9-10. Iron "Spanish style" horse/mule shoes with nails.

1 cm

Fig. 9-11. Brass flag staff or guidon base.

Fig. 9-12. Gilded Mexican eagle.

CHAPTER 10

Chaos

BY THE DAWN OF APRIL 30 the Mexican army in Texas was in total chaos. The army Filisola had gathered at Powell's, which arguably could have advanced on Houston and saved the day for Mexico, was now in a shambles. Urrea's division had occupied the Atascosito Crossing and was supposedly making preparations for the crossing of the army. Filisola, along with the other generals and most of the first and second brigades, had left the stranded artillery, wagons, baggage, and wounded, and was marching to join Urrea's troops. Pickets from each unit had remained in the rear to help Ampudia extract this ragtag remnant of a once proud army from the mud and get them to Atascosito. According to all the Mexican sources there was no longer any order whatsoever in their movements. This fact was verified by the Texans who trailed the Mexican army through the mud.

The individual units could not maneuver in the mud. Each time a wagon or cannon passed a certain point, the road became so chewed up that the next vehicle had to get off the road to avoid being mired in the ruts. The units became small bands of men and animals that, once they became separated, found it too exhausting to travel even a short distance to communicate with one another.

Today the land in question is nearly all rice fields. It is hard to imagine, but old-timers who used to traverse this prairie before it was farmed report that it used to be much worse. Joe Hudgins, a prominent rancher in the area, and past president of the Houston Archeological Society, tells that when he was a young man he was unable to ride a horse through this prairie when it was even moderately wet. The area was not only muddy but was overgrown by several varieties of bluestem grass that grew chest high. The prairie grass was so thick that one could not see the lay of the land well enough to tell where the higher ground might be.

It would seem logical to assume that there were more trees in the area in 1836 than there are now. However, this is not the case with the Mar de Lodo. Filisola reported that there was no wood on the prairie to use for firewood. Aerial photographs of the area from 1932 confirm that there were far fewer trees at that time than there are now.[1] It is believed that the fires that once plagued the prairies kept the trees from getting a foothold. Urrea reported that moving through the prairie, without landmarks, was similar to sailing.[2]

The only report from Urrea on April 30 was a short dispatch that he sent to Filisola that morning. The letter informed the commander-in-chief that the Atascosito Crossing on the Colorado was in Urrea's control. General Urrea was supposed to have been building rafts or otherwise providing passage for the army upon its arrival.

Filisola gave two accounts of April 30. They are quite different in the detail, though not contradictory. The first is from Filisola's May 14 letter to the government in Mexico.

> The night was horrible; artillery, cavalry, sick, baggage mules, everything that accompanied the army was a confused mess, without any distinction and without being able to move from the place where they were caught.
>
> With immense trouble it was hardly possible to assemble the brigade of infantry and form them in a place that appeared less miry: but the weight of the men very soon made us know that the surface of the ground was all the same, and the soldiers sunk up to their knees: to heighten our misery there was not a single splinter of wood to make a fire for cooking, and consequently less for watch-fires. This

1. Edgar Tobin Aerial Surveys, Wharton County, Texas, 1932 (in author's possession).

2. Urrea, "Diario de las operaciones militares," *Documentos para la historia de la guerra de Tejas;* translated in Castañeda (trans. and ed.), *The Mexican Side of the Texas Revolution,* 262.

want made me fear yet greater evils, and that the soldiers would, without distinction, lay hold of trunks or ammunition boxes to warm themselves; thanks to the zeal of the generals, chiefs and officers, and to the unparalleled endurance of a Mexican soldier, no disorder occurred during the whole night. The morning of the 1st of May [April 30] presented to my sight a spectacle truly horrible, and which can only be believed by those who were witnesses, because it is not possible for any one to imagine it who does not possess a knowledge of the topography of Texas, of the qualities of its surface, and of the inconstancy of its climate in continual changes of cold, heat, snow, rain and frightful hurricanes. The position of the army on this morning was the right bank of the principal rivulet of several which form the river San Bernard[3] and between the two roads which come from San Felipe de Austin to Bexar and to this town [Victoria], which are marked on the map of Texas of 1833; all the rivulets were swollen so as not to afford a passage before eight or ten days, and no other outlet remained but the road which leads to the pass of the river Colorado, called Atascosito; the land between the said rivulets is swampy and of the same kind as that on which we were encamped: the said pass was not five leagues off: cannons, wagons, mules, ammunition and men, were all buried in the mud. . . . I determined then to advance with everything that could follow, which

3. Once again Filisola reported that they were on the "principal rivulet of the several that form the river San Bernard." This statement supports the idea that when Filisola moved from the San Bernard to the Middle Bernard, probably on April 29, he likely did not realize that he had done so and thought he was still on the principal rivulet, which would have been the San Bernard. The only time he mentioned the Middle Bernard was in his representation to the government. As the Middle Bernard flows into the San Bernard just north of where Filisola likely turned toward the northwest, and began to follow the Middle Bernard, it is very possible that he did not know that he was now following a new creek. Even today it is difficult to realize that the fork is there unless you were to cross the Middle Bernard and then encounter the San Bernard. When questioning residents of the town of East Bernard, which sits just to the south of the juncture of the Middle Bernard and the San Bernard, it is apparent that even they are unaware of the location and differentiation of the two.

consisted only of men, and to leave all the rest to the zeal
and incomparable indefatigability of lieutenant colonel Don
Pedro Ampudia, commandant-general of the artillery, with
pickets of soldiers from each corps, so that they might assist
him in the work. At dark I encamped one league distant
from Atascosito.[4]

It should be noted that Filisola's statement about the troops not
using ammo boxes, etc., for firewood on the night of April 29 is possibly true. On the other hand, it is likely that the same could not be
said for the night of April 28. The spare muskets he doled out to the
troops to carry and those that he had thrown in the creek the morning of April 29 could have been loose due to their carrying cases
having been burned. In his declaration in the Filisola trial Col.
Agustín Amat, commander of the Zapadores Battalion, and Peña's
commander, verified that items were burned to make their mess.

The Army began the march and having passed the stream of
San Bernard, three downpours fell in one day that flooded
the terrain in order that they were not able to follow the
road that they were taking, and that they headed to the Atascosito Crossing, and the terrain was in such a muddy state
that men, carts, artillery, etc. became stuck, and that the mentioned crossing was only five leagues distant, they were
delayed for 11 days in passing them [the five leagues] with
the munitions, artillery and carts, having had to leave some
of them abandoned and others burned to make mess.[5]

The second Filisola account is from the Cumplido edition of his
Memorias and was written thirteen years after his first account. In it
he writes as if the soldiers did indeed burn some of the above mentioned items.

30th—This day we began to cross the lowland of which I

4. Filisola, May 14, 1836, letter to the Mexican government, *La rebelión de Texas,*
Anexo No. 22, pp. 284–285; translated in Filisola, *Evacuation of Texas,* 42–43.
5. "La guerra de Texas: Causa formada al Gral. Filisola por su retirada en 1836,"
Tomo X, No. 2, pp. 400–403.

have made mention. We were not able to make much progress the whole day, even though the generals, leaders and officers worked generally as persistently as the soldiers. It was still threatening to rain and there was no doubt that if it was another downpour like the previous ones, very few would have survived to tell about it. In this immense swamp of water and mud there was not a splinter of firewood, nor anywhere to get it, in order to have mess, unless it was taken by hand from the carts, gun carriages or the cases for the muskets. The soldiers working all day had no piece of cracker, nor any means to cook a few beans. Disgracefully, even the cattle that had been driven for eating vanished that gloomy night. For certain, you could not have had a more sorrowful situation, nor one more conducive to poor discipline, insubordination and disorder. However, it is necessary to say, to the glory of all, that as they went at this arduous and desperate situation, nobody professed a complaint. On the contrary, with a resignation full of heroism, they did no more than to encourage others to work and laugh at their extraordinary hardships.

More over, it is necessary to agree, that in these exertions they could not last without eating. It would have been a crime to continue. Consequently Filisola decided to order the first brigade, which had become the vanguard, to reunite with the second, which I have stated, they carried out under the same hardship that I have already given to understand.

To carry it out, I gave the order for twenty men with two officers from each unit to be placed under the command of the artillery commander, D. Pedro Ampudia. With this force from all the battalions, said leader would undertake the extraction of the stuck cargoes, carts, and artillery. He would continue the march until he found the army. He told Ampudia that he was dividing the cargoes in fourths to remove them from there, making it the responsibility of the owners for that material that was partitioned off and omitted. After this disposition he undertook the march with the two brigades, the treasury, the equipment in the best shape, the mess mules of the units and all the rest that could proceed at this time; until they found a more convenient spot where

Chaos

they could find provisions of firewood. Then they could return from there, carrying relief supplies of meat and firewood that they procured for those that were left behind. Then they would be able to emerge from this immense and barren mud hole as soon as possible.

As it was, with four leagues of marching, with continuos work, since from time to time they came upon mud holes and puddles to pass, they stopped in a forest of oaks which was situated on a low ridge that was almost imperceptible, as they commonly are in the territory of Texas. The elevation did provide ground that was better for making camp, at which they arrived from a gorge that formed two immense swamps.[6]

Filisola went on to report that as soon as he arrived at the campsite of April 30 he ordered the gathering of meat and firewood to be sent to the bogged-down troops in the rear. He sent one of his aides, Lt. Col. Juan Cuevas, along with as many cargo mules as could be spared, to deliver said supplies. Filisola was effusive in his praise for Ampudia in regard to his hard work in getting most of the wagons and all of the artillery through the quagmire. He reported that Ampudia himself was working in mud that was at times waist-deep.

There is other documentation that Ampudia, with the help of the pickets from each unit and Peña with his sappers [*zapadores*] stayed behind and worked to free the artillery. One document is from Ampudia. In the Peña memoirs, appendix No. 3, document IV is a dispatch written by Ampudia on June 22, 1836, in support of Peña's role in the Texas campaign.

> Pedro de Ampudia, Lt. Col. and Artillery Commander General, Army of Operations over Texas:
>
> I HEREBY SWEAR: That José Enrique de la Peña, Captain, with a Lt. Col. Grade, attached to the Engineer Corps, while acting as aide to Col. Francisco Duque, Commander of one of the columns during the siege at the Alamo, in the heat of battle, dodged in and out of the crossfire, and ran across the

---

6. Filisola, *Memorias para la historia de la guerra de Tejas* (Cumplido, 1849), I, 236–238.

∞

battlefield to fulfill his duty to inform that said Commander had been wounded, and that his second, General Manuel Fernández Castrillón needed to take over as had been earlier agreed. I personally watched this intrepid young man climb the palisade that formed part of the compound, inside the fort. He performed his duty like a fine officer.

During the crossings of the Guadalupe, Colorado and Brazos Rivers, he worked and assisted me through all those hardships with untiring and honorable energy. He furthermore contributed, under my orders, fifty-seven men from the Zapadores to help retrieve the batteries that had gotten stuck in the swamps that form during the rainy season between the Saint Bernard and the Atascosito. Finally, Peña's faultless conduct, in addition to his invaluable service that he has given during the Texas campaign, make him, in my judgment, worthy of the Supreme Government's consideration and esteem, at every level of society.

GENERAL HEADQUARTERS IN MATAMOROS,
JUNE 22, 1836
PEDRO DE AMPUDIA (SIGNED)[7]

In the same papers (appendix No. 3, document V, August 17, 1836), Agustín Amat, commander of the Zapadores Battalion, confirms Ampudia's statement.

Mr. Agustín Amat, Col. of the Army and Lt. Col. and Commander of the Zapadores Battalion.

I HEREBY SWEAR: That the Lt. Col. of the army, Captain José Enrique de la Peña, was in charge of the forces that Col. Duque sent to Béjar. Peña fulfilled his commission with the fine commitment that is well recognized in this officer. During the siege of the Fort of the Alamo, on the 6th of March of this year, he was one who most distinguished himself in the column led by the above-mentioned Col. [Duque].

He risked his life twice in the crossfire in order to fulfill an important order. Inside the fort, I am personally aware of his tireless service to bring order and efficiency [in the

7. Peña, *La rebelión de Texas,* Anexo No. 3, Documento IV, p. 236–237.

chaos], in an effort to reduce the number of victims and the confusion that usually ensues in those circumstances.

I SWEAR FURTHER: That in the section that I was commanding at the Brazos River, he performed the orders I issued with the same zeal. During the river crossings, where hardships were overwhelming, he performed with dedication and reliability. The same is true during our retreat when he helped the artillery commander to extract the equipment that had been left stuck in the mud by offering fifty-seven men from the Zapadores that I had actually assigned to him.

So that these facts are known, I give him the [commendation] in Matamoros on August 17, 1836.

Agustín Amat (Signed)[8]

ARCHEOLOGY OF THE MAR DE LODO

A stretch of four to five miles along the Middle Bernard Creek, starting from 41WH91, and proceeding to the northwest, generally paralleling the creek is the heart of the Mar de Lodo. The archeology of this area has been documented in *Tracking the Mexican Army through the Mar De Lodo (Sea of Mud) April 29–May 9, 1836*.[9]

In his *Representación* to the government Filisola indirectly pinpointed this area as having the worst conditions of any area in the retreat. In response to Urrea's claim to have saved the artillery, Filisola replied that the only risk the artillery ran in the whole campaign was when it was bogged down for about two leagues (5.7 miles), on the bank of the middle rivulet of the San Bernard. He reported that it took nine days to drag the artillery out.

Any attempt to exactly date any of the sites along the trail past the area described in chapter nine of *Tracking the Mexican Army through the Mar De Lodo* is probably futile. The trail of the Mexican army has been traced for approximately five and one-half miles along the Middle Bernard Creek. As the path heads to the northwest the artifacts abruptly stop. This is likely due to a slight elevation of

8. Ibid., Anexo No. 3, Documento V, p. 237.

9. Hudgins, Kieler, and Dimmick, *Tracking the Mexican Army through the Sea of Mud*.

the land that allowed the army to travel with less trouble and thus fewer artifacts were dropped.

All along the army's route there are pockets of artifacts. Logically, one would think that very few of these would be from Urrea's division, as they made a quick, one-day trip along the entire last leg of the trail to the Colorado. His division had no artillery or baggage to get stuck so is less likely to have left proof of its passing. The first and second brigades are likely to have come out of the worst of the Mar de Lodo by the night of April 30. Thus, they would have occupied the area for only two days and one night. The bogged artillery, wagons, carts, mules, etc., and the troops that were trying to free them were in the area from the morning of April 29 until around May 7. Much of the material that has been recovered is likely to be evidence of this salvage operation. The scattered concentrations of artifacts may well be the positions where the small groups of soldiers gathered to spend the night, or where soldiers tried to free a wagon or artillery piece that was stuck in the mud.

One other general statement about the overall trail of the army through the Mar de Lodo should be made. As the trail progresses toward the northwest there is more scatter side to side. This is an indication that as the soldiers got deeper into the mud they were more and more spread out, most likely due to the worsening condition of the road.

During excavations, in the spring of 2000, we were surprised and very excited to find what we first thought was an extremely large cannonball. It was later learned that this was actually a howitzer shell. After we were able to pinpoint exactly what this shell was, a safety issue became apparent. As described below, the hollow bronze shell had a fuse in place and still contained the original gunpowder. As far as could be ascertained the seal at the base of the fuse was still tight. The Office of the State Archeologist was contacted and recommended that we notify the U.S. Army bomb squad from Fort Sam Houston. The bomb squad instructed that the shell not be moved but, as it was in my garage and I did not want the neighbors to see the bomb squad at work there, we removed the shell to the country. The army was kind enough to remove the fuse; the gunpowder had solidified to a point that it could not be removed. The bomb squad loaded the shell with plastic explosive, which shook up

∞

the neighbor's cattle a bit when it blew the shell to smithereens. Needless to say we were in a deep depression for days as this had been the only known loaded shell of its kind. We did locate the fragments, in the bottom of the four-foot hole left by the explosion, and managed to reconstruct much of the bomb. From this we did get an idea of how sharp the shrapnel would have been, so a small piece of information was salvaged. Since this was a Mexican howitzer shell that was blown up by soldiers from Fort Sam Houston we could argue that this explosion qualifies as the very last shot of the Texas Revolution.

Luckily several more howitzer shells have been found. Rather than calling the army back, we took the shells to the local car wash. When no one else was there we stuck the nozzle into the shells and washed out the powder. We then dried the powder and placed a small sample on a piece of paper. To see if the powder was still combustible we burned the paper, but the powder would not ignite. Although we have given out two samples of powder for chemical analysis, we have not received either report at this time.

All the shells are made of bronze and are hollow. They all have a fuse opening and all had the fuse in place or pushed inside of the shell. All still contained gunpowder that was moist when first opened and had nearly solidified over the years. Four of the six shells have marks stamped on their sides. Two of the shells have the same mark. Although many inquiries have been made regarding these marks; their meanings remain unknown. Several theories have been postulated but none seems to make good sense. They do not appear to be manufacturer's marks as they are too different and two of the shells are unmarked. One idea is that the marks may have helped to increase the fragmentation of the shells. This is unlikely, due to the fact that they were individualized and the mark on one shell is quite intricate. Another theory is that they were to show which howitzer was to fire that particular shell. It is also a possibility that the marks were to indicate a variation in the amount of powder they contained. The only plausible idea is that they were personal inscriptions made by the crew, much like the crew of a modern-day air force bomber might personalize its bombs. Some of the shells also have a small rust mark opposite the fuse holes. These are likely from the manufacturing process.

A total of six howitzer shells were found at three sites. The first howitzer shell (later destroyed by the army) was found in 41WH92 at a depth of 26 centimeters (top of shell). It weighs 11.4 kilograms (25 pounds) and is 15.8 centimeters (approximately 6.25 inches) in diameter. The marking on this shell consists of three intersecting lines measuring 62 centimeters, 73 centimeters, and 74 centimeters in length, resembling an asterisk. The second shell was found directly under the first. The top of the second shell was at a depth of 53 centimeters. It weighs 10.9 kilograms (24 pounds) and is 15.7 centimeters (approximately 6.25 inches) in diameter. Fuse opening diameter is 2.2 centimeters and the casing is 2.1 centimeters thick. The mark chiseled into the casing on this shell consists of four lines. Two lines, 2.6 centimeters in length, converge to form the letter "V," with a smaller line, 1.4 centimeters in length, midpoint below the convergence, so it reads "A." A fourth line, 2.6 centimeters in length, is above and touching the apex of the "A."

The third howitzer shell was discovered at 41WH95. It was the only shell found at this site. The top of this shell was at a depth of 17 centimeters. It weighs 12.9 kilograms (28 pounds) and measures 15.8 centimeters (approximately 6.25 inches) in diameter. Fuse opening diameter is 2.1 centimeters and shell casing thickness is 2.8 centimeters. This shell has a much more elaborate marking than the others [Fig. 10-1].

The last three shells were unearthed at 41WH92. The top shell was found at a depth of 20.5 centimeters. It weighs 12.2 kilograms (27 pounds) and measures 15.8 centimeters (approximately 6.25 inches). Its fuse opening diameter is 2.4 centimeters and the shell casing thickness is 2.3 centimeters at the fuse hole. The middle shell was found at 36.5 centimeters and weighs 10.9 kilograms (24 pounds). It has a diameter of 16.1 centimeters (approximately 6.25 inches), with a fuse opening diameter of 1.9 centimeters and a shell casing that is 2.0 centimeters thick. The bottom shell was at a depth of 52.5 centimeters. It weighs 12.9 kilograms (28 pounds) and has a diameter of 15.8 centimeters (approximately 6.25 inches). The fuse hole is 2.1 centimeters and the casing is 2.8 centimeters thick at the fuse hole. These three shells were found in a vertical column; the top two shells were in contact with the shell below.

There is some doubt as to whether these shells would have been carried in a loaded state and, if so, whether the fuses would have been left in place during transport. The Royal Artillery Historical

Trust in London was contacted for an opinion on this subject.[10] They informed us that the howitzer shells of that day were usually loaded with gunpowder at the time of manufacture. They also reported that it would be unlikely that the shells would be primed (placing the fuse into the fuse hole) until a target was chosen. The fuse was usually cut to the proper length according to the distance to the target. Their expert opinion was that our shells being primed suggests that the gun positions were prepared for action and then later evacuated—perhaps in a hurry—leaving some ammunition behind. The fact that three howitzer shells were found together in a vertical column, and in another location two were stacked in a similar fashion makes it likely that the shells were intentionally buried. There is no way that the shells could have ended up in this configuration, unless they were buried. It is possible that when the Texans presented to the rearguard of the Mexican army the howitzer crews placed fuses in several shells, in case there was to be trouble. When the howitzer crews moved on they probably had no desire to carry potentially dangerous primed shells, so they buried them to keep the Texans from getting the shells. There is no record of the howitzers being in position during these days. In fact Filisola specifically commented that when the Texans presented to the rearguard of the Mexican army on May 2 the only thing Ampudia was able to do was swing around two four-pounders, the only cannons he could get out on the mud, to face the enemy.[11]

The fuses were wooden plugs that were hollow down the center. They were filled with a gunpowder/alcohol mixture that would burn as the shell was in flight toward its target. In *Artillery through the Ages,* Albert Manucy states that the cannoneer cut the fuse to the proper length. He also adds that a paper cap covered the head of the fuse and had to be removed before the shell was put into the gun.[12] One of the six fuses recovered from our site had remnants of the cover and the string that tied the cover in place [Fig. 10-2].

There is one more clue that the shells were not transported

10. Brig. K. A. Timbers, Historical Secretary, Royal Artillery Historical Trust (personal correspondence, Dec. 2, 1997).

11. Filisola, *Evacuation of Texas,* 44.

12. Albert Manucy, *Artillery through the Ages* (1949; reprint, Washington, D.C.: U.S. Government Printing Office, 1962), 66.

∞

primed. Two lead cylinders have been excavated that are the right size for plugs for the fuse holes [Fig. 10-3]. They are striated on the outside and some of the fuse holes of the shells appear to have matching scratch marks [Fig. 10-4]. It is possible that these lead plugs were for transporting the shells and were replaced with the fuses when primed.

The La Villita excavation at the Alamo in 1985 found a similar shell. That shell was 17.3–17.5 centimeters in diameter and weighed 10.65 kilograms. The author of that section of the La Villita report (Nesmith, pages 63 and 73) concludes that this was a seven-inch shell. A Spanish inch or *pulgada* is .916 inches; thus seven *pulgadas* would equal 6.412 inches. As the shells had to be smaller than the bore of the howitzer (the difference is referred to as windage), the size of our shells is very consistent with a seven-*pulgada*, or 6.5-inch howitzer shell.

There is ample documentation in the Mexican literature of the existence of four seven-*pulgada* howitzers participating in the 1836 Texas campaign. Filisola reported that the first division had two seven-*pulgada* howitzers and likewise the second infantry brigade of the second division.[13] The San Luis Battalion report noted that there were two howitzers that entered San Antonio with Santa Anna and the advance Mexican forces on February 23, 1836. When fired upon by the Texans' eighteen-pounder from the Alamo, the Mexicans responded by lobbing four howitzer shells into the midst of the Texans. The same report went on to detail the arrival of the other two howitzers in San Antonio between March 7 and March 10. It also documented the departure of one of the howitzers with the San Luis and Jiménez Battalions as they left San Antonio on March 11 to join General Urrea.[14] This last detail is important as it places at least one of the howitzers with Urrea and subsequently with the retreating forces that occupied our sites. Urrea mentioned that he took a howitzer with him on April 22 as he left Columbia for Brazoria. (Castañeda translated this as a mortar but the original Spanish shows that Urrea called it an *obús*. The other sources used the same term—

13. Filisola, *Memorias para la historia de la guerra de Tejas* (Rafael, 1848, 1849), Woolsey translation, *Memoirs for the History of the War in Texas*, II, 150–151.

14. San Luis Battalion Daily Log, Feb. 23, Mar. 11, 1836.

obús—when referring to the howitzers).[15] Both the Peña diary and the general orders for April 25 reported that the first brigade and the second brigade each had a howitzer with them as they departed Powell's on the morning of April 26.[16]

Howitzers were invented by the Dutch in the seventeenth century. They usually threw explosive shells or bombs and were normally lighter and more mobile and required only half the powder charge of regular cannons. They also had a higher trajectory similar to mortars. Mortars were even shorter than howitzers but they had a fixed elevation of 45 degrees. The only way to change the range of a mortar was to adjust the charge.[17] The range of a howitzer shell could be adjusted by changing the angle of the tube and by cutting the fuse to the desired length. The rate of burn of the fuse was constant so the gunner would cut the fuse based on the distance from the target. The fuse of the howitzer shell would ignite upon the firing of the tube and if properly timed the shell would explode just as it arrived at the intended target.[18]

An inventory of artillery munitions from the Mexican army dated February 6, 1833, has been provided to us by Kevin Young. The inventory lists many types and sizes of ammunition including "shells of bronze, 7 pulgadas (6.412 inches), loaded." There is also a separate listing for the same shells, unloaded. It is also noted that fuses are listed as a separate item. This fact supports the contention that the shells were not transported with fuses in place. It is interesting to note that, at that time, the Spanish word for a howitzer shell was *granada*. This is the same word used in the San Luis report for the shells that were shot at the Alamo in response to the Texans' first salvo from their eighteen-pounder.

Another source that mentioned howitzer shells is Andrade's list of items abandoned or destroyed as he withdrew from San Antonio. As mentioned previously, this list appeared in the unpublished clean version of the Peña diary but was omitted from the final draft.

15. Urrea, "Diario de las operaciones militares," *Documentos para la historia de la guerra de Tejas*; translated in Castañeda (trans. and ed.), *The Mexican Side of the Texas Revolution,* 249.

16. Peña, *La rebelión de Texas,* 183; ibid., Anexo 6W, pp. 252–253.

17. Wise and Hook, *Artillery Equipments of the Napoleonic Wars,* 14.

18. Manucy, *Artillery through the Ages,* 56.

Among the items on the list were: sixty-four unloaded shells for a seven-and-one-half-*pulgada* howitzer, sixty-three unloaded shells for a seven-*pulgada* howitzer, and twenty-seven cans of canister for a seven-*pulgada* howitzer. As all our shells were nearly the same diameter, it is believed that they were meant to be fired from a seven-*pulgada* howitzer.[19]

It is possible that two of the four Mexican howitzers used in Texas are now located at West Point. According to Walter Nock, museum specialist at the academy, there are two such howitzers listed in the 1914 Artillery Catalog. There is a 6.5-inch bronze howitzer inscribed "El Ecla" that was captured at Matamoros on May 18, 1846, and a 6.5-inch bronze howitzer inscribed "El Vesubio," which was captured at Contreras on August 20, 1847. El Vesubio likely means Vesuvius.[20]

A solid brass, or bronze, cannon ball was found about two hundred yards south of the three howitzer shells that were found in one unit at 46WH92. At this time it is the only such ball excavated from our sites. It is 3.34 inches (8.45 centimeters) in diameter and weighs 61.5 grams. Two additional solid iron cannon balls were found as well. They are 3.64 inches (9.6 centimeters) and 3.58 inches (9.4 centimeters) in diameter. They weigh 6 pounds, 2 ounces and 5 pounds, 14 ounces. As both of these were heavily rusted, the weights may not be accurate. Comparing these two iron balls with the two found at the original site (42WH91) indicates that they are probably for the same size cannon. The first two balls are 3.54 inches in diameter and weigh 6 pounds. The bronze ball mentioned above is .2 to .3 inches smaller in diameter. According to Filisola the retreating army had two four-pounders, two six-pounders, two eight-pounders, and two howitzers. It seems likely that the bronze ball was meant for one of the four-pounders and the iron balls were to be fired from one of the six-pounders. It is possible that the six-pounder iron balls were captured from the Texans at the Alamo or Goliad, considering that the Mexican artillery used bronze projectiles more frequently than iron.

A large variety of brass furniture parts from India Pattern mus-

19. Peña, unpublished clean copy of his diary, pp. 100-101, Peña Papers (CAH).

20. Walter J. Nock, museum specialist, West Point Musuem (personal correspondence, May 28, 1999).

kets were discovered. These are described in detail in chapter four. Another brass musket piece that was found is a butt plate. This thick plate would protect the stock from wear and tear. It had two holes though which two large iron screws attached it to the wood of the stock. Fragments of these iron screws have been found in some of the butt plates.

Many brass military buttons were found along the trail. Two buttons with the number "6" inscribed on them, the same type found at Madam Powell's, were unearthed. There were also two buttons with the number "1" on the face of the button [Fig. 10-5]. These are a different style than the number "6" buttons, as they are convex and have a raised ring around the "1." The number "1" on both of the buttons is stylized, and almost appears to be a letter "j." As mentioned previously, there were no numbered units in the Mexican army during the Alamo period. After 1832 the battalions were named for Mexican revolution heroes, famous battle sites, or the unit's place of origin. There was one unit, however, that may still have used a number in its uniforms. The First Active Battalion of Mexico was sometimes referred to as the "First" and could have had a "1" as its logo. These "1" buttons seem to be more in the "Spanish style" and are likely to be pre-1832, possibly even older than the flat "6" buttons. There are no backmarks on the "1" buttons and like the "6" buttons they are of one piece and have a pinched shank. These pinched shanks are more in the Spanish style as well.

One very unusual button was found that has an exploding bomb insignia on the front. It was likely the button from the uniform of a grenadier (or possibly from one of an artilleryman, as he used the same emblem as the grenadier). There is a design around the entire outer edge of the button, which is rare on the Mexican buttons recovered at our site. This is a one-piece button and has a complete shank. It is 23 millimeters in diameter [Fig. 10-6].

Several "bullet buttons" were found along the trail. These buttons are so named due to their similarity to a musket ball. One of the "bullet buttons" had no back, but was found to have two pieces of wood inside, which likely formed an insert that gave support to the button. There were two brass buttons with floral designs found, as well as one with a star pattern. The star button had one large star in the middle and several small ones around the edge [Fig. 10-7].

Several plain brass buttons were found with back marks that

indicated English manufacture. The backmarks read; "Fine Treble Gilt HG & CO," "Warranted Rich Orange," "Orange Gilt Colour," "Orange Colour," etc. The "HG" and "CO." most likely stood for the Henry Grillery Co., which produced buttons from 1807 to 1808. These buttons tended to be of one piece, with round shanks.

Another item added to our knowledge of the period Mexican army accoutrements. Initially felt to be a knife handle, it was later identified as a cane handle. It is eleven centimeters in length and is made of brass. The handle is broken where it would have turned down and attached to the cane. It has a simple design of parallel curved lines on the top and both sides [Fig. 10-8]. Mexican military artist Joseph Hefter illustrated several of his soldiers carrying canes in his images of Mexican army uniforms.[21]

A nosecap for a pistol holster was found on the trail. It is brass and 4.5 centimeters in diameter. At the top are two small holes with iron pins that attached it to the leather-and-wooden base of the holster. Several fragments of wood were found inside the object. There is a tip that projects out 1.2 centimeters. There are two parallel circles etched into the top and two pair of parallel circles around the side [Fig. 10-9].

An unidentified object is pictured in [Fig. 10-10]. It is brass and has a radiating design on the face. It is 6.1 centimeters in diameter and has an attached, raised circular center, which is 1.4 centimeters in diameter. There are 42 lines radiating outward from the center to the edge. It weighs 54.4 grams and is two millimeters in thickness. The back of the emblem is plain and has two connectors, one of which has been broken. The distance between the connectors is 5.4 centimeters. The thickness of this artifact, the size of its connectors, and the distance between the connectors is nearly identical to that of the cross-belt plate. It is possible that this is a cross-belt plate for a different unit.

Toward the northern end of the Mar de Lodo a brass candle-holder was recovered [Fig. 10-11]. It is 10.5 centimeters in height and the drip pan at the top is 4.7 centimeters in diameter. The round base is five centimeters in diameter and has an oxidized area on the bottom of the base, suggesting an attachment to an iron object. There is a knob and a slot on the side of the tube that allowed for

21. Nieto et al., *El soldado mexicano,* 33, 40, 46.

adjustment of the height of the candle. Inside the tube is an adjustable metal platform with a pointed center, on which to attach the candle. Another candleholder, of nearly identical construction and size, was discovered at Madam Powell's. It was bent to the point that it could not be accurately measured. It is possible that the candleholder found in the Mar de Lodo was a match to that at Powell's and may have even come from her home.

Several eating utensils made of brass were found throughout the site [Fig. 10-12]. Most were spoons; some were just utensil handles. The spoons and handles show remnants of silver plating, and several are quite decorative. None had any identifying marks or manufacturer's marks. It is possible that these were part of the plunder that Peña complained required the use of so many of the mules.

Two brass rosettes, designed to be bridle decorations, were recovered. The back of each rosette is concave and the face has a layered, gradually smaller series of four circles. The base of the lower circle is 3.4 centimeters in diameter and the pinnacle or top circle is .8 centimeters in diameter. One of the rosettes has two connectors on opposite ends that extend outward .9 centimeters from each edge and are .9 centimeters wide. Each connector has a five-millimeter hole near the distal end. The connectors of the second rosette are broken off [Fig. 10-13].

Three small, brass fragments were excavated [Fig. 10-14]. Two of these fragments fit together to form a letter "p." The third fragment appears to be part of a letter as well, but not part of a "p." All three fragments have small connectors extending from their backs. The letter may have served as a collar insignia, with the "p" possibly standing for *permanente*.

Brass tacks were found in several places along the route [Fig. 10-15]. The average length of the tacks is 1.8 centimeters and the average weight is 1.3 grams. The heads are about 8 by 8 millimeters. It is possible that the tacks were used to decorate musket stocks. They also may have been used to construct cases for holding munitions, as brass would not spark and cause an explosion.

Some of the more common artifacts found in the Mar de Lodo were brass/bronze canister shot. Occasionally they were found in clusters, suggesting that they came from a spilled can of canister. Unlike the first site at 46WH91 none of these cans was found intact. Neither were there any can fragments discovered. The size difference of the brass canister shot is even more pronounced than that of the lead. The smaller or light canister shot has a diameter range of 2.1 centimeters to 2.7 centimeters and weighs from 53.7 grams to 79.3 grams; average weight is 66.4 grams. There are several with casting lines visible and they tend to be poorly cast; many being off center. The larger brass canister shot measures 3.1 centimeters to 3.6 centimeters and weighs from 131.5 to 174.8 grams; average weight of the larger canister is 152.9 grams [Fig. 10-16].

The use of brass or copper shot by the Mexican army apparently caused heated feelings among the Texans and the Americans. A common belief at the time was that copper shot was extremely poisonous. It was generally accepted that even a slight wound from a copper ball would lead to death. One example of this belief is found in the account of the battle of San Jacinto by Dr. N. D. Labadie.[22] Dr. Labadie related that on the afternoon of April 20, during a skirmish with the Mexicans, a young private in the Texan Cavalry, Olwyn J. Trask, was brought in with his thigh bone broken by a ball. On examination Labadie felt that the ball remained in the leg and it was likely a grape-shot (canister) or a one-ounce musket ball. He later saw Trask at Zavalla's house, at which time Trask told him he was wounded when the cannon fired, but he was unaware whether the ball was lead or copper. Labadie wrote that he advised that the leg be amputated as he felt that it was a copper ball. He reported that he went so far as to call on the captured captain of the Mexican artillery who confirmed that the only canister they fired were four-ounce copper balls. By the time Trask was moved to Galveston his leg was too bad to amputate and he died of his wound three weeks later. After his death a copper ball was found in his right knee.

Another example of the feelings regarding the Mexican army's use of copper shot and canister is found in a letter written by George Dolson to his brother in Detroit. Dolson, a member of the Cincinnati Volunteers, arrived at San Jacinto just after the battle. Even though he had not participated in the fight, he gave a great deal of detail concerning the battle in his letter of May 24, 1836. The letter was published in the *Detroit Free Press* and the story was picked up by the *Morning Courier and New York Enquirer* of July 18, 1836.

22. Labadie, "San Jacinto Campaign," 171, 174–175.

At the battle of San Jacinto, there were six hundred Texians and about twelve hundred Mexicans. besides [*sic*] fifty officers. The engagement had lasted not more than ten minutes when the Alabama Riflemen boldly charged on the Mexican artillery, and so completely routed them, that, obtaining possession of their guns [*sic*], before they had time to discharge them, *quicker than Alabama lightning*, turned their own guns upon them; and dreadful was the fire for the Mexicans, for they had, themselves, loaded the guns with copper grape [canister], which is so poisonous that it is almost impossible to effect a cure even of the slightest wound. there [*sic*] are about two hundred of the Mexicans wounded in this manner [considering that one canister shot would have contained approximately forty balls and the Mexicans had only one cannon, this number is seemingly a great exaggeration].[23]

The unnamed writer of the story for the *Courier and Enquirer* expounded on Dolson's comments regarding the copper shot in his introduction to Dolson's letter.

Some of the incidents will be new to the reader. If, for instance, the Mexicans had really loaded their guns with copper shot, the *Lex Talionis*[24] was never more appropriately exercised than when the Texians captured the felon artillery and turned it against the savages who had provided themselves with such ammunition. The Seminoles are said to have shot silver at the beleaguered blockhouse in Florida, but it was left to the Mexican Goths to fire copper into the ranks of their "opponents," as Santa Anna politely terms the Texians after they had captured him.[25]

It is interesting to note that the Texans felt the Mexican army was depraved for the use of copper shot. The Texans claimed the high moral ground as they used lead shot. How ironic that lead is now known to be poisonous and copper innocuous. It is possible, how-

23. George Dolson, Letter, *Morning Courier and New York Enquirer*, July 18, 1836.
24. *Lex Talionis* is the law of equal and direct distribution, i.e., an eye for an eye.
25. Unknown author, *Morning Courier and New York Enquirer*, July 18, 1836.

ever, that the arsenic used in the extraction of the copper may have been present in sufficient quantities to have caused damage.

There were many musket balls found scattered through the area. The majority were for the .75-calibre India Pattern muskets. Some small lead shot was found that might have been for pistols. One other possibility is that these small shot were used for buck and ball. This was when two or three small balls were placed in the same cartridge with one large ball. Two of the musket balls were unique from the others. They were made of copper. They measure 1.73 and 1.88 centimeters in diameter and weigh 26.8 and 34.7 grams [Fig. 10-17].

A very interesting coin was unearthed on the trail. The date is illegible but it has been identified as a 1750s-style French coin [Fig. 10-18]. The wide variety of coinage found at the Mexican sites, as well as mentioned in the Mexican accounts, supports the fact that the army was desperate for coinage and used almost any that was available.

One flint for a flintlock musket or pistol was found on the surface. It is likely that there are many more in our site but as they are not metal we cannot find them with a detector. There was also a lead pad that was used to secure the flint in the hammer of the musket. It is broken into two pieces but was likely of one piece originally.

Since the site of the Mar de Lodo was first published in the *Houston Archeological Society Journal*, a unique artifact has been discovered. It is a totally different type of flaming bomb insignia. Due to its size it seems to be a cross-belt plate. The scroll on the face of the bomb has been associated with hat wear, so another possibility is that it is a shako plate. To the knowledge of the author no other similar flaming bomb insignia have been found. It is likely that different grenadier companies had their own style of bombs [Fig. 10-19]. There is also a possibility that this style of flaming bomb was used by the artillerymen.

Another button was discovered that might predate the Sixth Battalion button described in chapter four. This button is brass and is inscribed "B.D.L. No. 6" [Fig. 10-20]. In English this would be Battalion of the line—No. 6.

A brass cockade was excavated at our site. This is a very thin round item that connected to the top of a shako. It would have been painted red, white, and green, the national colors of Mexico [Fig. 10-21].

Chaos

Fig. 10-1. Bronze howitzer shell.

Fig. 10-2. Wooden howitzer fuse.

Fig. 10-3. Lead plug.

Fig. 10-4. Howitzer shell fuse hole.

Fig. 10-5. First Battalion brass button.

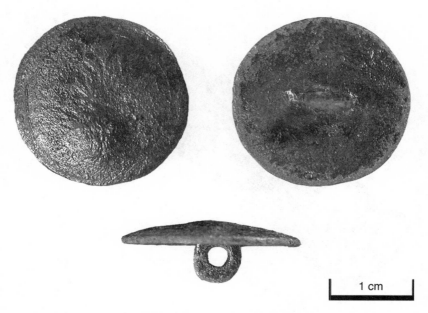

Fig. 10-6. Brass exploding bomb button.

Fig. 10-7. Brass "star" button.

Fig. 10-8. Brass cane handle.

1 cm

Fig. 10-9. Brass holster nosecap.

1 cm

Fig. 10-10. Brass emblem.

_1 cm_

Fig. 10-11. Brass candleholder.

_1 cm_

243

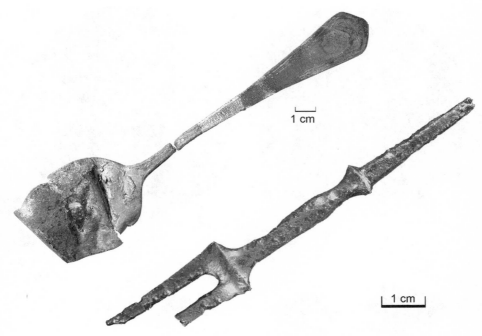

Fig. 10-12. Brass silver-coated spoon and iron fork.

1 cm

1 cm

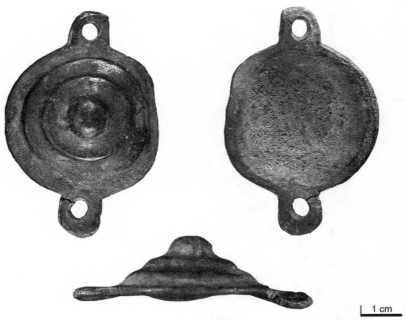

1 cm

Fig. 10-13. Brass bridle rosette.

Fig. 10-14. Brass letter "p" (collar insignia?).

Fig. 10-15. Brass tacks.

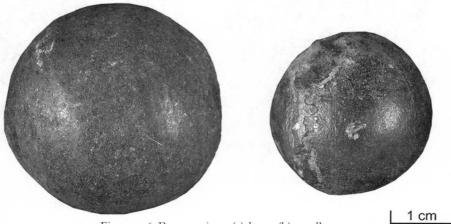

Fig. 10-16. Brass canister (a) large (b) small.

Fig. 10-17. Copper musket balls.

Fig. 10-18. French coin (circa 1750).

1 cm

Fig. 10-19. Brass grenadier or artillery exploding bomb insignia.

Fig. 10-20. Brass "Battalion of the line" button.

Fig. 10-21. Brass cockade.

CHAPTER 11

The Texans Arrive

AFTER THE BATTLE OF SAN JACINTO the Texans and the Mexican army had little interaction. Deaf Smith had sent Santa Anna's orders to Filisola by means of the captured presidial soldier on April 27th. Smith had no interaction with any other Mexican soldiers except the ones that shot at him.[1] Adrian Woll did arrive at the Texan's camp at San Jacinto. He was detained there for over a week so that he could not report back to Filisola regarding the strength and condition of the Texan army.[2] Other than these two minor events the two opposing forces had kept their distance from one another.

That all changed on May 1 when the Texans presented to the rear of the Mexican army. They found the remnants of the Mexican column in a miserable situation. At that location all that remained of the army was the bogged-down artillery and wagons, the wounded, and those pickets of troops that had been left, under the command of Pedro de Ampudia, to help clean up the mess.

In his letter to the Mexican government from Victoria on May 14, Filisola reported that about three hundred of the enemy had shown up at the rear, where the cannons and baggage were scattered. He wrote that the enemy had opened communications with

1. See chapter 7, footnote no. 5.

2. For an excellent discussion of Adrian Woll's trials and tribulations in the Texan camp and on his return to Mexico, see Dorothy Virginia Barler Montgomery, "Movements of the Mexican Army in Texas after the Battle of San Jacinto" (M.A. thesis, Sul Ross University, 1970), 146–151.

Ampudia. According to Filisola the artillery was so bogged down that Ampudia was only able to maneuver two four-pounders to face the enemy. He was able to muster only about one hundred infantrymen to prepare for a possible attack.

There are several letters between the Mexicans and Texans that tell of the interactions. The following letter tells of the reaction of Filisola to the Texans' appearance.

> To the commander of the Forces coming from Galveston:
>   Sir—
>   It is now 8 o'clock at night, and Mr. Joe Wells has presented to me a passport from His Excellency, the President of the Republic, Don Antonio Lopez de Santa Anna, with a pass from general Houston, stating that he is the bearer of dispatches; but had arrived without them, because Mr. Fulcher, who accompanied him, remained behind: I am consequently ignorant of the contents. By the couriers I learn that you are coming on with a force under your command: and I judge that the aforesaid dispatches contain advice of this movement, as, however, I am not certain of it, I trust that until I receive them, you will be pleased not to come within sight of my troops, for in this state of uncertainty, a disagreeable result might ensue; whereas this army is repassing the Colorado, pursuant to the agreement entered into by His Excellency the President, Don Antonio Lopez de Santa Anna, and which in good faith we wish to fulfill. In the enclosed paper, Mr. Wells requests his companion to send him the said dispatches, and I hope you will forward them to me, for the purpose of complying with the instructions contained in them, and to communicate them to the different divisions under my command.
>
> God and Liberty.
> Vicente Filisola
> River Colorado, May 2, 1836[3]

From this letter it is apparent that initially Filisola had no idea

3. Filisola to Commander, May 2, 1836, in Jenkins (ed.), *Papers of the Texas Revolution,* VI, 149.

who he was dealing with, what their force was, or even where they were coming from. Somehow the courier that was sent into his camp arrived without the dispatches that were intended for him. For this reason Filisola held him in his camp. This detention of the courier was later to become a cause of friction between the two forces. As no mention of the arrival of these dispatches is later documented it seems possible that this story was concocted by Wells in order to gain entry into the Mexican camp. It is interesting that General Woll, who had bent sent to spy on the Texans, and Joe Wells, probably sent to spy on the Mexicans, were both being held in the opposing camps.

Filisola claimed in his May 14 letter to the Mexican government that since he did not want to compromise himself with any treaties Santa Anna had made with the enemy, he gave only vague instructions to Ampudia to save all that he could of the rearguard and cross the Colorado. Ampudia wrote Juan Seguín on May 2. Juan Nepomuceno Seguin, a native of San Antonio, was a messenger for Travis from the Alamo, fought with his Tejano company at San Jacinto, and commanded San Antonio after it was abandoned by the Mexican army. It is apparent that the Texans were wise enough to leave their forces out of sight. Thus, the Mexicans were unaware as to their number.

From General Pedro de Ampudia
    To Juan Seguín (incorrectly addressed to Erasmo Seguín, Juan's father)
    Contraband Marsh, Quarter until eight in the evening, May 2, 1836

By way of a report from the officer charged with assisting the sick, I am informed that there is a large force in those woods, which, according to you, has its sole objective the recovery of black slaves and such as may belong to the citizens of this country. In regard to the former, I say to you that there are no slaves at this place and, with regard to the latter, that I have no knowledge of any property belonging to the individuals who accompany you.
    You assert that you come in peace, his Excellency the President being in negotiations, and therefore a suspension

∞

The Texans Arrive

of hostilities is presently being observed. Under such circumstances, I hope you will order or persuade whomever is in command to order that your force does not advance until permission has been received from his excellency, Commanding General Don Vicente Filisola, [and be] assured that on the part of the division under my command there will be no hostile acts. However, if without that permission your force wishes to advance, I will carry out my duty.

The said commander in chief, to whom I am giving an account at this moment, is with part of the army some four leagues distant. In any case these matters, as you must understand, should be resolved exclusively between the commanding generals of the contending forces.

God and Liberty
Pedro de Ampudia[4]

It is interesting that the adversaries were obviously posturing. The Texans were there to find out the numbers and positions of Filisola's forces. No doubt they were anxious to make sure the Mexicans were indeed retreating, as Santa Anna had ordered. Seguín claimed that they were not there for any hostilities but were only looking for escaped slaves and captured plunder. Ampudia knew there were slaves and plunder with the main force of the army but claimed that neither was to be found in the Mexican camp. Technically Ampudia may have been telling the truth. There probably were not any slaves with him at the far rear of the army. He also did not say the Mexican army had no plunder; just that he had no knowledge of it.

There was some disparity in the record as to exactly which, and how many, Texans showed up at the Mexican rear on May 1. One account, by one of the participating Texans, stated that Col. Ed Burleson commanded the three hundred Texans. Walter P. Lane, an eighteen-year-old private in the Texan army, who at the time had been in Texas for about two weeks, gave the following account of the initial contact of the two forces:

---

4. Jesús F. de la Teja, *A Revolution Remembered: The Memoirs and Selected Correspondence of Juan N. Seguín* (Austin: State House Press, 1991), 137–138.

A few days after the battle of San Jacinto, Col. Ed. Burleson started to find Gen. Filasola [sic], near the San Bernard. He had some three hundred men. He had an order from Santa Anna for Filasola to surrender or vacate the country. We camped on the San Bernard one evening, and some of our men, who were in bathing, swam over, and happened to go through a skirt of willows on the other side, and saw Gen. Filasola's army encamped on the prairie. They came back and gave the alarm, when Col. Burleson and some others swam their horses over. We were drawn up opposite the ford, with orders, if we heard anything to swim over and succor them. In about an hour they came back. Filasola, after reading Santa Anna's order, told Burleson he would give an answer next morning. At 9 o'clock next morning our officers went over again. In a few minutes Deaf Smith came back and told us Filasola had retreated in the night, and his camp was vacant. Quite a number of us swam over to see the enemy's camp. They had left wagons, muskets, lances, scopetes,[5] and every thing they could not carry on pack mules, and cut out at 12 o'clock the night before, burning the carriage of six pieces of artillery, and throwing the guns in a pond.

I was sauntering through the camp with the others, when we came to some big wagons with covers on them. While looking at them, I picked up a lance, and, to exercise my juvenile arm, threw it at one of them, when a loud yell came from the wagon: 'Por la amor de Dios no mortar usta dor!' [sic] ('For the love of God, don't kill us!').

Some twenty sick and wounded Mexicans were in the wagons, having been left by their comrades. We gave them something to eat and treated them kindly. We sent a detachment to follow Filasola, and see that he did not damage the settlers in his retreat. He made a straight march for the Rio Grande, via San Antonio, and never 'drew rein' till he got into Mexico.[6]

5. *Escopeta* is Spanish for a firearm or gun and was commonly used by the Texans to describe the Mexican carbines (shortened muskets).

6. Walter P. Lane, *The Adventures and Recollections of General Walter P. Lane, A San Jacinto Veteran* . . . (1928; reprint, Austin: Pemberton Press, 1970), 18–19.

Walter Lane wrote his memoirs nearly fifty years after the fact. He himself labeled his recollections as semihistorical. He had been in Texas only two weeks when this incident took place so it is likely that his knowledge of the geography of the area was lacking. The incident probably took place on the Middle Bernard and not the San Bernard. Lane may well have been confused by the two, as it seems, was Filisola. There can be little doubt that Filisola was already at the Colorado by the time the Texans showed up. Thus the claim that Filisola and the Texan commanders met in person could not have been true. The Mexican army did exit Texas but did so slowly and not through San Antonio, as Lane wrote. It is true that the Mexican wounded were abandoned, but the artillery that Lane claimed was dumped in a pond has not been documented by any Mexican sources, nor has it been discovered during the archeology done at the site.

There are two documents that make it obvious that Col. Burleson was not yet present at the time of the initial contact. It is possible that since one of the Texan commanders was Juan Seguín, Lane intentionally failed to mention him. At the time of Lane's writings Seguín was considered a traitor, by some, for fighting for Mexico in the Mexican American War. The first letter that sheds light on the makeup of this initial Texan force was from Sam Houston to Col. Burleson.

> Head Quarters of the Army
>> Battle Ground San Jacinto 30th April 1836
>> To Col. Edwd. Burleson
>> Sir
>> The commanding General directs your continued vigilance and activity with the Command under your direction—You have no doubt before this discovered the importance of the renewal of this precaution. You will use your discretion whether to remain at Fort Bend or return to the Main Army—In the mean time obtain such information as you can of the Enemy, without risking an action west of the Brazos—You can with your force keep the enemy from crossing, and it will be proper to keep all boats and crafts on this side of the river—The Steam Boat has not returned nor has the President yet arrived—Genl Woll who has come to

Camp does not give very satisfactory information—I do not know what force the Enemy have, nor whether they are falling back—We cannot trust the Enemy. We must watch them—

I have the honor to be
Sam Houston
Com. In Chief [7]

This letter shows that on April 30 Sam Houston felt that Burleson was still at Fort Bend. He gave Burleson two choices—stay and guard the crossing of the river at Fort Bend, or fall back and join the army. At that point Houston was obviously still worried about a possible enemy attack. He still had no idea where the Mexican army was or what it was up to.

A second Houston letter, to Henry Wax Karnes, further clarified which Texans had presented to the rear of the Mexican army.

> Headquarters of the Army, Camp on San Jacinto, 3d May, 1836.
>
> To Captain Karnes:
>
> Sir, I have received with great pleasure the intelligence communicated in your last favor. Colonel Burleson (who is directed to advance and with whom you will unite the forces under your command) has general instructions which I hope will be sufficient for your guidance. So long as the enemy are faithful in their retreat they will not be molested, but you are required to use utmost vigilance and not suffer surprise nor permit any unnecessary encroachment upon them or their property.
>
> Sam Houston, Commander in Chief [8]

From this letter it may be gleaned that as of May 3 Houston had ordered Burleson to join Karnes at the rear of the Mexican army. It is apparent that Houston did not believe that Burleson had yet

---

7. Houston to Burleson, Apr. 30, 1836, A. J. Houston Papers (Texas State Library, Archives Division, Austin, Texas).

8. Houston to Karnes, May 3, 1836, in Jenkins (ed.), *Papers of the Texas Revolution,* VI, 154.

arrived at that point. From these two letters and others yet to be discussed, it seems likely that the initial force of Texans was comprised of about a hundred men under the command of Karnes and Seguín. Most likely Burleson did not arrive on the scene until later. Only after his arrival was the Texan force composed of the three hundred men that Filisola and Lane reported.

Peña mentioned the appearance of the Texans at the Mexican rear as well. He confirmed that it was Karnes and Seguín who were initially involved. He also documented the detention of the Texan courier in the Mexican camp.

> On the 2nd and 3rd, Señor Ampudia had some disputes with Mr. Henry Karns and with Don Juan Nepomuceno Seguín regarding claims they made about the delay of A Texas courier in our camp, as well as about some Negroes and other properties. They were commanding a small force and promised not to interfere with us.[9]

In the Cumplido edition of *Memorias* Filisola gave a more detailed account of the interaction between the two forces. He remarked that on May 2 he sent the preferential companies of the Morelos and Guadalajara Battalions to reinforce Ampudia and the rearguard. He did this due to the fact that Juan Seguín, with a force of the Béjar rebels, had presented to the rearguard. It is interesting that Seguín was identified by Filisola as the commander of the Texans. It is certainly possible that Seguín corresponded with the Mexicans due to his ability to speak Spanish. It is also likely that Seguín was either in command or at least sharing the command with Karnes. Filisola went on to say that Seguín

> declared that he did not carry any orders for hostility and that they were only trying to reclaim those possessions and slaves that were in the control of individuals of the army. These were possessions of the proprietors of Texas, as it had been agreed upon in the armistice between their leaders and the president. They also were to expedite the re-crossing of

9. Peña, *La rebelión de Texas*, 189; translated in Perry (trans. and ed.), *With Santa Anna in Texas*, 170.

the Colorado by the troops, so that the colonists could return to investigate their homes and interests located on the left bank. He also requested that we accelerate our crossing of the river, because even though they [Seguín's troops] were under his command they were undisciplined. For the most part they were volunteers and it was difficult to contain them. Our reply was to tell them that the individuals of the army had no such possessions, and that the slaves who had shown up were considered free among us, and they had left to wherever they had wanted; and if he thought that he was incapable of controlling his volunteers he could leave their containment to the Mexican soldiers. [Subsequently] there were no other attempts at communication, and they [Seguín's troops] were content to remain as guards, without any attempt to engage, while we crossed the Colorado, and took our position on the right bank. And this is how our progress to the Atascosito Pass unfolded rather than how Mr. Urrea represents it, as having been driven by fear instead of by a prudent military precaution. Is it not possible to imagine that just as the enemy appeared at our rearguard, he [the enemy] could have easily appeared at our vanguard at the Atascosito?[10]

In this version, not only does Filisola present himself as the tough guy, but he is able to get in a dig at Urrea for stating that there was never any threat from the enemy to the rear. When evaluating the letters that passed between Filisola, Ampudia, and Seguín, the tough side of Filisola is not so apparent.

Camp on the Sandy Bernard, May 4, 1836.
    Col. N Seguín Sir—An officer from your camp came to me yesterday morning, acquainting me that his companions were surprised that their courier, and wished to know the reason of it [sic]. I informed him that he passed through our camp; that the affair was a very simple one, for even the despatches [sic] of the President were not answered within

10. Filisola, *Memorias para la historia de la guerra de Tejas* (Cumplido, 1849), I, 238–239.

one hour of their reception; nor do I believe that General
Filisola will, for the sake of one man, infringe the armistice,
and especially, when the honor of the chief magistrate of
Mexico, that of the whole army, and of General Filisola,
himself, is interested in carrying into effect these treaties. I
have written to the General, and the courier will certainly
return today.

Your attentive, obdt. Servt.
Pedro de Ampudia[11]

If Ampudia was telling the truth to Seguín in this letter, he
seemed to have been unaware of the fact that the Texan courier, Joe
Wells, did not even have the mentioned dispatches. He wrote a second letter to Seguín on the same day.

Col. John N. Seguín—Your communication of yesterday
informs us that the forces under your command, forming the
vanguard of that army, will not move from your present station, until the division under my command shall have
crossed the Colorado, agreeably to the armistice made
between His Excellency, the President of the Mexican
Republic, Don Antonio Lopez de Santa Anna, and the commander of the army to which you belong: and have no
doubt it will be complied with on your part. With Lt. Col.
Don Ygnacio Barragan, the bearer of the present despatch, I
forward to the sick the necessary supplies, until His Excellency, Don Vicente Filisola, can take measures for their
removal: and inasmuch as those sick men are on the ground
occupied by your camp, I hope you will in the future attend
to them, as I have been informed you will. General Filisola
has ordered me to preserve strict harmony, so that at no time
it may be said that we proceed in bad faith, and also because
it is not only comfortable for the laws of war, but to the
orders of our President.

God and Liberty.
Pedro de Ampudia

11. Ampudia to Seguín, May 4, 1836, in Jenkins (ed.), *Papers of the Texas Revolution,* VI, 159–160.

This last letter reaffirmed what Lane wrote about the Mexican wounded being abandoned. Filisola was later criticized by Urrea for leaving the sick and wounded at the mercy of the Texans, but Filisola responded with solid logic. He claimed that there were more than one hundred sick and wounded in the wagons mired at the rear of the army. By his account Ampudia ordered that mules be rigged to carry these men and that some of the incapacitated were actually carried on the shoulders of other soldiers. Only the most seriously affected were left in the wagons. He went on to ask what should have been done with these men. Ampudia's men could not extract their wagons from the mud and they were too seriously ill to move from the wagons. Filisola suggested that other than killing them the only option was to leave them, trusting in the humanity of the enemy. He pointed out that the enemy had, up to this point, repeatedly displayed their humanity.

Another member of the Texan unit that presented to the rearguard of the Mexican army, Sterling C. Robertson, documented his view of the action. Part of his account has been mentioned in chapter one because he was also with the Texan troops that followed Cos's wagon train as it fled toward Old Fort. He continued his account and related that he joined a detachment of mounted men and went on a reconnoitering trip in pursuit of Sesma and Filisola, on their retreat out of the country.

> From every appearance presented, by scattered baggage, muskets thrown away, and mules left bogged down in the mud the panic appeared even greater, than among the fugitives; from the field of battle. They left 50 mules, and 14 baggage wagons, in the mud in the distance of ten miles; buried one piece of cannon, and threw at least 1000 stand of arms in the river San Bernard. When the advance of the detachment came up with them, they said they were getting out of the country, as fast as they could; and would obey the orders of

12. Ibid., 159.

Santa Anna, and go to Monte Del Rey [Monterrey] by way of San Antonio. We could have taken at least 1000 men of them, with their mules, and baggage and cannon, if we had been allowed to do so, but as the treaty was on hand we were ordered not to molest them.

If I had had the command, I would have endeavored to have misconstrued my orders, and at least taken their cannon, and arms from them. They had ten pieces of cannon—six pounders: and an immense quantity of plunder, which they had taken from the houses of the citizens of Texas, after they had left them. Our men were all anxious for the contest; flushed with victory, and full of resentment against the Mexicans. On the other side, the officers and soldiers, were nearly frightened to death; and would have surrendered, in one moment, and I think without the firing of a gun. I have no doubt that Gen. Rusk regrets that it was not done, as nothing has been done with regard to the treaty; and he is now on his march after them to San Antonio; at which place I expect, we shall have them to fight, unless we can shew a respectable army.[13]

The above letter was dated May 26 from San Augustine, Texas.

Just as in Lane's version, there are several flaws in Robertson's account. One glaring weakness is that Robertson either failed to mention, or did not know, that the main body of the Mexican army was no longer in the area when the Texans arrived. It is likely that there were no more than 350 to 450 Mexican troops with the rearguard at this time.[14] Therefore it would have been very difficult to

13. Sterling C. Robertson letter, *Morning Courier and New York Enquirer,* July 8, 1836.

14. Filisola said that he sent 20 men from each unit back to help Ampudia (Filisola, *Memorias para la historia de la guerra de Tejas* [Cumplido, 1849], I, 236–238). As there were 8 infantry battalions in the retreat, this would have been 160 men. (This number may be a bit high as Filisola has also stated that Ampudia could muster only 100 infantrymen to face the enemy when they presented. Filisola, *Evacuation of Texas,* 43–44). Filisola states that he sent the preferential units of the Morelos and Guadalajara Battalions to Ampudia as reinforcements (Filisola, *Memorias para la historia de la guerra de Tejas* [Cumplido, 1849], 237–238). Taking the stated strengths of the Morelos—382—and the Guadalajara—254—and dividing by 8, then multiply-

∞

take a thousand Mexican soldiers prisoner. Additionally, the Mexicans, by all their accounts, had only eight pieces of artillery. Obviously they were not all six-pounders as Robertson implied. It is also interesting to note that Robertson, like Lane, stated that the Mexican army proceeded on to San Antonio. Considering that Robertson must have left the army soon after this encounter in order to have written the letter from San Augustine on May 26, it is likely that he assumed that Filisola obeyed the orders of Santa Anna and retreated to San Antonio. This was certainly not the case, as after they crossed the Colorado, the entire Mexican army retreated to Victoria, then Goliad, and on to Matamoros.

Another short description of the retreating Mexican army was given by Col. James Swisher. He remained with the main Texan army. They did not begin to trail the Mexican army until May 10. He stated that, judging from the signs along the way, the retreat must have been a hasty and disorderly one. He noted there were broken-down carts and abandoned plunder along the road. He added that here and there was seen an unburied carcass of a Mexican soldier.[15]

An anonymous account of the retreat of both the main Mexican army and the division in San Antonio was printed in the *Philadelphia Gazette* of July 5, 1836.

Natchitoches, June 13, 1836
    By Dr. _____, and two other gentlemen of Virginia, who reached here from our army yesterday, we have news up to the first of this month, when our army were near La Bahia.

---

ing by 2 (8 companies in each battalion, 2 of which were preferential) gives 95 from the Morelos and 63 from the Guadalajara. If there were 10 to 15 on each of the 8 artillery crews, that would account for another 100 or so men. We know there were 100 sick and wounded, but they would have been of little or no help. Ampudia and Amat documented that Peña had 57 men of the Zapadores Battalion (Peña, *La rebelión de Texas*, Anexo No. 3, Documento IV, pp. 236–237, and Anexo 3, Documento V, p. 237). This would have been an extra 37 men. When totaling these it seems that Ampudia had, at most, about 460 men with him in the rear. It should be remembered that the artillerymen would have been scattered throughout the prairie where their cannons were stuck.

15. John Milton Swisher, *The Swisher Memoirs by Col. John M. Swisher,* ed. Rena Maverick Green (San Antonio: Sigmund Press, 1932), 48.

The enemy had passed there, which was the last place there wos [sic] any apprehension of their making a stand.—The Mexican division at San Antonio had been insulted by the Cumanches [sic] in that place, who took from them all their mules and horses and left them no means to retreat. The enemy spiked all the cannon, threw them into the river, blew up the Alamo, left San Antonio, and joined the main army at La Bahia, as they had no means of conveying their baggage, to enable them to leave by a more direct route for Mexico. The main army, on their retreat between the Colorado and the St. Bernard, lost in one bog upwards of 100 mules, 14 baggage wagons, and made causeways of their muskets to get over the morasses,—burnt the carriages of their cannon, and also buried their guns. This is a true account of the glorious retreat of the Mexican army, consisting of between 4000–5000, who fled thus, lest they might be overtaken by our army of 6 or 700 men. The enemy have now left our country. San Antonio is entirely deserted by its citizens. They say there are not six souls in the place.[16]

There were other Texans who were not at the rear of the Mexican army. Some were actually prisoners who were forced to travel with the retreating army. One Texan's travails were so difficult that they rivaled the tribulations of the Morelos Battalion. Samuel T. Brown was a soldier in Col. William Ward's command. Ward had been sent from Goliad to Refugio by Fannin. At the chapel in Refugio he and his command were surrounded and attacked by Urrea's troops. The Texans were able to slip out of the chapel in the night and began to work their way back north. Brown was captured along with Ward and eighty-five men near Victoria on March 22, 1836. They were marched to Goliad and were part of the Texan troops that were executed on Palm Sunday. Brown was able to escape the execution and, along with John Duval and a man named Holliday, worked his way north. During this escapade he was actually captured once by Mexican cavalry but something spooked them off and he was allowed to go free. Brown reached the Colorado River with Holliday but was unable to swim it due to a bad arm. There he was

16. Reprinted in the *Morning Courier and New York Enquirer,* July 6, 1836.

∞

separated from Holliday but was able to find a canoe to cross the river.

He was within sight of the Brazos when on April 20 he was recaptured by twenty Mexican cavalrymen and taken to the Mexican camp at Fort Bend (Old Fort). Brown reported that he was placed under guard along with several other prisoners the Mexicans had gathered up. He could recall the names of only three, and he mentioned that the three had resided in Texas for several years—Johnson, from New York; Leach, an Englishman; and Simpson. He went on to report that the night after the battle of San Jacinto a Mexican officer brought the news of the defeat into camp and the army instantly retreated. (Once again, this disputes Filisola's claim that the news of the battle did not reach him at Old Fort until April 23.) After Brown was brought into camp he took off his boots to let them dry and to let his swollen feet rest. Soon his boots were stolen. He stated that he had to march barefoot through the mud and water, nearly knee deep all over the prairies, as the rain was falling in torrents pretty much all the time. So, according to both of their reports, he and Peña walked barefoot back to Mexico. At the 41WH91 site an iron piece was discovered that seems to be from a leg iron. Certainly this could have been for one of the captive Texans or for a deserter from the Mexican army [Fig. 11-1].

Brown marched with the Mexican army to Victoria and then on to Goliad. In May he left Goliad and was taken with about a dozen other Texan prisoners to San Patricio on the Nueces River. For some reason he was sent all the way to Mexico City with Filisola after the general had been dismissed as commander of the Mexican army. He remained in Mexico City as a prisoner until March 25, 1837. He was then brought back to Matamoros by Filisola and was allowed to board a ship for New Orleans on July 1.[17]

It is likely that the "Simpson" mentioned in Brown's account was one William Simpson. According to Isaac L. Hill, a sergeant in Capt. Moseley Baker's company, he, James M. Bell, and William Simpson were sent on April 5, 1836, to stand guard in San Felipe. Early the next morning, Simpson, who was supposed to be standing guard but was scavenging a vegetable garden, was surprised and captured by

17. Samuel T. Brown, "Fannin's Massacre—Account of the Georgia Battalion," *Texas Almanac, 1857–1873,* pp. 359–367.

⁂

The Texans Arrive

the Mexican cavalry. Hill and Bell were able to make good their escape.

Hill reported that after the war he was able to talk with Simpson and get the details of his capture. Simpson related that he was overtaken by a Mexican officer who struck him with the flat of his sword. He surrendered to the officer and was taken immediately before Santa Anna. Santa Anna assured him that his life would be spared if he told the truth about the strength, condition, and position of the Texian army—which he did. He was detained as a prisoner and put to work until a few days after the battle of San Jacinto. Simpson went on to relate to Hill that a wounded soldier informed Filisola of the defeat of Santa Anna. At that time a considerable portion of the division had already crossed the Brazos, but they immediately crossed back to the west bank and began their retreat. Simpson started on the retreat with the Mexican army but unlike Brown, he soon escaped. Simpson reported that while on the march he lay down in the prairie. The high grass concealed him from view and after the Mexican soldiers had passed he arose and proceeded on his way.[18]

The existence of one other prisoner captured by the Mexican army was documented in a Natchez, Mississippi, newspaper, *Mississippi Free Trader,* on December, 6, 1838. It was reported that a physician from that town, Dr. William N. Thorn, had been taken prisoner at Cópano by troops of Urrea's division. Thorn stated that he served as Urrea's division surgeon until they had returned to Matamoros. Doctor Thorn stayed in the tent with Urrea and claimed to have been present at nearly every Council of War. He said he became very familiar with Urrea and his feelings and goals as well as with the officers of Urrea's division. In spite of the fact that he was a prisoner he stated that he was strongly indebted to General Urrea for "many marks of kindness and courtesy."[19]

There was another encounter between several Texans and the Mexican army that was documented by both sides. While the Mexican army was camped on the Colorado River on May 7, several Texans spent the night in their camp.

18. "Recollections of Isaac L. Hill," in "Reminiscences of Early Texans: A Collection from the Austin Papers," *Quarterly of the Texas State Historical Association,* 7 (July, 1903), 40–46.

19. Nixon, *The Medical Story of Early Texas,* 201–202.

Peña mentioned that one of the rebels, Alejandro Alsbury, arrived in the Mexican camp on May 7. He described him as a man from the enemy army who confirmed the details of the battle of San Jacinto. Alsbury also gave Peña the particulars of the capture of Santa Anna. One of the details that Alsbury related to Peña was that the commander of the enemy cavalry had stipulated that Santa Anna was not to be harmed. Because of this stipulation the Texans had called out to the Mexican commander-in-chief from the woods. This was likely firsthand knowledge from Alsbury since, in his account of the capture of Santa Anna, William Taylor reported:

> Captain Karnes then called to Dr. Alsbury, who spoke the Spanish language, to call to Santa Anna in the thicket, (for he had no doubt Santa Anna was one of them,) and say to him, if he would come out and give himself up, we would take him prisoner and spare his life; for he had fears that he might get out of the thicket and escape, during the night, to Filisola's camp, some twenty miles distant, as he had not men enough to guard the thicket securely. Dr. Alsbury, called out to him, accordingly, to come out and deliver himself up, and his life should be saved. But no reply was made; all was as still as if there had not been a living soul in the thicket.[20]

Alsbury also told Peña of the ignition of a cartridge pouch and some rifles and pistols on the night of April 23. He noted that the enemy ammunition and ammunition captured from the Mexican army was on the point of catching fire. If Peña drew a connection between this fire and the glow that he reporting seeing on the eastern horizon on the night of April 22, he did not mention it.

Peña also told of a long night of discussions with Alsbury concerning the war, Santa Anna, tactics, etc. He reported that he repeatedly argued that it was necessary, at all costs, to maintain the integrity of the Mexican territory.[21]

The fact that Alsbury was in the Mexican camp on the Colorado was verified in the journal of Dr. James H. Barnard. Dr. Barnard was

20. Taylor, "Pursuit of Santa Anna and His Cavalry," 537–540.

21. Peña, *La rebelión de Texas*; translated in Perry (trans. and ed.), *With Santa Anna in Texas,* 169–170.

one of the doctors who was spared from the Fannin execution due to the fact that the Mexican army was desperately in need of surgeons. He was sent from Goliad to San Antonio to care for the Mexican soldiers wounded during the storming of the Alamo. In his journal entry for May 17 was the following:

> Tuesday 17th—Dr. Alsberry [*sic*] came in to town to-day with a pass from Gen. Fillasola, now Commander-in-Chief. Dr. A. is son-in-law to Angelo Navarro, with whom I live. His wife and sister, together with a negro, Bowie's, were in the Alamo when it was stormed. He had come in order to look after his family and take them off. He gave us all the particulars of the battle of San Jacinto, the capture of Santa Anna and the retreat of the Mexican Army, the number of volunteers pouring into Texas, stimulated thereto by the tale of Fannin and Travis.

The compiler of the journal, Hobart Huson, included the following information in his footnote on Alsbury:

> Dr. Horatio Alexander Alsbury was a Kentuckian who came to Texas in 1824 as an Austin colonist. While at the Siege of Béjar he won and wed Juana Navarro (then widow of Alijo Perez) daughter of Angel Navarro, and adopted daughter of Governor Juan Martín de Veramendi. She was at the Alamo during the Siege and was nursing Bowie when he was killed. Dr. Alsbury was then with General Houston's army, and was afterwards at San Jacinto.[22]

The fact that Barnard reported that Alsbury had a pass from Filisola proved that Alsbury stopped in the Mexican camp on his way from San Jacinto to San Antonio as Peña reported. Had he not been at the camp of the retreating Mexican army he would have had a pass from Santa Anna, not Filisola. It is also interesting to note that even though his first name was Horatio his middle name was Alexander, which would be Alejandro in Spanish. Alejandro is how

---

22. Joseph Henry Barnard, *Journal*, ed. Hobart Huson (Refugio, Tex.: Goliad Bicentennial, 1950), 42.

SEA OF MUD

Peña referred to him. On the list of the participants of the battle of San Jacinto there is no "H. Alsbury," but there is an "A. Alsbury." Thus it is likely that he preferred to be called by his middle name, Alexander (Alejandro). It also makes sense that he would have been returning to San Antonio to check on his family, and that he was a Spanish speaker, as he lived in San Antonio and was married to a Tejana.

There is more evidence that Alsbury stopped in the Mexican camp. In a letter from Rusk to Lamar, dated May 12, 1836, Rusk wrote to Lamar that he had

> received a letter from Mr. Allsbury [sic] who has been in the Mexican camp. He states that they were concentrated on the West Bank of Colorado river four thousand strong. Genl. Filisolo [sic] stated to him that he intended to obey the order of Santa Anna & take up the line of march by way of La Bahia [Goliad] in a body. That the officers all told him that they obeyed the order out of humanity to the prisoners in order to save their lives that the national honors had been compromised by their retreat and that there would be another Campaign but that this had closed.[23]

The statement quoted above was a description of the same meeting from the opposite viewpoint. Even though Alsbury did not specifically mention Peña, the information that is attributed to the "officers" is classic for Peña's train of thought. The fact that Alsbury put the Mexican army on the west bank of the Colorado is consistent with the date of May 7, by which time the majority of the Mexicans had crossed the river.

There is also the account of Alsbury's brother, Y. P. Alsbury,[24] who stated that his brother was a Spanish speaker. He also noted that his brother had spoken to Filisola at a later date. They talked about the Mexican officer who, though wounded, was able to deliver the news of San Jacinto to Old Fort.

There is also evidence that Alsbury was only one of several Tex-

---

23. Rusk to Lamar, May 12, 1836, in Jenkins (ed.), *Papers of the Texas Revolution,* VI, 249.

24. Y. P. Alsbury Reminiscences, Barker Papers (CAH).

∞

The Texans Arrive   269

ans who visited the Mexican camp on the Colorado River. In the *Morning Courier and New York Enquirer* of June 13th, 1836, the following story is printed:

TEXAS From the New Orleans Bulletin, May 27.

A gentleman of high respectability, arrived last evening in this city, informs us that Joseph Baker, formerly editor of the Telegraph, printed at San Felippe, having been sent after the battle of San Jacinto to the Mexican army, left the division under the command of Felasola, at the Colorado, on the 8th instant.

Felasola observed to Mr. Baker, that as Gen. Santa Anna was a prisoner, he did not acknowledge him as general of the forces then in the field, but would recognize him as President of the Mexican nation, and as such he would obey his order to withdraw the troops, and would execute it as soon as possible.

He said he had no doubt but Congress would acknowledge the independence of Texas, for it was a country the Mexican people did not want; and although it has been explored and known to them for one hundred and fifty years, and though a good country for the agriculturalist, it was not one adapted to the habits of the Mexican people, there being too many flies and musquitoes for the convenience of raising stock.

He acknowledged that the present campaign in Texas had terminated to the great disgrace of Mexico—that the cruel massacre of Col. Fanning's division was unjustifiable, and would meet with the indignation of the civilized world. He further said that the invasion of Texas was alone projected and carried on by the ambition of Santa Anna; that had it not been for this, Texas would have been admitted a state of the Mexican Republic at the time she made the application through her agent, General S. F. Austin, in 1833, and at this time would have had a local government suited to her wants.

He was well aware, he said, that the Texans were receiving

aid from the citizens of the United States, and that they had the sympathies of that nation.[25]

Two days later, on June 15, the same paper carried another story from Texas that included the following account:

TEXAS From the New Orleans Bulletin, May 30
We are very much pleased to learn from a highly respectable citizen of Texas, who arrived last evening by way of Red River, and who brings intelligence 8 days later than already received, that on the 16th inst. the Mexican army was retreating with the greatest precipitation and disorder, having thrown a large number of muskets into the San Bernard river. He also states that a large number of Texans had visited the Mexican camp on the Colorado, and slept there one night, and had been there treated more as men whom they looked upon as already their conquerors than as captives, which they had it in their power to make them had they been so inclined. Our informant says he has been assured by those persons after their return to the Texan camp from this visit, that the Mexicans said openly, if the Texans would only allow them to return unmolested, that they would never trouble them again.

From the same informant we learn that one of the Texans met Wall [Woll], the well known French general in Santa Anna's service, on the prairie, who stated on being questioned that he was proceeding to see what kind of a treaty Santa Anna was about to make with the Texans, on which he was taken into the camp and detained as prisoner, with all the other great folks.[26]

There is little doubt, from all these sources, that on May 7, 1836, a number of Texans came into the camp of the Mexican army located on the west bank of the Colorado River. They spent the

25. *Morning Courier and New York Enquirer*, June 13, 1836.
26. Ibid., June 15, 1836.

The Texans Arrive

night and some of them spoke with Filisola and his officers, including Peña. Filisola, and possibly others, gave the impression that they were obediently obeying the orders of Santa Anna and planned to leave Texas with their tails tucked between their legs. As will be discussed in the next chapter this may well have been calculated, on the part of Filisola, to buy time and carry out his original plan. However, when considering that the encounter took place after the journey through the quagmire of the Mar de Lodo, it is also possible that by May 7, this was exactly his plan.

Fig. 11-1. Iron leg iron.

Costumes Mexicaines. Lancier Méxicain. By Claudio Linati, 1828. Lithograph (hand-colored). 12 ⅛ × 9 ⅛ inches. *Courtesy of the Amon Carter Museum, Fort Worth, Texas.*

CHAPTER 12

Atascosito Crossing

O N THE MORNING OF MAY 2 Filisola left Gaona and the first brigade camped in the woods, and traveled with Tolsa and the second brigade to find Urrea at the Atascosito Crossing. There he expected to find the rafts that he had directed General Urrea to construct in order to assure their crossing of the Colorado. Instead he said he found only four wooden tie-ups in a square and one in the middle. Urrea's force had nearly finished crossing the river in two small canoes that had been discovered at the crossing. Filisola complained that one of the canoes could pass only three or four loads at a time. The other could carry twelve men, but only at great risk.

According to Filisola, he personally took over the task of arranging the crossing and, aided by the *zapadores* and some prisoners, was able to construct a raft that day that was capable of transporting twenty-four to thirty men per trip. This raft was sufficient to pass the artillery pieces as they arrived. The four-pounders could be ferried across along with their crew.[1]

In the Cumplido edition of *Memorias* Filisola claimed that about this time he noticed that General Urrea appeared to have a certain detachment and indifference. He stated that he was greatly surprised by this, as he had never seen him behave this way. He dated his acquaintance with Urrea back to when he had first known him as an aide to Gen. Miguel Barragán in 1821. It certainly is possible that Urrea was becoming aware that the chaos of the Mar de Lodo had

1. The Spanish term for the artillery crew was *armeros*.

left the army in shambles and that they were in danger of losing their ability to face the Texans in battle. It is likely that it was now clear that the army was not going to regroup and reassume the offensive. After this realization, Urrea may have regretted going along with the plan to regroup. It was at this point that he began proclaiming that he had opposed the retreat from the onset.

Filisola went on to comment that soon after Urrea's forces finished crossing the river, they set up camp on the plain at the exit of the road from the woods that bordered the bank. He was surprised that Urrea did not seem to feel that the distance that separated his force from the main army was a potential problem. Not wanting to upset Urrea, Filisola elected not to reprimand him, saying that he had great respect for the services that Urrea had performed on the campaign. In its entry for May 1 the San Luis Battalion daily log supported Filisola's claim that Urrea camped some distance from the crossing: "the Battalion San Luis passed and walked a quarter of a league from the woods. General Filisola arrived with the heads of the other divisions and occupied another point at the river" (on the opposite bank).

On this issue Filisola was nit-picking. It is unlikely that there was a decent spot to camp in the woods that skirted the river. He failed to note that the enemy would not have appeared on the west bank of the river, but from the east. Urrea would have been of little help if the enemy appeared on the bank opposite him, no matter where he had camped.

Not all was well for the cannons and wagons even after they had exited the mud of the prairie. Filisola stated that, prior to arriving at the Colorado, the artillery had to make its way through dense underbrush and thick woods, which contained a number of muddy creeks. It became necessary to make a road through the forest by cutting trees and using them to construct bridges over each of the creeks.

On May 3 Filisola decided that it was important to send someone to Mexico to give a verbal report of the true situation of the Mexican army. He said that he needed an intelligent leader who could assure that supplies would be sent from Goliad to Victoria, as well as seeing that supplies for the army would be sent to Matamoros. He elected to send Gen. Joaquín Ramírez y Sesma on this commission.

Another interesting event was reported by Filisola on May 3. He stated that on that day his aide, Capt. Juan Rivera, returned to camp from a mission that he had undertaken on May 1. Rivera's orders had been to proceed down the east bank of the Colorado in the direction of Cayce's Crossing (to the south). His goal was to find a homesite at which General Woll had confiscated corn as he advanced eastward toward Old Fort. Woll had reported upon his arrival at Old Fort that some supplies still remained at that homesite.

Rivera reported to Filisola that he had not found the homesite but had gathered two or three sacks of corn from a field. As he was doing this, he and his men were fired upon from the adjoining woods. In the ambush one muleteer was killed and another muleteer and two soldiers were wounded. Filisola went on to write that nothing could be more natural than this type of occurrence because, after the triumph of San Jacinto, the majority of the colonists had hurried west to inspect the remains of their homes. He elected not to send out new scavenging parties. It was clear that besides the fact that there was little to be found, it would be necessary to start a fight at each dwelling.

Rivera's tale is very interesting in light of a piece of local Wharton County lore. The small community of Egypt, Texas, is located just east of the Colorado River, about ten miles south of where the Atascosito Crossing is believed to have been located. According to oral history in Wharton County the Mexican soldiers raided a homesite at Egypt. Upon the approach of the Mexicans (Woll's soldiers?), the family hid all their valuables in a trunk and buried it in the family cemetery. They placed a grave marker on what appeared to be a freshly dug grave and listed the cause of death as smallpox, hoping the Mexicans would be afraid to investigate. After the war the family returned and recovered the valuables. The original trunk reportedly still exists.

A man from Egypt has reported that as a small boy he and his brother were digging near the family cemetery and found the skeleton of a Mexican soldier. He reported that his father made them cover the skeleton. It is interesting to note the similarities of the stories and that the location is south of Atascosito on the east bank. It is possible that this is the site that Woll raided and Rivera was sent to locate. It is also possible that the skeleton is that of the muleteer that was killed in the action.

∞

Atascosito Crossing

Peña noted in his memoirs that the days from April 29 until May 3 were, for him, the most painful of the campaign. He was able to travel only twenty to twenty-one miles (Mexican miles), and the days were spent on foot, in the mud, with nothing warm to eat because there was no wood for a fire. He was able to cross the Colorado on May 3.

When Peña had made the crossing he was greeted with a letter from a young lady in Mexico whom he had adored for the past ten years. He described her as beautiful, seductive, and endowed with many attractive gifts, but added that she was also deceitful, fickle, and inconstant. He went to great lengths in describing his anguish over her.

The perjurer of whom I complain is the only woman who has been able to chain my heart and fill it to overflowing. I have loved her with all my strength, I solemnly swear it, and since I have lost her, I feel completely alone in the universe. Should the sobs my heart emits grate upon her ears, she could not help but feel the painful remorse for having condemned me to such pain when she could have made me the most fortunate of mortals. But let it be known that although I am deeply offended, and despite my painful conviction that I cannot be happy with or without her, I weep for her and I pardon her, for I fervently wish her contentment. I shall not take the bitter revenge which is in order because of her horrible conduct toward me, in the hope that time or death will cure my deep wounds still oozing blood.

The stoics, men who have reached the winter of their lives, whose hearts have been frozen will say—What a fool! He wants to tell us about his affairs, which can be of interest only to him. But had they witnessed my vigils, my bitter anguish and anxiety; had they seen the bitter tears I shed without a friendly hand to wipe them; had they witnessed the constant torment that was piercing my soul, pricked by the infernal passion of jealousy; if these men, indifferent to their own sorrows as well as to those of others, could take hold of my sad reflections, my bitter recollections, and the terrible nightmares that at all hours, at all times, are pounding my imagination, depriving me of rest, they would then be indulgent. I ask no more of the reader than his indulgence and assure him that I am not ashamed to present myself as I am, rather than as I should be or would like to be.

Reason is of no use when an extremely sensitive soul finds itself deeply moved. A harsh destiny chained my life to an unfaithful woman, who could not appreciate my love for what it was worth.[2]

This baring of the soul by Peña proved that the men who composed the Mexican army of 1836 did just as Santa Anna liked to brag of them; they suffered well. This was an army of men shocked at the sudden turn of events at San Jacinto. Almost immediately they were dealt another disaster, in a long line of disasters, when they wandered into the quagmire of the Mar de Lodo. In the face of all this Peña was deserted by his lover and the floodgates of emotion opened up for all to witness. Those who have painted the Mexican army as being composed of ignorant, incapable, and heartless savages obviously were uninformed of the facts. There can be no doubt that both armies had their share of scoundrels. On the other hand, both armies had a goodly number of educated, caring, and honorable men, trying to do their best for the causes that they had embraced.

The San Luis Battalion daily log entry for May 3 reported that they were still camped on the prairie near the Colorado. It documented a message received from Santa Anna reporting that all Mexican prisoners from sergeant down were working on Galveston Island. A copy of this communication has not been located though Filisola did receive two letters from Santa Anna on May 5. Neither of these mentioned anything about the Mexican prisoners going to Galveston. Filisola did mention that he received other letters from Woll, with the same date, that reported on the same information as the Santa Anna letters.

2. Perry (trans. and ed.), *With Santa Anna in Texas*, 167–168. Apparently Sánchez Garza, the editor of *La rebelión*, did not feel that this declaration of love by Peña was important enough to include in his reprint of the memoirs. Since this quote contained no "facts" regarding the retreat, the original handwritten document was not consulted for accuracy. It is of interest that this subject was not included in the unpublished clean version of his diary but was added later in the final draft.

In the Cumplido edition of *Memorias,* Filisola reports the following two communications received from Santa Anna on the afternoon of May 5.

Army of Operations.—Esteemed Sr.—Today General
Adrian Woll arrived at this camp. He has placed in my hands
the communications of the 28th. As there is still no end to
the ongoing negotiations with this government, obviously,
General Woll needs to stay here to take the treaty that definitely will be concluded, and which, no doubt, will be satisfactory to both parties. Meanwhile, for no reason, should
you prolong your countermarch, and rather than cutting it
short, as I previously ordered, continue your march to Monterey, gathering all the detachments from Matagorda,
Copano, La Bahia, etc. You should leave in Texas only a garrison of 400 men with two light cannons, in San Antonio,
under the orders of a general of your choice, and the
wounded and sick that remain there.
    Arrange for the garrison at San Antonio to be provided
with three months advance pay and supplies, along with fifty
cases of cartridges.
    God and Liberty San Jacinto April 28th, 1836 Antonio
López de Santa Anna.—Esteemed General of the division
Vicente Filisola[3]

This second letter is more than likely the "personal" letter of the
two. Nearly every communication between the Mexican generals
would normally include a formal letter and a personal note.

D. Vicente Filisola.—San Jacinto, April 30th of 1836.—
    My esteemed friend and companion: I have received
your valuable [communication] from the 28th, past, and I
need to officially inform you that, since soon the ongoing
negotiations will be concluded, and at that time I should be
able to depart for Vera Cruz, you need to continue your
march for Monterey, leaving only one garrison of four hun-

---

3. Filisola, *Memorias para la historia de la guerra de Tejas* (Cumplido, 1849), I,
243–244.

dred men in Béjar with two cannons; in order that you can complete all that I want, I give you all the orders, in one.

Since I have no more clothes than what I am wearing, I want to remind you of your shipment of my baggage with all speed, remitting that of General Castrillón, not withstanding that he has died, as I have in it various things of which I have great need. Return the affections to the generals that gave them to me in your last correspondence and keep yourself in good health. Once again your affectionate servant. Q.S.M.B. Antonio López de Santa Anna[4]

It should be noted that it was only at this juncture that Santa Anna ordered Filisola to leave Texas. Up until this time he had merely ordered the army's divisions to withdraw to Victoria and San Antonio. Filisola offered no evidence, nor do any of the other Mexican sources, that he changed his plan due to the arrival of the new letters. In fact he went into great detail in his memoirs stating that the only reason he published the letters was the fact that Santa Anna later criticized him for not opening communications with the Texans and not protesting the detention of General Woll at San Jacinto. Filisola responded that he had no reason to communicate with the Texans, as it was to his advantage that the Texans did not know what he was doing or what he planned to do. He said that he was thinking of the six hundred prisoners. He argued that if the enemy believed that Santa Anna was still in charge, the prisoners were more likely to be safe. It was his belief that the extra time gained during the truce gave him more time to await the orders from Mexico City. He argued that he did not want to get involved in dealings with the enemy until he had heard the wishes of the government. It should also be noted that Santa Anna told Filisola that Woll would remain at San Jacinto—not that he was being detained by the enemy.

Santa Anna's order for the garrison of four hundred men and two light pieces of artillery to remain in San Antonio was curious. It was even more curious for Santa Anna to tell Filisola that this garrison should be given three months' pay in advance. Every Mexican source is in agreement that the *soldados* had been paid little or noth-

4. Ibid., 242–243.

∞

Atascosito Crossing

ing since the beginning of the campaign. This was classic for Santa Anna—boldly giving orders he knew could not be obeyed.

As with the earlier orders, Filisola did not obey the directive to garrison San Antonio. The only Mexican *soldados* left in San Antonio were those too sick or too badly wounded to be moved. On May 6 Ed Burleson wrote a letter to General Rusk,[5] who had taken command of the Texan army after Sam Houston left for New Orleans to get his wounded ankle attended to. Burleson's location at the time was given in the letter as "Campt at Bernard." The letter stated that Burleson did not know what Santa Anna was up to, leaving four hundred men and two cannons in San Antonio. He could not imagine why there needed to be such a force to guard a few sick and wounded. He was very much against permitting the Mexicans to do so.

Filisola responded to Santa Anna's letters with the following communication:

> Army of Operations.—Esteemed Sr.—At this moment, 2:00 in the afternoon, I have just received your communication of the 30th, dated at San Jacinto. In reply I wish to say that all of your orders will be carried out, notwithstanding that in so doing I am compromising my responsibility to the nation's government, in whose service I am employed.
>
> I wish that my march could be effected with the speed that Your Excellency recommends; but the present state of the roads and the worn out state of the trains and equipment, that you well know, do not allow it; nevertheless full effort will be given to this point.
>
> God and Liberty. Colorado River, May 5th, 1836.— Vicente Filisola.—Esteemed general, president Antonio López de Santa-Anna.[6]

His personal note to Santa Anna was as follows:

Esteemed general of the division, president of the republic

---

5. Burleson to Rusk, May 6, 1836, in Jenkins (ed.), *Papers of the Texas Revolution,* VI, 180.

6. Filisola, *Memorias para la historia de la guerra de Tejas* (Cumplido, 1849), I, 245.

Antonio López de Santa-Anna.—Atascosito, May 5th
1836.—Esteemed sir, friend and companion: I have already
officially replied to you all that is and will be my compliance
with the orders of your communications: [orders making]
demands of me that in fulfilling them, might in the future
cause me great pain. Even now, my friend, I'm having a difficult time of it, because I know well the profession to which
I belong, and [I know well] the obligation that my friendship
with you places on me, and [I know well] my duty to the
interior [government of Mexico]. Anyway, Señor, I will
retreat, because I don't ever want to be accused, by those
who view events from the outside, of having been the cause
of a disaster; but in carrying this out, I accomplish it with an
army of Mexicans, that is considerable in number, in discipline and in virtue, qualities about which you are already
aware. The army knows the positions in which you and your
worthy companions find yourselves.

The orders that you gave for the return of your baggage
were issued immediately, and are now being repeated, with
instructions to not use any excuses to delay, even in the face
of our lack of the most essential things.

Keep yourself well, and have the worthiness to accept the
sincere expressions of the senior generals, commanders, and
officers, giving the same to your companions that are
together with you, and prepare yourself as a friend for the
support and consideration with which I repeat to you as
your faithful servant. Q.S.M.B.—Vicente Filisola[7]

This last letter seems to hint that Filisola was very torn, but he
confirmed that he would comply with the orders. He stated several
times in his later writings that he was trying to give the impression
that he was obeying in order to keep the Texans from harming Santa
Anna and the other prisoners. It can easily be argued that Filisola
had every right to think that if indeed the Texans felt Santa Anna
had no authority with the Mexican army, they would have executed
the prisoners. Considering the fact that there were so many hard
feelings among the Texans, stemming from the Alamo and Goliad,

7. Ibid., 245–246.

the lives of Santa Anna and the prisoners were in a precarious balance. This danger to the Mexican prisoners was real, even when the Texans felt that Filisola was obeying Santa Anna. The risk to all the Mexican prisoners would have been even greater had the Texans felt that Santa Anna was powerless to help them. It is interesting to note that Filisola continued to refer to his obligation to the Mexican government and seemed to hint that he would be doing what the government desired and not as ordered by Santa Anna.

Filisola addressed the issue as to whether he was obeying Santa Anna's orders to retreat or was just giving the impression of doing so. He had several years to think about this version, as the Cumplido edition of his memoirs was not published until 1849.

> Everything that could be desired, under the circumstances, was happening, that is, to know our prisoners had been saved in the first moment of frenzy, and consequently, to discover their existence: that he [Santa Anna] had entered into negotiations without obligation or responsibility, which had remained with the command, and that these [negotiations] provided that the movement that had been agreed upon would be made more safely and comfortably. What other thing was needed, to make it better, when all the advantages that could be hoped for, under the circumstances, made it easier, and at the same time they were left with full freedom to later act in accordance with the new orders from the supreme government, and even better; everything, except for a deceptive submissiveness, that could have been suspended at any time. Without this deception, things would have been attributed to something inconsequential, because in no way could they have been called obligations, that is the conditions that a captured general has agreed upon with the rebels.[8]

Filisola brought up an excellent point in this quote. Considering the fact that the council of generals decided, at the meeting of April 25, to fall back and regroup, waiting for new orders from the supreme government, Filisola could not have asked for better rela-

8. Ibid., 246.

tions with the Texans. He had promised the enemy nothing. He was under no obligation to obey any directives from Santa Anna. Additionally, the truce that was in place, and was being respected by the Texans, was to his advantage in carrying out the above plan. The vulnerability of Houston and the Texans, immediately after San Jacinto, has been widely postulated; but what of the extreme risk to the Mexican army at the same moment? Filisola's forces were, for the most part, sub par (compared to those of Santa Anna), scattered and demoralized. None of the Mexican generals, with the possible exception of Urrea, had the leadership skills or the trust of the other generals, troops, etc., to quickly organize the scattered Mexican forces and attack. It is possible that had the Mexican army not been stuck in the Mar de Lodo the plan that was agreed upon at Powell's would have led to ultimate success in the conflict. The Mexican army did eventually receive orders from the government in Mexico City instructing them to hold the line at Goliad and retreat no further. The delay that the Texans allowed might have proven to be fatal to the Texan cause, had the Mexican army been able to arrive at Goliad in reasonably good condition. It is possible that on April 22, 1836, the Mexican army was as vulnerable to attack as the Texans. If either army had been able to move in a timely manner against the other, a positive outcome may have been within reach.

Filisola did mention that along with the letters from Santa Anna was a dispatch from Woll which told of his arrival at the enemy camp. Woll advised Filisola that he was awaiting the conclusion of negotiations prior to rejoining the army. Filisola also wrote that during the crossing of the Colorado the baggage of the president and the other generals was sent to the enemy camp.

Most of the artillery and wagons started arriving at Atascosito on or about the fifth and sixth of May. Filisola heaped praise on Lt. Col. Pedro Ampudia for his part in extracting the bogged-down equipment. He also noted that by this time the animals were in the worst of condition. He related that, even with a double team of mules, the artillery and wagons could not be moved, due to the extreme fatigue of the animals. He wrote that things were so bad that whereas he normally would have assigned one mule to carry the mess of each eighty soldiers, he was now limited to giving one mule for each eight companies (probably 300 to 400 men in their undermanned condition).

∞

Filisola also related that before he left the Colorado he released about forty individuals of various nations who had been captured in different places. He thought this would improve the Texans' treatment of the Mexican prisoners and would also free up the soldiers who were guarding these forty captives. In addition, it would help ration the small amounts of food that remained.

He also wrote that for the same reason, that is to placate the Texans and improve the situation for the Mexican prisoners, he approved a petition from the citizens of Matamoros for the lives of several Texans that had been captured at San Patricio and were under a death sentence from Santa Anna.

Urrea wrote Col. Francisco Garay several letters from the Atascosito Crossing. In one of these letters he once again gave a glimpse of his real feelings about the retreat. Things had reached the point that Urrea was suspicious that the army would not be stopping at Victoria or Goliad. On May 7 Urrea wrote Garay that he thought there was going to be a meeting of the generals that night. The subject of the meeting was to be the abandonment of the Goliad-Cópano-Béjar line of defense. Urrea called such an abandonment an act of cowardice and bad planning, and stated that, as a troop commander, he would not be able to avoid it. Therefore, he said, he would arrange the affairs of his division and go home. He asked Garay to make sure that his troops and those of Alcerreca advanced to Victoria and that they did so in good military fashion. He wanted his division to continue in orderly movement, as it had throughout that disgraceful campaign that had cost the republic so much and had been so horrendous to the military men. He said that his troops did not desire to retire with no trace of honor.[9]

In response, Filisola called this letter an act of insolence. He asked what information Urrea had obtained that even remotely hinted that the Goliad-Cópano-Béjar line was to be abandoned. He also wanted to know what happened to the meeting of generals that Urrea believed would take place that night.

Even though Filisola is correct in his opinion that Urrea was being premature in these suspicions, everything that Urrea feared turned out to be true. It seems that about this time Urrea not only

9. Filisola, *Análisis del diario militar del General D. José Urrea durante la primera campaña de Tejas,* 101.

realized that this was a retreat rather than a withdrawal, but also began to regret not openly opposing the movement from the start.

A listing of items that were abandoned by the Mexicans in the Mar de Lodo was documented by both Filisola and Peña. Their lists are quite similar and overall they mention fewer items than the Texans documented. Peña wrote that the eleven wagons that were leased from José Lombardero were abandoned, and in them some of the wounded. He also mentioned twenty-six cases of ammunition in addition to the quantity that had already been wasted. Also abandoned in the mud were a blacksmith's forge, a gun carriage with spare parts, a large transport wagon, another covered wagon belonging to the artillery train, as well as gun and rifle cases and lance handles that were burned as firewood.[10]

General Urrea's division left the west bank of the Colorado, heading for Victoria, on May 8. Filisola and the rest of the army were to follow on May 9 (see Map No. 1). This exit from the Colorado marked the true beginning of the long trip back to Mexico. There was little doubt by this time that if left unmolested the Mexican army was headed home.

10. Peña, *La rebelión de Texas*; translated in Perry (trans. and ed.), *With Santa Anna in Texas,* 171.

CHAPTER 13

The Aftermath

BY MAY 9, 1836, the Mexican army was totally disorganized. The divisions were functioning as totally separate forces. What had started as an organized withdrawal to Victoria to await orders from the Mexican army had developed into scattered groups of disheartened men. It was now obvious, at least for the near future, that there was little chance that they would be able to function as an army. The cause of this sudden change in fortunes was not the arrival of Santa Anna's orders or Filisola's lack of courage but the torrents of rain that transformed the Texas prairie into the Mar de Lodo.

Peña and Filisola documented that soon after leaving the Colorado River, Filisola called a meeting of the commanders and officers in response to all the gossip about the retreat. Peña's version of the event was that Filisola gave a lengthy speech trying to justify his decision to retreat. He also reminded them all that the army was "not a congress in which what is best should be discussed." Filisola went on to say that if any one of them would offer a plan that would convince him that the fate of the army could be reversed, he would submit to it. Peña gave the following statement about the response to Filisola's invitation for a plan to take the offensive:

> Señor Gaona objected that such a proposal could be made
> only in strong positions, an objection very much in accord
> with the current code. It is necessary to reflect, whenever
> this can be accomplished, that my censure is not so much for
> the retreat, to a certain point necessary once it had begun, as

it is for the way in which it was done. The wisest and best combined plan would hardly have any effect eighteen days after the first backward step had been taken. What can one do with soldiers who even now keenly feel the deprivations they have so recently suffered? What can be done, I repeat, after they have lost their moral will, after so much suffering and the conduct observed toward them? It is quite noticeable that none of the corps commanders were consulted when the retreat was agreed upon, who now are called and instructed to quiet the criticisms that are generally made against it.[1]

This statement from Peña gives great insight as to the state of mind of the Mexican officers after they had extracted themselves from the Mar de Lodo. Even those most vehemently opposed to the retreat seemed to realize that by the time they left the Colorado River there were no viable alternatives other than to continue the retreat. The major factor that had changed, between Powell's and the Colorado River, was not the numbers of troops, the strength of the Texans, or the Mexican leadership, but the fighting spirit and the equipment of the *soldados*, which had been decimated by nine days in the mud of the Mar de Lodo.

In the Cumplido edition of his *Memorias* Filisola told of the same meeting of the officers, but from a different perspective.

Tonight we stopped at the stream called San Diego: General Tolsa and Colonel Amat, informed me that among Captain Enrique de la Peña, and three other young officers were being poured out some rude comments that criticized the movements that had been carried out. To their knowledge this was the first time there had been slanderous talk of this type.[2]

The Texans did get precariously close to the Mexican army, especially to the forces under Andrade that were rejoining the main Mexican army as they withdrew from San Antonio. There was actu-

1. Peña, *La rebelión de Texas*, 191; translated in Perry (trans. and ed.), *With Santa Anna in Texas*, 172–173.
2. Filisola, *Memorias para la historia de la guerra de Tejas* (Cumplido, 1849), I, 251.

SEA OF MUD

ally a plan formulated by Filisola to attack the Texans with the force under his command. At the same time Andrade's division was to attack the Texans from the west flank. This plan was formulated because Filisola had been informed that the Texans intended to attack his flank.

On May 25, before this confrontation came to a head, the commissioners from the Texas government arrived with the treaty that had been signed by Santa Anna and the Texan government on May 14. After the arrival of the treaty Filisola seemed totally resigned to the fact that the only way to protect the Mexican prisoners was to continue the retreat. He noted that the only other option—to attack, was unavailable to him. He argued that the army had the soldiers and the will to do so but no means to allow them to succeed. His idea that the will of the *soldados* was still strong was probably bravado on his part. Considering the conditions of the Mar de Lodo, the lack of food, sleep, and shelter, and the deplorable weather, the chances that the soldiers remained in a fighting mood seem remote.

Urrea was now obviously bitter about the way the retreat had gone, and on May 11 he sent the following letter to the Mexican government complaining of the retreat and of Filisola in particular.

Army of Operations. Reserve Brigade—Concealed

Your Excellency:—At the moment I was given the complete plan for the operation that His Excellency the President General was kind enough to forward to me, I was occupying with the division under my command the valuable positions of Columbia and Brazoria, and already having situated one part of my forces on the other side of the Brazos River, I received the official communication, and special letter that are marked number 1 and number 2, that the 2nd in command of the army sent me, copies of which I have the honor of sending on to Your Excellency. In number 3 is the copy of the warning that General Mariano Salas sent me from Columbia. He inserted to me the order that caused him to leave there with the Jiménez Btn., which he commanded, and all the cavalry. Without losing time I arranged for my forces to march. The march was being forced when a special letter was received, copy number 4. It persuaded me that the purpose of my having been sent for so quickly was for a movement against the enemy. The movement was slowed by the annoying transportation of two large boats and a wagon that the soldiers had to swim across the river due to the failure of mules and oxen. The operation was also delayed in leaving that place while discarding and rendering useless more than 200 muskets. The reunion was achieved after one days march at the habitation of Madam Pawell, although at the beginning two quite long and difficult roads separated us.—Here, His Excellency gave me for the first time further details of the disgraceful incident of the 21st of last month and the ill-fated luck of the President General; no one wanted to question about the death of His Excellency. This was accompanied with so many brave desires to humiliate the enemy. It produced such a great depression on the morale of all the units that united that neither the thoughts that I felt I should make known to their leaders, nor the confidence that a gathering of all the troops should have instilled, could dispel or lessen it. *In this situation the order to begin the retreat to the Colorado River was given, without first making sure of the true fate of our worthy Premier Leader, without knowing the position of the enemy, and without making the smallest movements to scout for the dispersed that surely would be gathering in growing numbers on the bank of the river or Buffalo Bayou—* The new organization of the Army in brigades placed me at the head of the reserve, the only satisfaction I had on this day. Until one days march on this side of the San Bernard Creek I covered therefore the rearguard of our forces. At this position His Excellency the General in Chief judged it convenient that I advance with my brigade to secure the passes of the Colorado, and facilitate the troops, artillery and baggage crossing it. This commission, always tough, was double so in these circumstances due to the very bad state of the roads, the unexpected return of the waters and the shortage of almost all means for the construction of rafts or boats in which to cross. However, everything was done but not without cost. I will omit the details, not wanting this communication to be too long.—The crossing of all the army assured,

∞

His Excellency also arranged that I proceed to this place, at which I arrived last night, and to which His Excellency is headed with the main part of the troops. I do not know for sure to which point we will continue our retreat, nor the line of defense the Army will form, though when I separated from His Excellency he did not seem to place any importance on this intention, although it is true that he was inclined to establish one, supported by Monterrey and Saltillo, *I believe that he abandoned this idea, acting as though he had listened to my thoughts as to preferring to make it from Béjar to Goliad and the Port of Cópano, at which the troops could have received supplies for subsistence more regularly and in greater abundance and which could have avoided the desertions that resulted from the state of affairs. This also would have saved a small part of the honor of the Mexican Army, so badly blemished in the final action of this campaign.*—Allow me now, Your Excellency to give you the news that we have of His Excellency the President General, the state of the Army today and my ideas regarding the best arrangement or reorganization that we should give it, thus to restore its morale so that in any event it can work with energy and the efficiency worthy of the Mexican soldier, and that perhaps today more than ever requires the service of the nation.—Attached is, below in number 5, a copy of a letter with which His Excellency honored me from San Jacinto the 30th of April. In the letter it seems as though he was in negotiations with the insurrectionists and although I was ignorant of all of these and his intentions, I am aware through the official communication sent to his second in command that he had concluded an armistice with them. Therefore today the hostilities have ceased and the person of His Excellency will be treated with consideration. I also judge that he can embark from Galveston for Veracruz, for which reason it was decided not to send his equipment to him, which at that time had been ordered to be on its way and was very advanced toward this point. The Señor General Adrián Woll, has proceeded to the enemy camp to confer with His Excellency, and I also, for my part, have sent an official from my brigade for the same purpose. As soon as they return or I have any news from

∞

The Aftermath 293

them, I will hurry to make Your Excellency aware of it.—
The state of the Army is very sad, even lower is the spirit of
the troops, severely lacking clothing and footwear, and the
cavalry was virtually naked, and dismounted. The force, however, under my command, that is composed of the permanent Battalion of Jiménez, of the actives of San Luis, Tres Villas and Yucatán, of the Regiment of Cuautla, a Squadron of
Tampico, a picket of the active Squadron of Guanajuato (I
say of Durango) and auxiliaries of Guanajuato, although they
are poorly dressed, has not the least bit of weariness from the
campaign, I have the satisfaction to assure Your Excellency
that it does not participate in the discouragement that dominates the others, on the contrary it is indignant to what has
happened and desires an opportunity *to punish anew the
enemy and revenge the blood of their companions rescuing the Commander in Chief, which it would have gone and accomplished if not
for the constant hinder of the armistice that existed and the orders
from His Excellency that he sent us today.*—For the best service
of this Army it seems to me that it would be best to form
three separate corps, joining all the Infantry in one force and
reuniting in another all the Cavalry. This way we would get
rid of much material that burdens us today, it would reduce
the number of leaders to the precise ones of decree, the
operations would be more uniform and finally, more positive
passive and exact discipline that the service demands. With
the same frankness that I have taken the liberty of speaking
to Your Excellency, I should confess that in my concept the
poor spirit that today dominates many of our soldiers, would
cease the moment these changes are adopted, as it is no less
just to make some honorable exceptions in the conduct of
some of the leaders that I would demote.—Attached to Your
Excellency, with those cited documents, the copies of which
are designated numbers 6 and 7, so the concept that I have
made is better understood from a principle of the movements of the Army. The prudence of Your Excellency will
describe it as it deserves.—I remit to Your Excellency this
communication with extraordinary embarrassment, because
I consider it to be of the utmost importance that Your
Excellency is opportunely informed of the true state of these

things, to avoid the fatal consequences that the imprisonment of His Excellency the Commander-in-Chief and the
other sad events that have occurred this way, can have on the
fate of the Republic, leaving with this passage the freedom
of responsibility that an indiscreet silence would have
brought me.—I request that Your Excellency give an
account of the expressed information to His Excellency the
interim President, as he should be aware of it, repeating to
Your Excellency with this purpose the sureness of my consideration and esteem.—God and Liberty. Victoria, 11th of
May of 1836.—José Urrea.—His Excellency Secretary of
War and Navy General Don José María Tornel.[3]

This was the first documented instance that Urrea officially and
openly criticized Filisola. According to Urrea's writings he had been
doing so privately since the first word of Santa Anna's defeat. The literature that is available at this time, however, seems to confirm that
Urrea quietly went along with the plan hatched at Powell's until
after the crossing of the Colorado and the disastrous encounter with
the Mar de Lodo. The only exception to this was Urrea's complaints
in private letters to his own subordinate, Francisco Garay.

After the army had marched for Matamoros Filisola finally got
his orders from Gen. José Tornel, secretary of war.

Secretary of War and the Navy
    General Section.—First Desk.—Most excellent Sir.—
With the most profound regret His Excellency the interim
president has been informed by the official note from Your
Excellency of the twenty-ninth of the present month concerning the defeat suffered the twenty-seventh [sic] by the
division commanded in person by the president, commander
in chief of the army, with the very regrettable circumstance
of the fact that His Excellency was taken prisoner along
with other leaders and officers. His Excellency the interim
president is consoled to some degree by the fact that so
experienced a general as Your Excellency should be the one

3. "La guerra de Texas: Causa formada al Gral. Filisola por su retirada en 1836,"
Tomo X., No. 1, pp. 140–144.

to take the command, which he expressly confirms.

First, Your Excellency is charged to address the enemy general and to courteously demand the president and commander-in-chief's freedom; at least while arrangements can be agreed upon over this point. The consideration is due him, because of his dignity and of his distinction during the more auspicious times in America's history, because the entire Nation wishes it out of gratitude, as he is their leader; the Interim President depends on you to direct all of your wisdom and effort toward securing the rest of the army and regrouping it in order to preserve its integrity and presence, and to position it at a convenient point so that it can receive the supplies, that this body is immediately ordering to be delivered.

The preservation of Béjar is an absolute necessity so that the government in light of the circumstances may decide upon the most appropriate measures. The fate of all the prisoners is very important to the nation, and you are charged with trying to alleviate it, with authorization forthwith to propose exchanges. This is so that with this purpose and for the sake of humanity it may save the lives of the prisoners that have been or may be taken by the enemy.

Your Excellency is aware of the consequences that could come about from an oversight committed in these circumstances, but the government has no fear of this because it knows how great are the expertise and the skill of Your Excellency. With this message I have the honor of offering you my most distinguished consideration and esteem.

God and liberty. Mexico City, May 15th,—Tornel. His Excellency General Don Vicente Filisola, second general in command of the army of operation against Texas.[4]

Once again there was a private letter that accompanied the official letter. It reiterated the above letter but added at the end:

---

4. Filisola, *Memorias para la historia de la guerra de Tejas* (Rafael, 1848, 1849), reprint, *Historia de la guerra de Tejas* (1968), II, 499–500; Woolsey translation, *Memoirs for the History of the War in Texas*, II, 246–247; retranslated for G. Dimmick by Dora Elizondo Guerra.

SEA OF MUD

In no case will Your Excellency commit yourself to the independence of Texas, for this act is null and void in and of itself, and the nation will never allow it. However, everything is left to the wisdom of Your Excellency, and you are asked with all urgency again to realize how much the nation and the supreme government are interested in the saving of the president general.[5]

Both of these letters had to give Filisola the impression that the first priority of the Mexican government was not the holding of his position but the salvation of Santa Anna. Why this was the case is difficult to understand as Santa Anna was severely criticized on his return to Mexico. The only order regarding the holding of his position was that he not abandon San Antonio. However this had already happened by the time Filisola finally received the order. Even if he had gotten the order earlier it is most improbable that he would have been able to leave any troops in Texas and still protect Santa Anna and the other prisoners. Even with the apparent adherence of the Mexican army to the orders of Santa Anna there were strong forces in Texas that favored the execution of the captured commander-in-chief.

Another factor in the ultimate outcome of the war needs to be considered. The Texas navy had been legislated by the General Council of Texas in November 1835. In January 1836 four schooners were purchased. One of these, the *Liberty*, was sold in New Orleans in May 1836 for debt payment. By September 1836 the *Brutus* and the *Invincible* were in New York for repairs. Once again, debt held up their return. They did not get back to action until June 1837. In April 1836 the fourth Texan ship, the *Independence*, fought a four-hour battle with two Mexican vessels and was eventually captured. This captured vessel increased the Mexican navy to eight warships.[6] In 1838 the Texas navy was virtually nonexistent. The "fleet" consisted of

5. Filisola, *Memorias para la historia de la guerra de Tejas* (Rafael, 1848, 1849), reprint, *Historia de la guerra de Tejas* (1968), II, 501; Woolsey translation, *Memoirs for the History of the War in Texas*, II, 247.

6. "Texas Navy," The Handbook of Texas Online, http://www.tsha.utexas.edu/handbook/online/articles/view/TT/qit2.html (accessed June 18, 2003); "History of the Texan Navy," *Texas Almanac, 1857–1873*, pp. 389–394.

two ships. The first was only the hulk of a ship lying on its side on the mud flats offshore from Galveston. The second was the *Potomac,* which was seen to be rotting alongside a pier in Galveston.[7]

The condition of the Mexican navy may have been slightly better in regard to numbers but the condition of their ships may have been worse than that of the Texans. When Col. Juan Almonte was sent to Texas on a fact-finding mission for the Mexican government he reported that he was unable to arrange for one of the national sloops to take him to Texas. The port commander told him that there was not a boat that was seaworthy as there was no money available for repairs. He proceeded to look for passage on a merchant ship to take him to Texas but found that none would be sailing in the near future. He eventually made the decision to proceed by way of an American frigate to New Orleans and from that port find his way to Texas. It is interesting that a high official of the Mexican government on an important mission was unable to travel by sea from one port in his country to another without using an American ship and an American port.[8]

Almonte gave a further hint of the condition of the Mexian fleet in 1834 when he wrote to the Mexican government on March 4. Almonte informed the government that he had discovered that new ships could be built in New York at a very reasonable cost. He argued that repairing their old sloops cost nearly as much as a new ship. He added that even after the costly repairs, the Mexican ships could serve no more than four or five months.[9] From these two comments it can be argued that there was almost no chance that the Mexican navy could have transported Santa Anna's army to Texas in 1836.

Further evidence of a weakened Mexican navy is the fact that in 1838 the Texas congress passed a new law. It provided for purchasing Mexican ships that had been captured in the Pastry War from the French.[10] Thus it is likely that by 1838 the Mexican navy was no longer comprised of eight vessels.

7. Tom Henderson Wells, *Commodore Moore and the Texas Navy* (Austin: University of Texas Press, 1998), 3.

8. Jackson (ed.) and Wheat (trans.), *Almonte's Texas,* 56.

9. Ibid., 64

10. Wells, *Commodore Moore and the Texas Navy,* 4–5.

SEA OF MUD

Considering the above details, the slight naval advantage would have to go to the Mexican navy. Taking into account the distances involved and the fact that there were still only eight ships in the Mexican navy (and even fewer by 1838), it seems unlikely that naval superiority would have been a major factor in the final outcome. If Filisola had attacked immediately or had somehow avoided the Mar de Lodo, the only real advantage may have been that the Texans did have steamboats available to help them operate near the coast.

The Mexican army's retreat, however, was a significant blow to the Mexican navy as it did cost Mexico any ports that could serve in resupplying a subsequent army. A good example of the importance of the Texas ports took place at Cópano soon after the Mexicans had abandoned that position. The incident was reported in the *Morning Courier and New York Enquirer* of July 6, 1836.

The Brig *Good Hope*, arrived on the 21st of June at New Orleans, announces the capture of the schr. *Watchman* in the Bay of Copano, by a party of Texian cavalry, who took her by surprise. The *Watchman* had sent her boat on shore to land provisions for the Mexican army, (with which she was principally laden) while a party of the Texian cavalry, having intimation of it, concealed themselves in a convenient place close to the beach, and as soon as the boat struck the shore, jumped into it, leaving the crew behind, and then pulled for the *Watchman*. Upon approaching the schooner, those on board took them for their own boat's crew, and quietly permitted them to get on board. The *watchman* [sic] was released by order of Brigadier General Rusk, in consequence of being under American colors; the cargo, however, being Mexican, was confiscated.

With the Texans now in control of all the ports north of Matamoros, it would have been very difficult for the Mexican army to have been transported by ship for a second campaign against Texas.

Urrea sent a letter of protest to Filisola on June 1, 1836. It was written three weeks after his letter of protest to Tornel and the Mexican government. This certainly was not following the chain of command, as he should have addressed Filisola first and then the government. There certainly is the possibility that Urrea had done just that, repeatedly, as he later claimed. Unfortunately, for Urrea's argument, it was not documented in the dispatches of the early days of the retreat. Urrea's letter was very critical of Filisola and showed almost none of the friendship (feigned or not) of his earlier correspondence with his new commander.

Most Excellent Sir: From Mission Refugio, in a letter dated May 17 of this year, I expressed how important I considered it that the army's operation in Texas maintain its line along the San Antonio River, where it could count on the township of Béjar, fortifications at the Alamo and Goliad, and in addition on the Port of Cópano; and not abandoning it without orders from the Nation's Supreme Government. That line was our only option after having abandoned the Colorado River where I believed you would have headquartered the Army; as you had discussed it with me when I joined you at Madame Powell's, after your retreat from the Brazos River as a result of the debacle suffered by the portion of the forces that advanced under orders of the Commander-in-Chief of the Army.

In Guadalupe Victoria, before I began my march to this point, I spoke at length with you about this very issue, and I believe you had agreed with me regarding how important and urgent it was to maintain that line of defense. Even the Supreme Government's resolutions dictated the troops conduct.

After all Sir, it pains me to see the army marching toward this city [Matamoros]. As a general in the Mexican Army, and as a commander of one of its divisions in the operations in Texas, I would be remiss in my duty if I feigned to express my feelings and hide my opinions regarding this latest maneuver. In expressing myself Sir, I submit my protest and do so with no other intention than what is natural and laudable in refusing to be a party to what I feel will affect our Nation's honor and good name, simultaneously heaping upon it immeasurable harm. Harm that even a vivid imagination shudders to imagine.

In order to continue explaining myself with utmost clarity, so that at a later date my position will not require interpretation, I am compelled Sir, to turn my thoughts back to those more recent days when everything bode well for a happy ending to a war that has instead turned out to be the most painful that the Mexican Army has ever experienced.

The army had beaten a treacherous and traitorous enemy each time it dared to show its face; [an enemy] which had lost its principal strongholds; having to abandon their homes and their pursuits; having to hide their families in forests, and having their numbers reduced to an insignificant few, undisciplined, uninstructed and improperly guided, by leaders who didn't know how to lead. What an inexplicable state of affairs this is for us, to say nothing about its also being disgraceful; and not being able, in spite of everything, to bolster its [our army's] strength. You Sir are well aware that after that victory [San Jacinto] you assured your security by ending the hostilities and dispersing almost your entire force, terrified at their own losses.

What will be said of us Sir, when it becomes known that the Mexican Army in Texas has shown itself to be a weakling before its enemy; even with a force exceeding four thousand, backed by considerable artillery with a history of victory, it was yet incapable of attracting good fortune to its side. It wasn't even able to discover the fate of its most distinguished leader, or to regroup its dispersed forces, or return them to arms with the ardor they had had up until that disastrous journey of April 21.

On the contrary, you abandoned your position and began a retreat that, speaking with the candor of a soldier, was nothing more than a shameful runaway that has ended in the demoralization; with the exception of the division which I have had the honor to command, part of which is presently in your domain; has overtaken the greater part of the army.

I can see it now, and this sentiment is not the most painful. According to the dispatches that you have sent from Mujeres Creek, to General Francisco Vital Fernández, Commander of these districts; and as I understand it from your dispatches, you Sir have acknowledged that those Texas rebels represent a legitimate government. To the discredit and disgrace of the Mexican Nation you have established with that presumed government negotiations that lean toward the recognition of those Texas rebels, who this Nation has justly opposed, and has made untold sacrifices to resist and to put down.

I don't see that you have the authority to do this, neither does the Nation, or the Supreme Government, or the Army itself can allow seeing it trampled and disgraced in such a way. As for me, it is imperative for me to be explicit and to tell you Sir that such conduct will never have my approval. It never did and you know it well. That retreat that has been forced upon the army and was initiated from the Brazos River; and by the way, if I saw myself compelled to follow that order to join you; after having been left with only four hundred men in Brazoria, by the orders you issued to that part of my Division that remained in Columbia; without waiting for me to issue orders; leaving my rearguard unprotected; it was because it was my duty to follow your superior orders.

Could it be said that these events are dictated by his Excellency the President? But if indeed the President's orders are always sound, should they be as blindly contradicted today, when unfortunately and to our dismay, he finds himself a prisoner among the enemy? Who is to say, on the other hand, that while the President did issue those orders, he was really expecting us to follow our better judgment not to carry them out? I am inclined to think that is the case, because General Santa Anna has always looked toward the Mexican Army's honor. The army, especially lately, owes its existence to him. He was the one that rebuilt it from nothing after having been buried by so many political setbacks.

You had the means to reconcile the extreme differences, and to save us from such a responsibility and criterion. This was the Government's supreme decision, when it was informed of what had happened.

I pleaded with you in Guadalupe Victoria to await [the Government's decision], and to position the Army in Cópano, Goliad and Béjar, since there was nothing stopping our march. I now reiterate my request so that there won't be additional reasons to stain the Mexican Army's good name and reputation.

We are also taking into consideration the many Mexican families on both sides of Béjar's San Antonio River. They have little else but their existence, which they will surely loose if they remain in the country after they are abandoned by our troops. Maybe they would be forced to follow us, confirming throughout our scarce generosity toward them plus the non-existent support they received from us for their sacrifices.

In closing Sir, the course taken by the Army in Texas will give the entire Nation the message of a total defeat. A defeat that doesn't really exist, and that will probably cause the Nation, as it is moved to act, to involve itself all over again in the chaos of the revolutions that have caused it so much misfortune.

You cannot be a party to such a calamity, if you give yourself a chance to think about the devastating results. You, who have served the Nation, and who have made it proud, must, more than anyone else in these critical circumstances, especially now that you find yourself at the head of these forces; you must guard the Army's stability and harmony.

I am still convinced of it, but if toward the same end, the path you have adopted continues to be implemented, I want you to understand that I do not approve it. From this very moment I submit a formal protest against its adoption, and by informing the Supreme Government, I have cleared my conscience and have fulfilled my duty.

> I repeat my protest as I see it. You have my esteem.
> God and Liberty—Matamoros, June 1, 1836.
> From: José Urrea
> To: Don Vicente Filisola[11]

This letter is a fascinating study of the whole incident of the retreat. As has been the case in previous letters, the strong and heart-

---

11. Urrea to Filisola, June 1, 1836, included in Peña, *La rebelión de Texas,* Anexo No. 25, pp. 288–291.

felt emotions of Urrea are obvious. This is the earliest writing that is known in which Urrea begins to claim to have opposed the retreat from the outset. He wrote that the only reason that he joined Filisola at Powell's was because he was commanded to do so. If the letter is carefully read it is noticed that the event that seems to have been the last straw was the abandonment of the line of defense from Cópano to Victoria, Goliad, and San Antonio. Urrea offers no proof in the letter that he openly opposed anything prior to arriving at Victoria. It was there that he confronted Filisola and insisted that they must hold that defensive position. It is a telling fact that when Urrea wrote this letter about the extreme importance of not abandoning their line, he was already in Matamoros. If it was so critical to defend the mentioned position, why had Urrea already left Texas? One consideration has to be that Urrea realized there was going to be blame assigned for the disaster and, to the greatest extent possible, he intended to distance himself from the decisions that were made.

By late May the Mexican government had received the letter of complaint from Urrea and had learned that San Antonio, Victoria, and Goliad had all been abandoned. They were now aware that the Mexican army was falling back to Matamoros. The government ordered the removal of Filisola as commander of the army and replaced him with Urrea. In spite of Urrea's constant claims that he was in favor of stopping the retreat and attacking the rebels, he had no real choice, at this point, but to continue the retreat. It is likely that even though they now had their most aggressive leader at the helm, the effects of the fourteen days in the quagmire of the Mar de Lodo had destroyed the means, and likely the will, to press the fight to the Texans.

A letter written by General Andrade to Urrea on June 13, 1836, gives an idea of the deplorable condition of the army. Urrea had ordered Andrade to take the troops that were under his command (some who had been with him in San Antonio and some who had retreated with Filisola) and return to Goliad. Andrade respectfully wrote to Urrea that this was impossible. He reported that the five battalions in his command were barefooted and that the few clothes that covered their limbs were filthy since they had not been cleaned in three months. The commanders and officers were barefoot and many were on foot. The cavalry horses were worthless, with more than 150 cavalrymen on foot. Andrade wrote that the cavalry's gear was destroyed and the Dolores Regiment was incapacitated. Their weapons, like those of the infantry, needed to be totally reconditioned. This could not be done for lack of gunsmiths and the forges. He stated that the artillery was in poor repair, its quick matches of rope were rotting, and its ammunition needed to be thoroughly examined—which was to be expected after seven months of being loaded on the backs of the mules. This important branch of the army was neglected just like all the others. Andrade wrote that they had 150 sick and wounded following them who had no care other than a medicine chest that had only enough supplies for twenty men to be properly attended. He added that only assistant doctors were available to care for the men. There was no food in the stores except for a few pounds of lard. The men were given a ration of meat that was insufficient to keep them healthy or vigorous. General Andrade added in his report to Urrea that the troops had suffered immensely for seven months, suffering all types of intemperate weather. He felt that if they tried a retrograde movement at that time it would result in mass desertion.[12]

Urrea did not stop the retreat until the entire army reached Matamoros. He really had no other choice as the majority of the army had already reached that point by the time he was appointed commander-in-chief. He remained in command of the forces there as the Mexicans prepared for a second campaign against Texas.

The Mexican government was intent on retaking Texas. The Mexican secretary of war, José María Tornel, reported that the command of the "second" army was given to Gen. Nicolás Bravo. It is interesting to note that, according to Tornel, the elements of nature still pounded the Mexican troops as they marched toward Matamoros to begin the second campaign. He specifically wrote that ever since April 27 (he was likely using Filisola's dates) nature had hindered their movements. Tornel placed the strength of the assembled Mexican army at seven thousand men. He stated that the army even had a pontoon bridge floated from Yucatán to Matamoros to help them pass the large rivers of Texas. Five war vessels were purchased to prevent interference from the United States. The secretary of war claimed that the army was well supplied. He flatly stated that the

12. "La guerra de Texas: Causa formada al Gral. Filisola por su retirada en 1836," Tomo X, No. 3, p. 589.

only reason the second campaign failed to materialize was lack of money.[13]

In the meantime Filisola was court-martialed in September 1836 for his decision to retreat. The trial basically evolved into an Urrea versus Filisola affair. The majority of the senior generals aligned themselves with Filisola while many of the younger officers joined the Urrea camp. Filisola was eventually exonerated. The following report is the judgment handed down in the trial by the presiding judge.

Esteemed Commanding General

The summary proceedings that were ordered by the Commanding General is finished. It concerns the retreat carried out by the Army of Operations in Texas, which, due to the defeat and imprisonment of His Excellency President Antonio López de Santa Anna, was left to His Excellency General of the Division Vicente Filisola. I present my judgment hoping that it will meet with the approval of the superiors, so that this case will be closed once and for all; or if it is not approved, it can then be further examined by a Council of War presided by senior officers.

Certainly there were losses and damages that the Nation suffered with this retreat, and His Excellency the Secretary of the Office of War and Navy expresses this in his official introductory document. However, in the same document he says that as the Esteemed General did not enjoy total freedom of choice, it can not be clarified who should bear this responsibility.

The Señor Filisola has answered the charges that were made against him in the same document [the introductory document], in the statement that he made to the Supreme Government on the nineteenth of August last and is attached to the summary. His assertions are confirmed by the declarations of Generals Ramírez Sesma, Gaona, Tolsa and Colonel Amat.

13. José Maria Tornel, "Texas y los Estados-Unidos de América en sus relaciones con la Republica Mexicana," in Castañeda (trans. and ed.), *The Mexican Side of the Texas Revolution,* 366–368.

There is no doubt that when the disgrace at San Jacinto occurred one third of the Army that was assigned to the campaign was lost. Señor Filisola suddenly found himself commander-in-chief of a poorly organized corps of troops, without a base of operation, disseminated, in an unknown country, without the necessary supplies, *with a growing number of consuming non-combatants* [camp-followers] *besides the troops, from whom he could not separate,* whose units, like the majority of those that compose the Army of the Republic, have many surplus officers with respect to their strength, and finally with the hindrance resulting from the artillery train, wagons and mules. He was without a firm campaign plan and was not able to count on a plan that had been made in case there was a defeat. His situation had to have been extremely critical and pressured. In addition to this the position that he occupied was indefensible, so that no one could have achieved military actions. With great prudence he retreated to the habitation of Madam Pawell and reunited there the different units and decided to repass the Colorado and establish the army there to recover from the stated deficiencies and place it in a functioning state. This measure, besides the reasons that are supported by the cited testimonies, was approved by the Supreme Government as can be seen by the official order of May 15.

Up to here Gen. Filisola worked in accordance with the principles of the art of war, and even if the result did not show it, he did what he should have done. Gen. Urrea and some of the witnesses presented by him denied the lack of supplies and assured that they had the ability to advance against the enemy, but the first is made in very general terms and the evidence that has been gathered does not support it. At the least, what has been said in broad terms is that there assuredly was an abundance of supplies at Matagorda, Columbia and Brazoria; Lieutenant Ignacio Salinas said that at the first place there was about five hundred casks of flour, potatoes, chocolate, ham, coffee, about three hundred or four hundred packs of corn, eighteen barrels of rice and seven of crackers, and this is all that was inventoried; and at those [others] all that showed significant quantities are 178 packs of corn, 78 casks of flour, 121 sacks of salt, five barrels of brandy, sixteen barrels of whiskey, eight barrels of meat, likewise six of fish, eight packs of coffee and four boxes of tea. These are very small quantities for the needs of the Army and very different from what Lieutenant Salinas assured. In Columbia and Brazoria inventories were not performed and according to Colonel Salas there was corn in great quantity, about a hundred barrels of flour, various of potatoes and a little rice, although many oils and other effects; but as we have seen that the inventories did not concur with what was calculated to be at the first site, I believe that it will have to be reduced. We have less information of the existence of supplies in Brazoria, but according to the number of homes which were guarded, according to what Colonel Garay said in his declaration, I think that it is about the same as in Matagorda, but it is not a certainty.

But even if the supplies had been sufficient, it would not have made the retreat unavoidable for the purpose of finding a safe distance for reorganizing the army and remedy the rest of the maladies with which it was inflicted, in order to prepare it to take the offensive, working with prudence and caution. Although it might have been possible to mount a weak offensive that might have ended in a victory, especially against an army of amateurs, it is more likely that it would have ended in disgrace. And though a victory might have occurred, even with nothing to support it other than a probability, defeat could have also happened, and the responsibility of it would have fallen to him, with the probability that those circumstances would have been even more disastrous to the Republic.

The retreat until the right bank of the Colorado was approved by the Supreme Government, as is seen in the cited official order; the rains created increased necessities and obligated them to countermarch from point to point until they were able to gain control, and even there they could not remain due to the lack of supplies mentioned in the manifest of Gen. Andrade.

Allow me now to speak about the charge that is aimed at Señor Filisola because it seemed that he began the retreat or

∞

continued it because of the orders that he received from His Excellency Gen. Santa Anna, and that he abandoned the position of Goliad because he received the treaty agreed upon by that Señor General and the Leader of the rebels; but as it has been demonstrated that it was necessary to continue the retreat, I do not blame Sr. Filisola for having demonstrated to Sr. Santa Anna that they were retreating as per his command. Because the Texans were going to see his communications it was prudent to use this language, but I have never in my communications to the Government justified my conduct in similar commands or agreements, but if it is conceded that he was justified to act as he did, given the circumstances, of which we have abundant evidence, that motivated his actions, it is essential that those facts be included [in his defense], for he committed no crime, and since this case must be judged based only on his reaction and action, it does not follow [to accuse him]. It is my judgment that in absolving His Excellency, General of the Division Vicente Filisola, the Supreme Government should also take care to restore his good name and reputation.

Mexico, January 14 of 1837
Eulogio Villa Urrutia.[14]

After this decision was reached, Filisola returned to the army and was soon to replace Nicolás Bravo as commander-in-chief of the northern Mexican army in Matagorda. Urrea's *pronunciamiento* (uprising) failed, but he was later pardoned for this action. Peña, who supported Urrea in his revolution, was not so lucky and eventually ended up in prison. Peña may well have been punished more harshly than most of the participants of the uprising as he had made several VIP enemies in his public criticism of Filisola, Santa Anna, and Gaona.

Another interesting opinion offered after the fact is that of General Santa Anna. Even though he was only indirectly involved in the retreat and was a prisoner during much of the fallout from the retreat,

14. "La guerra de Texas: Causa formada al Gral. Filisola por su retirada en 1836," Tomo X, No. 3, pp. 597–599.

he presented strong thoughts on the subject when he wrote his *Manifiesto que de sus operaciones en la campaña de Texas y en su cautiverio; dirige a sus conciudadonos* (Manifest of his Operations in the Campaign of Texas and his Captivity; Directed to his Fellow Citizens):

> I had no doubt that in the early confusion caused during the first moments of a disaster with the magnitude of the one at San Jacinto, our troops' operations needed to be suspended temporarily. They needed to stop in order to renew the soldiers' ideal for avenging the recent outrage, and to convince them that justice and superiority were on their side. A new attack on the enemy should have been, and could have been attempted successfully. Faced with a force three times larger, as it was possible to organize, and due to a dispatch that should have been made and wasn't, respect for our lives would have been undoubtedly different. It was unbelievable, yet there it was. We were left stranded and abandoned to the mercy and agenda of our enemy.
>
> Nevertheless, General Filisola's retreat could not have come from any other idea than from his own. It was completely opposed to mine as regards this point. In his reply to my dispatch of the 22nd he said that he was moved by a concern for my safety, a desire to save my life and the life of the rest of the prisoners, in spite of knowing how advantageous it would be for our Army to continue the hostilities. I was filled with gratitude at such a noble gesture, even though later, in light of the public's disapproval of his choice, he attributed his action to other causes. In my judgment his first sentiment was the true one, and I shall always hold a deep respect for him in my heart. Unless of course it was the change in the reasons he later gave that has brought such censure upon my honor regarding the state of the army under my command.
>
> Much has been said about the lack of supplies. I'm ashamed to admit that a lack of resources was not, for me, reason enough to delay a march on San Jacinto by an army that was only sixteen leagues away, and by an army that has always been justly admired for its endurance and suffering, under all kinds of privation. However, there was meat and

other provisions in abundance. There were more provisions on the way, perhaps not of the finest quality, but sufficient enough to avert perishing from hunger, which was not the case on the retreat to Matamoros, that is to say, a retreat close to two hundred leagues long.

Two days would have sufficed for the forces at Thompson's, or for the entire army to have crossed the river at Brazoria under the protection of General Urrea. They could have struck the enemy and thus repaired the debacle of the 21st.

The Army's position beyond the Brazos would have been free of the obstacles presented by the terrain in the course of the retreat, and after the rains of the 27th. By that time the enemy could have been crushed, and the supplies that I took in New Washington and were later overtaken by the enemy could have remained in our possession. In my judgment, the above-mentioned option should have encouraged that General who took over my command to lead an attack. At the risk of sounding presumptuous and of flattering myself, I feel that if I had reached Thompson's three days before as I had intended, victory would have been in our hands.

I was greatly surprised, when I learned later about the retreat, mounted so precipitously and so against my true wishes. May I be allowed a bit of pride, as I make an observation about the lethargy that can only come to rest on the other person guilty of it. On the 20th of April, the major portion of the army was together, after it had crossed the Colorado River. Just two Divisions would have been sufficient to engage the enemy and to support each other had it not been for an unfortunate chain of coincidences.

We had had plenty of food, munitions and other supplies—even more than what was essential. We had won at every encounter. Our rearguard and our flanks were protected; yet from the instant that I was captured, the army retreats, food becomes scarce, our positions are abandoned, and the army concentrates its force two hundred leagues distant from where it should have been, and where it had left six hundred prisoners completely abandoned and left to their own fate. At what point did the army fulfill its objective and its duty?

I foresaw that the troops would be disconcerted and I seized the moment and Houston's proposal, buying the army the necessary time to regroup through the means of the armistice I concluded, and by which the army chose to use as a passport to retreat unmolested.

The only thing that was done for the prisoners by the leader into whose hands my command now rested was to send General Woll as an emissary rather than to conclude the armistice; or better yet rather than to appreciate it, given that a prisoner had crafted it. Woll did nothing more than to deliver and carry messages, and when that General was apprehended and treated badly, not a single protest was made. He was forgotten completely, and had only the efforts of the president prisoner to protect him.

I gave that general spoken instruction, so as not to place him in a vulnerable position regarding my judgment about what the army should do. The objective, of course, was to not allow the enemy to enjoy his victory. I also gave him a written directive in which I stated that the information he imparted in my name was to be trusted.

However, no other thought occupied the army except to retreat. Fear reached such a pitch as to have the army consider allowing the Texan prisoners in our possession, numbering over 100, to escape or to be set free without any thought to setting up a prisoner exchange for those of us captured at San Jacinto. Even our sick were abandoned. In short, the army's proximity, its mode of operation, its Commander's dignity to not allow himself to be overwhelmed by one small setback, anything the army could have done for those of us who were held prisoners would have given us hope and would have allowed us to raise our voices in defense of justice. Instead, the army's support was just not there, and we were left to the mercy of the victorious, in the midst of an undisciplined rabble, filled with pride of a significant but unprotested triumph.[15]

15. Santa Anna, "Manifiesto que de sus operaciones en la campaña de Tejas y en su cautiverio dirige á sus conciudadanos" (excerpt from), in Peña, *La rebelión de Texas,* Anexo No. 21, pp. 279–280; translated for G. Dimmick by Dora Elizondo Guerra.

The above statement by Santa Anna, written after his return to Mexico, is a masterpiece. It shows why Santa Anna was such an expert at staying on top of the Mexican political machine for all those years. He made gross exaggerations of the facts, i.e., that the Texans surely would have abandoned the prisoners and all their captured stores had Filisola only bothered to show up at the scene. He contradicted himself repeatedly, i.e., they should not have obeyed me; but when I sent word with Woll as to what the army should do they did not obey me. He totally ignored the fact that even with the best troops and with the commander who, in his own mind, would have still won the day, had he escaped, the Mexican army suffered one of the greatest one-sided defeats in the annals of military history. Yet, if one is to believe the above statement, none of the occurrences were his fault and he acted only in a way to allow Filisola to achieve a simple movement against an overmatched enemy. Pick any paragraph in the above statement and exaggeration, twisted logic, or outright lies are easily found. One has to respect the bombastic stylings of Gen. Antonio López de Santa Anna that are so apparent in his writings even after all these years. His statements made the biased barbs of Filisola, Urrea, Peña, and Ramírez y Sesma seem like the works of rank amateurs.

Santa Anna remained a prisoner in Texas for quite some time. The government of the Republic of Texas never could agree on whether to send him back to Mexico or to execute him. Finally they washed their hands of the affair and sent him to Washington, D.C., to meet with Andrew Jackson. Jackson allowed the fallen Mexican hero to return to Mexico but he was not well received in his native country. He was called back to power from retirement at his hacienda, Manga de Clavo, for the Pastry War but was eventually exiled to the United States. In 1846 the Mexican American war broke out and Santa Anna was smuggled back into Mexico by the Americans to help stop the war. On his return to Mexico Santa Anna was begged by the Mexicans to lead them in their fight against the Americans. On February 22, 1847, after a forty-mile forced march with very little to eat or drink, Santa Anna's army of over eighteen thousand Mexican soldiers attacked and nearly defeated Zachary Taylor and his American army at the Battle of Buena Vista.

The Pastry War, as it came to be known, was another development that very likely delayed the second Mexican campaign. The war got its name because one of the first French citizens to lose his wares to a rioting mob was a baker. The French, fed up with the poor treatment of their citizens during the many outbreaks of the Mexican federalist wars in the late 1820s and early 1830s, in 1838 blockaded Vera Cruz and several other ports; for a short time in December of 1838 Vera Cruz was occupied by the French. Santa Anna was reinstated as commander of the Mexican army and attacked the French as they were abandoning the city. He lost his left leg in the action but was able to convince the Mexican people that he had won a great victory. The Mexican government finally agreed to settle with the French. It was during this time that Urrea started a new *pronunciamiento* in Sonora. The Pastry War was but a small matter in the course of Mexican history but was very significant to the Texans in that it gave them precious time to strengthen their hold on newly conquered lands.[16]

The Mexican army did mount two invasions of Texas in 1842 but they were not serious attempts to retake their captured territory. The first was in March of 1842 and was aimed at San Antonio. At the same time a small Mexican army crossed the Rio Grande and advanced as far as Goliad. Both these incursions were short-lived and the Mexican forces quickly withdrew from Texas. The next incursion was in September of 1842 and was led by Gen. Adrian Woll. San Antonio was seized and many Texans were captured. After an encounter at Salado Creek the Mexican forces withdrew.[17]

16. Hubert Howe Bancroft, *History of Mexico,* Volume 5, 1824–1861 (6 vols.; San Francisco: A. L. Bancroft & Co., 1885), 186–205. This is volume 13 of *The Works of Hubert Howe Bancroft* (39 vols.; San Francisco: A. L. Bancroft & Co., 1882–1890).

17. Clarence R. Wharton, *History of Texas* (Houston: Turner Co., 1935), 217–218.

CHAPTER 14

Conclusion

AFTER THE BATTLE OF SAN JACINTO the Mexican army was in a very poor situation. They were spread all over the state of Texas—San Antonio, Refugio, Goliad, Victoria, Columbia, Brazoria, Cópano, and Old Fort. Santa Anna had been so confident of victory that he had formulated only a cursory battle plan. To make matters worse, he had not discussed the situation with his second in command, Vicente Filisola. Filisola had spent precious little time, face to face, with Santa Anna, since they had left San Antonio on March 31. Santa Anna had sent Gaona to the north, Urrea to the south and he would personally advance in the middle. That plan, however, fell apart when Santa Anna took off in pursuit of the Texan government, which had recently moved from Washington-on-the-Brazos to Harrisburg. The fact that Gaona managed to get lost east of Bastrop certainly contributed to the disruption of Santa Anna's strategy.

Even though Santa Anna had with him at San Jacinto only about twelve hundred of the six thousand or so soldiers that he brought into Texas, they were by far the best troops in his army. The only other capable division was that of Urrea and its effectiveness had been hampered by the losses suffered on its march north. The strength of the Mexican army, their cavalry, was mostly left in San Antonio, due to the deplorable condition of their horses after a terrible trip into Texas. As if all this were not enough, they had been hampered by not one, but two blizzards while marching north to meet the Texan uprising.

When Filisola got the news of the disastrous defeat suffered by

Santa Anna he acted immediately without considering his options. Apparently one of his primary concerns was to reunite with Urrea. The latter general was the undefeated leader of the southern force, and the only Mexican general who had been making decisions independently of Santa Anna. Filisola immediately formulated plans to unite with Urrea as quickly as possible. Even though he had already ordered Urrea to join him at Old Fort, Filisola sent Urrea a new order telling him to follow Filisola's guide to a point yet to be determined. Filisola would not even wait for Gaona to finish crossing the Brazos before leaving Old Fort. There is good evidence that he left in such a hurry that he actually got lost on the night of April 23 and ended up at Madam Powell's by mistake.

Retrospectively, this sudden knee-jerk reaction was probably Filisola's worst decision. As events eventually played out, this was likely his only real opportunity to confront the Texans with any reasonable hope of success. He had a large number of Gaona's troops across the Brazos at Old Fort and Urrea had, or was at least close to getting, some of his troops across the Brazos at Brazoria. Had Filisola immediately commenced the movement toward the Texans, it is possible that he could have reached San Jacinto by April 25. Had he done so he might have caught the Texans disorganized and unprepared for another battle.

There were many potential problems with this would-be course of action. First of all, it would have required a coordinated movement of two separate armies, one of which, Urrea's, was divided between Matagorda, Columbia, and Brazoria. Had the two divisions been able to pull off the maneuver, they would have arrived at San Jacinto after a difficult river crossing and two long days' march. They would have had to leave all the female camp followers unprotected or have used much needed soldiers to protect them. Even if they had been able to overcome all these obstacles, they still would have had to deal with the deluge that commenced April 26.

Another factor that would have come into play is the consideration that Houston likely would have known they were coming. He sent his spies out immediately to look for Mexican stragglers from the battle and watch for any Mexican reinforcements. If indeed Houston had known of their impending arrival, there is certainly no guarantee that he and the Texans would have stood and fought when Filisola arrived at the scene, ready to do battle. Other than the encumbrance of the Mexican prisoners there was nothing to prevent the Texans from withdrawing to Galveston or toward the Louisiana border. There was also the matter of the emboldened reinforcements that it has been documented were rushing into Texas daily. To make matters more difficult, American troops were soon to mass along the Texas-Louisiana border, supposedly to subdue rowdy Indians.

When all these dynamics are considered, it is apparent that Filisola's chances of victory, had he acted immediately, were slim at best. At the time, his decision to reunite all his forces in the surrounding area was without a doubt the right decision. This is true only because he was unaware of the upcoming storm and the devastating trek through the Mar de Lodo. Had he been able to see into the future, his best chance of victory would have been to attack immediately. The fact that he carried out the movement with such haste and confusion might reflect poorly upon him but that in itself does not make the decision a bad one. It is interesting to note that even the Mexican government, in its orders to Filisola and in its trial verdict, had no problem with his withdrawal to Powell's and subsequently on to the opposite bank of the Colorado.

From the Mexican accounts, as biased as they generally were, it seems as though all the Mexican generals, including Urrea, were in agreement that the best thing to do was to withdraw to Goliad, get resupplied, summon the troops from San Antonio, and await orders from Mexico City. At the time, this agreement, made at the meeting of April 25, was not an agreement to retreat out of Texas, or to discontinue hostilities. It is apparent that, at the time the decision was made, the generals had every intention of renewing the campaign, depending on the desires of the Mexican government. It is likely that this was the reason that Urrea did not initially seem to oppose the original plan as vehemently as he later claimed.

On April 26, while crossing the San Bernard River, the situation took a dramatic turn for the worse. It is hard to imagine how the situation could possibly deteriorate after months of forced marches, blizzards, dead and wounded at the Alamo and Coleto, lack of supplies, and the complete defeat of their commander-in-chief and twelve hundred of their premier troops—but it did. The downpour that commenced on that day was foreign to the Mexican soldiers. From the description of the storm it may have been one of those once-in-a-decade events. The Mexican forces were not equipped to maneuver in this weather. During the entire campaign they had been hindered by their lack of efficient means to cross major waterways. Now that weakness was to be greatly magnified by this horrendous storm.

To make matters even more intriguing, if that was possible, the news of Santa Anna's capture and his orders to withdraw were received on April 27—when the army was camped along the flooded West Bernard Creek and Filisola was trying to decide what his next move was to be. There is little doubt that the arrival of these dispatches had no effect on the plans of Filisola and his generals.

If anything, considering the fact that they had decided they needed time to hear from Mexico City, the temporary halt to the hostilities could only have helped them. The only factors that were changing their plans were the weather and the terrain. How ironic it is that the very land that they were fighting to preserve for their country turned out to be as much of an adversary as the Texan army. It was nature that forced the Mexican army to alter their planned route, which had initially been to retrace the path of Urrea during his advance up the coast. On the advice of Urrea's own guides, Filisola altered their destination to the Atascosito Crossing of the Colorado River. Unfortunately for the Mexican army this redirection steered them directly into the heart of the worst terrain they possibly could have encountered in wet weather. They bogged down in a sea of mud, or as Filisola called it, *un Mar de Lodo*. The Mexican army entered the prairie bog on April 28 and did not finish crossing the Colorado River, a mere twenty miles from where they had entered, until May 9.

It was a miracle and a testament to the determination of the Mexican officers and soldiers that they were able to traverse the Mar de Lodo at all. It seems almost beyond belief that they were able to cross this quagmire with 2500 men, 1500 women, eight pieces of artillery, 120 wagons, and 1200 to 1500 mules. Essentially, by the descriptions of those involved, this was accomplished for the most part with human power, as the mules and horses were barely able to move in the muck.

After extracting itself from the mud the Mexican army was in no shape to even think about mounting an offensive against the Texans. They were now in a survival mode. They had left much of their armaments, supplies, etc., scattered in the mud to be discovered by avocational archeologists 164 years later. In addition to the abandoned gear, the army seemed to have left its will to fight, as well. This was the moment when their leaders realized that they would eventually have to retreat all the way to Mexico and that there would be hell to pay when they got there. This is the point when the plan fell apart and the movement of the Mexican army was no longer an organized and calculated one but a slow drifting of individual groups toward Mexico. Thus, it was also the moment when the posturing and finger-pointing became the norm among the leaders.

Had there been no Mar de Lodo it is quite conceivable that Filisola and the Mexican army would have reached Goliad as a viable fighting force. They certainly could have maintained their position there long enough to allow the one thousand soldiers from San Antonio to join them. They could have been resupplied from the port of Cópano.

If not for the Mar de Lodo, it is possible that Filisola's decision to take the conservative approach and await further orders may eventually have led to victory. This scenario, however, seems almost as implausible as the scenario of the immediate attack. The Texan army would have had even more time to organize and get reinforced. The Mexican troops had less confidence and no significant financial resources from their government in Mexico. They had only been able to get the first campaign off the ground because of the power and backing of Santa Anna. How were they possibly going to refinance a second campaign, whether it was launched from Goliad or from Matamoros?

In 1828 General Manuel de Mier y Terán made an inspection tour of Texas.[1] At the time Mier y Terán reported to the Mexican government that it would need to take immediate action to prevent the loss of Texas. He recommended four steps and felt that if they were not enacted immediately Texas would be lost. First, he recommended immediate reinforcement of the garrison at Béjar. Second, he felt that the immigration of North Americans into Texas should be suspended. Third, that the eastern part of Texas, where the rivers were navigable, should be reserved for Mexican settlers. Lastly, that garrisons of troops

1. Mier y Terán, *Texas by Terán*, 27–39.

should be used to establish new colonies in Texas. General Terán was apparently a wise man and evaluated the situation well.

Unfortunately for Mexico, it did not have the will or the resources to carry out his plan. By the time Santa Anna entered Texas it is likely that the die was cast. Had he won at San Jacinto it certainly would have temporarily halted the advance of the Americans. However, in the long run, there seems to be little doubt that the flow of the Americans to the west would have continued. Several factors played a role in this seemingly unstoppable migration. The tremendous population explosion in the U.S. and the resultant land-hunger was fed by the supply of cheap labor that slavery provided. The climate of Texas was very similar to that of the southern United States making the adjustment for the Anglo settlers easier than that for an immigrant from Saltillo or Monclova.

The movements of Filisola and the Mexican army after the battle of San Jacinto were a major part of the Mexican campaign in Texas. The fact that the trials and tribulations of the Mexican army in the Mar de Lodo have been forgotten is a shame, especially considering that the episode played a major role in the outcome of the conflict.

After evaluating the various options available to Filisola on April 22, 1836, there are none that would have given him more than a slight chance at victory. Thus, even though the Mar de Lodo was a major factor in the outcome of the conflict, it cannot be classified as decisive. Accordingly, if one accepts the premise that the Anglo invasion of Texas was out of the Mexicans' control by 1836, one would also have to argue that the battle of San Jacinto was not decisive but merely a major factor. Although it is not true that the Mar de Lodo alone caused the downfall of the retreating Mexican army, it is true that it did rapidly speed up their exit from Texas. The mud and muck of the Mar de Lodo may well have saved the Texans from having to suffer further losses on the battlefield in forcing the Mexican army back to Mexico. It does seem ironic that by greatly slowing down their withdrawal the Mar de Lodo greatly hastened their exit from Texas.

There are many details of the Mexican army's trek though the Mar de Lodo yet unanswered. What was their exact path and where was the campsite of April 27? Did Urrea truly fight against the retreat from the outset, as he later claimed? Was Filisola truly feigning obedience to Santa Anna, as he later claimed, or was he remov-

∞

ing himself and the army from Texas with the greatest haste? Even though there are no definitive answers to these questions we at least have some insight into the issues. More importantly they are now at least known to be issues.

After a long hiatus the tale of the tenacious Mexican *soldados* and *soldaderas* in the Mar de Lodo has returned to the spotlight of historical awareness.

APPENDIX I

∞

Diary of an Anonymous officer
From José Urrea's diary

April 29: Today our bad luck reached its limit. Since the previous day, the wagons had fallen behind, and some of our sick, which were generally looked upon with disdain, died. It filled one with indignation to see the insult heaped upon these men in their misery. Even the generals viewed them with disdain, especially Gaona. As if men should not be allowed to fall ill, even under such miserable conditions. The vanguard began its march at 8:00. By 10:30 the rearguard had not yet begun its departure.

Before initiating the march, there was an effort to empty the wagons of their cargo. Munitions, rope and canvas, artillery quickmatch and numerous other items were discarded. The soldiers managed to salvage some of it. In contrast, some of the officers had three and four mules each, and the generals and other superiors took four times their share of plunder. Someday the cost of what was discarded will come to light.

I walked knee deep in mud, floundering endlessly until I lost my shoes. Without a choice, I continued thus. Barely did we give thirty or forty paces before having to stop to have the soldiers retrieve the wagons that were stuck in the mud up to their axles.

Between five or six in the afternoon, having traveled about five or six miles, each unit camped where they could, including the generals and officers. Clusters of soldiers could be seen all over, scattered one from the other. The artillery had been left behind, stuck in the mud two or three miles into the march. Loads of our ammunition, supplies and equipment remained scattered along our way, and what managed to make it through, at the cost of immense effort, ended up being useless. Much equipment was lost. Many of the mules were disabled, and the troops went without food because its shipment went missing. Nothing was found to eat. It is impossible to describe that day's march. It was a total loss.

General Urrea and his brigade were ordered to push forward toward the Colorado in order to prepare the means for crossing the river, and to safeguard it. The officers and troops were exceedingly frustrated. There was enormous discontent at the inability to inspect the roads before getting buried in them, while suffering untold hardship and hunger. The road to San Felipe de Austin is on high ground, and we had traveled it successfully during heavy rain. Why did we not take that road, if during rain, the condition of the present one was unknown?

30th: On the 30th the generals and infantry advanced, leaving behind a picket from each unit under the command of General Ampudia to retrieve the artillery and as much of the other equipment as was salvageable. And so it was that the march continued in whatever way it could. It was impossible not to grieve at the sight of over fifteen hundred mules scattered in every direction. No sooner were some pulled out, than others would sink, and this chain of events plagued us the whole distance. Everything went badly, everything was a struggle and a pain. Since the previous day's march had been as hard, the equipment, munitions and cans of canister were barely findable in the mud.

COLORADO RIVER, MAY 5: The 29th and 30th of April and the 1st, 2nd, and 3rd of May have been for me the most arduous of this campaign. In the last three days I was able to walk approximately twenty or twenty-one miles in mud and without a bite to eat. In addition, I had to deal with my unit's supplies and equipment. Mine were the first to arrive.

On the 3rd I crossed the river with all that was my responsibility and I was presented with a letter from Mexico City that caused me greater grief than all else I had just endured. Destiny has a way of unleashing its bitter blows to destroy those it has chosen as its victims. Today's general orders state that henceforth neither the officers nor the generals will have at their disposal any more mules than what the army regulations specify, and that there will be one mule assigned for each eighty men. It is just a directive, and had it been obeyed from the onset of the campaign, much money and many mules would have been saved. The disorder caused by these animals has been notorious. Some of their owners, under contract to the government, loaded them with corn they were picking along the way, and then selling to the soldiers. Some of these owners protested against this recent directive, because they needed the mules to carry whatever comestibles were found along the way. They weren't being unreasonable [in their objections]. However, a different means of transporting their goods could have been foreseen and provided, without increasing the number of mules. Ramírez y Sesma advanced on the 3rd, and rumor had it that he took with him 67 loaded mules.

MAY 7, Colorado River: Yesterday, Mr. Alexander Alsbury arrived at camp. He is a member of the enemy's army and confirms that our troops were indeed defeated in a surprise attack forty-five miles from the Brazos River, on the West bank of the San Jacinto. As of the day of his departure he declares that there were thirty senior and junior officers held prisoners, and about five hundred and fifty to six hundred troops. The rest are lying out in the fields unburied. He declares that the battle lasted twenty-two minutes, and that some officers like Francisco Aguado chose to die rather than turn over their swords. He (Alsbury) said that he was ordered by the enemy (Texan) cavalry commander to call out to Santa Anna, who was in the woods, and stipulate his safety.

A young enemy soldier found this general [Santa Anna] the day after the battle, around 1:00 in the afternoon. When the young soldier asked where General Santa Anna might be, he replied that the general had left and that he was one of his aides. Alsbury added that Santa Anna was disguised when he was found, and that is how he was presented to Houston, in whose tent he requested to be taken. That is what actually saved him, because those whose friends had been executed by his orders were very angry with him. It became known that one of the enemy's cavalry commanders was opposed to saving Santa Anna's life. Shouts could be heard from the forest to execute him.

Alsbury also has said that on the 23rd some of the enemies ammunition and that captured from us, was about to burn. This was due to a fire that started in some cartridges and set off some muskets and pistols. This caused great alarm. Accordingly, the sentinels surrounding Santa Anna held him at gunpoint. The aforementioned Alsbury agreed that we should have not taken the road we did. Instead we should have taken the Goliad road. He is a sensible man, but is passionately loyal to the enemy, and he is as presumptuous and as haughty as the rest of them, who consider themselves superior to us, notwithstanding what poor soldiers they all are.

∞

Appendix 1

We spent last night and today arguing. I have pointed out to him that the only one they have defeated is Santa Anna. I have agreed with him that they have the law on their side regarding the lands they own legitimately in Texas, but I have also told him, a thousand times, that it is our right to preserve the integrity of our territory at all cost, or cease to exist.

It was Santa Anna's weakness that accepted such an agreement. My opinion about this unfortunate general, in his present situation, is that he has neutralized his weakness by giving himself the power to act as mediator [between Texas and the Mexican Congress?]. Alsbury adds that he [Santa Anna] had had a conference with Zavala on the 26th, and had asked him why he hadn't waited for him in Harrisburg. He replied with a great deal of disdain that he wasn't so _____ [*sic*] to do that, since [Santa Anna], not satisfied with having chased him [Zavala] throughout Mexico, had had to come to Texas to persecute him. It is unkind of him [Santa Anna] to insult the man [Zavala] in his disgrace because of disputes they had had in the past.

Much of our foodstuff spoiled on the 28th, 29th and 30th of April, and on May 1st, 2nd and 3rd. The drovers carrying our goods stole much of it and threw the rest of it away. Because of one of the most outrageous orders, many of the officers traveling in clusters with soldiers, appropriated more than they really needed. The artillery brought in by the sweat of the soldiers began to arrive yesterday, and finally all of it arrived at camp around 1:00 or 2:00 in the morning. The artillery commander and his officers deserve to be commended for their successful achievement at the river crossing, as well as with their dealings with Karnes and with proceedings over property claims, a dispatch, and slaves. The enemy continues haughty. Our Commander-in-Chief's good standing plummets.

MAY 23: [After (part of the diary) describing Texas, its forests, rivers and meadows, He continues. (this is Urrea's note)] Yesterday, at five in the afternoon, Henry Karnes and W. D. Redd arrived at this camp. Redd is aide-de-Camp to Rusk, the American leader. They brought a letter informing us that our prisoners will be set free soon, and it talked further about a prisoner exchange. The commander-in-Chief, accompanied by Generals Tolsa, Colonels Amat, Montoya, Mariano Garcia and the officers, met the enemy emissaries at the point where our advance had been ordered to halt. Those who wished that the man who is now in command of our

∞

army possessed more dignity ridiculed the form this encounter took.

MAY 25: There is much to relate today. Our Commander-in-Chief had news the night before last that the Americans were in Victoria. Since Mr. Redd and his companions, who had left on the 24th, had assured us that there wasn't a force there, it was believed by some of the more skittish geniuses in our midst that they had lied to us, and that they were probably planning to surprise us. It was also murmured that when they [the emissaries] had gone to look in on one of their prisoners who was hospitalized, their true objective was to reconnoiter our camp. Some said they even saw them making observations.

Nothing had been mentioned in yesterday's orders about a march, but at dawn reveille was sounded, followed rapidly by all the successive calls. We arrived on the 17th at these ruins. It rained excessively all of that night and the following day. It hadn't rained again until today when in early morning the North wind began to blow hard, accompanied by very heavy rain that lasted three hours.

We had been here for eight days already, supposedly, as word had it, waiting for Señor Andrade to join us with his troops from Béjar; but what with the inopportune march in the worst weather, on top of the misgivings that sprung up last night—all this gave rise to some unfavorable reflection and conjectures. It was pouring down rain, and although the last bugle call had sounded, suddenly two soldiers and three other persons could be seen. Some of our men believed the enemy were upon us, and they prepared to take a stand.

It turned out to be Benjamin F. Smith, McPentire [sic], and Henry Teal, whose ranks were Colonel, Major and Captain in the Texas army. They were carrying the agreement crafted between the man who still considered himself at the head of the Mexican Army and with the President of what was now calling itself the Government of Texas. The two orderlies with them were the first and only two soldiers ever seen in uniform to date. Our troops thought it rather strange.

The essential points of the articles in said agreement began to become apparent, in spite of the subterfuge exercised to conceal them. Everyone who heard the terms was outraged; making it clear that there still exist Mexicans wishing to preserve the honor of being Mexican.

Nothing could be more dishonorable for us than this agreement, hatched by those who promoted the separation of Texas. But it is even more dishonorable for that one Mexican who signed it. General Santa Anna had done many despicable things in his political career, but never so base as to sell out his nation and abandon such a territorial jewel as was Texas, as if he had had the power to do so, posing as he did as if he were still the head of our republic. That is to what this agreement has brought us [a sell out].

Under the same circumstances, another man would have blown out his brains, rather than sign away his honor. It's impossible to see this in any other light. He should have had the courage to accept the consequences that his cruelty caused, turning this war into a savage blood bath. He should have refrained from giving a single order, given that he had a perfectly legitimate excuse for the captors who were obliging him to sign. His excuse of course was that his orders would not be obeyed, as indeed they should have not been obeyed.

General Filisola who had been saying Amen to everything the prisoner [Santa Anna] had ordered, once again uttered an Amen after having read this heinous agreement. He replied that the terms of the agreement would be met. However, if he uses condescending language with the enemy, it is my opinion that it is because he considers the response the more acceptable, and not because he wanted to please the prisoner general.

Nevertheless, the author of this account wished passionately that he [Filisola] would rise to the dignity of his position and to the dignity of the army he now commanded in his dealings with the commissioners. With the combined Andrade and Urrea Divisions, he had more than four thousand men under his command. The enemy at best has 1500. The enemy claims he has 2000, but we all know his penchant for exaggeration, even when there are statistics that point to the first figure as being the more accurate.

It is true however, that we are not in a position to arm an offensive for lack of food, supplies, the rain and mud, and other obstacles that will be mentioned subsequently. We were however in a position to use stronger language with an enemy who felt victorious over having surprised only one of the vanguard divisions.

Since one of the demands of the agreement specified that all property belonging to the colonists be returned, and that they be recompensed for the rest, General Filisola began to meet that demand by turning over a young Black boy he took when we crossed the Colorado. The boy had served him as a driver. [Filisola] said he would return everything they recognized as theirs, and to that end Smith, Teal and Filisola began their inspection, and settled other matters. Regarding payment of damages, Filisola had already said he didn't carry money, but that the Government would pay what would be owed.

We, on the other hand, did not have anything that we lost at San Jacinto returned to us. The only compensation our nation received after war was the loss of the territory we had come to defend, and we did not even have commissioners to speak for our side. We repeat that General Filisola is the finest, most honorable man, and if his conduct is to be reproached, it will be with pity. Maybe he could have done better, but he is, in the end, simply ineffective, and has no one around him to come to his aid. He would rather have turned over his entire pay to anyone willing to spare him his charge, unburdening him from the weight of what he is compelled to confront.

We have skimmed through the agreement, and we believe that he [Filisola] was under no obligation to obey until the Government stepped in. If Filisola would be so weak as to approve it [the agreement], though we don't dare to speculate, his shame would be greater than the shame of the man who signed it in the first place. His fall from grace would be inevitable, and from his ruin the national government will rise to vindicate the nation from this outrage.

I have written to Mexico on the 4th and on the 12th, urging them not to be faint in the face of weak men. Better to die than to give up this most beautiful territory. Neither the government nor the nation has even a notion of this land's value. But even if it wasn't worth anything, its honor precedes all, but first it is important to hold on to it, and later, if seen fit, it could be sold or given away.

[Translation by Dora Elizondo Guerra.]

Author's Note: This document is a translation of Appendix No. 33 in Urrea's diary. It is obviously the work of Peña as it is basically the same as the final draft of the Peña memoirs. There are slight differences, in regard to both the clean version of the diary that is included in the Peña Papers and the final draft of the memoirs. It

∞

Appendix 1   331

should be noted that there is material in this version that is not in the initial work but is in the final version. There is also material in this translation that is in the initial work but is not in the final version. Thus it is likely that there were at least three separate variations of Peña's account of the Texas campaign. It seems logical that the version given above was the "middle" version of the three.

Deposition of Cavalry Captain and Field Commissioned Lt. Col. José Enrique de la Peña[1]

COURT MINUTES:

On this day, month and year [1836], Lt. Col. José Enrique de la Peña was summoned to appear before the District Judge, and in my presence as Secretary, he was asked to place his right hand over the hilt of his sword and was asked the following questions:

QUESTION: Do you give your word of honor to tell the truth in everything asked of you during this interrogation?

REPLY: I do.

QUESTION: What is your name and occupation?

REPLY: My name is José Enrique de la Peña and I am a Cavalry Captain and Field Commissioned Lt. Colonel assigned to the Corp of Engineers.

QUESTION: Where were you in April of this year, and what was your occupation?

REPLY: I was in the Army of Operations over Texas in charge of a Sapper Company.

QUESTION: On the nineteenth, did you leave Hold-Fort with said Company by order of Colonel Agustin Amat, and what was the reason given for that departure?

REPLY: On said day, I left with the Sapper Battalion and about sixty men from various pickets from the infantry who had been attached to that battalion. We took a six pounder and fifty cavalry-men. We were ordered to go to Columbia to surprise a group of about sixty Americans, and to capture a store of food and supplies about which a group of Coaxtes Indians had informed us.

---

1. "La guerra de Texas: Causa formada al Gral. Filisola por su retirada en 1836," Tomo X, No. 3, pp. 543–547.

QUESTION: Did you carry out your objective, and if not, why not?

REPLY: We traveled all night of said day until about two in the afternoon of the following day. The commander of the section believed we had traveled beyond the distance to Columbia, but was unable to ascertain it, because our guides spoke only English, and the commander didn't quite trust the interpreter. He feared that the guides were not acting in good faith. The commander gathered all the captains of the sections and asked their opinions about our circumstances. Several were of the opinion that we should return to camp, but I and the Major attached to the Sappers did not think it would be appropriate to return without fulfilling our mission. I volunteered to advance with a cavalry escort to reconnoiter and determine whether it was true that we were about six or eight miles from Columbia. The Commander, based on his instructions, was empowered to act without consulting with anyone, and he decided to return to camp. We counter marched and reached the Army on the 21st.

QUESTION: When did you learn about the President's defeat, and how was the Army's morale affected? What measures were then taken?

REPLY: On the 22nd, I went to watch General Gaona's section cross the river. He was supposed to go to Nacogdoches. I saw that they were recrossing the river, and later learned that they had done so because the President had been taken by surprise and had been defeated on the banks of the San Jacinto. The reactions were mixed throughout. Some showed apathy and weakness, while others were, on the contrary, resolute, but it can't be said that either emotion was greater than the other. However, everyone believed that we would move forward, or at least hold ground where we were.

QUESTION: What was the status of the Army at that point with regard to armament, munitions, food and other supplies?

REPLY: I believe that the armament was in good condition; at least it was in my section, because we had been very careful with it, particularly because of the very cold weather. Most of the other sections also took very good care of their armament. We had sufficient munitions and they were in good condition, especially General Gaona's section. He had leather covers made for the ammunition boxes, and that kept them well protected. Food was scarce. When I left Béjar with my section, we had already consumed our rations, but as we approached the Colorado we found corn in the houses near Moctezuma and Atascosito passes. My section reserved about one hundred bushels of corn [and] some beans and salt taken from Béjar. Rice was very scarce, and there wasn't any lard or any crackers. We probably had food to last us about a month because a month earlier General Gaona had reserved enough food for two months. There was plenty of beef, given the abundance of livestock in the area that also provided sufficient milk. As for our access to shelter, there was none. The few houses along the way were used as hospitals or for other more essential needs.

QUESTION: Do you know why the Army abandoned Madam Powell's, and upon your retreat from there, are you aware if food and other property was burned or destroyed?

REPLY: The only thing I heard upon leaving Hold–Fort is that we were to join General Urrea. When we began the retreat, we had no means for transporting the barrels and casks of brandy, whiskey and wine that had been found there, and the troops began to drink. I reported this behavior to our commander, and he ordered me to destroy the barrels and casks with a pickaxe. In the process of this I found several loads of beans, and the personal belongings and back packs of our prisoners that were being left behind because we didn't have the means to transport them because, the commanders and other officers had appropriated a greater number of mules than they were allowed. Later, I learned from Corporal Cruz Cisneros of my battalion that several loads of things had been set on fire, and other things had been dumped into the river.

QUESTION: Do you know why a retreat was ordered from Madam Powell's, why it [the army] recrossed the Colorado, why it went to Goliad and why it continued from there to Matamoros? Feel free to say whatever you know regarding this event.

REPLY: On the 24th, when we were at Madam Powell's with General Urrea's Division, the consensus was to go after the enemy. A meeting was called with all the generals and senior officers. I went to see the Senores Ampudia and Juan Morales to recommend that they oppose a retreat. Senor Morales told me that it looked like the plan was set to run, and that neither of them had been asked to attend the meeting because instead they had been ordered to guard the camp. Word had it that we were retreating due to the shortage of food, and

∞

Appendix 2

335

because the soldiers were almost naked. It seemed the aim was to take a position across the Colorado to wait for orders from the Supreme Government.

However, some of the officers in General Urrea's Division said, and Gen. Urrea himself assured me that there was plenty of food everywhere his division had been. From what had been observed, his soldiers seemed to always have food.

As for clothing, it is true that none was left. When we initiated our march to cross the Colorado through Carey's Pass [sic], we crossed the first St. Bernard tributary. It had been raining very heavily and we got trapped in the mud. By the time we got to the second St. Bernard it was so overflowed that it was impossible to cross it. Since there were no bridges or any other means of crossing, the General decided to take the Atascosito road. That road was equally muddy due to the rain that fell on the 26th and 27th. It was so bad that we couldn't even move in it—not on foot or horseback.

The cannon and the battalions became trapped in the mud, and much of our food and ammunition was made useless. In the end it became necessary to leave behind twenty men from each battalion. I personally led a Company of Sappers and all of us were under the command of Lt. Col. Ampudia. It took us from the 28th of April to the 7th of May to retrieve the artillery and to reach the Atascosito. From there we continued our march until we reached Goliad. The word in Goliad was that we were to remain there to protect Cópano and Béjar. The Sapper Battalion was charged with repairing the fortification in Goliad, since it was in need of it. While in Goliad we received wagons and food from the Port of Cópano. I believed we had enough supplies to last us a month, except for crackers and bread, since flour was scarce, so we were receiving only half rations. On the 23rd, we had heard that the enemy had reached Victoria, and on the night of the 24th an alarm was sounded. On the 25th, at dawn, we heard bugle calls with orders to retreat. It poured down a hard rain. Col. Morales told me that the objective was to create a mock retreat in order to lure the enemy so as to engage and defeat him between Goliad and the Guadalupe River. Our operation was to be carried out alongside Senor Andrade.

The Division began the march, but I was ordered to remain in Goliad to guard the supplies that ended up having to be left behind because the mules had been sent to Senor Andrade. I had orders to turn over the supplies to him when he showed up, but before any of this happened, I received orders from the General, Commander-in-Chief to abandon the supplies and to join the Army's main body, which I did.

As to what else I can add, I can say that the general feeling of the Army was to not retreat. There was a lot of grumbling, even among the foot soldiers who were saying that it was better to finish this once and for all than to have to endure all their past hardship.

This atmosphere of discontent obliged General Filisola to call a meeting of all the generals and of the officers of all the units on May 10th. He urged them to put a stop to all the grumbling, or else to be punished for disobeying an order. He emphasized that he was in command, and that their only choice was to obey without question. General Filisola said that if there was anyone with a better proposal for protecting the National honor, then that plan would be followed. General Gaona raised the issue that Senor Filisola's stand regarding absolute and unquestioned obedience was effective only when engaged in a siege of battle.

I have nothing more to add. I swear that all I have said is true on the word of honor I have already given. I also swear that upon having my deposition read back to me, I agree that it is accurate, and I confirm that I am twenty-nine years old.

The witness and the judge signed this deposition in my presence as secretary.

Eulogio de Villaurrutia, Judge (Rubric)
José Enrique de la Peña, Witness (Rubric)
Miguel de Aponte, Secretary (Rubric)

[Translation by Dora Elizondo Guerra.]

APPENDIX 3

Unit Strengths of the Mexican Army, May 9, 1836

ARMY OF OPERATIONS

General state of the force of all the units that compose the army on this stated day.	colonel	Lt. Col.	1st Adj.	2nd Adj.	sub Adj.	Capt.	Lt.
Veteran Units							
Artillery		2					1
Zapadores Btn.		1	1			2	
Jiménez Btn.		1		1	1	7	7
Morelos Btn.		1	1	1	1	6	7
Active Units							
1st Active of Mexico	1		2	1		4	7
San Luis Potosi Btn.		1		1		3	7
Querétaro Btn.	1		1		1	3	3
Guadalajara Btn.		1			4	6	9
Aux. of Guanajuato			1			5	9
Permanent Cavalry							
Cuautla						2	2
Tampico						2	2
Presidial							1
Active Cavalry							
Active Durango						1	
Total	2	6	7	4	3	39	51

Camp on the Colorado River, May 9 of 1836.—Lt. Cayetano Montoya.—
[Vo. Bo.] Vicente Filisola.

From "La Guerra de Texas: Causa formada al Gral. Filisola por su retirada en 1836," Table no. 1.

sub Lt.	1st Sgt.	2nd Sgt.	gunsmith	bugler	musician	corporal	pvt.	total[1]
5	2	3		2		6	57	**70**
2	6	8			16	17	97	**144**
9	12	23	1	8	15	34	200	**293**
2	4	13	1		21	30	314	**388**
4	6	15		4	21	28	232	**306**
4	7	11		6	10	34	344	**412**
3	5	9		3	10	23	206	**256**
	3	18		5	7	31	190	**253**
	19			10	35	221		**285**
	8	2		5		8	91	**74**[2]
	1	7		2		15	88	**113**
				1		6	30	**40**
						1	1	
	57	**128**	**2**	**36**	**110**	**267**	**2031**	**2630**[3]

[1] Totals are given for enlisted men only.

[2] This is added incorrectly. It should be 114.

[3] The correct total should be 2675.

∞

Appendix 3

〜

Unit Strengths and Condition of the Mexican Army, May 14, 1836

Army of Operations against Texas—State of the force, armament, munitions, supplies, means of transport and health it had on the expressed day.

UNITS	Col.	Lt. Col	1st Adj	capt	2nd adj & lts	sub lts, sub adj'ens.	surg	sgt	musicians	cpl & pvt	total*
PERMANENT INFANTRY											
Sappers		1	1	2	2	3		15	16	140	171
Aldama Btn.			1	2	2			1	4	66	72
Jiménez Btn.		1		7	9	21		28	23	203	250
Morelos Btn.	1	1	1	7	10	14		20	21	389	430
Matamoros Btn.		1		1	1	2		4	5	39	48
Guerrero Btn.		1		2	2				15	15	
Unattached officers and troops	3	1	1	2	1						—
ACTIVE INFANTRY											
1st of Mexico Btn.	1		2	4	8	16		21	27	373	421
San Luis Potosi Btn.		1		3	9	4		17	15	409	441
Toluca Btn.	1			1		4		3	8	72	83
Guadalajara Btn.			1	4	7	11		27	18	259	304
Querétaro Btn.	1		1	4	3	9		14	15	246	275
Aux. of Guanajuato			1	5	9	7		19	10	261	290
Tres Villas Btn.			1	4	4	6		9	13	167	189
Yucatán Btn.			1	3	5	3	1	10	5	224	239
Unattached officers and troops			1								—
PERMANENT CAVALRY											
Dolores Reg.	1		1	6	10	12		34	17	216	269
Tampico Reg.	1	1		9	5	17		26	13	311	350
Cuautla Reg.				6	4	16		26	15	175	216
Unattached officers and troops	3	1	1	3	2	2					—

UNITS	Col.	Lt. Col	1st Adj	capt	2nd adj & lts	sub lts, sub adj'ens.	surg	sgt	musicians	cpl & pvt	total*
ACTIVE CAVALRY											
Guanajuato Reg.				2		3			1	20	21
Auxiliary Reg.				1		1	1			20	21
Unattached officers and troops						1					—
PRESIDIAL TROOPS & ART.											
Coahuila & Tejas Tamaulipas. and Nuevo León				2		1	1	3		36	39
ARTILLERY		2		1	2	6		9	6	110	125
TOTALS	12	11	13	74	95	163	2	288	232	3753	4273

*Total given is for enlisted men only.

Armaments—There is what is needed of all classes, however some needs repair and cleaning.

Munitions—This is sufficient, most needs to be totally remade.

Campaign Equipment—There is abundance with those seized from the enemy.

Supplies—There is scarcely enough for eight days and no means of procuring them from anyplace other than Matamoros.

Means of transport—There is all that is needed, however all the mules are in bad condition, due to the great amount of work.

Military Health—The army wants for medical men and medicines.

Money—Not one peso, all that was destined for the Army has been retained in Matamoros by the Commanding General of the departments of Tamaulipas and Nuevo León. Guadalupe Victoria, May 14 of 1836.—Vicente Filisola

From "La guerra de Texas: Causa formada al Gral. Filisola por su retirada en 1836," Table no. 2.

Bibliography

A NOTE ON TRANSLATIONS: Dora Elizondo Guerra has acted as the independent translator of Spanish-language documents researched in the writing of this book. As such, she has translated documents that have never before been translated and documents that have previously been published in translation. Those documents that have never been translated before are footnoted as "translated for G. Dimmick by Dora Elizondo Guerra."

Those documents that have previously been translated by others (Castañeda, Woolsey, Perry, etc.), Guerra has retranslated, comparing the older translation to the original Spanish-language document. In some instances she has corrected or altered the previous translation. This is indicated in the footnote by "retranslated for G. Dimmick by Dora Elizondo Guerra." This follows the citation of the original source and the previous translation of that source.

ARCHIVAL DOCUMENTS

Alsbury, Y. P. Reminiscences. In Eugene C. Barker Papers. Center for American History, University of Texas at Austin (CAH).

Houston, Sam, to Edward Burleson, April 30, 1836. A. J. Houston Papers. Texas State Library, Archives Division, Austin, Texas.

Morgan, James. Papers. Rosenberg Library, Galveston, Texas.

Peña, José Enrique de la. Memoirs. José Enrique de la Peña Papers. Center for American History, University of Texas at Austin (CAH). CAH has a first draft, untranslated version of Peña's memoirs, as well as a final draft. A variation of the first draft is included as "Diary of an Anonymous Officer" in the appendices of Urrea's published diary, *Diario de las operaciones militares* (cited below in Books and Pamphlets, under Urrea, José), and as Appendix 1 in this book. Peña's final draft was edited by J. Sánchez Garza and published in Mexico in 1955 as *La rebelión de Texas. . . .* The final draft was also translated by Carmen Perry and published in 1975 as *With Santa Anna in Texas. . . .* In 1997 an expanded edition of *With Santa Anna in Texas* was published, with an introduction by James E. Crisp. (See below in Books and Pamphlets, under Peña, José Enrique de la.)

Portilla, Nicolas de la. Diary. In José Enrique de la Peña Papers. Center for American History, University of Texas at Austin (CAH).

"Relacion de los senores, gefes y oficiales que perteneciente al ejército de operaciones sobre Tejas, pasaron revista en el mes de Marzo en la ciudad de San Antonio Béjar ("List of the senior commanders and officers who belonged in the army of operations over Texas that passed in review in the month of March in City of San Antonio." Archivo Historico de Secretaria de la Defensa Nacional (AHSDN), Operaciones, XI/481.3/1713, Tomo 2, f. 383v. Mexico City, Mexico. Provided by Thomas Ricks Lindley and Jack Jackson.

San Luis Battalion Daily Log. José Enrique de la Peña Papers. Center for American History, University of Texas at Austin (CAH).

NEWSPAPERS

Diario del gobierno de la República Mexicana (Mexico City).
El Mercurio del Puerto de Matamoros (Matamoros, Mexico).
El Mosquito (Mexico City).
Mississippi Free Trader (Natchez).
Morning Courier and New York Enquirer.
New Orleans Bulletin.
Philadelphia Gazette.

THESIS

Montgomery, Dorothy Virginia Barler. "Movements of the Mexican Army in Texas after the Battle of San Jacinto." M.A. thesis. Sul Ross State University, 1970.

Alcerreca, Agustín. *Manifiesto que publica el Coronel Graduado y Primer Ayudante Agustín Alcerreca, para justificarse ante el Supremo Gobierno de la Nación ante sus conciudadanos, de la nota con que ha pretendido en Matamoros, cuyo autor no se descubre y refiere hechos de la pasada campaña de Tejas.* San Luis Potosí, Mexico: Imprenta del Gobierno, á Cargo del Ciudadano José María Infante, 1836.

Bancroft, Hubert Howe. *History of Mexico.* Volume 5, 1824–1861. 6 volumes. San Francisco: A. L. Bancroft & Company, 1885. This is volume 13 of *The Works of Hubert Howe Bancroft.* 39 volumes. San Francisco: A. L. Bancroft & Company, 1882–1890.

————. *History of the North Mexican States and Texas.* Volume 2, 1801–1889. 2 volumes. San Francisco: The History Company, 1886. This is volume 16 of *The Works of Hubert Howe Bancroft.* 39 volumes. San Francisco: A. L. Bancroft & Company, 1882–1890.

Barnard, Joseph Henry. *Journal.* Edited by Hobart Huson. Refugio, Tex.: Goliad Bicentennial, 1950.

Bollaert, William. *William Bollaert's Texas.* Edited by W. Eugene Hollon and Ruth Lapham Butler. Norman: University of Oklahoma Press, 1956.

Brown, John Henry. *History of Texas from 1685–1892.* Volume 2. 2 volumes. St. Louis: L. E. Daniel, Publisher, 1893.

Castañeda, Carlos E., translator and editor. *The Mexican Side of the Texas Revolution, 1836, by the Chief Mexican Participants, General Antonio López de Santa Anna, Ramón Martínez Caro, General Vicente Filisola, General José Urrea, General José María Tornel.* Dallas: Graphic Ideas, 1970.

Darling, Anthony D. *Redcoats and Brown Bess.* Historical Arms Series, No. 12. Canada: Museum Restoration Service, 1971.

Day, James M., compiler and editor. *The Texas Almanac, 1857–1873: A Compendium of Texas History.* Waco: Texian Press, 1967.

Diccionario Inglés–Español y Español–Inglés. Edited by F. Corona Bustamonte. Paris: Casa Editorial Garnier Hermanos, no date.

Documentos para la historia de la guerra de Tejas. Mexico: Editora Nacional, 1952.

Filisola, Vicente. *Análisis del diario militar del General D. José Urrea durante la primera campaña de Tejas.* Matamoros: Mercurio a Cargo de Antonio Castañeda, 1838.

_____. *Evacuation of Texas: Translation of the Representation Addressed to the Supreme Government by Vicente Filisola, in Defense of His Honor, and Explanation of his Operations as Commander-in-Chief of the Army against Texas.* Columbia, Texas: G. & T. H. Borden, Public Printers, 1837; reprint, Waco: Texian Press, 1965.

_____. *Memoirs for the History of the War in Texas.* Translated by Wallace Woolsey. 2 volumes. Austin: Eakin Press, 1986, 1987. This is a translation of the Rafael edition cited below.

_____. *Memorias para la historia de la guerra de Tejas.* 2 volumes. R. Rafael, 1848, 1849. Reprint, *Historia de la guerra de Tejas.* 2 volumes. Mexico D. F.: Editora Nacional, 1968.

_____. *Memorias para la historia de la guerra de Tejas.* 2 volumes. Mexico: Ignacio Cumplido, 1849. This is a different book than the Rafael book by the same name. The Cumplido edition has not been translated into English.

Gray, William Fairfax. *The Diary of William Fairfax Gray: From Virginia to Texas, 1835–1837.* Edited by Paul Lack. Dallas: William P. Clements Center for Southwest Studies, 1997.

Haecker, Charles, and Jeffery Mauck. *On the Prairie of Palo Alto.* College Station: Texas A&M University Press, 1997.

Herring, Patricia Roche, *General José Cosme Urrea: His Life and Times, 1797–1849,* Western Frontiersman Series xxvi. Spokane, Washington. Arthur H. Clark Company, 1995.

Hogan, William Ransom. *The Texas Republic: A Social and Economic History.* Norman: University of Oklahoma Press, 1946.

Hudgins, Joe D., and Gregg Dimmick. *A Campsite of the Retreating Mexican Army, April, 1836, 41WH91, Wharton County, Texas.* Houston Archeological Society Report No. 13. 1998.

Hudgins, Joe D., Terry Kieler, and Gregg Dimmick. *Tracking the Mexican Army through the Mar de Lodo (Sea of Mud), April 29–May 9, 1836, 41WH92, 41WH93, 41WH94, 41WH95, Wharton County, Texas.* Houston Archeological Society Report No. 16. Fall, 2000.

Jackson, Jack, editor, and John Wheat, translator. *Almonte's Texas: Juan N. Almonte's 1834 Inspection, Secret Report, and Role in the 1836 Campaign.* Austin: Texas State Historical Association, 2003.

Jenkins, John H., editor. *The Papers of the Texas Revolution, 1835–1836.* 10 volumes. Austin: Presidial Press, 1973.

Jenkins, John Holland. *Recollections of Early Texas; The Memoirs of John*

Holland Jenkins. Edited by John Holmes Jenkins III. Austin: University of Texas Press, 1958.

Lane, Walter P. *The Adventures and Recollections of General Walter P. Lane, A San Jacinto Veteran, Containing Sketches of the Texian, Mexican and Late Wars, with Several Indian Fights Thrown In.* 1928; reprint, Austin: Pemberton Press, 1970.

Linn, John J. *Reminiscences of Fifty Years in Texas.* New York: D. & J. Sadlier & Co., 1886; reprint, Austin: Steck Company, 1935.

Lubbock, Francis R. *Six Decades in Texas; or, Memoirs of Francis Richard Lubbock, Governor of Texas in War Time, 1861–63: A Personal Experience in Business, War, and Politics.* Edited by C. W. Raines. Austin: Ben C. Jones & Company, 1900.

Manucy, Albert. *Artillery through the Ages.* Washington, D.C.: Government Printing Office, 1949; reprint 1962.

Mexicano. "Se nos ha entegado en Tejas como borregos de ofrenda" ("We Have Been Delivered Up in Texas Like Sacrificial Lambs"). *Imprint of the Testimony of Valdez.* Mexico: 1836. OCLC Number 9011153, pp. 3–4. Center for American History at the University of Texas at Austin (CAH).

Mier y Terán, Manuel de. *Texas by Terán; The Diary Kept by General Manuel de Mier y Terán on His 1828 Inspection of Texas.* Edited by Jack Jackson. Translated by John Wheat. Austin: University of Texas Press, 2000.

Moore, Stephen L. *Eighteen Minutes: The Battle of San Jacinto and the Texas Independence Campaign.* Dallas: Republic of Texas Press, 2004.

Neumann, George C., and Frank J. Kravic. *Collector's Illustrated Encyclopedia of the American Revolution.* Texarkana, Tex.: Rebel Publishing Company, 1975.

Nieto, Angelina, Joseph Heftner, and Mrs. John Nicholas Brown. *El soldado mexicano, 1837–1847: Organización, vestuario, equipo.* Mexico, D. F.: Privately printed, 1958.

Nixon, Pat Ireland. *The Medical Story of Early Texas, 1528–1853.* Lancaster, Penn.: Lancaster Press, 1946.

Ornish, Natalie. *Ehrenberg; Goliad Survivor—Old West Explorer.* Dallas: Texas Heritage Press, 1993, 1997.

Peña, José Enrique de la. *La rebelión de Texas: Manuscrito inedito de 1836 por un oficial de Santa Anna.* Edited by J. Sánchez Garza. Mexico:

n.p., 1955.

———. *With Santa Anna in Texas: A Personal Narrative of the Revolution.* Translated and edited by Carmen Perry. College Station: Texas A&M University Press, 1975.

———. *With Santa Anna in Texas: A Personal Narrative of the Revolution.* Translated and edited by Carmen Perry. Introduction by James E. Crisp. Expanded edition. College Station: Texas A&M University Press, 1997.

Salas, Elizabeth. *Soldaderas in the Mexican Military: Myth and History.* Austin: University of Texas Press, 1990.

Santa Anna, Antonio López de. *Manifiesto que de sus operaciones en la campaña de Tejas y en su cautiverio dirige á sus conciudadanos el General Antonio López de Santa Anna.* Vera Cruz, Mexico: Imprenta Liberal, á Cargo de Antonio María Valdez, 1837.

———. *See also* Castañeda, Carlos E. *The Mexican Side of the Texas Revolution.*

Santos, Richard G. *Santa Anna's Campaign against Texas, 1835–1836, Featuring the Field Commands Issued to Major General Vicente Filisola.* Waco: Texian Press, 1968.

Swisher, John Milton. *The Swisher Memoirs by Col. John M. Swisher.* Edited by Rena Maverick Green. San Antonio: Sigmund Press, 1932.

Teja, Jesús F. de la, editor. *A Revolution Remembered: The Memoirs and Selected Correspondence of Juan N. Seguín.* Austin: State House Press, 1991.

Tijerina, Andrés. *Tejanos and Texas under the Mexican Flag, 1821–1836.* College Station: Texas A&M University Press, 1994.

United States Department of Agriculture, Soil Conservation Service, Texas Agricultural Experiment Station. *Soil Survey of Wharton County, Texas.* Washington, D.C.: Government Printing Office, 1974.

Urrea, José. *Diario de las operaciones militares de la division que al mando del General José Urrea hizo la campaña de Tejas publicado se autor con algunas observaciones para vindicarse ante sus conciudadanos.* Victoria de Durango, Mexico: Imprint of the Government, 1838.

———. "Diario de las operaciones militares de la división que al mando del General José Urrea hizo la campaña de Tejas ..." *Documentos para la historia de la Guerra de Tejas.* Mexico: Editora Nacional, 1952.

∞

Wells, Tom Henderson. *Commodore Moore and the Texas Navy.* Austin: University of Texas Press, 1988.

Williams, Annie Lee. *The History of Wharton County.* Austin: Van Boeckmann-Jones Company, 1964.

Wise, Terence, and Richard Hook. *Artillery Equipments of the Napoleonic Wars.* Men-at-Arms series. London: Osprey Publishing Ltd. 1979.

Wharton, Clarence R. *History of Texas.* Dallas: Turner Company, 1935.

———. *Wharton's History of Fort Bend County.* San Antonio: Naylor Company, 1939.

PERIODICALS

Crisp, James E. "The Little Book That Wasn't There: The Myth and Mystery of the de la Peña Diary." *Southwestern Historical Quarterly,* Volume 98, October 1994, pp. 261–296.

Delgado, Pedro. "Mexican Account of the Battle of San Jacinto." *The Texas Almanac, 1857–1873: A Compendium of Texas History.* Waco: Texian Press, 1967, pp. 613–629.

Duke, Alan R. "Artifacts from San Jacinto." *Houston Archeological Society Newsletter,* No. 45, April, 1974.

Lapham, Moses. "Moses Lapham: His Life and Some Selected Correspondence, II." Edited by Joe B. Frantz. *Southwestern Historical Quarterly,* Volume 54, April 1951, pp. 466–468.

Mexico. "La guerra de Texas: Causa formada al Gral. Filisola por su retirada en 1836." *Boletín del archivo general de la nación.* Tomo X, Nos. 1, 2, 3, DAPP Mexico: 1939.

Ortega, Gabriel Nuñez. "Diario de un prisonero de la Guerra de Texas." *Boletín del archivo general de la Nación,* Tomo IV, November–December, 1933, No. 6.

"Recollections of Isaac L. Hill," in "Reminiscences of Early Texans: A Collection from the Austin Papers." *Quarterly of the Texas State Historical Association,* Volume 7, July 1903, pp. 40–46.

Taylor, William S. "Pursuit of Santa Anna and His Cavalry after They Had Commenced Their Flight from the Battlefield of San Jacinto." *The Texas Almanac, 1857–1873: A Compendium of Texas History,* Waco: Texian Press, 1967, pp. 537–540.

Index

(Illustrations are indicated by a page number in **boldface**.)

ment abandoned or destroyed by, 230–231; notified about Santa Anna, 172; on supplies, 308; troops with, 113; to Urrea on battle-readiness of army, 304–305; withdrawal from San Antonio, 290–291

archeological sites: April 28th site, 190–191; April 29 trail and campsite, 201–208; La Villita excavation at the Alamo, 229; maps showing locations of, **167, 173, 195**; Mar de Lodo, 224–237; Powell's homesite and tavern, 102–111; Urrea site on San Bernard River, 140–145; Urrea's route north, 64; west bank of San Bernard River, 179. *See also* artifacts

armistice, 153, 160, 285, 293

artifacts: brass tacks, 234, **245**; bridle rosettes, 234, **244**; buttons, 232–233, 237, **240–241, 248**; candleholders, 233–234, **243**; cane handle, 233, **242**; canister shot, 202–203, **209**, 234–237, **245**; cannon balls, 204, **210**, 231; chinaware, 208; coins, 105, 237, **246**; cross-belt plate, 204–205; eating utensils, 234, **244**; flag or guidon base plate, 207, **214**; flints for flintlocks, 237; "Granaderos" plate, 204; horse or mule shoes, 206–207, **213**; howitzers at West Point, 231; howitzer shells, 225–231, **238–240**; India Pattern Brown Bess musket parts, 103–104, **107**, 142, 191, 206, **212–214**, 231–232; knives, 208; leg irons, 265, **273**; locks, **108**, 204; Mexican eagle, gilded, 207, **215**; musket balls, 237, **246**; nails, 202; "P" fragments, 234, **245**; pistol holster nosecap, 233, **242**; unidentified objects, 233

artillery: abandonment allegedly proposed by Filisola, 179–181; Ampudia's defense of rearguard with, 228, 252; archeological evidence of, 129–130n17, 190–191, 202–204, **209**, 210, 231, 234–235; bogged down in Mar de Lodo, 199, 217, 219, 224, 336; as hindrance to troop movements, 307; howitzers, 225–231; inventory of

munitions, 230; at Old Fort, 35–36; poor condition of, 305; reorganization of at Powell's, 129–130n17; at San Jacinto, 31n3; Urrea leaves artillery with Gaona, 193; Urrea's claim to have saved, 224; in Urrea's division, 61; with Urrea's forces, 229–230

Atascosito Crossing: Contrabando Road route to, 171–172; as destination, 320; Urrea at, 217, 218, 292–293; Urrea sent to, 188, 326; Urrea's failure to construct rafts for troop crossings, 275

B

Baker, Joseph, 270

Baker rifles, 104

barges, ferries, and rafts: at Brazos river crossing, 12, 14, 48, 52–53; burned by Urrea, 79, 80; Urrea's failure to construct, 275

Barnard, James H., 267–268

Barragán, Marcos: account of battle (secondary source), 24; account of flight after San Jacinto, 12–15; rejoins army, 24, 98

Barragán, Miguel, 168n21

battalions: organization and names of, 30; reorganization of at Powell's, 129. *See also by specific name*

Bay Prairie Road, 63–64, 136n6

Béjar, 45, 296, 300, 321, 336

Bell, James M., 265

blacksmith equipment (forges), 181, 207, 287

Borden, Thomas H., 51

Bordentown (Louisville), 51

Bowie, Jim, 268

Bravo, Nicolás, 305, 309

Brazoria, 291, 308, 318; Urrea's occupation of, 66, 70–72, 73, 75–77; Urrea's route north to, 63–64

Brazos River: alleged destruction of ferry, 52–53; barges for crossing, 12, 14, 48; bridgehead fortifications constructed on, 49–51; difficulties crossing as motive for withdrawal from Powell's, 122–123; during flight from San Jacinto, 12; Santa Anna's crossing of,

Urrea and opposition to retreat, 45;
variations in accounts of, 135, 187; on
war council and subsequent plans, 113,
125–126; on West Bernard conditions,
150–151; on withdrawal from Old
Fort, 51. *See also Análisis* (Filisola);
Memorias (Filisola)
firewood, lack of, 218–221, 278
flag or guidon base plate, 207, **214**
flints for flintlocks, 237
Forbes, John, 172n1
forges, 181, 207, 287
forks, 234, **244**
Fulcher, Mr. _____, 252
fusileros, 30

G

Galveston, 74, 75
Gaona, Antonio, 306; on artillery abandonment controversy, 181–182; as
Cuban national, 115n2; as Filisola supporter, 194; joins Filisola en route to
Powell's, 91; on offensive options,
289–290; Peña on, 325, 334–335; at
Powell's, 97, 119–120; Santa Anna's
battle strategy and, 317; Santa Anna's
orders to, 153, 155; troop movements
of, 49; troops under, 129; on Urrea
as vanguard, 194; at war council, 119,
120
Garay, Francisco, 308; account of, 69–72;
artifact possibly associated with, 142;
assigned to return Santa Anna's baggage, 165–166; in Brazoria, 77; to
Casey's Crossing, 131; at Powell's, 95;
Urrea's correspondence with, 84
García, Mariano, 24
Goliad, 113, 126–127, 135, 163, 309,
336–337; Mexican army ordered to
hold line at, 285; Mexican incursion
(1842), 314; retreat through, 263. *See
also* Fannin Massacre
Goliad-Cópano-Béjar line of defense,
285, 286, 293, 302–303, 304
Grant, Dr. James, 62
Gray, William Fairfax, 66–67n8
grenadiers: artifacts associated with, 204,
210, 232, 237

Guadalajara Battalion, 23, 31, 49, 129, 133,
258
Guanajuato Battalion, 133, 294
Guerrero Battalion, 23

H

Hammeken, George, 176–178
Harrisburg road, 49–50
Harrison, Dr., 66–67n8, 66–68, 71–72, 73
helmets (shakos), 204, 205–206
Hill, Isaac L., 265
Hinojosa, Manuel: illustrations by, **6, 28,
60, 88, 112, 170, 216, 250, 288, 316**
History of Texas 1685–1892 (Brown), 163
Hold Fort. *See* Old Fort
Holfort. *See* Old Fort
Holliday, _____ (prisoner of war),
264–265
horses and mules: artifacts related to, 142,
143, 206–207, **213**, 234, **244**; condi-
tion of, 285; shortages of, 35, 173, 304,
326–327
House, Thomas, 9
Houston, Sam, 282, 318–319; defeat of
Santa Anna at San Jacinto, 7–8; orders
to Burleslon, 256–257; orders to
Karnes, 257–258; Texans supporting
Urrea at Galveston, 68; as unable to
determine Filisola's intentions, 162
howitzers and howitzer shells, 225–231,
238–240

I

Iberri, María Castillo (José María Castillo
y Iberri), 13–14n6, 14
immigration into Texas, 322
India Pattern Brown Bess muskets: as
artifacts, 103–104, **107**, 142, 191, 206,
212–214, 231–232; British *vs.* American manufacture of, 206; musket balls
as artifacts, 237, **246**; stripped and
culled during retreat, 196
Infansón, Miguel (Infanzon), 183n14, 185
Infante, N., 183
Ingram, Mary Belle, 131n19
insignia, 105–106, **110–111**; "flaming
bomb," 237, **247**; "P" fragments, 234,
245

munitions: canister shot, 190–191, 202–203, **209**; cannon balls, 204, **210**; culled and abandoned, 196, 202; destroyed by Texans, 267; destroyed by Urrea, 79; howitzer shells, 225–231, **238–240**; inventory of, 230; musket balls, 103–105, 237, **246**; powder analysis, 226

musket balls, 103–105, 237, **246**

muskets: New Land Series, 104. *See also* India Pattern Brown Bess muskets

N

Nacogdoches, 49, 86, 263–264

nails: abandoned, 196; as artifacts, 106, 202

Navarro, Juana, 268

navies, 297–300, 305

New Land Series muskets, 104

Nock, Walter, 231

noncombatants: deaths during march to Monclova, 32–33; as hindrance, 58, 122, 307, 318; at Old Fort, 36–40; as refugees, 26; with Urrea's command, 65

Nuñez (unidentified captured officer), 21n24

O

Old Fort: artillery in, 35–36; barges constructed to cross Brazos, 12, 14; Brazos crossing, 49; equipment and supplies abandoned or destroyed at, 52; Filisola on reasons for withdrawal from, 51; Filisola's forces at, 29, 318; Gaona's arrival, 49; Peña's account of withdrawal from, 55–56, 318; Rodríguez and dragoons sent to, 98; strategic value of, 58; supplies at, 41–45; Urrea on withdrawal from, 79, 82, 83

Ortega, Gabriel Nuñez, 90–91

P

Pastry War, 298, 313–314

Peña, José Enrique de la, 14; accounts of, 24, 100–101, 135, 200–201; on M. Aguirre, 18; on Dr. H. A. Alsbury, 267, 327–328; Amat's dispatch in support of, 222–223; Ampudia's dispatch in support of, 222–223; on arrival of Texan forces, 258; on artillery abandonment proposed by Filisola, 180; deposition of, 117, 333–337; diary excerpt in Urrea's diary, 325–332; on distances traveled, 57, 134–135; on equipment abandoned, 196–197; on Filisola's decision to retreat, 165; on Filisola's proclamations and subsequent withdrawal, 92–94; on foreign influence in Mexican army, 114–115; imprisoned, 309; lover's rejection of, 278–279; on meeting about retreat decision, 289–290; on morale, 46–47, 334; on mud, 198–199; on noncombatants, 36–37; on Old Fort, withdrawal from, 55–56; Portilla on, 47; on prisoners of war, 199; on retreat, 115–117, 165, 289–290; on San Bernard crossing, 138; on Santa Anna, 328, 330; on sick and wounded, 198; similarities in account to Urrea's diary, 100–101; sources used for memoirs, 135; on stragglers, 50; on supplies, 42–44, 52, 328, 330, 334–335; on treaty, 329–331; Urrea supported by, 115–117, 309; on war council, 99–100, 123–125, 335–336; on weapons supply and condition, 42–44

pistol holster nosecap, 233, **242**

Portilla, José Nicolas de la, 18–19, 50; on ferry's destruction at Old Fort, 53; on Urrea's division, 47

Portilla, Manuel, 50

Post West Bernard, 141

Powell, Elizabeth, 53, 89–90

Powell's homesite and tavern: abandonment of, 122, 335; archeological research at site, 102–111; burned, 133; Filisola's description of, 91, 103; historical marker at, 64, 102; Urrea's arrival at, 96; visits of Mexican army to, 89; war council called at, 99–102; withdrawal to, 53

presidial soldier, **146**

Pretalia, Rafael: dispatched to Filisola by Urrea, 77–79, 80, 81, 85

Primero Battalion, 31

prisoners of war: artifacts associated with, 265; Filisola criticized regarding, 154; Filisola on, 281, 284, 296; Filisola's release of, 154, 286; with Mexican army, 264–266; at San Jacinto, 126; from San Jacinto, 126; Santa Anna as, 152–153, 270; Santa Anna orders release of, 154, 155, 163

proclamations, issued by Filisola, 92–95

property: Brazoria spared by its citizens, 73; destruction of Texan property, 154; Filisola on destruction of, 161, 162–163; Louisville (Borden homesite) burned, 51–52n32; munitions destroyed, 267; Peña on burning of structures, 56; Powell's tavern burned, 133; scorched earth policy, 45; Texans demand return of, 253–254, 330–331; valuables buried as smallpox victim, 277

Q

Querétaro Battalion, 65, 133

quicksand, 188

Quitman, John A., 86

R

rafts. *See* barges, ferries, and rafts

Ramírez y Sesma, Joaquín, 48–49, 306; as Filisola's second-in-command, 129; as Filisola supporter, 117, 156; at Powell's, 97; sent to Mexico by Filisola, 276; Urrea's correspondence with, 75–76, 82–83; at war council, 119–120

ranks, 15n11

rearguard, 133; Ampudia as, 228, 252, 258; Gaona on need for, 119, 120; Urrea as, 174, 186

reconnaissance: couriers as spies, 252–253, 329; by Mexican forces, 150–151; by Texans, 318–319, 329

Redd, W. D., 328

Refugio, 113, 264

Reminiscences of Fifty Years (Linn), 25–26

Representación (Filisola), 138; on April 28 campsite, 175–177; on artillery, 35, 224; on distance to San Jacinto, 56–57; on supplies, 69–73; on Urrea, 121; on

Urrea as encouraging attack, 78; on Urrea's April 26 position, 138–139; on Velasco, 74–75; on war council at Powell's, 121; on withdrawal to Powell's, 53

retreat: countermarch to Powell's, 128; as difficult to define, 82; as disorganized or hasty, 54–55, 217–224, 261–264, 271, 289; Filisola's decision to withdraw, 58, 319; forces divided during, 195–196; government's approval of, 308; as inevitable, 289–290; as majority decision, 319; marching orders, 133; meeting to discuss, 289–291, 319; motives for withdrawal, 126; mud as disorganizing and demoralizing, 198, 217–224; opposition to, 102, 289–290, 319, 335–336, 337 (*See also* Urrea's opposition to *under this heading*); Peña as agitating against retreat, 99–100; as pivotal decision in Texas Revolution, 60; planned relocation across the Colorado, 128–129; as ploy to deceive Texans, 336; ports lost as result of, 299; reconnaissance missions during, 149–151; as regrouping or orderly withdrawal, 113–114, 121, 139, 182; route of (map), **16**; Santa Anna on, 309–313; Santa Anna's orders and, 2, 153, 158, 166–167, 280–281, 283–284, 309, 320; as series of actions, 127, 128–129; strategic maneuvers during, 138–139; Urrea in charge of final stage of, 305; Urrea's opposition to, 45, 83, 85, 87, 115–118, 276, 291–295, 299–304, 322

Reyes, María Francisca de los, 45

Ricoy, José Maria, 47

Rivera, Juan, 277

Robbins, Thomas, 9, 20n21

Roberts, _____, 20

Robertson, Sterling C., 24, 261–263

Rodríguez, Pedro, 98

Rodríquez, N., 173–174

routes: alternatives to Mar de Lodo, 326; April 24–26 (map), **149**; April 27 (map), **167**; April 27 travel, 167; April 28 (map), **173**; April 29, Urrea's divi-

sion, 173; April 29 (map), **195**;
April–May retreat (map), **173**; archeological evidence of, 136; difficulty in
locating, 147–148; from Fannin battle
site to Brazoria (map), **64**; Filisola on
choices of, 189–190; from Goliad to
Powell's, 135; north to Brazoria, Urrea,
63–64; from Old Fort, 95–96; from
Powell's to Cayce's Crossing, 133–136;
remaining questions about, 322; traced
along middle Bernard Creek,
224–225; Urrea's division (map), **64**;
weather and change in, 320
Ruiz, 79, 80
Rusk, Thomas, 163, 262, 282; on Alsbury,
268

S

Salas, Mariano, 70, 183, 291, 308; Filisola's
orders to, 76–77; joins Filisola, 79, 91
Salinas, Ignacio, 80; on retreat during
deposition, 117; on supplies, 307–308
San Antonio, 32, 113, 172, 229; as
deserted, 264; Mexican incursions,
314; as retreat destination, 262, 263;
Santa Anna's orders regarding,
281–283; withdrawal from, 290–291,
297
San Bernard system: as confusing,
148–149, 163, 177, 219n3, 256; crossing
of San Bernard, 134, 137–138, 319–320;
flooding on, 168; Lissie Prairie terrain
described, 187–188; route around
source of West Bernard, 171; West
Bernard flooding, 150–151, 171
Sánchez-Navarro, José Juan, 32
San Jacinto, battle of: anonymous Mexican account of flight after, 12–13;
artillery captured at, 31n3; as decisive,
1–2, 7–8; Dolson account, 235–236;
element of surprise at, 7, 58; Filisola
informed of defeat, 23–24; Labadie
account, 235; Mexican survivors of,
25–26; noncombatant refugees after,
26; Peña on impact of defeat, 334; as
pivotal, 322; potential for attack on
Texas forces after, 31, 77–78, 128, 318;
prisoners of war taken at, 126; reports

after, 98; Santa Anna on, 310–313; Taylor account, 9–12, 15–17, 267; Urrea's
perception of, 87
San Luis Battalion and Battalion log, 129,
133; April 28 travel distances, 175; on
Atascosito Crossing detail, 194–195;
on Barragán, 15; on distances traveled,
134–135; on location of Urrea's camp
at Atascosito Crossing, 276; for May 3,
279; route from Goliad to Powell's,
135; Santa Anna's orders to be ignored,
163–164; troop strength of battalion,
73n15; on Urrea's route, 63
San Patricio, battle of, 62
Santa Anna, Antonio López de: advance
to capture Texas Cabinet, 29–30;
authority while prisoner of war,
163–164, 168, 270, 281, 283–285, 330;
battle-readiness of forces under,
29–32; as believed dead, 98–99; capture of, 21; exiled to U.S., 313; fate of
as unknown, 120, 292; during federalist wars, 314; Filisola, communications
with, 155–156, 160–163, 279–281,
282–284; Filisola on risk to, 297; instability in Mexico after loss of leadership, 121; Karnes's pursuit of, 11; during Mexican American War, 313;
orders to Filisola, 151–156; Peña on,
328, 330; personal baggage requested
by, 155–156, 164–165, 283, 285; at Powell's, 90–91; as prisoner of war,
152–153, 270, 313; prisoners ordered
released by, 154, 155; on retreat,
309–313; retreat ordered by, 153, 158,
166–167, 280–281, 283–284, 309, 320;
at San Jacinto, 7, 13–14; on San Jacinto
defeat, 310–313; troops under command of, 317; Urrea on, 302
Secrest, Field, 9
Secrest, Washington, 9
security of Mexican interior, 121
Seguín, Juan, 253–254, 256, 258, 259–261
shakos, 204, 205–206, 237
sick and wounded: Ampudia on,
260–261; with Andrade, 113; as hindrance, 58; lack of medicines and doctors, 305; left behind, 217, 251, 255,

305; total Mexican soldiers in Texas, 113; unit strengths of Mexican army, 338–340

truce (armistice), 153, 160

Turnage, Shell, 9

U

Ugartechea, Domingo, 126–127, 173

uniforms, **ii, 132, 146, 192, 274**; artifacts related to, 204, 205–206, **211**; buttons used on, 105–106, **107–111, 240–241, 248**; of dragoon, **132**; insignia, 105–106, **110–111**, 234, 237, **245, 247**; lancer's uniform, Mexican army, 274; shakos, 204, 205–206; Texas army and, 325

Urrea, José de: Andrade, communication with, 304–305; on April 28 campsite, 178–179; on artillery abandonment, 179–180; artillery with, 229–230; at Atascosito Crossing, 188, 193, 217, 218, 275, 276, 292–293, 326; battle-readiness of troops, 34, 61, 62, 64–65, 86; Brazos crossing by, 49–51, 69, 85, 128, 291; as commander, 304; contradictions and inconsistencies in accounts of, 75–76, 77, 85; failure to construct rafts for river crossing, 275; Fannin massacre and, 62–63n3, 73; on Filisola, 126, 138–139, 188, 291–295; Filisola, communication with, 81–82, 299–304; Filisola's orders to, 54–55, 69, 74, 80–81, 86–87, 149–150, 150, 188, 193–194, 318; Galveston attack plans and, 74, 75; Garay, communication with, 84, 165–166, 286, 295; interactions with Filisola at Powell's, 96–97; on meeting to discuss Santa Anna's orders, 158–159; Mexican government, complaint to, 291–295; notified of San Jacinto defeat, 69, 72; as obedient to Santa Anna, 166; on Old Fort, withdrawal from, 79, 82; as openly critical of Filisola, 291–295; pardoned for *pronunciamiento,* 309; Portilla on Urrea's division, 47; Pretalia dispatched to Filisola by, 77–79; on proclamations issued by Filisola,

92–94; Ramírez y Sesma, communication with, 75–76, 82–83; as rearguard, 174, 186, 194; relationship with Filisola during retreat, 81–82, 85, 96–97, 125, 137, 195–196, 300; reluctance to share information with Filisola, 173–174; retreat opposed by, 45, 83, 85, 87, 115–118, 121, 127–128, 159, 276, 291–295, 322; route from Goliad to Powell's, 135; route north to Brazoria, 63–64; route of division (map), **64**; route taken exiting Old Fort, 95–96; San Bernard crossing and, 137; Santa Anna's battle strategy and, 317; on Santa Anna's dispatches and troop's response to, 152; Santa Anna's orders to, 153, 155; stragglers as concern of, 83, 126–127; summary of case against Filisola in diary of, 126; on supplies and equipment, 52, 79–80; as suspicious of planned retreat, 286; Thorn on, 266; troops under, 34, 129, 294; as unsuitable for mission to Houston, 160; Velasco assault planned by, 72–73, 75–77; at war council, 118–119. See also *Diario* (Urrea)

Urrea site, archeology at, 141–145

V

Vega, Romulo Dias de la, 47

Velasco, 72, 73, 75–77

Vera Cruz, 314

Victoria, 113, 127, 133, 172–173, 263, 286

Vince's Bridge, 7–8, 9–10, 13, 19, 251

W

war council at Powell's: documentation of events at, 117–118; location and circumstances of, 124–125; security of Mexican interior as issue, 121

Ward, William, 62

wax stamp, 142, **145**

weapons: Baker rifles, 104; condition and supply of, 31–32, 41–44; howitzers and howitzer shells, 225–231, **238–240**; New Land Series muskets, 104. *See also* artillery; India Pattern Brown Bess muskets; munitions

weather: Allision (tropical storm), 139;
blizzards, 317; as decisive factor, 289,
319–320; delays caused by, 86; documentation of storms, 140; as obstacle
to Mexican forces, 8, 86, 317; rainfall
during April 26–27 storm, 139–140;
storm while crossing San Bernard,
137; as unpredictable factor, 59, 190
Wells, Joe, 252–253, 260
West Bernard Creek: archeological evidence from, 136
West Point, 231
Woll, Adrian: as French national, 115n2;
detained by Texans, 251, 253, 271, 281;
as emissary, 159, 160, 172, 293–294,
312; Filisola, communication with,
285; as major general of army, 129; at

Powell's, 95; reconnaissance by,
150–151, 172; report on upper West
Bernard terrain, 172; San Antonio
incursion, 314; at war council, 119; on
withdrawal, 121–122
women and children. *See* noncombatants
Woolsey, Wallace, 3

Y

Young, Kevin, 230
Yucatán Battalion, 61, 294

Z

Zapadores Battalion, 129, 133, 275. *See
Also* Amat, Agustín
Zavala, Lorenzo de, 29

SEA OF MUD

COLOPHON

The typeface used for the text is Adobe Bembo. The display
faces are Adobe Madrone and Monotype Latin.

Two thousand copies printed at Sheridan Books,
Chelsea, Michigan, on 50 lb. Natural.